Arts & Crafts Architecture

Arts & Crafts Architecture

History and Heritage in New England

Maureen Meister

UNIVERSITY PRESS OF NEW ENGLAND

HANOVER AND LONDON

University Press of New England
www.upne.com
© 2014 University Press of New England
All rights reserved
Manufactured in the United States of America
Designed by Dean Bornstein
Typeset in Adobe Jenson by The Perpetua Press, Peacham, Vermont

For permission to reproduce any of the material in this book, contact Permissions,
University Press of New England, One Court Street, Suite 250, Lebanon NH 03766; or visit
www.upne.com

Furthermore:
a program of the J.M. Kaplan Fund

This book has been published with the generous support of Furthermore: a program of the
J. M. Kaplan Fund.

Library of Congress Cataloging-in-Publication Data

Meister, Maureen.
  Arts and crafts architecture : history and heritage in New England /
Maureen Meister.
    pages cm
  Includes bibliographical references and index.
  ISBN 978-1-61168-662-3 (cloth : alk. paper) — ISBN 978-1-61168-664-7 (ebook)
  1. Architecture—New England—History—19th century. 2.
Architecture—New England—History—20th century. 3. Arts and crafts
movement—New England. I. Title.
  NA715. M45 2014
  720.974'09034—dc23
                              2014013798

5 4 3 2 1

Contents

Color illustrations follow page 112

Illustrations

Color plates appear after page 112

Preface

On a late-summer morning in 2012, I drove to Lawrence, Massachusetts. For many months, while finishing the manuscript of this book, I had wanted to spend a day in this gritty industrial city. Lawrence was not unfamiliar to me. But what piqued my interest and drew me north were some special programs and exhibitions taking place at this time. Finally, there I was, first at the visitor center and then standing before the enormous doors of the Everett Mill, an intimidating brick pile that extends the length of several city blocks. Here was where the city's textile workers had reached a breaking point in January of 1912, walking off their jobs in what became known as the Bread and Roses Strike. Not settled until March, the walkout focused the nation's attention on the brutal conditions endured by its mill workers.

I have long been awed by New England's factories and their histories. In the early 1980s, I spent a summer employed as a guide at Slater Mill in Pawtucket, Rhode Island, and another summer at the National Park Service in the mills of Lowell, Massachusetts. While I was writing this book about turn-of-the-twentieth-century architecture in New England, images of the region's mill buildings sometimes flitted through my mind. Harsh sites, places of misery, they represent one of the many topics I have not pursued in providing a context for this study. The historian confronts seemingly endless numbers of intriguing avenues to explore and passes by them, mindful of the need to stay on course.

The subject that I have chosen to investigate has been ambitious enough. What has guided me has been a desire to examine the buildings and ideas of a group of architects, eleven men and one woman, who practiced in Boston a century ago while dedicating themselves to promoting a shared interpretation of the English Arts and Crafts movement. They participated in a rich discourse, centered in the region, about art and labor, and it permeated their work. My topic is the outgrowth of a book that I published in 2003, *Architecture and the Arts and Crafts Movement in Boston: Harvard's H. Langford Warren*. Warren, an architect, had trained under Henry Hobson Richardson, established the architecture program at Harvard, and in 1897 helped found the Society of Arts and Crafts, Boston, leading it through the better part of its first two decades. In examining Warren's career, I considered how his ideas about design and history contributed to the region's largest and most influential Arts and Crafts organization. At the same time, I recognized that Warren was not alone in this endeavor. I wanted to learn more about the architects and their fellow advocates who advanced Arts and Crafts theories in New England.

In the course of my research, I have been surprised to discover how often these architects and their projects have touched me personally. One example is William E. Putnam Jr. He and his partner, Allen H. Cox, were the architects of the dormitory where I lived when I arrived in Massachusetts at age eighteen to study at Mount Holyoke College. My first classes were held in a lecture hall that Putnam and Cox also designed. Several other architects in this group left their mark at Mount Holyoke. R. Clipston Sturgis was responsible for a portion of the college's campus plan, and the firms of Newhall and Blevins and Ralph Adams Cram were employed for various projects. Many years later, when I settled in Winchester, a suburb of Boston, I became interested in the architect Frank Patterson Smith, who moved to the community in 1895 and soon became Warren's business partner. Together they designed Epiphany Church, just up the street from me. As a result of this investigation, I see the influence of the architects in this circle virtually every day, whether I'm in Boston or Cambridge, in neighboring suburban towns, or traveling to another part of the region.

In writing this book, I have sought to provide a broad understanding of these individuals and the buildings that are their legacy—town halls and libraries, churches and houses, and schools and campus buildings. Stylistically, they reflect England's and New England's architectural traditions, designs that are Gothic Revival and Colonial Revival. Less obvious are the ways in which the designs are based in theory as well as history, ideas that originated in England's Arts and Crafts movement and then were blended with the rich cultural and architectural heritage of New England. Studying and visiting these buildings over the past few years has been a pleasure because they are beautiful. But this experience has also been uplifting—very different from visiting the region's sprawling mills. These Arts and Crafts buildings were erected in a spirit of idealism, and when they survive, that spirit is still embedded in them.

. . .

Dozens of people have made contributions to this book, and I wish to extend my thanks to them. First I want to acknowledge the wonderful staff of the Winchester Public Library, the arts desk of the Boston Public Library, and the Boston Athenaeum. Time and again, they have located references and sources for me that have been more than a little challenging to track down. I also received help, always with a warm reception, from the Library and Archives of Historic New England. Many more dedicated librarians, archivists, and members of preservation offices answered my queries. Their knowledge and commitment have been remarkable, and I want to let them know how much I have valued their assistance. I am further indebted to the many people who answered my calls and opened buildings to me—home-owners, ministers and priests, and more than one church music director.

My knowledge about the region's built environment has been enriched by my students at Tufts University as together we have examined the build-ings, landscapes, and public places of Greater Boston. My long association with the Department of Art and Art History at Tufts has been most re-warding, and I am grateful for the support I have received from the faculty as well as from Rosalie Bruno, Christine Cavalier, and Amy West.

Several academic societies and organizations have provided me with opportunities to share my research, and I want to express my appreciation to the people who have given generously of their time to make these ex-periences possible. At the 2007 conference of the Society of Architectural Historians, I was pleased to present a paper in a session that was organized by Jeffrey Karl Ochsner. In 2010 I participated in the "Useful and Beautiful" conference at the University of Delaware. Co-chairing a session with Kath-ryn Brush at the 2011 conference of the College Art Association was espe-cially satisfying. I also wish to thank Florence Boos and the William Morris Society in the United States, whose 2013 meeting gave me another oppor-tunity to present my work; and Lisa Koenigsberg and the Initiatives in Art and Culture, which included me in the 2013 conference held in Boston.

Most recently, I have been heartened by the good wishes and prompt response of the many individuals who have provided me with illustrations. I am happy to add that in the course of obtaining a photograph of A. W. N. Pugin's house, the Grange, in Ramsgate, Kent, I learned that it is available for holiday rentals, preserved through the impressive work of the Landmark Trust in the United Kingdom.

Many are the friends and colleagues who have taken an ongoing interest in my subject of study, and their encouragement has meant more to me than they may ever imagine. In particular I wish to recognize those colleagues who are experts in areas closest to my own field of research and have of-fered me their insights and gleanings: Edward R. Bosley, Beverly K. Brandt,

Edward S. Cooke Jr., Peter Cormack, Marie Frank, Marilee Boyd Meyer, Jeffrey Karl Ochsner, James F. O'Gorman, Roger Reed, Annie Robinson, and Albert M. Tannler. I have read their publications with admiration and continue to share their excitement when they tell me about their own research and discoveries.

In returning to publish a second time with University Press of New England, I am as grateful as ever for the talented people there. Phyllis Deutsch, editor-in-chief, has been enthusiastic about my subject and has provided me with exceptional guidance to shape the manuscript. This book has been further enhanced through the generous grant awarded to UPNE by Furthermore, a program of the J. M. Kaplan Fund.

Above all, I wish to express my heartfelt appreciation to my husband, David Feigenbaum. In serving as my tech support, he has responded to my requests for help with endless patience, not to mention talent. Together we have traveled to the corners of New England, where he has taken photographs to satisfy my ideas about what should be documented. When we encountered trees and stop signs and similar intrusions, he maneuvered around them and found angles that managed to satisfy us both. Through it all, spanning several years and many miles, we have shared some great Yankee cooking in some unforgettable settings—from Lake Champlain to Casco Bay. David has been a wonderful companion and truly my partner in this project.

Introduction: Grappling with Modernity

In April of 1897, a group of Boston craftsmen, architects, and supporters presented a groundbreaking Arts and Crafts exhibition featuring more than 1,000 objects in a building near Copley Square. The inspiration for their endeavor came from England, where the Arts and Crafts Exhibition Society had organized its first show in London in 1888. Significantly, the display in Boston was accompanied by a second exhibition, this one sponsored by the Boston Architectural Club. From the beginning, the Arts and Crafts movement that germinated in Boston was associated with architects.

The opening of the tandem exhibitions marked the first of several major cultural events that occurred in the city that spring. On May 26, 1897, senators and representatives of the Commonwealth of Massachusetts convened at the Massachusetts State House to celebrate the return from London of William Bradford's seventeenth-century manuscript, "Of Plymouth Plantation."[1] Less than a week later, on a drizzly Decoration Day, at the edge of Boston Common and across from the State House, the monument to Robert Gould Shaw was unveiled, the culmination of a lengthy parade.[2] This bronze relief, a major work by the sculptor Augustus Saint-Gaudens, honored the memory of the young Brahmin colonel who was killed leading the first black regiment raised in the North during the Civil War. Surviving veterans from the 54th Massachusetts Volunteer Infantry marched, the "Battle Hymn of the Republic" was played, and salutes were fired by warships in Boston harbor and an artillery unit on the Common. In a nearby hall, orations were delivered by Mayor Josiah Quincy, Professor William James of Harvard, and President Booker T. Washington of Tuskegee Institute. James emphasized that Shaw's legacy was not the courage of the soldier in battle, but rather his "civic courage" in accepting a commission in which "loneliness was certain, ridicule inevitable, failure possible."[3]

Meantime, along the opposite side of Boston Common, construction of the nation's first subway was under way. Stations at Park Street, Boylston Street, and the Public Garden would open on September 1. That same summer, further to the west, behind Henry Hobson Richardson's Trinity Church on Copley Square, framing began on Westminster Chambers, a ten-story, 120-foot-tall apartment building. The building would be the subject of protracted battles and litigation, ending with a ruling by the United States Supreme Court in 1903, upholding the legality of height restrictions.[4]

Against this backdrop, the organizers of Boston's first Arts and Crafts exhibition were debating their next steps. Energized by their success, they ultimately agreed to establish a Society of Arts and Crafts, which was incorporated in late June 1897. Its leaders were especially close to the theorists who gave rise to the movement in England, including John Ruskin and William Morris. Both men had been disheartened by the effects of the Industrial Revolution, observing how it had degraded the workers who toiled in factories that churned out cheap, mass-produced goods. Both Ruskin and Morris championed a preindustrial way of life and encouraged support of the craftsman.

For the architects, craftsmen, and advocates who founded the Society of Arts and Crafts in Boston, the region's colonial history was compelling, as demonstrated by the excitement over the return of the Bradford manuscript. There also was an idealism in the region's heritage that the society's founders would have appreciated in Shaw. These men and women were committed to improving life in New England as the new century was about to dawn. At the same time, the leaders of the Society of Arts and Crafts steered clear of several controversial concerns then emerging, which revolved around issues relating to innovations in mass transportation, tall buildings, and—above all—the plight of labor. On these topics, the society's leaders and members were not united. The environment that produced the Society of Arts and Crafts was both backward looking and forward looking.

Upheaval and Reform

The ideas that grew into an Arts and Crafts movement in New England found fertile ground in a region where the population confronted many of the same conditions of upheaval and calls for reform that were present in England. Both England and New England faced a rapid expansion of industry and the protests of labor, and both nurtured well-educated cultural elites who would critique these developments.

In one important way, however, the American experience during the second half of the nineteenth century was dramatically different from the English experience, and as a result, the American response to the Arts and Crafts movement took on a distinctive cast. Americans had endured the trauma of the Civil War, and they would require years to heal. In *The Brown Decades: A Study of the Arts in America, 1865–1895*, published in 1931, Lewis Mumford paints a picture of a country living with lost sons, crippled survivors, and a scorched landscape.[5] He describes a people desperately in need of regeneration, a nation focused on itself. This self-examination was reinforced in 1876 when the country celebrated its centennial. For the future of American architecture, a pivotal event was the Centennial Exposition in Philadelphia, which celebrated the nation's founding decades and contributed to the Colonial Revival.[6] Thus, while Ruskin and Morris were exhorting their countrymen about the degradations of industry, Americans were focusing on rebuilding the union and defining a national identity.

At the same time, by the close of the Civil War, New England had developed a tradition of moral outrage. For many decades, the region's textile mills had been a target of criticism. New England was where the American textile industry had originated, with the earliest mills erected at the end of the eighteenth century and in the first decades of the nineteenth century along the rivers of Rhode Island, Massachusetts, and New Hampshire. During the antebellum period, Yankee abolitionists condemned the factories for spinning cotton imported from the South and excoriated the mill owners for indirectly supporting slavery. Abolitionists such as the poet John Greenleaf Whittier repeatedly denounced the Northern businessmen who profited from textile production. "Shut the mill-gate," he penned in 1844, imploring, "Liberty for all!"[7] By the late nineteenth century, New England had become accustomed to individuals who spoke out for the oppressed. Within Boston's Society of Arts and Crafts, several leading members would consider such social activism to be their primary mission.

As in England, the growth of corporations in nineteenth-century New England provoked a reaction that was absorbed into Arts and Crafts thinking. After the Civil War, in New England as in other parts of the nation, those who excelled at organization and administration grew wealthy through the consolidation of companies. In Lowell, Massachusetts, as early as the 1840s, business investors who were engaged in large-scale textile production had launched related enterprises including power companies, insurance companies, banks, and railroads.[8] By and large, Americans admired the self-made men who were models of individualism; however, more and more people recognized that big business could abuse the individual.[9] Americans were torn by this paradox. In general, they were deeply attached to the concepts of the individual and self-realization, long personified by the colonial farmer and the craftsman—a commitment to the individual that would be shared by Arts and Crafts leaders.

By the end of the nineteenth century, organization and corporation had come to characterize not only businesses, but also educational and cultural institutions.[10] In Boston, ambitious leaders oversaw construction and institutional expansion at Harvard, Massachusetts Institute of Technology, the Museum of Fine Arts, and the symphony orchestra with its hall. The leaders of the Society of Arts and Crafts sought to attract a national membership to their organization, and they then led the effort to found a national league of handicraft societies. Bringing together large numbers of people under one banner was the new way.

Waves of immigrants, mainly from southern and eastern Europe, entered the United States at this time, crowding into cities everywhere, but especially in the Northeast. In the Boston of 1890, more than four-fifths of the residents were renters.[11] Immigrants transformed Boston's North and South Ends, where they settled, while frame three-deckers proliferated beyond the inner city.[12] Architects involved with Boston's Society of Arts and Crafts designed urban schools and bathhouses that served the influx of residents.

American laborers never saw a counterpart to William Morris to champion their cause. Nevertheless, the workers' struggle to improve their conditions was a subject that American Arts and Crafts proponents, including those in Boston, were compelled to contemplate. Organized labor grew dramatically in the 1880s. By 1886, the Knights of Labor claimed more than 700,000 members.[13] Recognizing the political significance of this population, President Grover Cleveland established Labor Day as a national holiday in 1894.[14] American workers continued to rebel, and by the turn of the century, the United States was experiencing more strikes than any other nation.[15] Uneasy about the power of large corporations and repulsed by socialism, America's prospering middle class embraced progressivism.

The rise of the Progressive movement, which emerged around 1900 and gained momentum over the next decade, coincided with the creation of Arts and Crafts organizations in the United States. The leaders came from similar backgrounds and grappled with many of the same issues. Increasing numbers of professionals and educated individuals concluded that the time had come for social and economic reform. The adherents of progressivism were moderates, and they believed in effecting change through government—ideally a government led by enlightened, educated men from their own ranks.[16] Their faith in government resulted in its expansion, especially at the federal level, while this outlook also gave rise to a more general interest in governance. Soon after the Society of Arts and Crafts was founded in Boston, its leaders established an elaborate organizational structure with several levels of membership, a governing council, and even a jury.

The spirit of the Progressive movement was propelled by energy and optimism.[17] Education was a priority for progressives, and they encouraged the country's dramatic increases in high school enrollment as well as the expansion of colleges and universities, including graduate degree programs.[18] The focus on education would be a defining characteristic of Boston's Society of Arts and Crafts, which offered lectures and published a serious magazine. The architects who were members designed large numbers and types of educational facilities. The turn of the twentieth century also experienced a boom in church building, with mainstream churches commonly becoming outlets for their members' desire to serve the needy.[19] The Boston architects designed many houses of worship, typically planned with meeting halls and schools.

For a large segment of the American populace, the turn of the twentieth century offered much to enjoy. New parks and playgrounds attracted residents during their leisure hours. So too did commercial entertainment, including family-oriented vaudeville theaters.[20] With consumer goods becoming abundant, more and more department stores opened, enticing customers to shop as well as to buy.[21] During the 1890s, now-familiar treats came on the American market, including Cracker Jack, Tootsie Roll, and Jell-O.[22] For many in New England, whether Yankee or immigrant, daily life presented pleasures and improvements over the experiences of earlier generations. As for Boston's intelligentsia and cultural leaders, their views were mixed; even those traveling in the same circles could evaluate the period in opposite ways. In Boston, one of the most critical judges was Charles Eliot Norton, a Harvard professor who became the first president of the Society of Arts and Crafts. Another Bostonian, Henry Adams, living in Washington, D.C., wrote about an industrial society that he believed had lost its soul. But for the most part, those involved with Boston's Society of Arts and Crafts were optimistic about the country and the modern age. They radiated a Progressive Era confidence in their writing and in their work as they faced the sunrise of the twentieth century.[23]

Arts and Crafts Architecture in New England

The prominence of architects in the Society of Arts and Crafts distinguished it from other Arts and Crafts groups in the United States. The architects promoted an ongoing collaboration with the craftsmen, turning to them to ornament buildings and encouraging patrons who would buy their wares. As officers, committee members, and jurors, the architects strived to create the nation's most successful group of its kind. During the first two decades of the society's history, from 1897 through 1917, twelve architects served in leadership roles. Because of their commitment to the organization and its mission, their work provides a meaningful basis for investigating the Arts and Crafts architecture in the region.

The twelve architects in this group did much to influence the physical character of New England. Although the popular image endures of a place dotted by towns oriented around white wooden churches that are colonial, federal, or Greek Revival in style, in reality, most of the region's communities include at least one or two churches that date from the turn of the twentieth century. Many are built of rust-tinged granite, in English Gothic style. Others are Colonial Revival, in which case they are usually red brick. Often these houses of worship are complemented by a Colonial Revival town hall, a library along the same lines, and Colonial Revival schools crowned with cupolas. These structures are now celebrating their centennials. Recently researched and often restored, many have been listed on the National Register of Historic Places. They are beloved for their ornament, embellished with sculpture, carved wood, wrought iron, tile, and stained glass. Yet although they have been documented and described, they have not been placed in a broader historical context. These are the buildings that represent the architecture that accompanied the Arts and Crafts movement in New England.

New England's Arts and Crafts architecture has languished in the shadows in histories of the larger movement. Among studies of American architecture, attention has been devoted to Gustav Stickley and his Craftsman houses, Frank Lloyd Wright and the Prairie Style, and Greene and Greene and their California bungalows. Delightful, to be sure, these better-known buildings illustrated new stylistic directions of the early twentieth century, and in so doing they have appealed to historians who have been attracted to their original qualities.

The architects in Boston, on the other hand, were more closely aligned with developments in England. They were in contact with contemporary English architects and generated many of their designs in response to English trends. On the whole, Boston's architects sought to affirm New England's English and Anglo-Colonial past. In this way, they contributed to a new direction in American architecture. During the late 1880s and early 1890s, Boston architects began designing Gothic Revival and Colonial Revival churches, houses, campus buildings, and municipal buildings well before the styles became popular across the country in the early twentieth century. At the same time, like their counterparts in England, these architects sometimes simplified their forms, studying vernacular traditions to produce more forward-looking designs.

But for the most part, Boston architects favored revival styles, and today their work may be fairly labeled conservative. Indeed, their buildings do not call attention to themselves. "Sobriety" and "restraint" were watchwords of the Society of Arts and Crafts, and the architects subscribed to this ideal. They objected to the French-influenced, Beaux-Arts architecture that was popular in New York City, finding it ostentatious. They also rejected the more radical stylistic developments emerging in Europe, including Art Nouveau from France and Belgium and the architecture of the Viennese Secession.

To examine a selection of buildings by the architects who were central to Boston's Arts and Crafts movement would be enlightening, yet it is also important to realize that their projects reflected shared ideals. The hopes and concerns that inspired the English Arts and Crafts movement, formulated by Ruskin and Morris, acquired a distinctive cast in New England. Charles Eliot Norton, the Harvard professor and the society's first president, was central to the development of the region's movement—a direct link between the English theorists and sympathizers in Boston. He was a close friend of Ruskin and knew Morris and his circle well. Like them, Norton expounded on the relationships between aesthetics and morality. According to Norton, simplicity and sincerity were essential to all creative expression.

In advancing their cause, the leaders of the newly formed organization in Boston turned to the writings of Ralph Waldo Emerson, blending his thoughts with Arts and Crafts theory. Emerson's regard for the plain Yankee meshed comfortably with Arts and Crafts values. His belief in the individual also was embraced, providing a rationale for the more dominant figures in the organization to nudge it away from English socialism.

Unlike Norton and Emerson, the architects were running businesses, and most of their clients were businessmen. Within their practices and in the governance of the Society of Arts and Crafts, they attempted to reconcile their ideals with pragmatic considerations. Many Boston professionals, working in other fields and other forums, faced similar challenges. One such man in the city at this time was Louis D. Brandeis. Best known for his role in later years as a United States Supreme Court justice, he was a contemporary of the architects and a fellow professional whose social circle overlapped with theirs. Like the architects, Brandeis accepted capitalism. Nevertheless, he also recognized the hardships experienced by labor, and by the turn of the century, he became more and more engaged with issues that would be associated with the Progressive Era. The same was true of the architects who helped lead the Society of Arts and Crafts.

The four decades from the 1890s through the 1920s produced an extraordinary flowering of architecture in New England. Yet the architecture of this period, intertwined with the Arts and Crafts movement emanating from Boston, has received scant treatment as a coherent body of work. This neglect may be explained by the fact that for much of the twentieth century, studies were focused on the rise of Modernism. In recent decades, however, monographs have appeared on several leading architects and firms from Boston of this period, notably books relating to Ralph Adams Cram, Lois L. Howe, Alexander W. Longfellow Jr., and H. Langford Warren.[24] In addition to these studies, two publications have made major contributions to an understanding of the history of the Society of Arts and Crafts: *Inspiring Reform: Boston's Arts and Crafts Movement*, for which Marilee Boyd Meyer was consulting curator; and *The Craftsman and the Critic: Defining Usefulness and Beauty in Arts and Crafts-Era Boston* by Beverly K. Brandt.[25] The pages that follow represent the first study to examine this Boston-based architecture in a comprehensive way, locating the architects and their buildings within the social, political, and philosophical contexts of turn-of-the-twentieth-century New England.

Virtually anyone who has spent time in New England has encountered the legacy of these architects. Their influence was considerable as they spread their ideas through professional organizations, including the Society of Arts and Crafts. The views that they advanced were adopted by many of their colleagues in the region and affected much of what was erected at the turn of the twentieth century. These buildings are not the quaint colonial churches and houses lodged in the American imagination. These buildings are larger and more elaborately finished, usually constructed of masonry, not wood. They are everywhere, scattered across the towns and campuses of New England. Today they have become historic buildings—handsome and substantial, admired for their craftsmanship, honored by those who live with them. Yet they also embody certain principles, ideals that guided their design. They are expressions of simplicity and sincerity, values at the heart of the Arts and Crafts movement in New England.

CHAPTER ONE

Dramatis Personae:
Twelve Architect-Leaders

From ENGLAND TO NEW ENGLAND, the theories and values of the Arts and Crafts movement crossed the Atlantic, resonating with the men and women who contributed to an emerging Arts and Crafts sensibility in Boston. In England the movement was inspired by the views of John Ruskin and William Morris, and from an early date, their writings were published and read in the Massachusetts capital. At the turn of the twentieth century, when English architects were designing buildings that reflected Arts and Crafts themes, Boston architects stayed current with the work of their overseas colleagues and were receptive to English trends—trends that became the basis for the Arts and Crafts architecture in New England.

The Arts and Crafts movements in England and Boston took shape in different ways. In England the movement was promulgated by the formation of guilds, leading to the show sponsored by the Arts and Crafts Exhibition Society in 1888. The movement in Boston, on the other hand, began with the exhibition held in the spring of 1897.[1] Perhaps the people in Boston first organized an exhibition rather than a guild because they understood that an exhibition would involve a finite time commitment. Then, too, the fact that the Boston exhibition was organized by a craftsman printer, Henry Lewis Johnson, and not an architect may have been relevant. Johnson was motivated by a desire to showcase the finest work then being produced by his fellow artisans. Yet as in England, architects in Boston were involved from the start, and ultimately they would promote the cause through a variety of activities. In 1897, when the prospectus for an exhibition of the Arts and Crafts was circulated, thirty-seven Bostonians signed on as endorsers. Among them were nine architects: Robert D. Andrews, Clarence H. Blackall, Francis W. Chandler, Charles A. Cummings, Bertram G. Goodhue, Alexander W. Longfellow Jr., R. Clipston Sturgis, C. Howard Walker, and H. Langford Warren.[2]

Johnson was an effective organizer, and much of the success of what became the nation's first major Arts and Crafts exhibition must be attributed to him. At the same time, he was able to achieve what he did because of the widespread interest in the Arts and Crafts ideas that had taken hold in Boston by the late 1890s. Charles Eliot Norton, who taught fine arts courses at Harvard, had created an awareness of Arts and Crafts concerns and sympathy for the movement's goals; and to a lesser extent, the architect Henry Hobson Richardson, who ran his practice in the Boston suburb of Brookline, contributed through his admiration of Morris and other English craftsmen. Also important were Boston's institutions and organizations that brought the design community together: Harvard, MIT, the Museum of Fine Arts and its school, the Boston Society of Architects, and the Boston Architectural Club. In March of 1897, shortly before the exhibition opened, Candace Wheeler, president of the Associated Artists of New York, commented that an attempt had been made for several years to organize such an event in New York City. But she believed that Boston had "the best nucleus for industrial art work" because of its many schools.[3]

Advocacy for the craftsman was regularly expressed at the meetings of the Boston Society of Architects. At an 1893 meeting, Andrews presented a paper in which he spoke about the need to reunite architecture with artistic crafts.[4] Two years later, he went further by declaring to his colleagues that the craftsman was a more vital man in art than the architect. Greek and Gothic buildings, he argued, were mainly the work of craftsmen, unlike the less admirable Roman and Renaissance buildings in which the architect was the "dominating power."[5] One may wonder how Andrews's colleagues reacted when he told them that "the decline of art in any period was contemporaneous with the appearance of the architect." This remarkable view did not seem to provoke any objections—at least any that were recorded. Whatever the case, Andrews's desire to bring together the craftsman and architect was widely shared.

As for the logistical demands of organizing the Arts and Crafts exhibition, the architects provided Johnson with a successful model. Beginning in 1890, architectural exhibitions had been presented by the Boston Architectural Club, sometimes sponsored jointly with the Boston Society of Architects.[6] When the Arts and Crafts exhibition opened to the public on April 5, 1897, the accompanying exhibition on architecture was organized by the club. Andrews chaired the exhibition committee and was assisted by a team that included architects George Edward Barton of Boston and Walter Cope of Philadelphia. On the catalogue cover was a wash drawing of the restored

FIG. 1.1 Cover of Boston
Architectural Club
exhibition catalogue,
wash drawing by A. C.
Fernald, 1897.

Massachusetts State House (fig. 1.1), designed by Charles Bulfinch and dating from 1795 to 1798, a recent preservation victory achieved mainly through the efforts of the architectural community.[7]

Before the Arts and Crafts exhibition came to a close, a group of men and women met to consider whether to hold another exhibition and form a sponsoring organization.[8] By June 1897, the Society of Arts and Crafts was chartered. The architects among the founders were Andrews, Barton, Longfellow, George Russell Shaw, Walker, and Warren. Founding craftsmen included Johnson, along with carvers Hugh Cairns, John Evans, and Johannes Kirchmayer, and the printer Daniel Berkeley Updike. Academic supporters included Charles Eliot Norton and Denman Ross, and patrons included Arthur Astor Carey and Samuel D. Warren II (not closely related to the architect, if related at all).[9]

Once the society was established, a governance structure was adopted. Members voted for individuals to serve on a council, and then the council elected its officers and made the decisions for the organization. Three tiers of membership were created: Apprentices, whose designation was soon changed to Craftsmen; Masters, who were distinguished designers; and Patrons, who were supporters and paid higher dues. Most of the architect members were promptly advanced from the level of Craftsman to Master, whereas most of the craftsmen never became Masters. By 1900 the society had opened a salesroom to display and sell its artisans' work. In order to evaluate the entries and maintain a high standard, a jury was appointed. Among its thirteen members were the architects Longfellow, Shaw, Sturgis, Walker, and Warren. Ross also held a seat.[10] The jury readily offered criticism and rejected work, which frustrated the craftsmen but enhanced the reputation of the organization. Within a few years, the society had attracted some of the nation's most prominent craftsmen as members, including Henry Chapman Mercer from Doylestown, Pennsylvania; Adelaide Alsop Robineau from Syracuse, New York; and Artus and Anne Van Briggle from Colorado Springs, Colorado.

Nevertheless, most of the members who joined the Society of Arts and Crafts came from New England, and the organization reflected the region's culture in many respects. To begin with, the way in which many of its leaders maintained close connections with England became a recognized characteristic of the society. Its mission, dedicated to promoting "mutually helpful relations" between architects and craftsmen, was written by Norton and directly derived from his friendship with Ruskin and Morris. Through the early twentieth century, the goal of bringing together architects and craftsmen continued to be supported by England's Arts and Crafts leaders, and the Boston organization excelled in this effort as well. Indeed, in 1910 the English architect C. R. Ashbee wrote a letter on behalf of a countryman visiting Boston, asking the society's salesroom manager to show the guest projects in which "the craftsmen actually work *for* and *with* the architects."[11]

As the Society of Arts and Crafts flourished, it reflected the culture of Boston in other ways. For example, its leaders shared the desire to emphasize education. The society maintained a library, sponsored lectures, presented large and small exhibitions, and published the magazine *Handicraft*.

Education to the society's leaders meant the study of history, whether of architecture or the applied arts, following the lead of the region's educational institutions. Less obvious, yet also a reflection of Boston's character, was the orientation of the society's leaders toward law and governance. To be sure, this interest became widespread in America during the Progressive Era. Yet a regard for the law permeated Boston's professional and academic communities at the turn of the century. By this time, the members of the Boston Society of Architects revised their bylaws almost every year.[12] In Cambridge, Harvard Law School was expanding and emerging as a nationally prominent institution. Oliver Wendell Holmes Jr. also generated interest in the law as he delivered public lectures and wrote about the workings of the courts and judges. Boston's professionals mixed with each other. In fact, Holmes and his wife, as well as Boston attorney Louis D. Brandeis and his wife, visited the 1897 Arts and Crafts exhibition.[13] When the leaders of the Society of Arts and Crafts established their jury in 1900, at least some of them would have been responding to the contemporary discourse on jurisprudence.

With the opening of the society's salesroom that same year, the organization asserted its commitment to free enterprise. Carey, the second president of the society, hoped to advance the socialistic goals of Morris, but the society's other leaders would not subscribe to this direction, and Carey resigned late in 1903. That November, Warren, in his role as the group's third president, explained to the members, "The fact of William Morris's socialism and the socialism of his friends has led both the friends of the arts and crafts movement and those who are indifferent to it to lay too much stress on socialism as connected with artistic production."[14] In the following year, the society moved its salesroom from 14 Somerset Street to 9 Park Street, and by 1905, it had become self-supporting. In Boston, the Arts and Crafts movement was tempered by an Emersonian emphasis on the individual. For the architects who served in leadership positions, the society was not a charity. It had to succeed, and it did succeed by developing a market for beautifully crafted products.

From 1897 through 1917, forty architects joined the Society of Arts and Crafts.[15] Twelve of them moved into leadership roles, serving as officers and members of the governing council, members of committees, and members of the jury.[16] All twelve became Masters, another indicator of their prominence in the organization. As practicing architects, they demonstrated their commitment to "mutually helpful relations," collaborating with the artisan

FIG. 1.2 Robert Day Andrews.

members of the society by embellishing their buildings with the craftsmen's sculpture, carved wood, tile, and stained glass. Their buildings also were conservative, notable for their restraint. Several of the twelve architect-leaders had lived and trained in England. Several were educators and historians. In terms of their personalities, all twelve were self-confident and energetic. Short biographies of these twelve individuals document the roles they played in governing the Society of Arts and Crafts and highlight some of the more important buildings that they designed during the late nineteenth and early twentieth centuries.

ROBERT DAY ANDREWS (1857–1928), a charter member of the Society of Arts and Crafts, served on its council and sat on the Workshops and Classes Committee (fig. 1.2).[17] A graduate of Hartford High School in Connecticut, Andrews entered the office of Peabody and Stearns in 1874.[18] During the 1875–76 academic year, he was a special student at MIT, and he then worked with other architects and traveled through Europe. When he returned to Boston in the early 1880s, he was hired by Richardson.[19] Cheerful and entertaining, Bob Andrews was described as "always a brainy man."[20] From 1884 to 1890, he worked in partnership with the architect Herbert Jaques; they were then joined by A. Neal Rantoul, the firm becoming Andrews, Jaques, and Rantoul.

Andrews's leadership in restoring Bulfinch's Massachusetts State House (1896–98) was much admired, and this success led to his restoration, with H. Hilliard Smith, of the Bulfinch State House in Hartford, Connecticut (1918–20). Assisted by Sturgis and William Chapman, Andrews oversaw the design and construction of the wings added to the Massachusetts State House (1914–17). He designed a number of school buildings, including Massachusetts high schools in Brookline (1894) and West Roxbury (1898–1901). Government buildings included the Worcester County Courthouse (1897–99) and Nahant Town Hall (1912), both in Massachusetts. Andrews also designed campus buildings, including an athletics center for the University of Vermont in Burlington (1901; now the Royall Tyler Theater) and a dormitory for the Women's College of Brown University (Miller Hall), Providence, Rhode Island (1910), as well as the Connecticut School for the Blind in Hartford (1913–17). Like several of his colleagues, Andrews was hired to work on clubhouses, including the Hartford Club (1901–4). Unlike most of his colleagues, he designed commercial buildings, such as the State Mutual Building in downtown Boston (1902–3). Typical for architects during this period, Andrews and his partners designed many large residences, a number of them in Maine. In Hartford, his firm's Williams house (1909) was especially notable and today serves as the Connecticut governor's mansion. Although most of the firm's projects were located in New England, the architects designed several buildings in Colorado, including office buildings in Denver and campus buildings for Colorado College.

GEORGE EDWARD BARTON (1871–1923), a charter member of the Society of Arts and Crafts, was its first secretary, a member of the council, and a member of the Workshops and Ecclesiastical Work Committees (fig. 1.3). Barton trained as a draftsman under Henry Vaughan, and he was employed for several years by the firm Cram, Wentworth, and Goodhue.[21] In 1895 Barton traveled to England to study domestic and church architecture.[22] Early in his career, probably during this sojourn, Barton spent time in London with Morris. Later he credited Morris with arousing his enthusiasm "for sociological study."[23] Returning to Boston, Barton entered Sturgis's office, and in 1902 they formed the partnership of Sturgis and Barton, which lasted seven years.[24]

While in England, Barton evidently befriended Sydney Cockerell, who had worked for Morris in acquiring a collection of medieval manuscripts. Once he returned home, Barton played a small but key role in putting the trustees of the Boston Public Library in touch with Cockerell.[25] Following

FIG. 1.3 George Edward Barton.

Morris's death in 1896, Cockerell worked as an agent, and between 1900 and 1901, he purchased several medieval manuscripts for the library, two of which had belonged to Morris.[26]

Like many of the founders of the Society of Arts and Crafts, Barton pursued a range of interests. Early in the twentieth century, he wrote a libretto for an opera, *The Pipe of Desire*, composed by Frederick S. Converse and performed in Boston in 1906. In 1910 it received attention as the first opera written by Americans and the first opera in English to be performed at New York City's Metropolitan Opera House during the regular season.[27]

Barton's many endeavors are all the more impressive considering that by 1901 he had contracted tuberculosis.[28] Eleven years later, he left Boston for Colorado to recuperate. He improved, but then his energy and attraction to social causes got the better of him. While investigating starvation among farmers, one of Barton's feet froze, leading to a partial amputation and paralysis on the left side of his body. This time, Barton entered a sanitarium in Clifton Springs, New York, where he doggedly pushed himself to recover by engaging in carpentry and gardening. In 1914 he bought a house in Clifton Springs, renovated it, and opened its doors to convalescents. Called Consolation House, it was a school, workshop, and vocational bureau. Three years later, Consolation House was the setting for the founding of the National Society for the Promotion of Occupational Therapy (later renamed the American Occupational Therapy Association), and Barton was elected its first president.[29] Today he is internationally recognized for his role in the

history of occupational therapy and for advancing recovery through craft work.[30]

In Barton's relatively short architectural career, he pursued an interest in design with a social mission. He won the Roger Shattuck Prize in 1898 for a plan for worker housing, and he wrote in *Architectural Review* about the model worker village of Port Sunlight, near Birkenhead, England, established in 1888 by Lever Brothers.[31] With Sturgis, Barton designed the South Bay Union (1901–3), a community center; and the Franklin Union (1906–8), a technical training school. Both served the immigrants living in Boston's South End. In Colorado Springs, Barton designed the Myron Stratton Home (1913), a refuge for the poor of Colorado.

RALPH ADAMS CRAM (1863–1942) served on the council of the Society of Arts and Crafts, belonged to the Exhibitions Committee and Workshops and Classes Committee, and chaired the Ecclesiastical Work Committee (fig. 1.4).[32] Born in Hampton Falls, New Hampshire, Cram moved to Boston in 1881 to apprentice with the architectural firm of Rotch and Tilden.[33] During this period, he began writing as an art critic for the

Boston Evening Transcript. He would become a prolific author, publishing twenty-two books and dozens of articles, some scholarly and some philosophical. After an apprenticeship of five years, Cram left Boston to travel in England and on the Continent. In Italy he was stirred by the Roman Catholic liturgy, leading him to break with his Unitarian upbringing and convert to Anglo-Catholicism.

Cram and his partners attracted attention for their contribution to the Gothic Revival. In 1889 Cram and Charles Wentworth opened an office in Boston, and three years later, they brought Bertram Goodhue into the partnership, becoming Cram, Wentworth, and Goodhue. After Wentworth died in 1897, Cram and Goodhue formed a partnership with Frank Ferguson. The first major success for Cram and his colleagues was the design of All Saints Church, Ashmont, in the Dorchester area of Boston (1891–94), inspired by English country churches of the fifteenth century. In the coming decades, Cram would design churches of this type for congregations across the United States. A prominent critic of the age, Montgomery Schuyler, admired the simplicity of the Ashmont church and its refined decoration, observing that the "mutual knowledge" shared by the architects and their craftsmen produced superior work.[34] In his reverence for medieval craft, Cram was influenced by contemporary English architects as well as by Ruskin and Morris. In 1892, he and Goodhue published a magazine called the *Knight-Errant*, emulating Morris's fine art printing that was inspired by medieval manuscripts. Cram also was attracted to medieval faith and religious ritual. Through the Society of Arts and Crafts, he encouraged craftsmen to produce high-quality liturgical objects.

Although Cram and his partners became best known for their churches, they also received recognition for an Elizabethan apartment building, Richmond Court, in Brookline, Massachusetts (1898), and the Gothic Revival Hunt Library in Nashua, New Hampshire (1901–3). In 1898 Cram, Goodhue, and Ferguson were hired by Wheaton College in Norton, Massachusetts, to develop a campus master plan. Campus work, involving supervisory positions as well as the design of individual buildings, would become another major area of Cram's practice. In New England, he was the supervisory architect for Mount Holyoke and Wellesley Colleges, and his firm designed buildings for Williams College in Massachusetts, Phillips Exeter Academy in New Hampshire, St. George's School in Rhode Island, and Taft and Choate Schools in Connecticut. Cram and his partners also made substantial contributions to the campuses of the United States Military

Academy at West Point, New York; Sweet Briar College and the University of Richmond in Virginia; Princeton University in New Jersey; and Rice University in Texas. As in their ecclesiastic work, Cram and his partners excelled in designing collegiate Gothic buildings, but they designed campus buildings in the Georgian Revival style, too. For Rice University, Cram turned to Italian Byzantine architecture to establish an image that seemed appropriate for the sultry Houston climate.

In 1914 Cram was invited to head the architecture program at MIT, where he would teach through 1922. His medievalist sympathies were valued for offering an alternative point of view to the program's Beaux-Arts teaching tradition.[35] Cram had become a widely respected leader of the profession. He was president of the Boston Society of Architects and had served six years as chairman of the Committee on Education for the American Institute of Architects. Also in 1914, Cram was appointed the first chairman of Boston's City Planning Board. At the end of 1913, Goodhue broke with Cram and established an independent practice in New York City while Cram and Ferguson carried on in Boston. Through his later years, Cram remained passionate about religious architecture, overseeing a new design and construction of the Cathedral of St. John the Divine in New York City. Perhaps surprisingly, he also began accepting commissions for office buildings. The National Life Insurance Building in Montpelier, Vermont (1921), is typical of the restrained classicism that he favored for projects of this genre.

Like his colleagues in the Society of Arts and Crafts, Cram valued scholarship as the basis for his work. In 1925 he joined eight others to found the Medieval Academy of America. He was its first clerk, and he later served as president. Whether in his practice, his publications, or his organizational activities, Cram sought to disseminate his ideas to the nation. On December 13, 1926, Cram appeared on the cover of *Time* magazine as its man of the year.

Lois Lilley Howe (1864–1964) was a member of the council of the Society of Arts and Crafts, sat on the Salesrooms and Windows Committee, and chaired the Library and Entertainment Committee (fig. 1.5). She was born and raised in Cambridge, Massachusetts, and graduated from Cambridge High School.[36] Although she was accepted to enter the Harvard Annex, the program for young women that became Radcliffe College, Howe chose instead to study design at the School of the Museum of Fine Arts. Entering in 1882, she spent four years there and was one of C. Howard

Walker's first students. When her father died in 1887, her mother decided to sell a large house and build a smaller one, commissioning a family friend, the architect Francis W. Chandler, to design it. Howe already had developed an interest in architecture, and participating in her mother's venture convinced her that she wanted to pursue this career. She presented her case to the president of MIT, Francis A. Walker, who agreed that she should be admitted. In 1888 she began the "partial" or two-year program in architecture—the only female student among the sixty-six entering students.[37] By a fortunate coincidence, Howe received further mentoring from Chandler when he was appointed head of the MIT program at just this time.

After leaving MIT in 1890, Howe worked as a draftsman for the firm Allen and Kenway. She also entered the competition to design the Woman's Building for the World's Columbian Exposition in Chicago, placing second to her friend Sophia Hayden. With the prize money, Howe made her first trip to Europe. During the economic downturn of the 1890s, Howe managed to receive small commissions. By 1900 she had opened an office in Boston, and a year later, with Robert Swain Peabody as her sponsor, she was elected to the American Institute of Architects, becoming its second female member.[38] In 1913 Howe and Eleanor Manning formed Howe and Manning, and in 1926, they expanded the partnership to include Mary Almy.

As a complement to her practice, Howe studied the region's early houses and documented them with measured drawings.[39] She and MIT graduate Constance Fuller published *Details from Old New England Houses*, and Howe published a monograph on the 1785 Colonel Robert Means house, located in Amherst, New Hampshire.[40] In 1931, the American Institute of Architects elected Howe a fellow, making her the third woman to attain this distinction.[41] She also was devoted to the Museum School, serving on its council from 1897 through 1931 and as secretary from 1897 through 1912. From 1932 to 1947, Howe was a member of the Housing Association of Metropolitan Boston, and in her later years, she was active in the Cambridge Historical Society and the Cambridge Plant and Garden Club, the oldest garden club in the country.

Howe's architectural practice focused on residential projects, many of which involved the reconstruction and expansion of colonial and federal houses.[42] She also worked on club houses, including the Business Women's Club in Boston (1912 and 1918), and small commercial buildings. She rebuilt an existing colonial house for the Concord Art Center (1922–23) and an old brick barn for the Fitchburg Art Center (1926), both in Massachusetts.

FIG. 1.5
Lois Lilley Howe.

FIG. 1.6 Alexander Wadsworth
Longfellow Jr.

Most of Howe's projects were in New England, but her best-known commission is probably Denny Place, a group of houses that she designed for Mariemont, Ohio (1923–25), the model garden suburb outside Cincinnati planned by John Nolen.

ALEXANDER WADSWORTH LONGFELLOW JR. (1854–1934) was a charter member of the Society of Arts and Crafts and served for many years as its vice president, a member of the council, and a member of the jury (fig. 1.6). He was chairman of the Membership Committee and sat on the Exhibitions Committee. Born in Portland, Maine, Longfellow was known as Waddy. He attended Harvard College, graduating in 1876.[43] In the fall of that year, he entered MIT as a special student in architecture and completed the program two years later. The firm of Cabot and Chandler provided him with some practical experience, and then he continued his studies at the École des Beaux-Arts in Paris from 1879 through the end of 1881. When Longfellow returned to Boston, he joined Richardson's studio and stayed for four years. By this time, he was ready to start his own practice and began working with Alfred Harlow. In 1887 they were joined by Frank Alden, forming Longfellow, Alden, and Harlow. In addition to devoting time to the Society of Arts and Crafts, Longfellow held prominent positions with several other Boston organizations. He was a director of the Boston Cooperative Building Company, dedicated to providing decent housing for the working poor. Longfellow also was a trustee of the Museum of Fine Arts and a member of the Boston Art Commission, serving on both boards alongside Sam Warren, his friend from the Society of Arts and Crafts.

The first major project for Longfellow and his partners was Cambridge City Hall (1888–91), a Richardsonian Romanesque building. During this period, Longfellow designed a model tenement block for the Cooperative Building Company, erected in Boston in 1889. From 1890 to 1893, he remodeled and expanded a federal period brick dwelling in Cambridge, Fay House, to accommodate a library, music hall, and classrooms for Radcliffe College. Longfellow's approach was sympathetic with the original structure and represents an early example of his interest in the Colonial Revival. Fay House also turned out to be the first of many buildings that Longfellow would design for Radcliffe and Harvard. His Phillips Brooks House (1897–99) was noteworthy for introducing the first fully developed example of Colonial Revival architecture in Harvard Yard. His Colonial Revival Agassiz House (1904) contributed to the emerging character of Radcliffe Yard. In Boston, Longfellow won the competition in 1898 to design the first elevated railway stations. He also designed public schools, including two in Boston—the Oliver Wendell Holmes and Abraham Lincoln Schools, both from 1912.

Alden, like Longfellow, had worked for Richardson, and through this experience, the partners established connections in Pittsburgh. They met with much success there and won the competition for the Carnegie Institute (1891–95). Eventually, maintaining offices in two cities proved untenable, and the partners dissolved the firm in 1895. Alden and Harlow developed their practice in Pittsburgh while Longfellow remained in Boston. In addition to working on large institutional projects, Longfellow designed houses and remodeled existing colonial and federal dwellings in the Boston area, New Hampshire, and Maine. Among his many clients were J. Templeman Coolidge Jr. and Arthur Carey from the Society of Arts and Crafts. In Maine, Longfellow designed several libraries, including the Merrill Memorial Library (1902–5) in Yarmouth, which was built on land donated by Sam Warren.

CHARLES DONAGH MAGINNIS (1867–1955) served on the council of the Society of Arts and Crafts and was a member of the Ecclesiastical Work Committee and Workshops and Classes Committee (fig. 1.7). Born in Londonderry, Ireland, Maginnis studied art at Cusack's Academy in Dublin and the South Kensington Museum School of Art in London.[44] While still in

FIG. 1.7 Charles Donagh Maginnis.

his teens, he immigrated with his widowed mother and siblings to Toronto and began working in an architect's office. From there, he moved to Boston, where he worked for William P. Wentworth and Peabody and Stearns.[45] In 1888 Maginnis was hired by Edmund Wheelwright, who also was an alumnus of the Peabody and Stearns office.[46] When Wheelwright was appointed to the new position of city architect by the mayor of Boston in 1891, he took his young assistant with him. Four years later, Maginnis began teaching pen-and-ink drawing at Cowles Art School in Boston. His teaching experience led to his publishing *Pen Drawing* in 1898, a well-received book that went through seven editions.[47] Also in 1898, Maginnis established a partnership with Timothy Walsh, who had trained with Peabody and Stearns, and Matthew Sullivan, who had trained with Wheelwright. Sullivan left the partnership in 1907, and the firm of Maginnis and Walsh lasted from 1908 through 1954. Maginnis held a seat on the Boston Art Commission, and he served as a trustee of the Museum of Fine Arts. As a native of Ireland, Maginnis faced challenges because of his ethnicity, but he succeeded in his profession and became a national leader. From 1937 to 1939, he was president of the American Institute of Architects. In 1948, the institute awarded Maginnis the gold medal for achievement, an honor that had been given to just fourteen other members in the prior forty-two years.[48] That same year, the Society of Arts and Crafts presented him with its gold medal.

Maginnis and his firm received many major commissions from Roman

Catholic churches, schools, colleges, seminaries, and convents across the country.[49] Like the other architects who were active in the Society of Arts and Crafts, Maginnis admired English Gothic churches and turned to them as a starting point for some of his designs. But he also was attracted to Lombard and Italian Byzantine churches, believing they offered an appropriate tradition when building for Catholics.[50] In 1909 Maginnis and Walsh won the competition to design a new campus for Boston College. Gasson Hall, the central administration and classroom building, featured a soaring Perpendicular tower that would inspire numerous interpretations of the theme on American campuses. The firm designed buildings for the College of the Holy Cross in Worcester, Massachusetts, as well as the University of Notre Dame in South Bend, Indiana. In the 1940s, the architects oversaw several projects for Saint Patrick's Cathedral in New York City, including the design of bronze doors and a new high altar.

Although Maginnis worked primarily for Catholic clients, he also was retained for municipal buildings—extensions of his experience under Wheelwright. His firm designed the North Bennet Street Bathhouse, Boston (1904–6), a police station in the Hyde Park neighborhood of Boston (1918), and several public schools in and around the city. More remarkably, in his later years Maginnis contributed to some of Boston's old-guard institutions. In 1937 Maginnis and Walsh won the competition to rebuild the chancel of Richardson's Trinity Church, an icon of Brahmin Boston.[51] A decade later, the firm designed Moors Hall to anchor the Radcliffe Quadrangle, a Colonial Revival building that comfortably harmonizes with Longfellow's earlier Bertram and Eliot Halls across the lawn.

Louis Chapell Newhall (1869–1925) held a seat on the council of the Society of Arts and Crafts and served as chairman of the Exhibitions Committee (fig. 1.8). A native of Malden, Massachusetts, he graduated from the local high school, enrolled at Tufts College, and then transferred to MIT, where he studied architecture from the fall of 1887 through the spring of 1889.[52] He continued his training in offices, working for J. Merrill Brown, J. Williams Beal, and Arthur H. Bowditch. One of Newhall's important early experiences was assisting Bowditch in the design of Hotel Somerset (1897), an expansive residential hotel at the far end of Commonwealth Avenue in Boston's Back Bay. In 1898 Newhall won the Rotch Traveling Scholarship, enabling him to travel through Europe. Three years later, he formed a partnership with Albert H. Blevins. In 1914 Newhall published a book titled *The Minor Chateaux and Manor Houses of France*.[53] His greatest achieve-

FIG. 1.9 William Edward Putnam Jr.

FIG. 1.8 Louis Chapell Newhall.

ment, however, was his role in supporting the Boston Architectural Club. From 1905 to 1915, he served as its president, and after that, he served as the organization's treasurer, continuing in this capacity until his death. He left a substantial bequest to the club that later was credited with its survival through the Great Depression.[54] While Newhall was president, he oversaw the organization's move in 1911 into a clubhouse at 16 Somerset Street, and he guided the board in developing a curriculum of classes for working architecture students.[55] Over the decades, the club expanded its educational mission and evolved into Boston Architectural College.

Most of the buildings by Newhall and Blevins are located in the Boston area. Their work in the city included the East Boston Gymnasium and Public Baths (1909); William Lloyd Garrison School, Dorchester (1910); and the Boston City Club (1913; now a Suffolk University building). They designed several Gothic Revival churches, such as Third Congregational Church, Cambridge (1911), and Payson Park Congregational Church, Belmont (1915–19). Their Tudor apartment houses and residential hotels were especially successful and received attention in the architectural press. One distinguished example was Burton Halls, Cambridge (1909). Newhall also designed houses, including an unusual Swiss-style chalet (1910–12) in Little Good Harbor, Maine, for F. Holland Day, a leading Boston photographer and member of the Society of Arts and Crafts.[56] In 1916 the firm designed Faculty House (renamed Dickinson House) for Mount Holyoke College in South Hadley, Massachusetts.

WILLIAM EDWARD PUTNAM JR. (1873–1947), the youngest architect in the group of twelve, served the Society of Arts and Crafts for several years as a member of the Craftsmen Membership Committee (fig. 1.9). He was born in the Boston suburb of Newton Centre, attended Chauncy Hall School in the city, and spent four years at Harvard College, graduating in 1896.[57] Putnam then enrolled at MIT, receiving a bachelor of science degree in architecture two years later. When he finished his studies, he worked as a draftsman for Walter H. Kilham.[58] In January of 1900, Putnam opened an office in Boston. When a competition was announced in 1902 for a new Athenaeum building, Putnam partnered with Allen H. Cox, who had been a special student in architecture at MIT when Putnam was there. Several prominent architects competed for the Athenaeum commission, including Peabody and Stearns; Andrews, Jaques, and Rantoul; and Longfellow. However, in what amounted to an upset, the special committee chose the plans of young Putnam and Cox.[59] Although the winning entry was never built, and the existing Athenaeum building was eventually renovated, the partnership between Putnam and Cox proved durable, lasting until Cox's death in 1944.

Putnam's most important buildings were Angell Memorial Animal Hospital (1915), a monumental Colonial Revival veterinary clinic on Longwood Avenue near Harvard Medical School in Boston, and the Unitarian Universalist Society headquarters (1925) on Beacon Street overlooking Boston Common.[60] Putnam was the senior partner in the firm, but Cox attracted many desirable commissions in the Connecticut River Valley where he had grown up. In Amherst, the firm designed seven Amherst College fraternities, all Colonial Revival (1911–1922); the Lord Jeffrey Inn (1925–26); and Jones Library (1927–28). At Mount Holyoke College, the firm designed several Elizabethan buildings, including a classroom building, Skinner Hall (1915); Clapp Science Building (1922–24); two dormitories, Hillside Hall (renamed the Mandelles) and Rockefeller Hall (both 1923); and the New Physics Building (1932; renamed Shattuck Hall). In Boston, Putnam and Cox were the architects of the small but influential Toy Theater, located on Dartmouth Street near Copley Square (1914), and the Kirstein Business Branch of the Boston Public Library (1930), inspired by the central pavilion of Bulfinch's Tontine Crescent, elegant row houses that were long demolished but still admired.

GEORGE RUSSELL SHAW (1848–1937) was a charter member of the Society of Arts and Crafts and served on the Exhibitions Committee (fig.

I.IO).[61] Born in Parkman, Maine, he spent his youth there and in Portland before continuing his studies at Harvard College, graduating in 1869.[62] His brother, Robert Gould Shaw, was younger by two years but also graduated with the class of 1869. Though most of the architects in this circle came from modest Yankee backgrounds, the Shaws descended from wealthy Boston Brahmin families. Their first cousin was the Civil War hero Robert Gould Shaw, who died commanding the first black regiment recruited in the North. In the spring of 1897, the regiment's valor was commemorated with the inauguration of the monument by Augustus Saint-Gaudens on Boston Common.

After Harvard, George Shaw studied architecture at MIT for a year and then traveled to England and France, enrolling at the École des Beaux-Arts.[63] During this period, his brother Robert studied architecture in Munich for three years.[64] In 1873 George launched his architecture practice in Boston, and a year later he and his brother formed a partnership called Shaw and Shaw. By the early 1880s, Robert's satisfaction with his chosen line of work had faded, and he moved on to other pursuits. George, on the other hand, was committed to architecture and went into partnership in 1882 with Henry Sargent Hunnewell, a member of Harvard's class of 1875. By this time, Henry's sister had married Robert, making the connections between the two families especially tight.

The firm of Shaw and Hunnewell lasted twenty years, disbanding in 1902.[65] After he retired, George became a skilled leatherworker. In fact, from 1904 onward, he identified himself in the listings of the Society of Arts and Crafts as a leatherworker rather than as an architect. A related interest led to a book, *Knots: Useful and Ornamental*, which he illustrated with 193 drawings.[66] Released in 1924, it was extremely successful and continues to be published. Shaw's main interest, however, was his research on pines, and he wrote books and articles on the subject.[67] Perhaps influenced by the exhibitions of the Society of Arts and Crafts, to which he contributed, Shaw organized a permanent display of conifers for Harvard.[68]

Much of the work of Shaw and Hunnewell reflects the partners' many connections to Boston's leading families and the Harvard community. The architects also were drawn to projects relating to science and medicine. In 1880 George Shaw was hired to develop an addition to the Harvard University Museum, a natural history museum, and the firm was hired for another addition to the same building in 1900. Shaw and Hunnewell designed Harvard's Jefferson Physical Laboratory (1882–84), an early physics building that was a gift of Thomas Jefferson Coolidge. More important buildings followed during the 1890s. The firm designed four buildings for McLean Hospital for the mentally ill in Belmont (1893–95), Free Hospital for Women in Brookline (1894–95), Convalescent Home of Children's Hospital in Wellesley Hills (1894), and Massachusetts Eye and Ear Infirmary in Boston (1897). In 1900 Shaw and Hunnewell designed Pierce Hall at Harvard, a large Georgian Revival building dedicated to the study of engineering. In the early 1880s, the firm designed a library for Watertown and a library and town hall for Wellesley. Their experiences with libraries and medical clients would have been relevant when they were hired to design the Boston Medical Library (1901; now owned by Boston Conservatory), located in the Fenway, to the west of the city.

In the 1880s, Shaw and Hunnewell set themselves apart from most Boston architects in the way they designed buildings in a restrained classical style at a time when Richardson's Romanesque prevailed. During the 1890s, they shifted direction and for the most part designed buildings that reflected the enthusiasm of Boston architects for the Colonial Revival. This interest was pursued by a younger generation of Boston architects, including George Shaw's son, Thomas Mott Shaw, whose firm Perry, Shaw, and Hepburn would gain widespread recognition for its work at Colonial Williamsburg during the 1930s.[69]

FIG. 1.11 Richard Clipston Sturgis.

RICHARD CLIPSTON STURGIS (1860–1951) was appointed in 1900 to the first jury of the Society of Arts and Crafts, indicating his colleagues' esteem for him (fig. 1.11). For some reason, he never attended the jury's meetings, yet he was devoted to the society, serving on the Library Committee, the Exhibitions Committee, and the Workshops and Classes Committee. From 1917 to 1920, he led the society as its fourth president.

Like George Shaw, Sturgis descended from Brahmin families and was well connected in the city through a web of family relations and friends. He was born in Boston, attended St. Paul's School in Concord, New Hampshire, and then entered Harvard College, graduating with the class of 1881.[70] That fall he took his first step toward becoming an architect by working for his uncle, John Hubbard Sturgis, whose firm of Sturgis and Brigham designed the original 1876 building for the Museum of Fine Arts. In the summer of 1883, young Clip, as he was known, left Boston for London, where he apprenticed through December of 1884 in the office of the architect Robert W. Edis. Capping this experience, he traveled extensively in England and on the Continent before he returned to Boston and rejoined his uncle's office in the fall of 1886. When the senior Sturgis died in 1888, Clip took over the business, entering into a partnership with William R. Cabot. The firm of Sturgis and Cabot lasted until 1893. From 1902 to 1909, Sturgis worked in partnership with Barton. The fact that Barton had trained under Vaughan and Cram would have appealed to Sturgis; all of them as designers were oriented toward English architects such as George F. Bodley and John D. Sedding.

During the first decade of the twentieth century, Sturgis's career took off. In 1902 the mayor of Boston appointed him to the three-man Boston Schoolhouse Commission, an independent board that had just been created to oversee the process of erecting school buildings for the city, including hiring architects and shaping the plans. From the beginning, Sturgis was chairman, serving until 1908, and he led the commission in a major national study of school design.[71] Meantime, in 1903 Sturgis was designated the architect to the Board of Trustees of the Museum of Fine Arts when it prepared to relocate the museum to a new site in the Fenway. The following year, Sturgis traveled with a team of museum leaders, including Sam Warren, to examine European museums, and Sturgis summarized their findings in a report that became the basis for the new building. Sturgis was a prolific writer, contributing entries to Russell Sturgis's *Dictionary of Architecture and Building* (1901–2) as well as many essays for periodicals. He wrote on English gardens, English buildings, and Christopher Wren.[72] From 1914 to 1915, Clipston Sturgis served as president of the American Institute of Architects, and under his leadership, the organization established its headquarters in Washington, D.C.[73]

Buildings by Sturgis may be found in every New England state.[74] Early in his career, he demonstrated an interest in designing school buildings, such as the Willard School in Quincy, Massachusetts (1889–91). Private schools employed him for campus work, including the Winsor School in Boston (1908–10) and his alma mater, St. Paul's, which hired him for several projects, most notably the Armour Infirmary (1912–14). From 1909 to 1912, he designed a new campus for the Perkins Institution for the Blind in Watertown, Massachusetts. Mount Holyoke College hired him to direct campus planning from 1915 to 1918. With Barton and on his own, Sturgis pursued an interest in buildings that served the working class and the poor. These included bathhouses for the Boston Parks Commission (1896); South Bay Union in Boston's South End (1901–3); Franklin Union (Benjamin Franklin Institute of Technology), also in the South End (1906–8); Elizabeth Peabody Settlement House, Boston (1912–13); and worker housing for the Bridgeport Housing Company and the United States Housing Corporation in Bridgeport, Connecticut (1917–19). Municipalities hired Sturgis for projects such as the public library in Brookline, Massachusetts

(1909), and the town hall for Arlington, Massachusetts (1912). He designed a number of bank buildings, including the First National Bank of Boston (1906) and the Federal Reserve Bank in Boston (1919–22).

Over the course of his career, Sturgis enjoyed residential work and was commissioned for some large and elaborately finished houses. Although most of his clients were located in New England, he was hired to renovate a New York City town house for J. Pierpont Morgan Jr. (1891–92) and to design a large country house in Green Lake, Wisconsin (1906–8), for Victor F. Lawson, editor and publisher of the *Chicago Daily News*. Like many of his architect colleagues in the Society of Arts and Crafts, Sturgis admired colonial and federal architecture, including the work of Bulfinch. Between 1912 and 1914, Sturgis oversaw the restoration of Boston's Old North Church, and he worked with Robert Andrews and William Chapman in designing new wings for the Bulfinch State House (1914–17).

CHARLES HOWARD WALKER (1857–1936) was a charter member of the Society of Arts and Crafts (fig. 1.12). He belonged to its Library, Exhibitions, and Workshops and Classes Committees, was a member of the council, and became a vice president. Between 1922 and 1925, he served as president, at a time when the society had nearly 1,100 members; he served as president again from 1930 to 1933.[75] When the first jury was created in 1900, Walker was among those appointed, and he held the position of critic of the jury starting in 1909, meeting weekly with craftsmen and writing evaluations about their work to help them improve.[76]

Walker became recognized as one of Boston's leading educators and authorities on design, yet his own formal education was limited. Called Howdy by his family and friends, he was raised in the city, attended its public schools, and entered the office of Sturgis and Brigham, training under John Hubbard Sturgis.[77] In 1879 he went to New York City, training for two more years. He then left the country to join the expedition to Assos in Asia Minor that was sponsored by the Archaeological Institute of America. Walker also traveled extensively in Europe.[78] By the mid-1880s, he was back in Boston and opened his practice. In 1889 he formed a partnership with Herbert R. Best, who soon left for Omaha and established an office there. Two years later, Thomas R. Kimball joined the partnership. When Best died that spring, Kimball moved west to take over the office. In 1900 Walker and Kimball dissolved amicably, with Kimball staying in Omaha. In 1919 Walker began working in partnership with his son Harold.

Walker was the consummate teacher. In 1884 he began lecturing at MIT

FIG. 1.12 Charles Howard Walker.

on the history of ornament, and he continued teaching there until his retirement in 1933. A year after he met his first students at MIT, he began teaching
a course on decoration at the Museum School. He also lectured at the Lowell Institute, at Harvard, and at New England Conservatory of Music. With
Katherine B. Child, he founded the Child-Walker School of Fine Arts in
1913. He expanded on his teaching through his editorial and writing activities. In addition to serving as an editor of *Architectural Review* from the time
of its inception in 1891, Walker published *Parish Churches of England* in 1915,
and the monograph "Some Old Houses on the Southern Coast of Maine"
in 1918.[79] He wrote the chapter on classical architecture and the epilogue
for *The Significance of the Fine Arts*, published by the American Institute of
Architects in 1923. He also wrote the book *Theory of Mouldings*, published
in 1926 and reissued in 2007.[80]

Like several of his architect colleagues, Walker was appointed to the
Boston Art Commission, serving from 1898 to 1899. Like Cram, Walker
was interested in the emerging field of planning, and supported the cause as
president of the Metropolitan Improvement League, Boston, from 1904 to
1912. The American Institute of Architects awarded Walker its gold medal
in 1922, and he received another gold medal from the Society of Arts and
Crafts in 1929.

Walker worked on a wide variety of building types. Like Longfellow,
Walker designed a model tenement house for the Boston Cooperative
Building Company, erected in the South End in 1886. Along with city
houses and country houses, he designed a residential hotel, Hotel Ludlow,
overlooking the apse of Richardson's Trinity Church, for Denman Ross

(1888–89). He also designed the Congregational Mount Vernon Church on Beacon Street in the Back Bay (1891–92). Like his colleagues, Walker was hired to build public school buildings in and around Boston, including the Longfellow School in Roslindale (1897). He designed several small libraries, two of which are in Maine: William Fogg Library in Eliot (1906–7) and Baxter Memorial Library in Gorham (1908), both Colonial Revival. Like Andrews, Walker accepted commercial projects and designed office buildings. The Niles Building (1915) and the Oliver Ditson Building (1918), both in Boston, are distinguished by their restrained classicism. Beyond New England, Walker's most important work involved the planning of two large expositions: the Trans-Mississippi Exposition in Omaha (1898), for which Walker and Kimball were architects-in-chief; and the Louisiana Purchase Exposition in St. Louis, Missouri (1904), for which Walker served on the board of architects. He also designed the Massachusetts Building and the Electricity Building for the St. Louis exposition. When Walker died, he was described not only as an architect but also as a pioneer automobile designer.[81] Design of all things interested him.

HERBERT LANGFORD WARREN (1857–1917) was a charter member of the Society of Arts and Crafts, became a vice president, and then served as its third president from late in 1903 until his death in 1917 (fig. 1.13). He sat on the Library and House Committees and was chairman of the Exhibitions Committee. He also was appointed to the first jury, and he was an associate editor of *Handicraft*, the society's magazine.

Warren was born in Manchester, England, to an American father and an English mother, and was raised mainly in England.[82] Between 1869 and 1871, however, he attended the gymnasia in Gotha and Dresden, attaining fluency in German. Returning to England, Warren studied until 1875 at Owens College in Manchester, where his courses included watercolor painting and drawing with William Walker. Both Walker and Ruskin had been taught by J. D. Harding, and Warren shared their interest in natural detail. He then spent a year training under the Manchester architect William Dawes.

While Warren was still in England, his parents relocated to Boston, and he decided to join them. In the fall of 1877, he matriculated at MIT, where he stayed for two years. Between 1879 and 1884, he worked in Richardson's studio, establishing lifelong friendships with Andrews and Longfellow. Also during this period, he enrolled as a special student at Harvard to attend Norton's lectures. A year of travel in Europe followed, and he embarked on

FIG. I.13 Herbert Langford Warren.

his practice in Boston in 1885. During the early 1890s, Warren maintained an office in Troy, New York, and from 1894 to 1895, he worked in partnership with Lewis Bacon. In 1900, Warren entered into the partnership of Warren, Smith, and Biscoe, which lasted until Maurice Biscoe left for Denver in 1906. From that time forward, Warren and Frank Patterson Smith enjoyed a successful working relationship until Warren's death.

After lecturing on Renaissance art for a year at the Museum School, Warren was hired in 1893 by Harvard president Charles W. Eliot to develop an architecture program. Over time, the undergraduate program became a master's degree program, and in 1912, the School of Architecture was established with Warren at its helm. Two years later, he became the dean of the faculty of architecture. He also was a member of the fine arts department, advising on the department's first doctorate. In addition to his regular duties at Harvard, from 1916 to 1917, he was a lecturer at MIT and the Cambridge School of Architectural and Landscape Design for Women.

Early in his career, from late 1885 through 1887, Warren handled the architectural coverage for *Sanitary Engineer*. In addition to editing *Handicraft*, he directed the *Architectural Quarterly of Harvard University*. He contributed entries to Russell Sturgis's *Dictionary of Architecture and Building* and Edmund Buckley's *The Fine Arts*.[83] At the time of his death, Warren was finishing *The Foundations of Classic Architecture*, intended to be the first of a multivolume history of architecture.[84] Thanks to the efforts of Fiske Kimball, a former student, the work was published posthumously in 1919.

Warren and his firm designed Colonial Revival municipal buildings, including Massachusetts town halls in Lincoln (1891–92) and Billerica (1894–95), as well as the city hall in Concord, New Hampshire (1902–3).[85] Also in Massachusetts, the firm designed Gothic Revival churches in Cliftondale (1892–93) and Winchester (1904 and 1911), as well as the chapel for the New Church Theological School in Cambridge (1899–1901). Warren and his firm designed a residential compound, Renfrew Park, in Middleton, Rhode Island (1890), and campus buildings for Proctor Academy in Andover, New Hampshire (1909). The architects also undertook several projects for Harvard, including the Soldiers Field gates, gatehouse, and Carey Cage (1897–1900), and a large 1906 addition to Gore Hall, the Harvard library that was demolished and replaced in the next decade by Widener Library. Between 1914 and 1917, Warren and Smith built Harvard's Germanic Museum (renamed the Busch-Reisinger Museum, now the Minda de Gunzburg Center for European Studies), following the conceptual designs of German Bestelmeyer. Beyond New England, Warren's major projects were the Troy Orphan Asylum (1891); National Church of the Holy City in Washington, D.C. (1894–96); and the campus plan and main building for Women's Methodist College (now Huntingdon College) in Montgomery, Alabama (1909–11).

Warren's contribution to the Arts and Crafts movement in New England cannot be overstated. His upbringing was ideal in many ways. Reared in the Swedenborgian faith, he was receptive to Emersonian thought. His English background gave him insight into the English Arts and Crafts movement as it was emerging, and also would have given him a bit of cachet among his colleagues in Boston and at Harvard. The fact that Warren was fluent in German would have appealed to President Eliot and to Norton, and it would have been respected by others in the Harvard community. A natural leader, Warren embraced a national perspective for the Society of Arts and Crafts and its cause. He also served as the first president of the National League of Handicraft Societies from 1907 to 1911. Warren believed that architecture and design more generally had to be based in scholarly study, an essential aspect of Arts and Crafts architecture in New England. Inspired by Norton, Warren promoted the ideals of sobriety and restraint, simplicity and sincerity. At the same time, as president of the Society of Arts and Crafts, Warren managed to modify these ideals with a pragmatic business perspective—an outlook shared by Progressive Era professionals.

CHAPTER TWO

Arts and Crafts Advocates, Arts and Crafts Architects

THE IDEAS THAT GENERATED THE Arts and Crafts movement in England churned through the early nineteenth century, stirred by several compelling theorists. During the second half of the century, architects, craftsmen, and their supporters began organizing formally in guilds while the architects promoted the craftsmen in the decoration of Arts and Crafts buildings. Toward the end of the century, Arts and Crafts concepts were attracting followers throughout the United States. Among them were architects who embraced the movement and developed distinctive regional styles. By examining these contexts, we may better understand how Boston's Arts and Crafts advocates and architects were distinguished by their English orientation.

The Arts and Crafts Movement Takes Root in England

The impetus for the Arts and Crafts movement may be traced to the late eighteenth century and the beginning of England's Industrial Revolution.[1] Accompanying the rise of manufacturing and the rapid expansion of cities, a struggling underclass of laborers emerged and grew. Over the course of several decades, working conditions worsened and the situation became volatile. At the same time, mass production led to an outpouring of consumer goods that were shoddy and depressingly uniform. As a result, critics started to voice concerns that were both social and aesthetic.

The end of the eighteenth century is also recognized as a time when the Romantic period emerged. Romantic thinking was characterized by a longing for a simpler, gentler past, and in England, authors, artists, and architects turned their attention to the Middle Ages, which came to be identified as a golden era. Another Romantic period phenomenon was a desire to investigate and affirm national identity—an enthusiasm that soon spread through Europe. In England this focus contributed to studies of England's Gothic monuments and the construction of new buildings in English Gothic styles. As people confronted the ills of industry and city life, they grew more appreciative of nature—an appreciation that contributed another dimension to the Gothic Revival. Gothic architecture was considered more natural than neoclassical architecture in its expression of structure, its irregularity, and its ornament. The Romantic regard for nature also stimulated England's well-to-do to purchase rural estates and erect country houses. By the mid-nineteenth century, the opening of commuter rail lines enabled many more people at a range of income levels to move into suburban towns where residents could enjoy swaths of lawn and cultivate gardens.

In the early nineteenth century, the groundwork for the Arts and Crafts movement was laid in writings by the Gothic Revival architect Augustus Welby Northmore Pugin. His major books were *Contrasts: Or, a Parallel between the Noble Edifices of the Fourteenth and Fifteenth Centuries and Similar Buildings of the Present Day; Shewing the Present Decay of Taste*, published in 1836, and *The True Principles of Pointed or Christian Architecture*, from 1841.[2] An ardent reformer, Pugin considered the classicism of early nineteenth-century British architecture to be barren and heartless, contrasting with the embellishment and kindness that he identified with the architecture of the Middle Ages. He also introduced the idea that architectural beauty could be correlated to the "fitness" of a design to its purpose, and he argued that Gothic architecture was beautiful because it met this standard.

All of these concepts would reverberate through the century in the writings of England's Arts and Crafts theorists. Prior to the publication of *Contrasts*, Pugin had converted to Catholicism, adopting the faith of pre-Reformation England, and his advocacy of the Gothic Revival was expressed in a tone that reflected his religious fervor. Through his architectural practice, Pugin explored ways in which his Gothic buildings could be enhanced by artisans whose working conditions and designs revived the practices of the Middle Ages. In the 1840s, he started specifying medieval-style floor tiles produced by Herbert Minton, and a few years later, the men began collaborating.[3] Also important was Pugin's collaboration with John Hardman Jr., whose firm supplied metalwork and stained glass for Pugin's buildings.[4]

Pugin warrants attention as a leading early theorist, but John Ruskin was more widely read and central to the emergence of the Arts and Crafts movement in England. Not an architect, Ruskin was trained as an artist. He subsequently turned to writing and teaching, becoming known as an author and the first Slade Professor of Fine Art at Oxford. Between 1843 and 1860, Ruskin published *Modern Painters*. Through its five volumes, he encouraged fidelity to nature, rejecting the neoclassicism of Sir Joshua Reynolds and the Renaissance concept of idealized nature. In volume 3, dating from 1856, Ruskin set forth four elements that he considered essential for "great art": a noble subject, a love of beauty, sincerity, and invention.[5] His call for sincerity is of particular interest as it would be emphasized by theorists in Boston's Arts and Crafts movement. According to Ruskin, sincerity reflected "the largest possible quantity of Truth in the most perfect possible harmony. If it were possible for art to give all the truths of nature, it ought to do it." But he recognized the impossibility of this ideal and accepted that choice "must always be made."[6] Sincerity, then, meant capturing some aspect of the truth that exists in the natural world.

In 1849 Ruskin published *The Seven Lamps of Architecture*, in which he identified virtues that contribute to great buildings. As in *Modern Painters*, he revered Truth and Beauty, along with five other "Lamps," namely Sacrifice, Power, Life, Memory, and Obedience.[7] Truth embraced two concepts: It meant that a building's design should express its structure honestly, a reference to the visible structure of Gothic architecture. It also was expressed in the workmanship of the individual and not the product of a machine. For Ruskin, Sacrifice referred to society's duty to enrich its buildings with ornament. In the Lamp of Memory, Ruskin urged the preservation of historic buildings, pleading that they be left untouched—a response to his distress over the damage that had occurred in early nineteenth-century restorations of England's Gothic monuments. His Lamp of Obedience also reflected his regard for England's architectural heritage. In this section, he condemned the English architects who called for originality, promoting the invention of a new style. "We want no new style of architecture," Ruskin declared. "But we want *some* style."[8] He exhorted his readers to respect common laws, by which he meant native architectural traditions. In England, such laws were embodied in the nation's Gothic monuments. Ruskin's regard for precedent would be a recurring interest for Arts and Crafts architects, both in England and in New England, several decades later.

Ruskin's chapter "The Nature of Gothic" in *The Stones of Venice*, written from 1851 to 1853, provided more support for the Arts and Crafts movement.[9] In this chapter, he identified "moral elements" that he found present in Gothic buildings. One of those elements was Savageness, which he equated with imperfection. Ruskin praised the irregularity of Gothic or

"Christian architecture" while he disparaged the regularity of Greek and Roman designs. Imperfection, according to Ruskin, is "essential to all that we know of life."[10] No architecture, he wrote, could be noble that is not imperfect. In this way, Ruskin presented imperfection as an aesthetic standard with a moral dimension that would be repeated by Arts and Crafts proponents.

Design became a subject of widespread interest in Britain in the mid-nineteenth century. In 1851 the Great Exhibition was held in an enormous iron and glass hall that came to be known as the Crystal Palace. When British commercial products were scrutinized, the consensus was that they were neither well made nor well designed. The superintendent of works for the exhibition was Owen Jones, who published *The Grammar of Ornament* in 1856.[11] In this book, Jones set forth visual vocabularies that were rigid and regularized, an approach that supported the very opposite of the naturalism and variety endorsed by Ruskin. Yet the book's systematic examination of design contributed to an expanding national discourse.

As the century moved forward, more theorists began campaigning for design reform, culminating in the Aesthetic movement of the 1870s.[12] Its leaders, including Oscar Wilde, were mocked for their self-conscious striving after beauty. But like Pugin and Ruskin, they believed that excellence in art corresponded to excellence in life. Their particular target was the home, and they crusaded to reform interior decoration. They sought to rid Victorian parlors of their heavy drapery and clutter while introducing superior products such as Japanese fans and ceramics to replace crude bric-a-brac. Japanese interiors and furnishings were admired for their spare lines and overall restraint. The Aesthetic movement spawned many preferences that England's Arts and Crafts theorists would advance.

More important than anyone else in defining the Arts and Crafts movement was the multitalented William Morris. Energized by Ruskin, Morris railed against the evils of the industrial age. Like Ruskin, Morris sought to improve the life of the worker by reviving handicraft. Morris also took up the cause of design reform. In 1859, he and his wife built Red House in Bexleyheath, Kent, commissioning the architect Philip Webb for the project (fig. 2.1). With lancet arches and irregular massing, the red-brick house recalled vernacular Gothic architecture of rural England. Inside, it was decorated by Morris's artist friends, including Edward Burne-Jones and Dante Gabriel Rossetti. Soon afterward, in 1861, Morris entered into a business partnership, Morris, Marshall, Faulkner and Company, a decorating firm

FIG. 2.1 Philip Webb, Red House, Bexleyheath, Kent, 1859–61.

based in London that employed artisans who produced wallpapers, textiles, and furniture.[13]

Morris was an accomplished writer, too, and in 1877 he applied this talent to lecturing and publishing on art and society. In his first lecture, he proclaimed that nothing can be a work of art if it is not also useful. Utility and beauty were thus conjoined, a theme that would become fundamental to the Arts and Crafts movement and often repeated. In furthering his point, Morris castigated his audience for the "tons upon tons of unutterable rubbish" that decorated their London houses—an outgrowth of Aesthetic movement thinking. He continued, "Simplicity of life, begetting simplicity of taste, that is, a love for sweet and lofty things is of all matters most necessary for the birth of the new and better art we crave for; simplicity everywhere in the palace as well as in the cottage." The lecture was promptly published in *The Architect*, and then was reprinted frequently, becoming a touchstone for Arts and Crafts architecture.[14] Morris's call for simplicity would be heard and reiterated in Boston.

Also in 1877, Morris spoke against the damage being done to Britain's medieval buildings in the name of preservation, a concern that had troubled Ruskin. Distressed by what he encountered, especially Sir George Gilbert Scott's work on Tewkesbury Abbey, Morris founded the Society for the Protection of Ancient Buildings.[15] Preservation of a nation's patrimony became connected with the Arts and Crafts movement, and the desire to preserve historic buildings would be intertwined with the movement that emerged in New England.

Like Ruskin and Pugin, Morris believed that the arts are a reflection of a society, identifying it as humane or harsh. Echoing Ruskin, Morris wrote that art "is and must be, either in its abundance or its barrenness, in its sincerity or its hollowness, the expression of the society amongst which it exists."[16] Sincerity, a virtue of great art in Ruskin's *Modern Painters*, was similarly promoted by Morris as a quality that captures what is true. As time went on, Morris despaired over the lives of those who toiled in drudgery, harnessed to machines. Though not condemning machines entirely, he believed that the machine should serve man, not master him. Morris hoped to see a revival of handicraft to restore the spirit of the downtrodden working class.[17] For him, socialism and the Arts and Crafts movement were bound to each other.

Gothic architecture appealed to Morris for many of the same reasons identified by Pugin and Ruskin. Most of all, Morris admired the way Gothic buildings mirrored a unity between art and life. He admired the Middle Ages as a time when builders and craftsmen worked cooperatively, designing together. He also appreciated the way that Gothic buildings, constructed with ribs and buttresses, combined utility and beauty—an idea shared by Pugin and Ruskin. Finally, Morris believed that Gothic architecture allowed its builders to work with greater freedom than the classical tradition. Because Gothic was more open to interpretation, Morris viewed it as a "living" style that could evolve.[18] Well into the twentieth century, a younger generation of Arts and Crafts architects would embrace these ideas in their writing and their work.

The third quarter of the nineteenth century in England saw a proliferation of guilds that brought together designers and craftsmen.[19] Morris's firm, reorganized under him as sole proprietor in 1875, became a model. Architecture was understood to be the branch of the fine arts that brought the various arts together, and architects provided much of the leadership in organizing the guilds. In 1882 the architect Arthur H. Mackmurdo joined fellow designers to found the Century Guild. Mackmurdo knew Ruskin well, but he was a selective follower. The Century Guild rallied for design reform but not for Ruskin's social concerns. Two years later, the Art Workers' Guild was organized by a group of architects from Richard Norman Shaw's office, including Gerald Horsley, W. R. Lethaby, Mervyn Macartney,

Ernest Newton, and Edward S. Prior. As advocates for the unity of the arts, they allied themselves with craftsmen, producing wallpaper, textiles, stained glass, and books. The guild also attracted members who were artists and designers, including Morris.

This energy culminated in the launching of the Arts and Crafts Exhibition Society, whose members presented a major display of craft products in a London gallery in 1888. Here was the first time the term *Arts and Crafts* was used. Through the early twentieth century, the society held exhibitions intermittently, complemented by lectures by Morris, Walter Crane, and other prominent figures.

Also in the late 1880s, the architect C. R. Ashbee established the Guild of Handicraft in London's impoverished East End. Sympathizing with the socialism of Morris, Ashbee sought to improve the lives of the working poor. He opened a school and provided training and employment opportunities for craftsmen, whose wares were sold in a London shop. In 1902 Ashbee led the guild in relocating to the picturesque town of Chipping Campden in the Cotswolds, where members lived communally until disbanding in 1909.[20]

English Arts and Crafts Architecture

What makes the architecture of the Arts and Crafts movement in England both fascinating and challenging is the way in which it was so varied.[21] Yet like the movement in general, it can be defined by an array of values realized in material forms. First and above all, the architects associated with the movement shared an appreciation of handicraft, cherished for its intrinsic beauty and for the joy it gave the craftsman. In architecture, handicraft was apparent in a building's details, such as hinges or door handles of wrought iron, casement windows with leaded glass, or carved stone and wood.

A second value was unity of expression. The idea sprang from an image of medieval craftsmen who collaborated with others to produce a harmonious whole. Arts and Crafts architects sought to provide a unified effect in their buildings through their coordinating positions, often taking charge of a project's decoration and furnishings. A third value was respect for regional traditions. This interest, which began with the rise of nationalism in the Romantic Era, led English architects to turn to vernacular buildings for inspiration.

A fourth value, repeated by virtually all of the architects associated with the Arts and Crafts movement, was simplicity. Simplicity, however, was invoked to advance a range of objectives. For Morris, calling for simplicity was a plea to the Victorian middle class to clear their cluttered parlors. The plea was also an attack on consumerism, as Morris associated cheap decorative goods with the sweat of toiling factory workers. For others, calling for simplicity meant advocating for building designs that reflected vernacular architecture, designs that were unpretentious and informal. As with the theory that girded the Arts and Crafts movement, Arts and Crafts architecture in its early stages was based in the Gothic Revival. But eventually, English classicism managed to find a place for itself under the movement's umbrella. As time went on, the call for simplicity supported designs that were reductive and freestyle, tending toward Modernism.

In eighteenth-century England, the first buildings that revived the Gothic past were eye-catchers erected in expansive landscape gardens. Constructing follies became a fad among the landed gentry, whose sheep grazed on lawns embellished by sham castles.[22] The revival was firmly established with Strawberry Hill, a house that Horace Walpole began to transform in 1749. Its exterior silhouette was animated by towers and crenellations, and inside, it featured ersatz fan vaulting, constructed not of stone but of papier-mâché. Strawberry Hill was artificial and whimsical, but its sources were English, and it evoked a Romantic love for a medieval past that was foundational for the development of an Arts and Crafts architecture.

Although the Gothic Revival attracted a small following, by the early nineteenth century, it was the classicism of Rome and Greece that provided guidance for much of what was built throughout Britain and on the Continent. Confronting this scenario, Pugin published his treatises to argue for the superiority of Gothic. He also attracted attention when he assisted Charles Barry in decorating the new Houses of Parliament, London (1836–68), where he demonstrated his commitment to handicraft inspired by Gothic examples. When Pugin designed his own house, the Grange, Ramsgate, Kent (1843–44), he chose building materials that had been used in the Gothic architecture of the region, constructing the house in a local buff brick (fig. 2.2).[23] Pugin was not alone in his examination of regional traditions. During the 1830s and 1840s, antiquarian societies were organized to investigate and document England's medieval architecture. In 1841 a monthly journal, the *Ecclesiologist*, was launched. Its aims were theological, seeking to invest the English church with a greater spirituality, but it also advanced the study of Gothic monuments, including small parish churches.[24]

FIG. 2.2 A. W. N. Pugin, the Grange, Ramsgate, Kent, 1843–44.

By midcentury, English architects had recognized the potential of applying Gothic forms to new building types. Architects designed Gothic museums, a trend set by Deane and Woodward's University Museum at Oxford (1854–60), and train stations, such as George Gilbert Scott's St. Pancras Station, London (1868–77). These buildings were vast masonry halls attached to sheds covered in iron and glass. Following the publication of *The Stones of Venice*, English architects turned away from their own heritage and for a few years flirted with the polychromy of Venetian Gothic architecture, designing buildings that were patterned with various colors of stone or red and tar-blackened brick. William Butterfield's All Saints Church on Margaret Street, London (1849–59), distinguished by its bands of red and black brick, exemplified the style that came to be identified with the High Victorian period (fig. 2.3).[25]

While the drama of polychromy and pattern played out, other architects pursued a quieter approach to Gothic, based on vernacular buildings. Among the most influential architects were Richard Norman Shaw and Philip Webb. Along with Morris, Shaw and Webb had worked for George Edmund Street, an architect who was committed to an integrated approach to building and handicraft.[26] After leaving Street's office in 1862, young Shaw packed his sketchbooks and traveled the countryside, paying special attention to vernacular cottages that became the basis for his Old English style.[27] He published his work frequently. Shaw's designs were not revivals based on a particular period, but rather were amalgamations—typically

FIG. 2.3 William Butterfield,
All Saints Church, Margaret Street,
London, 1849–59.

brick or stone on the first story and half-timbering or tile on the upper stories, with banks of mullioned windows and tall chimneys. In his design for
the country house Leyswood, in Groombridge, Sussex (1867–69), he realized his ideas in brick and half-timbering on a rambling scale (fig. 2.4). Just
a few years later, during the 1870s, Shaw began incorporating classical elements into his work, contributing to the Queen Anne Revival. His houses,
notably those for Bedford Park (1877) outside London, featured Palladian
windows and classical pediments, yet they retained the picturesque massing
of the Gothic Revival. As time went on, Shaw's office proved to be a major
training ground for architects who would become leaders in the Arts and
Crafts movement.[28]

Given that Webb was the architect who designed Morris's Red House,
he is routinely and justifiably recognized as a key figure in the emergence of
Arts and Crafts architecture.[29] Like Shaw, he turned to regional architecture for inspiration, but he produced houses that were plainer than Shaw's.
Webb ignored Ruskin's advocacy of architectural ornament and created interest in his designs through variegated materials and textures.[30] In 1861
Webb helped found Morris, Marshall, Faulkner and Company, and over
the years, he guided his clients in decorating their houses with Morris products, including wallpapers and textiles. Webb never used the term *Arts and*

FIG. 2.4 Richard
Norman Shaw,
Leyswood,
Groombridge,
Sussex, 1867–69.

FIG. 2.5 Philip Webb,
Standen, East Grinstead,
West Sussex, 1891–94.
Drawing room with
William Morris
wallpaper and textiles.

Crafts to describe his own buildings.[31] Yet Clouds, in East Knoyle, Wilt-shire (1877–86), and Standen, in East Grinstead, West Sussex (1891–94), contributed to the English Arts and Crafts movement, with Morris products used extensively in their interiors (fig. 2.5).[32] In his embrace of English vernacular traditions, Webb, like Shaw, found a place for classicism in his work. Although he rejected the Palladian revival, he designed a number of houses that were marked by symmetry and formal elevations.[33]

After the establishment of Morris, Marshall, Faulkner and Company, George F. Bodley provided the firm with its first commission, turning to

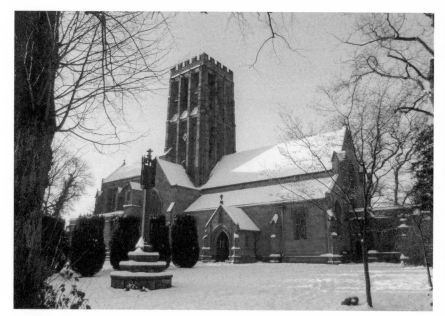

its artists for stained glass and decorative painting for the church of St. Michael and All Angels, Brighton.[34] Bodley became known for churches with brilliant chancels that incorporated stained glass, rood screens, and painting—rich ensembles that set a standard for a generation of architects. Although Bodley never joined the Arts and Crafts guilds, his buildings captured the movement's ideals.[35] He also was influential for establishing a new direction in late nineteenth-century church design, reworking English Perpendicular sources. Bodley's churches were horizontal in their massing while dominated by lofty square towers, an approach that would be pursued through the early twentieth century in England as well as by architects working in Boston.[36] Bodley's ornament was elegant and light, and the effect was restrained yet compelling. These qualities could be found in Bodley's Church of the Holy Angels, Hoar Cross, Staffordshire (1871–76) (fig. 2.6). During the years when Holy Angels was being designed and built, one of the men working in Bodley's office was Henry Vaughan, who would arrive in Boston in 1881 and bring his former employer's aesthetic concepts to New England.[37]

By the turn of the twentieth century, architects associated with the Arts and Crafts movement in England—and throughout Britain—were heading in two directions. Some of the movement's central figures, including Lethaby, were attracted to vernacular forms, which the architects reduced to their essentials. Other architects also examined native building traditions

FIG. 2.7 W. R. Lethaby, the Hurst, Four Oaks, Sutton Coldfield, Warwickshire, 1893–94.

but favored a more scholarly approach, resulting in a new wave of revival styles.

Lethaby worked in Shaw's office between 1879 and 1889, the heady period when Lethaby and some fellow pupils founded the Art Workers' Guild and launched the Arts and Crafts Exhibition Society.[38] A year after the 1888 Arts and Crafts exhibition, Lethaby and Ernest Gimson founded Kenton and Company, a furniture firm.[39] Furniture design, writing, and teaching absorbed Lethaby's time so that he ended up producing just a few major buildings over a little more than a decade. He shared Morris's commitment to bringing together artists and craftsmen, and like Morris he admired the Middle Ages as a period of collaboration.[40] Although he trained under Shaw, Lethaby's greatest admiration was for Webb and his spare regionalism. This approach was exhibited in the Hurst (1893–94), a red-brick house in Four Oaks, Sutton Coldfield, Warwickshire, designed by Lethaby with a gabled tile roof, tall chimneys, and two-story bays (fig. 2.7). It was clearly a product of its region, yet not a revival of a particular period style.[41] In his book titled *Architecture, Mysticism and Myth*, published in 1891, Lethaby argued that historical forms could not be separated from the authoritarian cultures that had generated them, and they should not be revived. He believed modern architects would find new forms from vernacular traditions that would convey "sweetness, simplicity, freedom, confidence, and light."[42] Like Morris, Lethaby valued simplicity and believed this idea

FIG. 2.8 C. F. A.
Voysey, Perrycroft,
Colwell, near Malvern,
Worcestershire,
1893–94.

would provide a direction for the architecture of the future—a spare, free-style architecture.

The reductive designs of C. F. A. Voysey also reflected a commitment to simplicity. During the 1870s and 1880s, he trained under architects who favored Gothic Revival and vernacular styles.[43] When the Art Workers' Guild was organized in 1884, Voysey was elected a member within the year, and he exhibited with the Arts and Crafts Exhibition Society.[44] Once he began working on his own, he specialized in residential designs that were indebted to the Gothic tradition, although for the better part of his career, they were not overtly Gothic. His houses were asymmetrical, with deep eaves, banks of casement windows, and tall chimneys. Perrycroft, in Colwell in the Malvern Hills, Worcestershire (1893–94), was Voysey's first major commission and contributed to his reputation (fig. 2.8).[45] Constructed with brick walls and finished in roughcast, the house has prominent chimneys and a flaring hipped roof. Buttresses run the full height of the walls, and the second story jetties over the first. Although the house is austere, it acquires a human dimension from its windows with small panes and doors with long strap hinges.

In a 1909 essay, Voysey elaborated on his philosophy of design. He wrote, "This sincerity, simplicity, and directness we feel to be good, because fitness is a universal law of nature, and these qualities tend towards it, and it is also essential to beauty."[46] Through his choice of words, including "fitness," "sincerity," and "simplicity," Voysey conveyed his commitment to the ideals of Pugin, Ruskin, and Morris. By stating that "fitness" follows the ways of the natural world and also is the basis for beauty, Voysey echoed the arguments that were made through the nineteenth century in support of the Gothic Revival. But simplicity was most important to Voysey, and he called for it repeatedly. Further on in the same essay, he declared, "We cannot be too simple."[47] Two years later, in discussing "The English Home," Voysey wrote that "simplicity, sincerity, repose, directness and frankness are moral qualities as essential to good architecture as to good men."[48] As with his predecessors in the Arts and Crafts movement, he believed there was a moral dimension to architectural design.

While Lethaby and Voysey were producing reductive, freestyle designs, other Art Workers' Guild members pursued an entirely different course, becoming known as the Neo-Georgians. Leading the movement toward a new classicism was Reginald Blomfield, along with Macartney, Newton, and Prior. Why these guild men tacked in this direction may be explained by their conviction that their work should be an outgrowth of English architectural tradition. By the turn of the twentieth century, the rise of French Art Nouveau and its variants may have encouraged them to be more explicit in designing buildings that were English in character.[49] Defining a native tradition in terms of Gothic architecture came to be seen as problematic, however, especially in urban settings where most preindustrial architecture was a vernacular Georgian.[50] Regard for local context won out.

Accompanying this new appreciation for the seventeenth and eighteenth centuries was a new admiration of the work of the architect Christopher Wren. Blomfield paved the way with the publication of his *Short History of Renaissance Architecture in England* in 1897. In 1906 Macartney became architect to Wren's St. Paul's Cathedral, while in the same year, he became editor of the London-based *Architectural Review*, enabling him to promote the shift toward classicism.[51] The designs of the Neo-Georgians were balanced, generally symmetrical, and refined. Their work was characterized by the regularity that Ruskin found objectionable, although their buildings had a charm derived from their craftsmanship and small-scale ornament—Ruskin's legacy. Newton's design for Luckley, a country house in Wokingham, Berkshire (1907), is a red-brick example of the Neo-Georgian revival, with a relatively small front entrance and banks of leaded windows under a roof inspired by Wren (fig. 2.9).[52] Arts and Crafts theory still provided a foundation for designs such as Luckley.

The stylistic developments in architecture on the Continent were of little interest to Boston's Arts and Crafts architects. Because much of New

England had been settled by people of English stock, and because most of
the architects were of English descent, they viewed English architectural
traditions as their logical models. "By heredity we are English," wrote Boston architect Robert Andrews in 1904.[53] The architects adopted Ruskin's
view that striving for a new style was undesirable, and they objected vehemently to Art Nouveau as it spread through France and Belgium. Similarly,
the inventive architecture emerging in Austria and Germany seemed at best
irrelevant and at worst debased.[54] Boston architects were respectful of the
training provided by the École des Beaux-Arts in Paris, especially its rigor-
ous methods of design and planning. Beaux-Arts ornament, on the other
hand, was considered too florid and too French.[55] Therefore, the influence
of English architecture on the Boston architects was considerable, whereas
the stylistic trends in Europe at the turn of the twentieth century were relevant only in that they represented directions to avoid.

The Arts and Crafts Movement Crosses the Atlantic

During the 1890s, several American Arts and Crafts groups were established, fashioned after the English examples. When Henry Lewis Johnson
organized Boston's first Arts and Crafts exhibition in April of 1897, followed by the formation of the Society of Arts and Crafts in June, he and his
colleagues believed they had presented the first such show in the country

and that they had launched the Arts and Crafts movement in the United States.[56] Several decades later, Johnson wrote, "It was logical that in this country, the Arts and Crafts movement should begin in Boston with its heritage of colonial craftsmanship in furniture, weaving, silverware, wrought iron, and other crafts."[57] He also stated explicitly that their inspiration was the English Arts and Crafts Exhibition Society.

In fact, several other Arts and Crafts groups had formed in the United States prior to 1897, although Johnson apparently was unaware of them, and their influence was limited. In 1894 some San Francisco artists and architects established a Guild of Arts and Crafts, which sponsored two exhibitions before breaking up in 1897.[58] In 1895 Charles Keeler, a poet, naturalist, and philosopher, formed a Ruskin Club in Berkeley, California. The same year, a group in Minneapolis established the Chalk and Chisel Club, which led to the creation of the Handicraft Guild and then the Minneapolis Arts and Crafts Society.[59] In 1896 women in Deerfield, Massachusetts, located in the Connecticut River Valley, founded a Society of Blue and White Needlework to revive "the spirit of the Colonial work."[60]

Historians of the Arts and Crafts movement in America generally identify 1897 as the watershed year, noteworthy because the Boston organization was launched in June and the Chicago Arts and Crafts Society was founded in October.[61] The Chicago society was based at Hull House, a settlement house established in 1889 by Jane Addams and Ellen Gates Starr to serve a community of impoverished immigrants. A year earlier, Addams had visited Ashbee's Toynbee Hall in London's East End, and it became a model for the Chicago women. By the late 1890s, Hull House offered courses in bookbinding and pottery, and in 1898 the society sponsored its first Arts and Crafts exhibition, held at the Art Institute of Chicago.[62] One of the society's charter members was the architect Frank Lloyd Wright. In 1901 he delivered what has become a well-known lecture titled "The Art and Craft of the Machine," in which he emphasized the machine's liberating aspects.[63] Thus in Chicago, Morris's socialism was embraced while his regard for handicraft over machine production was challenged.

As in England, American Arts and Crafts leaders struggled to sort out their idealistic, even utopian, objectives with their desire to succeed financially in a capitalist economy. This difficulty was especially pronounced for those involved with Arts and Crafts communities. One early and relatively successful community was Roycroft, the vision of Elbert Hubbard.[64] For the first two decades of his adult life, Hubbard had prospered as an executive with the Larkin Soap Company in Buffalo, New York.[65] Financially secure, he turned to writing and publishing, traveling in 1894 to Ireland and England, where he visited Morris's Kelmscott Press in Hammersmith.[66] A year later, Hubbard founded Roycroft in East Aurora, outside Buffalo, as a printing center. Hubbard erected buildings and attracted artisans who specialized in printing, leatherwork, metalwork, glass, and furniture production. The quality of the wares was mixed. But because of Hubbard's talents as a salesman who excelled in both publishing and lecturing, the community prospered, and it grew to about 500 workers during its peak years.[67] Hubbard was benevolent but autocratic, and he held the Roycrofters together. When he died on the *Lusitania* in 1915, the Roycroft community fell into decline.

Rose Valley, Pennsylvania, was an Arts and Crafts community where commercial interests were subordinated to the idealistic aims of its founders. Located to the southwest of Philadelphia, Rose Valley was established in 1901 under the leadership of the architect William L. Price.[68] Here artists joined craftsmen in an enterprise that was committed to a more consistent aesthetic standard than was maintained at Roycroft. Located in a rebuilt textile factory complex, shops were dedicated to furniture production, bookbinding, and metalwork, while studios were provided for potters and artists.[69] By 1906 the venture was deemed unsustainable, and the shops were closed.[70] Within a few years, Rose Valley evolved into a picturesque artists' colony.

Byrdcliffe, located in Woodstock, New York, was more like Rose Valley than Roycroft—an art colony more than a business venture.[71] In 1902 Ralph Whitehead, a wealthy Englishman, and his American wife pursued their dream of establishing an Arts and Crafts community on the farms that they bought.[72] Within a year, several structures were built, and Whitehead began the task of luring artists and artisans to the idyllic community. One of his recruits was Hermann Dudley Murphy, a successful artist and frame maker who taught painting in the architecture program at Harvard and was active in Boston's Society of Arts and Crafts. Murphy spent three summers at Byrdcliffe, from 1903 to 1905.[73] But in the end, the success of the colony was impeded by its rural location, a place where artists and craftsmen visited mainly during the summer.

Gustav Stickley may be the individual most closely identified with the Arts and Crafts movement in America.[74] Best known for his furniture, he established the Gustav Stickley Company outside Syracuse, New York, in

1898. In 1901 he began publishing a magazine, the *Craftsman*, to promote design reform, and he changed the name of his company to United Crafts, settling on the name Craftsman Workshops by 1904. Devoted to the ideals of Ruskin and Morris, in 1908 Stickley bought farmland in New Jersey where he planned to establish a farm school for boys.[75] Although he managed to construct several buildings and moved his family to the site, the dream of a self-sufficient, cooperative community ended with Stickley's bankruptcy in 1915.

Ultimately, the handicraft societies rather than the Arts and Crafts communities engaged the greatest number of Americans. Thousands of such groups were formed across the country at the turn of the century, and the Society of Arts and Crafts in Boston provided a model for many of them.[76] The fact that the society's leaders were writers and lecturers augmented their influence. Craftsmen read the society's magazine *Handicraft*, and they welcomed the speakers who were sent from Boston to local groups around the nation. Boston's shop and its jury system also were admired and imitated. When delegates from twenty-five groups convened to form the National League of Handicraft Societies in 1907, Boston architect Langford Warren was elected the first president.[77] Artistic, handcrafted work appealed to a wide spectrum of Americans, who participated in craft production and supported it through their purchases. By contrast, the socialist and utopian ideals of the Arts and Crafts movement never gained much traction.

American Arts and Crafts Architecture

From colonial times and well into the nineteenth century, developments in English architecture provided the framework for American building designs, especially on the East Coast, while to varying degrees, French, Dutch, Spanish, and German architecture contributed to regional approaches. Beginning in the 1860s, America's high-style buildings reflected their designers' increasing interest in French trends.[78] Travel to Paris was becoming more common, and Americans on the grand tour examined and admired the Visconti and Lefuel additions to the Louvre (1852–57). Imposing Second Empire buildings were constructed in the United States, such as Bryant and Gilman's Boston City Hall (1861–65) (fig. 2.10), John B. Snook's Grand Central Depot in New York City (1869–71), and Philadelphia's City Hall by John MacArthur (1871–1901). Second Empire architecture was symmetrically planned, and featured mansard roofs, projecting pavilions, and a pro-

FIG. 2.10 Bryant and
Gilman, City Hall,
Boston, 1861–65.

fusion of columns and sculpture. In the United States, few craftsmen were
trained to carve ornament, and what they did produce was cut mechanically
and in repetitious patterns.[79]

Meanwhile, American architects, especially on the East Coast, kept a
close watch on England, took notice of the Venetian Gothic Revival, and
responded with Venetian Gothic buildings of their own. An early example
was Peter Bonnet Wight's National Academy of Design in New York City
(1861–65), which was modeled after the Doge's Palace in Venice and was
enlivened by the polychromy introduced in England (fig. 2.11).[80] Well versed
in their Ruskin, the American architects of these Gothic buildings sought
to embellish them with hand-carved stone sculpture. Wight attracted two
English carvers to New York to work on the National Academy building,
and in the early 1870s, the Welsh carver John Evans moved to Boston, where
he worked on the sculpture for Henry Hobson Richardson's Brattle Square

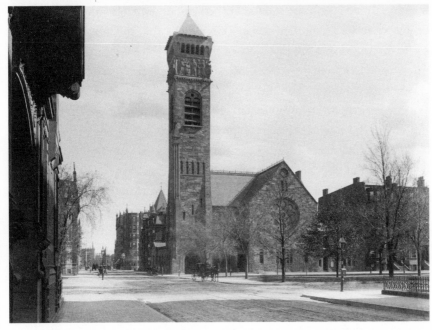

FIG. 2.12 Henry
Hobson Richardson,
Brattle Square
Church, Boston,
1870–72.

Church (1870–72) (fig. 2.12).[81] Soon Wight's English artisans joined Evans
in Boston to carve the sculpture for the Ruskinian Gothic New Old South
Church by Cummings and Sears (1874–75). Richardson returned to Evans
for the sculptural carving at Trinity Church (1872–77), and from then on,
the architect and sculptor collaborated regularly. Two decades later, when

Boston's Society of Arts and Crafts was organized, Evans became a founding member.

As the 1880s unfolded, American architects developed their own version of the English Queen Anne Revival. Their attraction to medieval architecture continued unabated; they favored fanciful, irregular massing and incorporated picturesque towers and Old English half-timbering into their work. Also at this time, the appreciation that emerged in the 1870s for America's seventeenth- and eighteenth-century buildings gained momentum. As a result, Colonial Revival designs began appearing in which colonial allusions were mixed with medieval elements in imaginative ways.[82]

By the end of the century, the influence of Arts and Crafts theory on American architecture increased, and architects responded to the movement's many tenets in their building designs and as members of local societies. Yet surprisingly little has been written about the influence of the Arts and Crafts movement on American architecture.[83] This situation may be explained by the fact that the buildings indebted to the Arts and Crafts movement are so diverse stylistically that their underlying relationships have not been appreciated. Another explanation may be that the buildings are more easily discussed in a broad review of the period's eclecticism. Nevertheless, this eclecticism may be better understood as reflecting two traditions that dominated American architecture at the end of the century. One tradition was the French, often intermingled with the Italian tradition; the other tradition was the English, which produced the Arts and Crafts movement.[84]

As the nineteenth century drew to a close, many American architects had studied at the École des Beaux-Arts in Paris, where buildings were lavishly ornamented with classical motifs derived from the Italian Renaissance. This approach carried aristocratic connotations and appealed to the Gilded Age aspirations of robber barons and the expanding ranks of the well-to-do. Beaux-Arts classicism was popular for urban and country residences in New York City and Newport, Rhode Island, as well as for grand hotels and theaters in cities across the nation. Other architects, including those who had studied at the École, turned to the English tradition when they set up their practices in the United States. Some of them revived English Gothic styles, while some were drawn to the ideals of the Arts and Crafts movement, especially the emphasis on simplicity and handcrafted ornament. The interest that many English architects shared in reviving the vernacular heritage of a given region also struck a chord with American architects, who were eager to develop regional styles in response to local building traditions as well as the local landscape. In 1899 Boston architect Langford Warren wrote approvingly about the "marked growth of distinctive local character in the architecture of our principal cities."[85]

The elite communities of Boston and Philadelphia were most like each other, with their members sharing Anglo-Saxon backgrounds and a strong sense of their English heritage. Architects in both cities were regularly in contact with their peers in England and kept abreast of new developments there. In the 1880s, Henry Vaughan in Boston and Cope and Stewardson in Philadelphia followed the lead of George F. Bodley, with whom Vaughan had worked, and began designing English Perpendicular buildings.[86] This direction was pursued in Boston by the architects who became leaders in its Arts and Crafts movement and in Philadelphia by Wilson Eyre and Frank Miles Day. Warren praised the Philadelphia architects for work that "shows an originality, a delicacy of feeling, and a scholarly quality."[87]

Delicacy—that is to say, fine, elegant detailing—characterized the designs of both Boston and Philadelphia architects. Architects in both cities also took an academic approach, measuring and drawing their colonial buildings and advocating for the buildings' preservation. These architects admired simple rural farmhouses as well as urban survivors. Boston architects designed houses in shingles, clapboard, and red brick, while Philadelphia architects were partial to native fieldstone.[88] In both cities, studies of English architecture led to designs for large Tudor Revival country houses. Philadelphia was especially recognized for having more houses of this type than any other part of the country.[89] On the other hand, Boston architects caught the spirit of England's Neo-Georgians and transferred the English regard for Wren to native son Charles Bulfinch, designing buildings after his work.[90]

In New York City, the French influence was predominant. Warren decried the style that he considered "full of bad taste," although he suggested that its lavish display could be rationalized because it expressed "the luxury-loving New Yorker."[91] Boston's Clipston Sturgis also associated New York architecture with ostentation. Following a meeting with *Chicago Daily News* owner Victor F. Lawson and his wife about a house they were building in Green Lake, Wisconsin, Sturgis drafted a letter to them in which he wrote that he would add glass-and-iron outside doors if they wished, although "I think them rather New Yorky, & so look down on them accordingly."[92] Not everything built in New York was indebted to the French, however. The Arts and Crafts ideal found a place there, too, as was demonstrated by

St. Thomas Church in Manhattan (1905–13), designed by Boston's Ralph Adams Cram and Bertram Goodhue, and elaborately decorated with wrought iron, sculpture, and stained glass. On the last day of 1913, Goodhue left the partnership and opened an independent office in New York City, where he designed several more Gothic Revival churches.[93] Though the city's Beaux-Arts mansions and Arts and Crafts churches reflect entirely different philosophies, they were informed by a thorough understanding of the major historical styles of Western Europe and were interpreted with a refinement that appealed to sophisticated New York clients.

The Arts and Crafts house designs that Gustav Stickley sold in the pages of the *Craftsman*, entirely unlike the ornate buildings favored in Manhattan, were distinguished by their simplicity and moderate cost to construct (fig. 2.13). It may seem paradoxical that in 1905, Stickley relocated his company headquarters to New York City. Sympathetic to the social ideals of Ruskin and Morris, while also an ambitious businessman, Stickley was selling his Arts and Crafts vision not to urban New Yorkers, but to a broad and middle-class segment of the American public.[94]

When C. R. Ashbee visited the United States in 1900, he singled out Boston, Philadelphia, and Chicago as cities where architects were encouraged to see an ethical responsibility in their practices.[95] From an aesthetic standpoint, Ashbee especially admired the new architecture in Chicago and the designs of Frank Lloyd Wright. By the turn of the century, Arts and Crafts houses routinely featured broad, overhanging roofs, open interior plans, and rooms that opened to porches and terraces. But Wright took these ideas farther, eliminating walls and cantilevering roofs through the use of steel. His houses of the early twentieth century seemed to hug the ground, as if responding to the Midwestern prairie (fig. 2.14).[96] Rather than develop his design ideas from any local architectural tradition, he developed his Prairie Style from the region's landscape. Wright and Ashbee formed a lasting friendship. Despite this relationship, Ashbee's wife Janet had reservations about Wright's architecture, writing that much of it was "too bizarre and away from all tradition to be beautiful."[97] This attachment to tradition ran deeply among the English.

The leading Arts and Crafts architects on the East Coast believed that different approaches to tradition made sense for different regions of the country, and they accepted the idea that the architecture in the Midwest and California could be less tied to the past. Writing about American domestic architecture, Philadelphia's Wilson Eyre observed that "we are settling down gradually to a few styles that seem best to suit the various parts of our varied country." He described how architects in the East were indebted to the English and French, "but especially the English," whereas architects in the Midwest were "experimental," and those in California were inspired by the state's climate and natural scenery.[98] In the San Francisco Bay Area, with the wide availability of redwood, architects favored weathered shingled houses that were simple in plan and massing. The Arts and Crafts call for

FIG. 2.15 Greene
and Greene, Gamble
house, Pasadena, CA,
1907–9.

simplicity was advanced by Charles Keeler, who published *The Simple Home* in 1904, dedicated to Bernard Maybeck, the architect of Keeler's house.[99]

In Southern California, Pasadena architects Charles and Henry Greene designed houses that were not simple at all, if "simple" suggests plain designs (fig. 2.15). Their houses, however, exemplified the Arts and Crafts devotion to craftsmanship and were enriched with carved wood panels, stained glass, and tile. The architects' commitment to developing a native style, suited to the region, also reflected their Arts and Crafts outlook.[100] Although the brothers' designs were unlike the more traditional styles promoted in Boston, Cram admired their houses for their low roofs, wide eaves, and "curious combinations of horizontals and verticals."[101] Goodhue, Cram's onetime partner, was another contributor to Southern California's architecture. He introduced Spanish Colonial–inspired buildings at the Panama-California Exposition, which opened in San Diego in 1915.[102] During these same years, California architect Irving Gill turned to the Spanish missions as a starting point for his designs, which he reduced to stark, cubic masses punctured by rectangular door and window openings and occasional round arches. Gill's Walter Luther Dodge house in West Hollywood (1914–16) may be seen as representing the call for simplicity in Arts and Crafts architecture taken to its ultimate conclusion (fig. 2.16).[103]

FIG. 2.16 Irving Gill, Dodge house, West Hollywood, CA, 1914–16.

As Americans considered the numerous social and aesthetic issues raised by the Arts and Crafts movement in England, their responses differed considerably. The emphasis on social reform, so important to Morris and Ashbee, was shared by Arts and Crafts leaders in Chicago but found little support in Boston. Yet in many respects, Boston's Arts and Crafts leaders were extremely close to the English movement. At an early date, they became familiar with Ruskin and Morris. They responded to the Arts and Crafts Exhibition Society's venture with a major exhibition of their own, and they organized what became the country's largest society of Arts and Crafts. When Boston's Arts and Crafts architects developed their ideas about building design, they were closely aligned with their English colleagues, favoring Gothic and Anglo-Colonial styles. Like the English, the Boston architects became advocates for the preservation of historic buildings, which informed their work. And when the English architects turned their attention to Wren, Boston's architects identified Bulfinch as their own illustrious forebear and source of inspiration.

CHAPTER THREE

An Intellectual Stew: Emerson, Norton, Brandeis

W<small>HEN THE</small> S<small>OCIETY OF</small> A<small>RTS AND</small> C<small>RAFTS</small> was organized in 1897, some exceptional minds in and around Boston were contributing to the intellectual discourse of the period. During the first half of the nineteenth century, the region had produced many of the nation's influential writers and lecturers, and they were followed by yet another generation of individuals who confronted fundamental questions about modern life in America. A rich intellectual stew simmered in New England, a discourse that helped to shape the region's Arts and Crafts movement, its architects, and their work.

By examining the lives of three men, we encounter salient concepts and concerns that circulated in late nineteenth-century Boston. Senior among the three was the author and lecturer Ralph Waldo Emerson (1803–1882), who lived to the west of the city in Concord and was a leader among the transcendentalists. Short excerpts from his essays appeared in *Handicraft*, the magazine published by the Society of Arts and Crafts between 1902 and 1904. From the beginning, the periodical featured pithy insights by British authors including Morris, Ruskin, Carlyle, and Crane. In January of 1903, Emerson was quoted for the first time, and after that, his thoughts appeared regularly, both on their own and in the articles of others. By the turn of the twentieth century, Emerson's persona and writings had become ingrained in New England culture.

The second man to warrant examination is Charles Eliot Norton (1827–1908), the Harvard professor of fine arts who was the first president of the Society of Arts and Crafts. Norton knew Emerson well. He struggled with Emerson's optimism yet still admired him and advanced some of the elder man's ideas. Norton also maintained enduring friendships with Ruskin and Morris. Because of his relationships with these men, Norton may be regarded as the guiding spirit of the Arts and Crafts movement in New England.

A third person to consider is Louis Dembitz Brandeis (1856–1941), one of Boston's leading attorneys, an advocate for progressive reforms at the turn of the twentieth century who would become one the nation's distinguished Supreme Court justices. Although Brandeis was not directly involved with the Society of Arts and Crafts, he was a contemporary of most of its founders and the architect-leaders. He studied at Harvard; lived on Beacon Hill, the heart of Brahmin Boston; and worked in the city when the society was organized. After finishing law school, Brandeis entered into a partnership with his former classmate, Sam Warren, who would become a founder of the Society of Arts and Crafts. Brandeis faced some of the same issues the architects faced—questions about how to promote reform through his professional expertise, as well as questions at the core of the Arts and Crafts movement relating to free enterprise, industry, and labor.

Emerson, Norton, and Brandeis strove to articulate how the individual should negotiate a path through a rapidly changing world marked by hardship and opportunity. All three were outspoken and influential thinkers, driven by strong moral convictions. Educated at Harvard and residents of New England, these three men addressed the nation through lecturing, teaching, and writing. An examination of their views helps us better understand the ideas that the architect-leaders in the Society of Arts and Crafts debated and promoted in the organization and in their practices.

Ralph Waldo Emerson

For several architects in this circle, Emerson was one of their own—a sage from an earlier generation, but not at all remote (fig. 3.1). One of the architects, Waddy Longfellow, was the nephew of the poet Henry Wadsworth Longfellow, an Emerson friend. Waddy also was the nephew of Rev. Samuel Longfellow, a second-generation transcendentalist and comrade of Emerson.[1] After Emerson died on April 27, 1882, Waddy joined the contingent from Cambridge who traveled to the funeral in Concord. In his diary, he described "passing through the streets each door with its badge of mourning for their best friend." From the church, Waddy went to Sleepy Hollow cemetery where, as Emerson was laid to rest, he observed the setting sun casting its rays on the pine trees over Hawthorne's and Thoreau's graves. When young Longfellow returned to Cambridge, he accompanied Norton.[2]

The architect Langford Warren also was connected to Emerson through family relationships. Warren was married to the former Catharine Reed, a granddaughter of Sampson Reed, recognized for introducing Emerson to

FIG. 3.1 Ralph Waldo Emerson.

the ideas of the philosopher Emanuel Swedenborg.[3] Over the course of his lifetime, Emerson compiled lists of men he admired, and Reed was regularly among them. Emerson included Reed on such a list in 1841, and when Emerson drew up his final list thirty years later, Reed was still there.[4] Warren, a practicing member of the Swedenborgian faith, would have taken a personal interest in Emerson's appreciation for Swedenborg's writings, which proposed correspondences between the natural and spiritual worlds. Emerson's *Nature*, published in 1836, reflects the influence of Swedenborg and Reed, and Emerson's *Representative Men*, published in 1850, devotes a chapter to Swedenborg.

When Cram was born in 1863, he was named Ralph in honor of Emerson.[5] Cram's father, a Unitarian minister, knew Emerson and subscribed to transcendentalist thought.[6] As would be expected, Cram read the works of his namesake. In a diary, he wrote that during his teens he read Carlyle and Ruskin, who reinforced his own gloomy outlook, and then he turned to Spencer, Darwin, and Emerson as he entered his twenties and became more at peace with the world.[7] In the years that followed, Cram pushed himself to achieve wide recognition and professional success, perhaps encouraged by Emerson's emphasis on self-cultivation.[8]

By 1897, when the Society of Arts and Crafts was organized, Emerson had been dead for fifteen years and had become a subject of historical interest. That same year, Caroline Healey Dall published *Transcendentalism in New England*, and the following year Thomas Wentworth Higginson published *Cheerful Yesterdays*, in which he examined American authors including Emerson.[9] In 1903 the 100th anniversary of Emerson's birth was celebrated in Concord, and shortly afterward, the tributes and reminiscences were published, including a speech by Norton.[10]

The fact that Emerson was first quoted in *Handicraft*, the society's magazine, in January of 1903 reflects the attention given to him during this anniversary year. The editor of *Handicraft*, Arthur Carey, and two assistant editors, Norton and Langford Warren, almost certainly selected the quotes that appeared in large type at the front of each month's issue. The magazine was published for almost two years, from April 1902 through March 1904. Seven Emerson excerpts were chosen, taken from just a few sources: "Art" and "Self-Reliance" from *Essays* (first series), 1841; and "Beauty" and "Considerations by the Way" from *The Conduct of Life*, 1860. Emerson also was quoted in *Handicraft* in an essay by Sarah Wyman Whitman in 1903, and by Frederic Allen Whiting in 1910 when the magazine was briefly revived.[11]

The first Emerson selection to be published was perfectly suited to the mission of the Society of Arts and Crafts: "Beauty must come back to the useful arts, and the distinction between the fine and the useful arts be forgotten."[12] The quotation was excerpted from "Art," and its message and words anticipated the more famous epigram to be written by Morris four decades later, in 1880:[13] "Have nothing in your houses that you do not know to be useful, or believe to be beautiful."[14] Emerson's words reflected his Spartan way of living and a resistance to luxury, typical of New England culture. Morris in 1880 was addressing different conditions. In response to the growth of cheap consumer goods, he was calling for broad social change. Unlike Morris, Emerson did not focus on the home; this emphasis on the domestic realm was Morris's contribution, a concern that would be taken up by leaders of the Arts and Crafts movement on both sides of the Atlantic.

In April of 1903, *Handicraft* quoted Emerson as saying, "It is a rule of largest application, true in a plant, true in a loaf of bread, that in the construction of any fabric or organism, any real increase of fitness to its end, is an increase of beauty."[15] Emerson's essay "Beauty" was the source of this statement. Published in a book in 1860, the essay had taken shape much earlier, having originated as a lecture that dated to the early 1850s. Emerson evidently was influenced by his travels in England between 1847 and 1848. In linking function and beauty, and specifically using the word "fitness," Emerson may have been influenced by Pugin, directly or indirectly. Whatever the case, his choice of words would have attracted both the architects and the craftsmen in the Society of Arts and Crafts.

The following month, readers opening their copies of *Handicraft* encountered this encouragement from Emerson: "Genial manners are good, and power of accommodation to any circumstance; but the high prize of life, the crowning fortune of a man, is to be born with a bias to some pursuit which finds him in employment and happiness,—whether it be to make baskets, or broadswords, or canals, or statues, or songs. I doubt not this was the meaning of Socrates, when he pronounced the artists the only truly wise, as being actually, not apparently so."[16] Promoting joy in labor was a constant refrain among Arts and Crafts theorists, including Ruskin and Morris, who both recognized the joy of the artist. At the same time, this passage is distinguished by a soaring quality that is distinctly Emersonian, language that would have been appreciated by those familiar with his writing. The source of the excerpt was "Considerations by the Way," and the editors drew from it again for the August issue. This counsel appeared: "The wise workman will not regret the poverty or the solitude which brought out his working talents."[17] The implication was that labor of the right sort would nourish one's soul. Although such a perspective would have been shared by the English Arts and Crafts theorists, it was firmly grounded in Yankee values.

During the last three months of 1903, quotations from Emerson appeared in issues of *Handicraft*. In the October and December selections, the reader was encouraged to think about how art of any period builds on the past yet achieves greatness by expressing the spirit of its time. In October, the editors returned to "Art" for wisdom: "But the artist must employ the symbols in use in his day and nation, to convey his enlarged sense to his fellow-men. Thus the new art is always formed out of the old. The Genius of the Hour sets his ineffaceable seal on the work and gives it an inexpressible charm for the imagination."[18] Emerson's next sentence in the essay appeared in the December magazine: "As far as the spiritual character of the period overpowers the artist and finds expression in his work, so far it will retain a certain grandeur, and will represent to future beholders the Unknown, the Inevitable, the Divine."[19] For the leaders of the Society of Arts and Crafts, whether they were contemplating architecture or the decorative arts, the conundrum was how to reconcile their view that history must be the basis for good design with their belief that originality was important as well. This question continued to be problematic, but Emerson's writing supported their conviction that in the final analysis, great art and great architecture had to reflect their own age.

Emerson's faith in the individual was perhaps his most important legacy, famously articulated in "Self-Reliance." In the November 1903 issue of *Handicraft*, these lines from that essay were chosen:

> Do that which is assigned you, and you cannot hope too much or dare too much. There is at this moment for you an utterance brave and grand as that of the colossal chisel of Phidias, or trowel of the Egyptians, or the pen of Moses or Dante, but different from all these. Not possibly will the soul, all rich, all eloquent, with thousand-cloven tongue, deign to repeat itself; but if you can hear what these patriarchs say, surely you can reply to them in the same pitch of voice; for the ear and the tongue are two organs of one nature.[20]

When the context for this excerpt is examined, one finds that the paragraph begins with Emerson telling his readers, "Insist on yourself; never imitate."[21] This directive follows a paragraph in which he criticizes American houses "built with foreign taste" and questions copying "the Doric or the Gothic model."[22] Emerson's underlying belief that people can find truth in themselves led him to urge Americans to build an architecture from "the climate, the soil, the length of the day, the wants of the people."[23] In his way, he set forth ideas that would take hold in New England at the end of the century with the emergence of the Colonial Revival.

Of all of Emerson's essays, his treatise "Art" was the favorite source to be quoted in *Handicraft*. When Sarah Whitman published an essay titled "Stained Glass" in the magazine, she concluded by referring to Emerson and shared his confidence: "Beauty will indeed come unannounced, springing up at the feet of noble and just men."[24] In 1910, when *Handicraft* was revived, Frederic Allen Whiting, the administrator of the Society of Arts and Crafts, quoted more extensively from the same passage from "Art," reiterating Emerson's call for beauty to return to the "useful arts."[25] The similarity between Emerson's language and that of Morris was appreciated by the leaders in the Society of Arts and Crafts, and Emerson's words provided a native dimension to the region's movement.

Although the quotations captured several themes that were advocated by the Arts and Crafts architects, Emerson's essays offered further support for their views. In "Beauty," Emerson wrote, "We ascribe beauty to that which is simple; which has no superfluous parts," and in another passage he observed that "all beauty must be organic."[26] Simplicity in design and design based on function were interrelated concepts, and they were restated by many European and American theorists through the nineteenth and early twentieth centuries. In the same essay, Emerson wrote, "All high beauty has a moral element in it," articulating a perspective that was characteristic for New England and the antithesis of the aestheticism—art for art's sake—that was advanced in Europe and the United States during the second half of the nineteenth century.[27]

Other Emersonian ideas would have inspired the Arts and Crafts architects or would have reinforced their way of thinking. Emerson's concept of nature as restorative would have appealed to them. In this respect, Emerson was consistent with the outlook of European Romantic writers, artists, and musicians. Yet his contribution was to locate nature in the country towns of New England. Early in his career, he described his delight in crossing a bare common under a clouded sky.[28] Decades later, the architects and their clients would turn to the same towns as retreats from city living.

Emerson pointed the way to specific stylistic developments that the Boston architects would promote. Most important was his assertion that American architecture should not be derived from foreign sources. After stating this opinion in "Self-Reliance," he repeated it in "Considerations by the Way," writing, "One day we shall cast out the passion for Europe by the passion for America."[29] Looking for appropriate models, the architects turned to surviving buildings from the seventeenth and eighteenth centuries. Just as Emerson admired the "sturdy lad from New Hampshire or Vermont," the architects appreciated rude weathered buildings clad in shingles or clapboards as well as the region's more refined brick buildings with cupolas and columns.[30] At the end of the nineteenth century, these buildings inspired Shingle Style houses in the Boston suburbs and resort towns of New England, as well as Colonial Revival town halls and campus buildings.

The architects shared Emerson's identification with England, which he expressed in his book *English Traits*.[31] Although they were determined to develop American-inflected designs, the architects considered English styles acceptable. Indeed, they were proud to descend from the Saxon race, which Emerson praised for "its commanding sense of right and wrong."[32] In their admiration of Gothic buildings, the architects would have found that Emerson again offered support. In his essay "Progress of Culture," he described the Middle Ages as "the feet on which we walk, the eyes with which we see," and in identifying the achievements of medieval society, he included the Gothic monuments.[33]

Finally, Emerson opened the way for the study of Japanese culture that intensified in Boston at the end of the nineteenth century, converging with the Japan craze that entered the United States via England and France. In 1844, when serving as editor of the transcendentalists' magazine the *Dial*, Emerson published the first American translation of a Buddhist text, the labor of Henry David Thoreau.[34] In the succeeding decades, others in Boston contributed to the fascination with Japan, and at the end of the century, Japanese architecture and design were favorite subjects for members of the Society of Arts and Crafts and its architects, most notably Cram.

While Emerson offered a foundation for many of the architects' interests and beliefs, he also advanced views that they would have been inclined to overlook. Emerson was skeptical at best about formal education.[35] Yet the architects were employed as educators, promoted educational endeavors in the Society of Arts and Crafts, and designed buildings for educational institutions. Another difference may be noted in the way that Emerson repeatedly criticized the enthusiasm of Americans for foreign travel, which was much valued by the architects.[36] Also worth noting is the fact that Emerson had little use for organized religion, whereas many of the architects were committed to a particular faith, and they designed a substantial number of churches.[37]

More than anything else, what Emerson offered was a confidence about the trajectory of modern life. At the end of "Art," Emerson explained how a steamboat crossing the Atlantic could be "a step of man into harmony with nature."[38] In "Progress of Culture," he asked, "Who does not prefer the age of steel, of gold, of coal, petroleum, cotton, steam, electricity, and the spectroscope?" He continued, "All this activity has added to the value of life, and to the scope of the intellect."[39] Against the gloom that weighed upon Ruskin and the misery that concerned Morris, Emerson's optimism provided an antidote. He believed the changes of the nineteenth century represented progress, and he challenged the individual to find pleasure in life. In "Considerations by the Way," he wrote that "power dwells with cheerfulness," and he was impatient with people who were generally despondent.[40] The transcendentalists were not unified in their thinking, however; Emerson represented one group whose members focused on self-culture and spiritual growth, whereas other members were more attentive to the downtrodden, devoting themselves to social reform.[41] Nevertheless, as the twentieth century was about to begin, it was Emerson with his confidence in the individual and faith in progress who appealed to the Boston architects.

Over the course of his lifetime, Emerson had become known to Britain's Arts and Crafts theorists. His optimistic outlook was entirely different from that of Carlyle or Ruskin, but both men admired him. On his first trip to Europe in 1833, Emerson met Carlyle, and the two established a lifelong friendship.[42] Ruskin rejected Emerson's belief that good will always win out, yet he still considered Emerson a great teacher.[43] In 1848, the artist Dante Gabriel Rossetti and his fellow Pre-Raphaelites listed Emerson as one of their "Immortals."[44] Walter Crane and C. R. Ashbee also appreciated Emerson's writing, and both men visited Concord after his death.[45]

Emerson's works offered enough breadth that people with differing views could find ideas that reinforced and clarified their own. To be sure, even his admirers did not subscribe to everything he wrote. For those living in New England, Emerson was valued for drawing upon the culture of the region to contribute to an international discussion about nineteenth-century issues. For those who knew him, he was admired for being unassuming yet thought-provoking, caring yet demanding.

Charles Eliot Norton

When the architects, craftsmen, and their friends assembled in Boston in April of 1897 to determine whether to organize a Society of Arts and Crafts, Norton was in attendance (fig. 3.2). He said he would be willing to support creating such a group, but only if "two things can be avoided—advertising and commercialism." Further, he stressed that the organization would need a strong executive committee whose members would not be "overawed" by large manufacturers.[46] On June 28 the society was incorporated "to develop and encourage higher artistic standards in the handicrafts," and Norton accepted the position of president.[47] Yet he was not a driving force behind the initiative. It was the architect Langford Warren who ran the preliminary meetings and kept the discussions focused.[48] But Norton, at age sixty-nine, was venerated as the dean of fine arts in America and was widely identified as the American counterpart to Ruskin.[49] Norton was chosen to inspire the society's members and contribute to its platform.

Through his years of teaching art history at Harvard, Norton had established a place for himself alongside Boston's architects. This relationship was recognized in 1885 when he was elected an honorary member of the

FIG. 3.2 Charles Eliot Norton.

Boston Society of Architects.[50] As a member of the Tavern Club and its president from 1890 to 1899, he also was well known by the many architects who belonged to this private social organization. Several would play key roles in the Society of Arts and Crafts, including Andrews, Barton, Long-fellow, Sturgis, and Walker.[51] In the spring of 1893, when Harvard's president Charles W. Eliot decided to establish an architecture program, Eliot solicited advice from Norton about who might take on the task. Norton recommended Langford Warren for the faculty position, and in the fall of that year, Warren became Norton's junior colleague.[52] Thus Norton was more than a little sympathetic to the architects who were promoting the creation of a Society of Arts and Crafts. By accepting the role of president, he helped them assert the importance of architecture that from the beginning was connected with the enterprise.

As a young man, Norton had pursued a career in business, but even in his early years, he demonstrated an inclination for teaching and embracing social causes. Born in Cambridge, Massachusetts, in 1827, he was the son of Andrews Norton, a prominent Harvard Divinity School professor, and Catharine Eliot, the daughter of a wealthy Boston merchant.[53] After graduating from Harvard College in 1846, Charles Norton found employment at a counting house in Boston. Later that year, he started teaching evening classes in a program he established for working men and boys, held in a Cambridge school building.[54] He also recruited other teachers to join him in what probably was the first night school in Massachusetts. The project went well, convincing him that evening schools should be opened across the country and run at public expense.

In 1852 Norton published "Dwellings and Schools for the Poor" in the *North American Review*.[55] By this time, the issue of housing the needy had become one of his related interests. Slums were growing in the eastern cities, including Boston, with great numbers of immigrants entering the country from Ireland and Germany. A year later, Norton developed a plan for a model housing project, and through a subscription, he raised the money to build two lodging houses in the city. The effort proved viable for both the investors and tenants, although it was limited in its influence due to the fact that developers could invest in more profitable buildings.[56] In 1854 Norton joined the board of the New England School of Design for Women, which had been founded the previous year, and he served as its treasurer.[57] The school's mission of training young women in art education was consistent with Norton's effort in running the evening school in Cambridge and anticipated his support for art education in the programming of the Society of Arts and Crafts. Both Norton and the architects would share a fervent commitment to education.

During the 1850s, Norton met Ruskin, Morris, and Emerson, establishing lasting friendships with them all. In 1855, when Norton was traveling in England, he called on Ruskin, ostensibly to see his paintings by J. M. W. Turner.[58] The meeting was brief, but in 1856, Norton and Ruskin ran into each other at Lake Geneva, and this time they found they had much in common. A year later, Norton spent a week visiting Ruskin outside Oxford, and in the years that followed, they wrote to each other often and spent time together whenever Norton was in Europe. Both men were troubled by the human suffering that they encountered during the middle of the nineteenth century. Ruskin believed that a sense of morality could be encouraged through art, a concept that appealed to Norton.[59] It was Ruskin's view that the individual should be urged to observe nature closely to become more sensitive not only to the physical world but also to its ethical dimensions. These ideas guided the English Pre-Raphaelite painters, advocates of "truth to nature," befriended by Ruskin and Norton. The desire to connect art and morality also guided Ruskin in shaping his theories about architecture.

Morality inspired his admiration of medieval cathedrals, which he praised for having been built as communal efforts, and it inspired his admiration of the buildings' ornament, which he felt reflected the freedom enjoyed by the craftsmen. In 1857, just before leaving England for the United States, Norton visited the Art Treasures exhibition in Manchester. When he returned home, he published a review in the *Atlantic Monthly* that concluded with his endorsement of the Pre-Raphaelite painters.[60] Two years later, Norton published *Notes of Travel and Study in Italy*. In it he expounded on the beauty of the Gothic cathedral at Orvieto, which he considered the embodiment of a flourishing republican polity.[61] Ruskin's influence on Norton was especially evident during this time.

Norton met Morris in 1856, and thereafter they saw each other often when Norton was in England.[62] Norton also developed friendships with people who were close to Morris, including the artists Dante Gabriel Rossetti and Edward Burne-Jones. In January of 1862, Rossetti wrote to Norton about the new decorating firm of Morris, Marshall, Faulkner and Company, and he enclosed the firm's prospectus.[63] Through such correspondence and his sojourns in England, Norton observed the Arts and Crafts movement as it gestated. Morris impressed him. In an 1868 letter to Ruskin, Norton assessed Morris as a "man of practical affairs, with the fine perceptions and quick fancy of the poet," a man who was simple and "so little of a prig."[64] Yet in 1899, when analyzing Morris, Norton wrote that although his friend had passion, he lacked insight. Morris's shortcoming, Norton believed, was that he failed to appreciate "all that Italy affords."[65] Norton thought that Morris was a man of the Middle Ages, a man of Northern Europe. Norton, on the other hand, loved Italy. He had become a leading Dante scholar, and he grew to appreciate the Italian Middle Ages. In Boston, Norton's preferences would encourage the architects to study the buildings of Italy and would lead them to consider the early Italian Renaissance as a foundation for their classicism.

The fact that Norton did not meet Emerson until the 1850s is noteworthy. In fact, Emerson had studied at Harvard under Norton's father, known in his day as the "Unitarian Pope." In 1838 Emerson challenged Andrews Norton's judgment on how to read the Bible, and in response Andrews denounced him.[66] Given the enormous respect that Charles Norton had for his father, one may assume that the young man felt obliged to steer clear of Emerson. But in 1852, when an English friend asked Charles to communicate with Emerson on his behalf, Norton proceeded to do so. Emerson responded cordially, thanking Norton for his mailing and expressing the hope that they might become acquainted.[67] By the late 1850s, the two men saw each other frequently. They dined together with fellow contributors to the *Atlantic Monthly*, and after 1860 Norton met Emerson at the monthly gatherings of the Saturday Club.[68] In his correspondence, Norton conveyed his admiration for Emerson and his views. When Emerson's *The Conduct of Life* appeared in 1860, Norton wrote that it "is full of real wisdom" and praised it for confirming "the moral principles of men."[69] In 1903 Norton told a gathering in Concord that of all the men he had known, Emerson impressed him for his "consistent loftiness of character." Emerson earned Norton's respect for the "natural simplicity of his manners and demeanor."[70]

Norton's feelings about Emerson were complex, however. Norton considered Emerson exemplary as an individual and a friend, yet he could not abide some of Emerson's core beliefs. Throughout his life, Norton was sensitive to the ways in which industrialization had degraded people's lives, concerns he shared with Ruskin and Morris. Even when Norton was living with his family in Europe in the late 1860s and early 1870s, contentedly digging in the archives of the Middle Ages, he was mulling over "the main social problems" of modern times. In 1870 Norton concluded that the United States had outgrown Emerson, that the nation needed "rational understanding, not that of the intuitions."[71]

Two years later, in February of 1872, Norton's wife died after giving birth. Making matters worse, he and his six young children could not return to Cambridge for another year because of a lease on their house.[72] When Norton and his family finally left for home, they were joined by the kindly Emerson, who had also been in England, recognized Norton's depression, and deliberately booked passage on the same boat. Each night as the steamer headed westward, Emerson and Norton spent a couple of hours together in the saloon before the lights were extinguished. In his journal, Norton commented on Emerson's purity, even as he observed "the limits of his mind."[73] Emerson's persistent optimism "is dangerous doctrine for a people," wrote Norton. "It degenerates into fatalistic indifference to moral considerations, and to personal responsibilities."[74] Yet Norton's affection for Emerson endured. Nine years later, when friends and family assembled for Henry Wadsworth Longfellow's funeral, it was Norton who offered support to a feeble Emerson. At Mount Auburn Cemetery in Cambridge, Emerson took Norton's arm to walk "up the path to the grave,—and his arm shook as we stood together there."[75] A month later, in April of 1882, Emerson was dead, and Norton rode the train to Concord to bid a last farewell to the perennial optimist.

Although Norton did not set out in life to become an academic, he became one of Harvard's legendary professors. Late in 1873, when he had just returned to the United States and was grieving over the loss of his wife, his cousin Charles W. Eliot, who four years earlier had become Harvard's president, proposed to Norton that he teach a course.[76] Norton was intrigued by the possibility and encouraged by his cousin's energy and liberal views. Harvard, Norton felt, was a civilizing institution, a moderating force against the American plutocracy.[77] For his part, Eliot appreciated the fact that Norton was knowledgeable in both art and literature.[78] Norton taught his first course in the fine arts in the fall of 1874 and would deliver his last lecture to a packed classroom in the spring of 1898 when he was seventy years old.

Even after his official retirement, Norton taught a small class on Dante for several more years.[79] Harvard was his calling. For Norton, exposing young minds to the ideals of Western civilization was his best hope to counter the corruption and oppression of the modern age. He did not present the history of art as solely a progression of formal developments. Rather, as he traced succeeding periods, he related them to the rise and fall of ethical values. His students learned that the first golden age emerged in Periclean Athens, followed by a long decline, after which a second cultural flowering took place in medieval Venice and Florence. Norton ended his lectures by examining the early Italian Renaissance, when society again blossomed during the Quattrocento. From the sixteenth century onward, as far as Norton was concerned, art and society became debased. His courses never considered later periods, which he would have regarded as unified, a continuum into modern times.[80] In teaching his classes in the fine arts, it should be emphasized, Norton was not an aesthete. Indeed, when Oscar Wilde arrived in Boston in 1882, Norton had little interest in meeting this man who loved beauty "for the sake of selfish enjoyment."[81] It was Ruskin's example as a professor at Oxford that was pertinent to Norton. Ruskin had demonstrated what might be achieved in teaching courses in the fine arts, and Norton kept Ruskin informed about his plans.[82]

Although Norton took a synthetic view of any given culture, probing its various branches of artistic production, he was especially attentive to architecture, whether the Parthenon of ancient Greece or the cathedrals of Italy. Having undertaken scholarly research, in 1880 he published *Historical Studies of Church Building in the Middle Ages: Venice, Siena, Florence*.[83] As for the architecture of New England, he loved the old farmhouses and the unpretentious dwellings in country towns. In 1864 Norton and his wife bought an eighteenth-century house with a barn and outbuildings in the western Massachusetts village of Ashfield.[84] He was enthusiastic about its "air of rural comfort and pleasantness," and observed how the settlement nestled into the surrounding hills, at one with nature.[85] Norton's appreciation of the vernacular buildings of the New England countryside was parallel to the interest in vernacular architecture developing at this time in England by Morris and English Arts and Crafts architects. In 1889 Norton published an article about the appeal of America's early houses.[86] Boston's architectural community shared this view, and several of the architects bought colonial houses for themselves. They also were retained by clients who wanted to renovate similar houses for their families.

On the other hand, Norton had little good to say about the buildings of his own time. Nothing exasperated him more than the construction he saw around him on the Harvard campus. In 1859 Norton wrote scathingly about the new natural sciences museum, designed by architects George Snell and Henry Greenough.[87] The museum's sheer, bare walls and lack of any embellishment such as columns or sculpture could not be excused. In 1867 Norton criticized Ware and Van Brunt's Memorial Hall, which had just been designed.[88] The weakness of this building, as Norton saw it, was its lack of unity and simplicity. He held out hope, however, that it could be improved over time with additional decoration. Richardson's buildings at Harvard, Sever Hall (1878–80) and Austin Hall (1880–84), did not meet with Norton's approval either, and he vented his frustrations in lectures to his students.[89] When Robinson Hall, designed by Charles McKim, was completed in 1901 for the School of Architecture, Norton published his objections in a 1904 essay in the *Harvard Graduates Magazine*.[90] The problem with Robinson Hall, he wrote, was that it failed to harmonize with Sever Hall. That same year, in a letter to President Eliot, Norton complained about Guy Lowell's new lecture hall, completed in 1902.[91]

In addition to criticizing specific buildings, Norton chastised Boston's architects directly, taking them to task for producing designs that lacked "refinement and poetic sense."[92] To some extent, the architects seem to have accepted the criticism as accurate. They were frustrated, as Andrews wrote, that they were inadequately compensated for their time, which thwarted their ability to do their jobs well. Yet even as Norton found fault with the designers, he emphasized the importance of their work. At a meeting of

FIG. 3.3 H. Langford Warren, proposed design for Harvard University Press, Cambridge, MA, watercolor and pencil, 1906.

the Boston Society of Architects in 1895, he reminded them of the high moral duties of their profession, stating, "Upon no class of men does greater responsibility rest today than upon the architects."[93] They understood that Norton was in their camp.

The question, then, was this: What approach to architecture did Norton favor? In light of his displeasure with so many of the buildings erected in his day, a project that he praised deserves examination. Such a building was designed by Langford Warren in 1906.[94] Norton and the Boston printer Daniel Berkeley Updike, another founding member of the Society of Arts and Crafts, had been hoping to encourage Harvard to establish a university press. With some privately donated funds, they asked Warren to prepare renderings, elevations, and plans. When Warren finished the drawings, the next step was to seek President Eliot's support. On March 2, Norton wrote to Eliot that the project "seems to me thoroughly well thought out, and to be exceedingly pleasing, and altogether a satisfactory design."[95] A few days later, after the president had met with Warren and Updike and reviewed the drawings, Norton followed up with another letter. He wrote, "Mr. Warren's plans seemed to me uncommonly good in design and well thought out."[96] In the end, the funding for the project never materialized. In 1913 Harvard University Press was established without Updike and without a new building.

Warren's drawings survive, however, to document Norton's idea of "uncommonly good" architecture (fig. 3.3).[97] Sited at the front of a lot was a two-and-a-half-story administration building, including offices and a library, which connected to a composing room, press room, and bindery at the rear. To the modern eye, the proposed design may look like a bland, brick Colonial Revival affair—agreeable yet forgettable. The administration building was massed with a projecting bay at each end, defining a forecourt. A slate hip roof was to support a cupola, similar to the one on Harvard Hall, dating from 1764 and located just beyond the main gates to Harvard Yard. The entrance to the building, aligned with the cupola, was designed with a fanlight and hood, while the flanking windows were divided into small lights. The overall effect was balanced and restrained, virtues to Norton's way of thinking, with architectural elements that were refined. The fence in front of the complex would have featured wrought iron, and the administration building's ornament outside and inside would have been hand carved and based on historic sources. Here was a building that represented the ideal vision of Norton, Warren, and Updike—a reserved yet elegant design that also embodied the Arts and Crafts movement in New England.

When the Society of Arts and Crafts was incorporated, the mission statement was written by Norton.[98] According to the statement, the society was committed to bringing designers and workmen into "mutually helpful relations" while encouraging workmen to develop their own ideas. This objective was consistent with Ruskin's concern for the spirit of the worker. It also promoted the collaborative approach that Norton observed when Morris and his friends founded their firm. The society's statement went on to explain that the organization would insist on "sobriety and restraint." It condemned "over-ornamentation and specious originality" and held that the form of an object should relate to its use. These were concepts that the English theorists would have endorsed, but the ideas also were supported by Emerson's essays, "Art" and "Beauty." In March of 1898, Norton lectured to a gathering of the Society of Arts and Crafts. Every craftsman, he believed, "should be able to express the thought, feeling and culture that are in his soul, as well as the capacity of the eye and hand."[99] In Norton's calling for the worker to look inward to his soul, one hears reverberations of Emerson. Indeed, through the later years of his life, Norton paid close attention to Emerson's writing. In 1883 Norton edited and published the correspondence between Emerson and Carlyle.[100] In 1899 he would edit and publish Emerson's letters to one of their mutual friends.[101]

When the Society of Arts and Crafts assembled in Boston's Mechanics Hall for the annual meeting in November of 1898, Norton as president gave the keynote address. His topic was "The Craftsman as Artist," and excerpts from his remarks were published in the December issue of *Architectural Review*.[102] From the start, Norton focused on the craftsman; craft itself was a secondary interest. He was concerned, he said, about the modern workers who labored without pleasure—a subject that was dear to him as well as integral to the Arts and Crafts movement. To redeem the worker from this condition, he continued, was the object of the society. Norton explained that it was essential for the worker to call upon his "moral nature," how he must train himself to perceive beauty, and how he must cultivate his imagination—ideas that had been advanced by Norton's Pre-Raphaelite friends as well as by Ruskin. Norton went on to state that by "self-respect and self-culture," the individual could express what was best in himself. In his reasoning and his choice of words, by calling for "self-culture," Norton drew from Emerson as well as the Unitarian background that he and Emerson shared. Norton urged the young craftsman to read poetry and to study photographs of great works of art. Self-culture to Norton meant the pursuit of a liberal education, and to him this education was a moral obligation, even if the individual had to educate himself.

Then Norton advised the craftsman to be guided by two ideals. "Simplicity and sincerity are the fundamental principles of good art," he said. These words and values were fixed in Norton's mind by this time. As far back as 1857, when Norton wrote his review of the exhibition in Manchester, England, he admired the simplicity in Giotto's painting and in Raphael's early art.[103] Norton also valued sincerity. He disapproved of Joshua Reynolds when the painter encouraged the study of other artists' works—an academic approach—but praised Reynolds when he "gave himself, with honest sincerity and affection, to the study of Nature."[104] Norton also would have encountered these words in the writings of Emerson, as in the essay "Beauty" from 1860, which encouraged simplicity, and in "Progress of Culture" from 1867, in which Emerson wrote that great men are sincere.[105] In 1889 Norton published an essay on architecture as a fine art, in which he urged architects to remain faithful to their ideals, exhorting them that "beauty and strength reside in simplicity, sincerity, proportion, and harmony."[106]

Nine years later, when Norton addressed the Society of Arts and Crafts, the words *simplicity* and *sincerity* had become widely used by Arts and Crafts leaders, for whom simplicity was equated with purity as well as clarity, and sincerity was equated with integrity. By the end of the nineteenth century, Norton had refined his ideas about what he meant by simplicity. In his address to the Society of Arts and Crafts, he illustrated his point by referring to the revival of fine printing. Norton told his audience that the books printed by Morris, with their heavy, dark typeface and borders based on medieval manuscripts, were full of faults. Far better was the printing from fifteenth-century Venice that was "simple, easily read, and adorned with initial letters elegant in design."[107] Updike, the printer, had embraced this lighter approach in the work of his press, and Warren's proposed building for Harvard was an equivalent expression in architecture. In fact, in the same 1898 issue of *Architectural Review* in which Norton's address appeared, Warren published a review of current architecture periodicals in which he observed that the most successful architects are those who "are guided by the great principles of sincerity and simplicity."[108] Although the meanings of these two words may have varied over the course of the nineteenth century, invoked to promote different designers' ideals, the gathering in Boston in 1898 understood Norton's preferences.

In his remaining comments, Norton encouraged the craftsman to avoid imitation. His audience may have recalled Emerson's dictate, "Insist on yourself; never imitate," published in "Self-Reliance." But Norton also admonished the craftsman to resist aiming for originality, reiterating an important tenet of the Society of Arts and Crafts. He assured the audience that the craftsman "cannot help being original if he be a man whose soul is really alive." The soul must be cultivated—Emerson again. In closing, Norton advised the young craftsman that his craft should be "the expression of the good that is in him," the beauty that is "the image of his character, his intelligence, and his imagination," all of which would produce not merely a craft, but a work of fine art.[109]

Norton created an intellectual framework for an Arts and Crafts movement in New England, blending the ideas of Ruskin and Morris with those of Emerson. Like Ruskin and Morris, Norton recognized how industry bore down on a growing working class in the nineteenth century. Like Ruskin and Morris, Norton was dismayed by mass production, and he supported the organized effort in Boston to promote a revival of craftsmanship. And like Morris and other English Arts and Crafts leaders, Norton subscribed to the idea of "mutually helpful relations." Some of the ideas favored by Ruskin and Morris were also of interest to Emerson, and these Norton adopted. One idea was a belief that "fitness" should be the basis for design; excess was to be avoided, while beauty was to be sought in designs that were functional. All four men were advocates for simplicity. They also were impassioned about morality, which Norton identified with sincerity as a basis for life and art. Emerson offered other ideas that Norton advanced. Emerson's love of the New England landscape was developed by Norton, as was Emerson's confidence that an American architecture could emerge from native, vernacular traditions. Emerson's interpretation of self-culture, indebted to Unitarian teaching, appealed to Norton, too.

The architects who aligned themselves with Norton were committed to designing buildings based on the guiding principles of simplicity and sincerity. They developed a shared understanding about what these concepts meant, and it gave a distinctive cast to the Arts and Crafts movement in New England. The architects leading the Society of Arts and Crafts strived to design buildings that were unassuming yet pleasing, informed by the study of architectural history as well as by the heritage of the region.

Louis Dembitz Brandeis

At the turn of the twentieth century, Louis Brandeis was a successful corporate lawyer and one of the most prominent men in Boston (fig. 3.4). Whereas Emerson and Norton had devoted the better part of their lives to lecturing and writing, Brandeis was first and foremost a man of business. Because of this orientation, he approached the world from a perspective that in some ways was more like that of the architects. The concerns that Brandeis and the architects addressed revolved around many of the same social, economic, and political issues that rose to the forefront in the Boston area at this time.

Shortly before his nineteenth birthday, in the fall of 1875, Brandeis arrived in Cambridge and enrolled at Harvard Law School. Born and raised in Louisville, Kentucky, he had just spent three terms studying in Germany. There he had met an American doctoral candidate, Ephraim Emerton, who had encouraged Brandeis to pursue his studies in Cambridge.[110] Harvard during these years was in flux. In 1870 President Eliot, one year into his position, had hired Christopher Columbus Langdell as dean of the law school.[111] Langdell launched something of a revolution in legal education, replacing rote learning with the reading of cases that were analyzed through Socratic dialogue. Langdell's objective was to encourage students to identify underlying principles in the law. Brandeis excelled in this environment,

FIG. 3.4 Louis Dembitz Brandeis.

finishing the two-year program first in his class, and then he returned for another year of graduate study.

During his law school years, Brandeis encountered some of the region's luminaries and emerging leaders. He met revered men of letters, including Longfellow and Emerson.[112] He also established a friendship with his classmate Sam Warren, who would become his law partner.[113] Warren's father had made a fortune in paper manufacturing, and the family lived in a grand manse on Beacon Hill. His mother directed her considerable energy to buying art, including paintings by contemporary Europeans and Americans along with old masters. As Sam Warren's closest friend, Brandeis frequented the family home, where he was exposed to the impressive collection.

Another friendship that Brandeis established during the late 1870s was with Denman Ross, who would amass a different type of art collection— one that would support Ross's investigations into design theory.[114] On visits to the Ross house in 1877, Brandeis studied photographs of Italian architecture and examined one of Ruskin's sketchbooks that had been acquired by Norton. During this period, Ross welcomed Brandeis into a group that was reading Ruskin's *Seven Lamps of Architecture*, augmented by a discussion led by Ross on the evolution of Gothic architecture.[115] Brandeis felt inadequate in these gatherings, yet he was inspired to read more of Ruskin's works.[116] From the time he arrived at Harvard, Brandeis was encouraged to appreciate art and architecture. Through Ross, Brandeis began thinking about the built environment, which would engage his attention in later years. Reading about Ruskin's concern for the laborer also must have left an impression on him.

The values of Harvard and Boston meshed with those of the young Jewish attorney from Louisville. He read and admired Emerson, and one may surmise that he was attracted to the essayist's devotion to self-culture and individualism.[117] Yankee restraint would have appealed to Brandeis, along with the Unitarian passion for justice. The region's commitment to education was another distinction that would have attracted him.[118] More specifically, Brandeis shared Eliot's desire to improve and expand Harvard's professional schools.

In 1879 Brandeis joined Warren in opening an office in Boston, and they developed a practice in corporate law. Eschewing the newer neighborhood of the Back Bay, Brandeis lived on Beacon Hill, where he would remain until his appointment to the United States Supreme Court in 1916.[119] On two occasions, he dedicated time to teaching, first at Harvard Law School during the 1882–83 academic year, and then at MIT, 1892–93. When he suggested to Eliot that Harvard offer a course such as the one he had just given at MIT, the president asked him to teach it. But Brandeis declined, preferring to stay focused on his practice.[120] Nevertheless, he was deeply committed to Harvard Law School. In 1886, he and six other graduates founded the law school's alumni association, with Brandeis serving as its secretary and offering his office for their meetings. The association's mission was to raise the money that would support Langdell in positioning the school as a national leader.[121] This ambition to influence the country through education—shared by Eliot, Langdell, and Brandeis—pervaded Boston and would drive the leaders of the Society of Arts and Crafts.

In 1889 and again in 1891, Brandeis assisted the Boston Society of Architects. On the first occasion, he helped the members incorporate the organization, which had been launched in 1867. On the second occasion, he drafted a standard building contract that the members could use.[122] Brandeis's relationship with the architects probably came about through Sam Warren, who had joined the group as an associate member in 1886.[123] Two years later, Warren's father died, and he abandoned the practice of law in order to run the family business. It seems likely that when the architects needed legal assistance, they came to Warren, who in turn asked his former partner to step in.

This relationship was typical of a widespread phenomenon at the end of the century in which professionals in various fields actively supported each other.[124] Through his efforts on behalf of the Boston Society of Architects, Brandeis crossed paths with some of the members who would soon be involved with the Society of Arts and Crafts. One of the architects was Langford Warren, who had been elected secretary of the Boston Society of Architects a couple of months before Brandeis drafted the building contract.[125] Other members of the Boston Society of Architects during this period who would play active roles in the Society of Arts and Crafts included Andrews, Longfellow, Shaw, and Walker. By the time the Society of Arts and Crafts was founded, the respect for professional counsel was such that its leaders saw that the organization was legally incorporated. The general respect for the professional also manifested itself when the society introduced a formal arrangement to offer counsel to its craftsmen from experts on design.

During the 1890s, new intellectual currents moved through Boston and Cambridge that penetrated various disciplines. One of the era's most influential individuals was the jurist Oliver Wendell Holmes Jr. Between 1880 and 1881, Holmes began formulating his ideas in a series of Lowell Institute lectures on "The Common Law." Brandeis attended at least one of them.[126] In these lectures, Holmes challenged the widely held view that law is unchanging, logically interpreted over time to reinforce fixed beliefs. Instead, he proposed that law is organic, changing with society's customs and needs. In 1897 Holmes sharpened his views in an address called "The Path of the Law," now famous in the annals of American jurisprudence.[127] His conclusion was that law is nothing more than what the courts will do, based not on fixed ideas but on the desires of society at a given time. A year later, in 1898, William James, one of Harvard's most renowned professors, introduced his philosophy of pragmatism. Like his longtime friend Holmes, James was interested in the way people think, and James concluded that what is considered true at any given time emerges from a social process.[128] Brandeis was greatly influenced by both men, and at the turn of the twentieth century, their ideas enabled him to find a way to work through the courts to achieve major reforms. Because these concepts were taking shape when the Society of Arts and Crafts was organized, one may observe how its leaders sought to create a social process for reaching a shared understanding of what constituted good design.

Ross was another figure who was attracting recognition in Boston and

Cambridge during the 1890s. After graduating from Harvard College in 1875, he began studying for his doctorate in history, receiving his degree five years later. Ross also trained as a painter, and eventually he turned his attention to the fine arts. His close reading of Ruskin stimulated his thinking, yet he distanced himself from Ruskin's moralistic interpretation of art history and started investigating how a scientific approach might be applied to design studies.[129] With this objective, Ross began acquiring works of fine and decorative art, striving to identify principles that contribute to beauty. Over the years, he accumulated more than 16,000 works.

In January of 1897, Ross was among the eleven men who assembled at the original Museum of Fine Arts on Copley Square to discuss organizing an Arts and Crafts exhibition.[130] When it was held in April, Ross served on the advisory board.[131] It is not surprising, then, that Brandeis and his wife attended the show.[132] By this time, both Ross and Sam Warren were trustees of the Museum of Fine Arts, and in June, both men signed on as founders of the Society of Arts and Crafts. After helping to establish the society, Ross extended his influence there as a lecturer and contributor to *Handicraft*.[133] In 1899 Ross was hired by Langford Warren to teach the architecture students at Harvard, where he would become one of the distinguished professors in the early decades of the twentieth century. In 1907 Ross published *A Theory of Pure Design: Harmony, Balance, Rhythm*.[134] The collection of art objects that Ross amassed suggests a parallel with Langdell's case studies, brought together to encourage the student to probe and learn. Because he was close to Ross and Langdell, Brandeis must have recognized similarities in their teaching.

During the first two decades that followed the establishment of the Society of Arts and Crafts, its leaders, including the architect members, and Brandeis devoted their attention to three broad areas of shared interest: education, the public realm, and the plight of the laborer. These individuals took up the banner for causes that were especially compelling to progressive-minded Bostonians.

A commitment to public education was firmly entrenched in New England's culture, and ideas for improving the schools were regularly advanced. In 1901 Brandeis assisted a group that was advocating for legislation to create a Boston Schoolhouse Commission, separate from the Boston School Committee and City Council.[135] With the city's population swelling, many school buildings were being constructed, and Brandeis supported the view that professionals should provide oversight of this work. In 1902 a three-man commission was established, and the architect Clipston Sturgis, a leading member of the Society of Arts and Crafts, was appointed to it, serving as chairman through his tenure until 1910.[136] Like Sturgis, many of the architects in the Society of Arts and Crafts were attracted to school building design and developed an expertise in the specialty.

Promoting museums was another interest during this period that related to the commitment to education. In 1901 Brandeis became a vice president of the Germanic Museum Association, which opened a museum at Harvard that spring in an old gymnasium.[137] In this role, he would have encountered Langford Warren, who produced a design for a permanent museum building and then, when a design was commissioned by a German architect, oversaw the museum's construction.[138] In 1901 Brandeis's friend Sam Warren, who had been serving as a trustee of Boston's Museum of Fine Arts, was elected president of its board. Under his leadership, the museum prepared to erect a new building on Huntington Avenue in the Fenway. Sturgis was retained to advise on the design.[139]

Educational efforts took a variety of forms. Bostonians frequently organized lecture series, and lectures were central to the programming of the Society of Arts and Crafts. In much the same way, in 1904 Brandeis joined the retailer Edward A. Filene in establishing the Boston City Club, which sponsored lectures on topics of interest to business leaders.[140] When the Boston City Club erected a building, it was designed by Newhall and Blevins.[141] Louis Newhall, the senior member of the partnership, was an active member in the Society of Arts and Crafts. In yet another educational endeavor, the Society of Arts and Crafts undertook an ambitious campaign in 1905 to encourage industrial education throughout the state. The society organized a conference at the Massachusetts State House, which resulted in new policies mandated by the state board of education.[142] Brandeis was among the prominent citizens who were called upon to endorse the proposals.

The public realm, including buildings and entire neighborhoods, was the subject of great interest in Boston at the turn of the twentieth century. For the architects, there were wide-ranging concerns. They became involved in issues relating to preservation, with Andrews leading the effort to save the Bulfinch-designed State House. Another cause promoted by the architects was building-height restrictions.[143] Brandeis was drawn into similar battles and some of the same ones. In 1893 he joined several of the city's leading citizens to oppose the West End Street Railway and its plan to run a trolley line across Boston Common. He later described this campaign as his "first important public work."[144] Six years later, he addressed the legislature in a citizens' campaign to impose height restrictions on Beacon Hill that would preserve the dominance of the State House dome.[145] At the turn of the century, a protracted fight was being waged over the height of Westminster Chambers, a new apartment building on Copley Square. Brandeis assisted a citizens' group that supported a height restriction.[146] As time went on, Brandeis became increasingly interested in the public realm, including working-class neighborhoods. In 1905 he wrote to his father about developments in German cities, observing how playgrounds were being constructed, streets lined with trees, and height restrictions imposed.[147]

Four years later, Brandeis joined Filene, who was director of the Boston Chamber of Commerce, in forming an organization called Boston-1915 to bring together civic-minded groups and individuals to encourage improvements for the city.[148] In November of 1909, Boston-1915 sponsored a major exhibition in the old Museum of Fine Arts building on Copley Square, showcasing ideas relating to everything from urban design to child labor laws.[149] Newhall was chairman of the City Planning Committee. More than 200,000 people attended, and hundreds of organizations participated. In the end, the second exposition, scheduled for 1915 to celebrate the city's achievements, never took place. Yet a significant outcome of the 1909 exhibition, with its focus on the future of the city, was the establishment of Boston's City Planning Board. Cram became its first chairman.

A concern for the laborer was shared by Boston's professionals, yet their sympathies were tempered by their inclinations as businessmen. Also, many of them adhered to Emersonian individualism. Soon after the Society of Arts and Crafts was organized, it began holding classes for workers. *American Architect* praised this approach to training, observing that it contrasted with that of the unions, which tried to restrict education and entry into the craft trades.[150] In 1903 the leadership within the Society of Arts and Crafts engaged in a tug-of-war over whether the organization would advocate for the social principles of Morris.[151] Although Carey, the society's second president, held views that were aligned with those of Morris, he was thwarted in his desire to focus on the conditions of labor. After he resigned in November and Langford Warren assumed the presidency, the society steered farther away from the larger social problems relating to industry. The strength of the Society of Arts and Crafts, Warren believed, was its "keeping those questions entirely out of our midst."[152] The organization excelled at training the craftsman and encouraging higher artistic standards, and Warren would emphasize these priorities in the years that followed.

During this same time, Brandeis also was trying to sort out how to help the worker. In May of 1905, the Harvard Ethical Society invited him to speak to the undergraduates at Phillips Brooks House, a center for social service groups that had opened in 1900, designed by Longfellow. The address that Brandeis delivered, "The Opportunity in the Law," criticized lawyers for having allowed themselves to become adjuncts of large corporations while neglecting their ability "to use their powers for the protection of the people." He continued, "We hear much of the 'corporation lawyer,' and far too little of the 'people's lawyer.'"[153] By this time, Brandeis was devoting more and more hours outside his practice to helping groups that focused on assisting the working class. One crusade was the passage of legislation to allow savings banks to offer life insurance to workers.[154] In 1908 Brandeis represented Oregon before the United States Supreme Court, convincing the justices that they should uphold the state's statute limiting the number of hours a day women could be employed in certain jobs.[155] Brandeis always believed in free enterprise, but he saw that the people needed representation, too. Brandeis and those steering the Society of Arts and Crafts ended up adopting very different approaches to helping labor. They shared a conservative belief, however, in leadership by the elite.[156] They believed in their expertise and their roles as champions for reform.

In an age of activism, the debates of the period were often heated and led allies to break apart. This was the situation confronted by the Society of Arts and Crafts when Carey resigned. Similarly, Brandeis found some of his early friends turning on him and vilifying him.[157] Yet Sam Warren and Denman Ross never abandoned him. Tragically, in 1910, Warren committed suicide, apparently in response to a struggle involving the family business. To honor Warren's memory, Ross donated a fifteenth-century Spanish panel to the Museum of Fine Arts.[158] Warren, Ross, and Brandeis shared many of the same values, and they held each other in high esteem.

In 1916 President Woodrow Wilson nominated Brandeis to the Supreme Court, sparking a firestorm. Harvard president Abbott Lawrence Lowell collected fifty-five signatures from prominent Boston citizens urging the Senate to reject Brandeis.[159] But Boston's elite was not united. Brandeis had his supporters, and they enlisted Harvard's former president, Charles W. Eliot, to submit a letter on the lawyer's behalf. In it, Eliot wrote that he had known Brandeis for forty years and praised his keen intelligence. Eliot continued, "He has sometimes advocated measures or policies which did not commend themselves to me; but I have never questioned his honesty and sincerity, or his desire for justice."[160] Well into the twentieth century, "sincerity" was an honored trait.

Years later, writing to his brother in 1927, Brandeis identified three men who "excelled in the art of living."[161] Perhaps surprisingly, considering his career as a lawyer and a Supreme Court justice, Brandeis named Ross as one of the three. Although the Arts and Crafts movement was not Brandeis's cause, it was an important cause for two friends he admired and cherished. Idealists all, Brandeis and the society's leaders were fellow travelers in Boston.

CHAPTER FOUR

An Arts and Crafts Movement Emerges in New England

O VER THE COURSE OF THREE DECADES, from the late 1860s through the 1890s, a variety of ideas took root in Boston that would produce an Arts and Crafts architecture throughout New England—an architecture that would be nourished by the region's culture and traditions. The most distinctive aspect of this culture was an almost religious faith in formal education, which had manifested itself in 1635 with the founding of Boston Latin School, the first public school in America, followed by the founding of Harvard College in 1636. An emphasis on education would characterize the Arts and Crafts movement centered in Boston and would influence the architecture related to it. Another distinctive trait was the attention to history shared by the educated members of the region's populace. By the second half of the nineteenth century, Boston's architects were actively supporting investigations into the past—studying the region's colonial and federal era buildings as well as underwriting an archaeological expedition in the eastern Mediterranean. A third characteristic of the regional culture was the reverence held by members of its elite for their English heritage. At the end of the century, the view was widely promoted that this heritage was shared by everyone, despite the presence of a large population of Irish descent and an influx of immigrants from eastern and southern Europe. Like Emerson and Norton, Boston's architects knew England well, traveling there and tracking English trends in architecture and design.

The most influential architect in Boston during the 1870s and 1880s was Henry Hobson Richardson. Among the rising stars were Robert Swain Peabody, Charles McKim, and Henry Vaughan. By the 1890s, most of the architects who would become leaders in Boston's Society of Arts and Crafts had befriended each other and were working together in educational institutions, professional organizations, and publications. A movement was coalescing.

Education and Organization in the Late 1860s and 1870s

After the close of the Civil War, Boston architects saw two important developments in their community, both contributing to the professionalization of the field. In 1865 the nation's first collegiate architecture program was founded at MIT, located in Boston's Back Bay. William Robert Ware was hired to direct the architecture school, and it opened in 1868.[1] From the beginning, those who enrolled were required to study architectural history in order to enhance their understanding of the principles of building.[2] By 1874 Ware had determined that the city's Georgian churches could offer some worthwhile lessons, and he assigned his advanced students to draw them, paying special attention to the towers.[3] Well before the national centennial celebration, Ware and other Boston architects demonstrated an appreciation for the region's oldest surviving monuments.

While Ware was busy launching the MIT program, some of his colleagues organized the Boston Society of Architects in 1867.[4] Its members also took an early interest in the region's colonial architecture. In 1869 one of the architects, William Ralph Emerson, voiced his concern about the destruction of old New England houses, which he pronounced "the only truly American Architecture which has yet existed."[5] During the late 1870s, the architects assembled to hear talks about colonial architecture, illustrated by drawings and photographs. On one occasion, members examined a portfolio of sketches by Bulfinch.[6] In 1879 the society held a competition for documenting a colonial building in New England.[7] Almost always, these meetings included an educational component featuring presentations and discussions. In 1875, at the instigation of Henry Van Brunt, the group sponsored a series of public lectures for students and anyone interested in architecture.[8] Van Brunt spoke about interior decoration, reflecting his knowledge of the English Aesthetic movement. In his remarks, he described the architect who, after completing a building, was mortified when his work was compromised by an owner who suffered from a lack of taste. Van Brunt, like his English counterparts, promoted the idea that the architect should have more say in the decoration of his buildings. Other lectures in the series addressed mosaics and terra cotta, stained glass, sculpture, and furniture. This focus on craftsmanship in mid-1870s Boston was parallel to incipient Arts and Crafts interests in England.

In addition to the founding of MIT's architecture program and the Boston Society of Architects, other developments during the 1870s raised the study of architecture and design to a new level, in both the region and the nation. Charles Eliot Norton's first fine arts lectures at Harvard in 1874 were important for their influence on the formal study of art and architectural history. Over time, Norton taught thousands of undergraduates and also attracted auditors.[9] Once ensconced at Harvard, Norton became interested in advancing scholarly studies, especially investigations of the ancient world.[10] By 1879 Norton had raised the funds to found the Archaeological Institute of America. He was elected its first president, with Ware serving on the executive committee. These men were ambitious, and they determined that the new organization would not be local, but rather national in scope. Such national ambitions were becoming pervasive in the world of Harvard and Boston, and this ambition would extend to the Society of Arts and Crafts.

Another initiative of the decade was the opening of the School of the Museum of Fine Arts in 1877.[11] The museum had been founded in 1870, and a new building, designed by Sturgis and Brigham, was finished six years later. Located in the Back Bay, it was a short walk from MIT and served the architecture students as well as the art and design students in the Museum School. The energy of the city's architects during this period was considerable, and they stepped forward to assist James R. Osgood when he began publishing the *American Architect and Building News* in Boston in 1876.[12] Ware was among the architects who served on the editorial staff, and he even supported it financially. Issued weekly, the journal was read by architects across the United States. Great buildings from the past were regularly illustrated and discussed—monuments selected not for imitation but to illuminate fundamental principles, the approach advanced by Ware at MIT.

The emergence of New England's Arts and Crafts architecture may be traced to certain architects who were active in the region during the 1870s. Henry Hobson Richardson claimed center stage.[13] Born in Louisiana in 1838, Richardson attended Harvard, graduating in 1859. During the Civil War years, he studied architecture at the École des Beaux-Arts in Paris, where he acquired his method of design. But he also traveled in England and was familiar with stylistic trends in the architecture there. When he returned to the United States, he began his practice in Manhattan while living on Staten Island. Although French qualities may be identified in Richardson's early projects, his buildings for the most part were consistent with the High Victorian Gothic direction favored in England.

When Richardson won the design competition for Trinity Church in

FIG. 4.1 Henry
Hobson Richardson,
Trinity Church,
Boston, 1872–77.

1872, his future in Boston was set (fig. 4.1). His bold, weighty style was widely admired by architects across the country. "Richardsonian" buildings were massive piles that seemed to grow from the ground, typically constructed with quarry-faced stone cut in large blocks, with windows and doors framed by low, round arches, inspired by French Romanesque precedents. Consistent with English architects of the period, Richardson insisted on high-quality ornament and decoration. At Trinity Church, dedicated in 1877, he brought together an exceptional team to embellish both the exterior and interior. On the facade, the sculptor John Evans carved foliate column capitals and a frieze, while inside the young John La Farge oversaw a stable of painters, one of whom was Augustus Saint-Gaudens. In addition to stenciling the church walls, La Farge and his crew executed murals that established a new standard in America for large-scale painting in a public building. La Farge also designed stained-glass windows, including a spectacular blue Christ in Majesty, dating from 1882 to 1883, installed after the church was completed.

In his orchestration of this symphony, Richardson was working in an Arts and Crafts fashion before the movement had been given a name. While the church was under construction, in 1874 Richardson moved to the nearby Boston suburb of Brookline. Within a short time, he had built drafting rooms and a library attached to the house where he and his family lived. Richardson and his wife welcomed into their home the young architects he employed, and they dined together on a weekly basis. This relationship between master and apprentices was unusual, and the young architects would warmly remember the experience years later.[14] Richardson returned to his alma mater to design Sever Hall (1878–80), a classroom building for the Harvard campus. Evans ornamented the building with organic patterns cut into the brick.[15] Designed with a modest Georgian doorway on the elevation that faced the street, Sever Hall alluded to the college's oldest surviving buildings, located on the opposite side of Harvard Yard—simple red-brick structures, dating from the colonial era.

The architect Robert Swain Peabody, never as widely known as Richardson, also rose to prominence in Boston during the 1870s.[16] After graduating from Harvard with the class of 1866, he worked for architectural firms in Boston and studied briefly at MIT before heading to Paris in 1867 to attend the École. His reaction to the experience was mixed. "Although we rendered the French projects, the thought of England and the picturesque was ever present with us," he later recalled.[17] Much as he valued his École training, Peabody preferred the Victorian Gothic styles. In the spring of 1869, he journeyed to London and implored the architect Alfred Waterhouse to take him on as an unsalaried hand. Peabody was persuasive, and once he settled in, he was pleased to be assigned to country house projects. He stayed only until early July, but the experience provided him with a knowledge of English residential work that would inform his own designs when he returned to Boston.

In 1870 Peabody and John Goddard Stearns Jr. established their partnership and began attracting commissions for residential, institutional, and commercial projects. Their buildings generally drew upon English fashions and were decidedly picturesque in character. In their free time, Peabody and members of the office staff started exploring New England, sketching colonial and federal period architecture. From the mid- to late 1870s, they shared their work with a growing audience. An office draftsman, William Edward Barry, published a small book called *Pen Sketches of Old Houses* while Peabody published his drawings in the *American Architect and Build-*

ing News, and Arthur Little, another staffer, published a book titled *Early New England Interiors*.[18] At a meeting of the Boston Society of Architects held in 1878, Peabody discussed the pre–Revolutionary War architecture of Philadelphia.[19] Reflecting the architects' studies of Georgian buildings, the firm began applying classical ornament to its designs. One such example was the Breakers (1877–78), a summer residence erected in Newport, Rhode Island, for Pierre Lorillard IV (fig. 4.2).[20] With its picturesque massing and profusion of steeply pitched roofs and tall chimneys, the house was typical of the 1870s. But its garlands, pediments, and urns were unusual and pointed the way to the Colonial Revival.

Mention also should be made of Charles McKim, who by the 1870s was known among Boston architects even though he was not from Boston.[21] After spending his childhood in the Philadelphia area and New Jersey, he enrolled in the Lawrence Scientific School at Harvard. Once he began his course work, however, he decided he wanted to study architecture, so he left Harvard. He served a brief apprenticeship and then proceeded to Paris in 1867 to enroll at the École. There he and Peabody struck up a friendship.[22] When he returned to the United States, McKim began working for Richardson in New York City. In the years that followed, this experience would connect him with the architects who worked for Richardson in Boston, as an informal network of alumni would develop.

By the mid-1870s, McKim had become fascinated by the colonial architecture of New England. In 1874 he published a photograph of the Bishop George Berkeley House (1729–31) located in Middletown, Rhode Island, in the *New-York Sketch-Book of Architecture*, which Richardson and he edited. The image was the first photograph of colonial architecture to appear in an American architecture periodical.[23] Three years later, McKim traveled around Boston's North Shore, sketching and making measured drawings of old houses.[24] At the end of the decade, he entered into the partnership of McKim, Mead, and White. Although the firm was based in New York City, McKim would play a major role in popularizing Colonial Revival architecture in New England.

1880s Boston during the Heyday of Richardson

Richardson's buildings commanded attention in Boston and around the nation for the way they demonstrated how the Romanesque architecture of the Middle Ages could be adapted to modern building types. Across the continent, government buildings, commercial buildings, and campus buildings were erected in what turned out to be a wildly popular style.[25] Yet by the beginning of the 1890s, the interest in Romanesque architecture waned—a decline that occurred most swiftly in Boston. In later years, the next generation of architects acknowledged Richardson's influence, but they considered his legacy to be his outlook, not the style that he introduced. Other architects and the organizational activities they were pursuing during the 1880s also would prove influential.

Richardson nurtured three young architects who would take on leading positions in Boston's Society of Arts and Crafts: Warren, Longfellow, and Andrews. Richardson also employed Herbert Jaques, who would become a member of the society. While assisting Richardson, the staff gained experience in working with the artists and craftsmen who embellished and furnished the firm's buildings. Richardson also served as a conduit in bringing Morris's ideas and products into Boston.[26] Although Norton provided the more important connection to the English leader, having established a friendship with him while abroad, Richardson's interest in Morris was influential, too. In 1882 Richardson, accompanied by Jaques, met Morris in England, and the men corresponded. Richardson decorated his office with

Morris textiles and promoted the use of Morris fabrics and wallpapers in many of his projects.[27]

In other respects, Richardson contributed to an Arts and Crafts way of thinking. Richardson encouraged his staff to spend time in his library, where he had accumulated an extensive collection of books and postcards.[28] From these materials, his assistants expanded their knowledge of architectural history. Historical sources were not studied for strict models, however; like Ware, Richardson urged the young designers to think about applying the lessons of the past to address modern building problems.[29] The men in his office embraced this concept and would repeat it time and again. Richardson also promoted an interest in developing an architecture that was distinctly American.[30] Romanesque architecture was a starting point for him, and he transformed it. His Romanesque architecture was bold and lithic, expressing his vision of a powerful and dynamic nation. The younger architects ultimately rejected their master's aesthetic, but they would pursue the quest to identify a suitable direction for American architecture.

Richardson's interest in Morris and his firm was shared by other architects and individuals during the 1880s. In 1882 Catharine Lorillard Wolfe selected Peabody and Stearns to build her enormous Newport seaside cottage, Vinland, on a site next to the Breakers.[31] Under the direction of Boston decorator Richard Codman, uncle of Ogden Codman, Morris and his fellow artists were commissioned to create some of the finest interiors to be found in the United States. Stained-glass windows were designed by Burne-Jones for the staircase hall, and Crane designed windows for the library and a frieze for the dining room.[32] Vinland's decoration was widely publicized and presented compelling possibilities for the Arts and Crafts movement in New England.

During the 1880s, Boston's architects engaged in new academic enterprises, enabled by growing organizations. Between 1881 and 1883, the Boston Society of Architects sponsored investigations at Assos, an acropolis located on the Aegean coast of Turkey, the first expedition in the ancient classical world run by the newly formed Archaeological Institute of America. Championed by Norton, the project was directed by Joseph T. Clarke and Francis Bacon, assisted by several young men including Walker.[33] All were trained as architects, and they surveyed, measured, and drew the site, which included a sixth-century BC Greek temple, an agora, and a theater.[34] Walker's encounter with ancient Greek ruins provided him with a keen appreciation of the relationship between a building and its ornament. Years later, as critic of the jury for the Society of Arts and Crafts, Walker would encourage designs that connected the forms of craft objects with their decoration. One more educational project was embraced by the Boston Society of Architects during the 1880s: the Rotch Traveling Scholarship, the nation's first such travel grant.[35] After receiving private funds in 1883, the group selected its first winner in 1884.

In the meantime, the Museum School was becoming established as a professional training ground for serious artists. In 1885 a course on decoration was introduced, with classes taught twice weekly by Walker and lectures given on a third day by Longfellow on decoration as applied to architecture.[36] Among the students was Lois Howe, who would take on a leadership role in the Society of Arts and Crafts. She later recalled that Walker would share his sketchbooks and photo albums "of strange foreign places" with his students.[37] Such images were still rare at this time, and they impressed her. Walker's new course also intrigued his colleagues, and in the fall of 1885, he presented a paper to the Boston Society of Architects on decorative design at the Museum of Fine Arts.[38] The ties between the museum, the schools, the artists, and the architects had grown close.

By the end of the decade, Boston's architectural community had identified the need for an organization that was open to everyone interested in learning about architecture. The Boston Society of Architects was selective, admitting its members through a process of nomination and election. In 1889 a group of architects founded the Boston Architectural Club.[39] Its first president was Clarence H. Blackall, a former draftsman with Peabody and Stearns and the first recipient of the Rotch Traveling Scholarship.[40] Soon the club was offering classes as well as lectures, and by the mid-1890s, it was the largest organization of its kind in the country. The twelve men who were incorporators included established architects such as Edward Clarke Cabot and Peabody, and young men who were just getting started such as Andrews, Sturgis, and Walker.[41]

Even during the years when Richardsonian Romanesque buildings were most sought after, new directions were being explored for the revival of colonial architecture. Between 1882 and 1883, McKim designed a house in Newport for Henry A. C. Taylor that was closely modeled after eighteenth-century examples (fig. 4.3).[42] Completed in 1886, it was much larger than its colonial sources, but it was like them in its symmetry, its fine classical ornament, and its center-hall plan. Similarly, McKim captured the essence of Boston's Beacon Hill town houses in his design of the John F.

FIG. 4.3 McKim, Mead, and White, Taylor house, Newport, RI, 1882–86.

Andrew house (1883–86), which was erected on a corner of Commonwealth Avenue in the Back Bay (fig. 4.4).[43] The walls of the house swell expansively on either side of the main entrance, reminiscent of the city's early nineteenth-century bowfronts.[44] The severity of the facade also recalls early Boston buildings. Yet McKim drew upon other sources, too. In the design of the Andrew house, he incorporated allusions to Italian Renaissance architecture, such as the heavy Florentine cornice, the balconies supported by consoles, and the buff-colored Roman brick walls.

Throughout the 1880s, interest in the Colonial Revival solidified. In 1886, Peabody and Stearns designed a town house at 246 Beacon Street, also in the Back Bay, that illustrates how Peabody was continuing his own study of local architectural traditions (fig. 4.5).[45] The house is remarkable not for its grandeur but for its simplicity. Constructed of stone and brick, it is enlivened by a bowfront to the left of the main entry and tall windows on the *piano nobile*. Minimally ornamented, Peabody's design does not incorporate Renaissance references as in the Andrew house. The Colonial Revival was not a coherent style then or in the decades to follow.

Another new direction during the 1880s was the appearance of a restrained Renaissance revival, introduced in the facades of two Back Bay houses designed by the firm of Shaw and Hunnewell. The Elizabeth Skin-

ner house (1886) and the Charles Head house (1887) are equally austere (fig. 4.6).[46] The fronts of both are white limestone, a choice of building material that anticipated the lighter palette of the 1890s. The ornament on the Skinner house, probably supplied by John Evans, is restricted to panels with swags between the windows and lion heads in the frieze, while the facade for the Charles Head house is treated in a similar fashion. This controlled classicism would be favored by architects in the Society of Arts and Crafts at the turn of the century. George Shaw, whose firm designed these two houses, would be a charter member. The key point is that even during the heyday of Richardson and his Romanesque, entirely different stylistic directions were being explored in Boston.

Along with the Colonial and Renaissance revivals, an English-inflected Gothic Revival arose in New England in the mid- to late 1880s. Looking back at this development, Cram attributed it specifically to Henry Vaughan. Cram called Vaughan "the apostle of the new dispensation"—the new dispensation being the revival of Perpendicular-style churches that was ad-

FIG. 4.5 Peabody and Stearns, 246 Beacon Street, Boston, 1886.

FIG. 4.6 Shaw and
Hunnewell, Skinner
house, Boston, 1886.

vanced in England by George F. Bodley, Vaughan's one-time employer.[47]
This alternative approach was warmly received by Cram, who belonged to
the first wave of architects to reject the Richardsonian Romanesque and
embrace the new ideal. Cram found Richardson's style alien, "with no historic or ethnic propriety."[48] Yet Cram always respected Richardson. Writing
in 1901, Cram praised Richardson for his enormous vitality as well as "his
splendid sincerity and honesty."[49] Even as Cram and his Boston colleagues
sought to distance themselves from the master's signature style, they honored Richardson in the moral language of Ruskin and Norton.

When Vaughan arrived in Boston in 1881, Richardson hired him. Soon,

FIG. 4.7 Henry
Vaughan, St. Paul's
School chapel,
Concord, NH,
1886–94.

however, Vaughan established his own practice, designing a Bodley-type chapel for St. Paul's School (1886–94) in Concord, New Hampshire (fig. 4.7).[50] Its most stunning component was its square tower, recalling the towers of Somerset, England, especially the one at St. Cuthbert's in Wells. Cram identified the St. Paul's chapel as the real beginning of the Gothic Revival in America.[51] In fact, also in 1886, McKim, Mead, and White designed an English Gothic church inspired by the same sources as those that influenced Vaughan. Yet St. Peter's Church in Morristown, New Jersey, was far more modest, without the pinnacles and other ornament that distinguished Vaughan's work.[52] Three years later, Peabody and Stearns designed another early example of the fifteenth-century English parish church, St. Stephen's, in Pittsfield, Massachusetts (fig. 4.8).[53] It, too, was far plainer than Vaughan's chapel. Nevertheless, Peabody's church is important as an indication of the fading attraction to Richardson's Romanesque and the rising interest in the new church type. Boston architects would adhere to the type for roughly forty years, designing Perpendicular churches and chapels for towns and campuses throughout New England and across the United States.

FIG. 4.8 Peabody and
Stearns, St. Stephen's
Episcopal Church,
Pittsfield, MA,
1889–92.

The 1890s and a Solidifying Arts and Crafts Ethos

In addition to the links formed by Norton and Richardson with Morris,
two more members of the Boston community met with Morris—encounters that would have contributed to the solidifying Arts and Crafts ethos.
The trip that George Barton made to England in 1895 affected him deeply.[54]
Although the purpose of his journey was to study architecture, Barton
spent time with Morris and was aroused by Morris's social concerns.[55]
When Barton became the first secretary of the Society of Arts and Crafts,
he hoped to address these issues. Another young architect welcomed by
Morris was Bertram Goodhue, who would become an early member of
the Society of Arts and Crafts. In May of 1896, Goodhue visited Morris at
Kelmscott House.[56] Most likely Goodhue wanted to learn more about the

Kelmscott Press, given his attention during this period to typefaces and the graphic arts.

Through the 1890s, the architects who would be instrumental in forming the Society of Arts and Crafts were investing much of their time to initiatives that would prove relevant. Three stand out: the launching of *Architectural Review*, the establishment of the architecture program at Harvard, and a preservation campaign under the aegis of the Boston Society of Architects. Common themes connected them all.

In 1891 *Architectural Review* was founded in Boston by young men associated with MIT.[57] The new publication differed from the *American Architect and Building News*, which, as its name suggests, was news oriented. By contrast, *Architectural Review* presented one or two long articles as well as reports and commentary on other architecture periodicals, both American and European. It also included illustrations of current architectural work.[58] Walker and Cram were the first editors, and then in 1894, Andrews took charge, assisted by Walker.[59] From the beginning, Walker, Cram, and Andrews were regular contributors. Warren was another participant, and within a few years, Sturgis was writing articles, too. Throughout this period, the architects also supported the *American Architect*. In 1894 the Boston Society of Architects appointed Walker, Sturgis, and Longfellow to serve as its advisors to the magazine, and by the end of the decade Warren was named an advisor.[60] Yet *Architectural Review* was directly controlled by these young architects through their editorial roles, and its pages consistently record their voices.

At the outset, Walker and Cram favored articles that encouraged an interest in the English Gothic Revival. The first issue of *Architectural Review*, published in November of 1891, featured a lead essay titled "Notes on Wenlock Priory," written by Warren.[61] It included a history of the medieval compound in Shropshire as well as illustrations of measured drawings and capital and molding profiles. The next month, the author of the lead article was Cram, who wrote about the life and work of the English Gothic Revivalist John D. Sedding.[62] While ostensibly a tribute to Sedding, who had recently died, the article also promoted Arts and Crafts thinking. Cram recounted the state of affairs, architectural and otherwise, in England at the end of the eighteenth century when the nation "had sunk to its lowest ebb" in its religious, industrial, and artistic conditions. By the beginning of the nineteenth century, Cram wrote, "The moral sense of England was revolting against the degradation in life which was due to the introduction of 'labor-saving machines,' and the acceptance of the theories of competition and laissez-faire." After summarizing the architectural highs and lows that followed, Cram expressed his admiration for Sedding. He praised the English architect for embracing Perpendicular Gothic and for laboring "to reunite the artist and the workman, the designer and the craftsman."[63] In early 1893, Warren reiterated this Arts and Crafts tenet in another *Architectural Review* article, stating that perfect art would be achieved when the architect comes into "close and intimate contact with the artisan."[64] As in England, the Boston architects linked the Gothic Revival to their goal of advancing the architect-artisan relationship. At the same time, they encouraged this relationship for classical buildings. In writing "Notes on the Sculpture and Architecture at the Columbian Exposition," Walker discussed how architects and sculptors could collaborate to ennoble designs in the classical tradition.[65]

A running concern in the pages of *Architectural Review* was how the architect should incorporate a knowledge of historical precedent into designing buildings. In his essay about Sedding, Cram praised the English architect for starting with English Perpendicular and guiding it onward, producing "a new theory of modern architecture."[66] Warren, in his article "The Use and Abuse of Precedent," wrote at length about the topic, urging architects to learn from the spirit, "not the letter," of times that generated great work.[67] But Warren did not take a hard line on this point, and conceded that rather than produce a design of poor quality, an architect might do better to copy something good. This suggestion apparently shocked Andrews. In the next month's issue of *Architectural Review*, Andrews responded with vehemence, invoking the sacred memory of Richardson. "Every student under him will remember his way of saying, 'Go in and spend an hour with the books, and have a good time. You may find something in that 'Picardy' that will help you,'" Andrews wrote. Yet, he explained, there was "literally no copying, although there was the most constant use of the library."[68] Andrews argued that studying precedent should provide inspiration, but not particular forms. New designs, he believed, should develop logically from modern conditions. This perspective was one that Warren, in fact, also favored. In the years ahead, Andrews, Warren, and their colleagues all would produce buildings that were heavily indebted to the past while striving to address their own age.

At the end of his essay on precedent, Andrews took a surprising turn. Departing from the question of how precedent should be used in designing buildings, he concluded, "The broadest use of precedent is self-culture." With these words, he invoked another revered memory—that of Emerson. Before arriving at this conclusion, Andrews acknowledged that he expected the architect would study precedents from Greece and Rome, but he went on to urge the designer to keep a special place in his heart for the "homely and unpretentious virtues of the land of our birth."[69] It was Andrews's hope that the region's architecture would reflect the "straightforward, unpretentious, scrupulous New-Englander."[70] From this point, Andrews made the transition to express his belief that by holding fast to Yankee character, architects could improve their own lives along with the lives of others.

In November of 1893, *Architectural Review* published Andrews's address to the Boston Architectural Club, a speech he had recently delivered as the organization's president.[71] Over the course of the year, Andrews must have been cogitating on Emerson's views and what they might mean to the modern architect. In his lecture, Andrews referred explicitly to Emerson and quoted him: "I embrace the common; I sit at the feet of the familiar and the low."[72] To Andrews, this outlook meant that architects should not try "to set our art on a high pedestal and fence it round with fine-spun sophistries to bar the public out." Although Andrews did not elaborate, he was criticizing an effete approach to architecture, most obviously the ornate architecture of Beaux-Arts classicism. He called on his fellow architects to "lift ourselves up, to make character, and not art, our ambition; and then its influence will flow into our art."[73] How such self-culture would be made manifest in bricks and mortar, Andrews did not say. But he was presenting a case for designs based on New England traditions, which his audience would have understood to be Colonial Revival and English-accented styles.[74]

Almost certainly, Norton inspired Andrews in his thinking. Yet whatever Norton's influence, by 1893 Andrews saw how an Emersonian outlook could provide a moral foundation for architecture—an outlook that Bostonians would soon fold into the Arts and Crafts views of Ruskin and Morris. By urging his fellow architects to design buildings that would be appreciated by the public, Andrews endorsed an attitude similar to that expressed by Brandeis a decade later when he lectured on "The Opportunity in the Law," encouraging lawyers to work on behalf of "the people."[75] Both leaders in their professional communities, Andrews and Brandeis shared a respect for the common man that resonated among progressive Bostonians.

Over the course of the 1890s, articles in *Architectural Review* covered Arts and Crafts themes and individuals associated with the movement.

Cram wrote articles including "The Interior Decoration of Churches" and "Good and Bad Modern Gothic."[76] Sturgis published an essay titled "The Garden as an Adjunct to Architecture" and reviewed *The Bases of Design* by Walter Crane.[77] And in 1898, the editors published Norton's "The Craftsman as Artist," drawn from his address at the first annual meeting of the Society of Arts and Crafts, in which he singled out simplicity and sincerity as fundamental to good art.[78]

A second major initiative of the 1890s was the creation of the architecture program at Harvard. In 1893 President Charles W. Eliot contacted Warren about establishing an undergraduate course of study.[79] Along with a recommendation from Norton, Eliot had received endorsements for Warren from Ware, Peabody, and Andrews.[80] Norton by this time was a senior member of the Harvard faculty, and his endorsement would have been especially influential. Like Ruskin, Norton believed the study of architecture should be allied with the fine arts rather than engineering, and that it should expose the student to a wide range of humanistic subjects.[81] During the 1892–93 academic year, Warren had lectured on Renaissance art at the Museum School, so his ability as a lecturer in addition to his talents as an architect made him an attractive candidate for the new position.[82]

Warren accepted the offer with excitement and started teaching in the fall of 1893. Significantly, the first course he presented was not in design but rather in the history of Greek and Roman architecture. Once the program took shape, Warren taught a regular cycle of yearlong courses on ancient, medieval, and Renaissance architecture. He believed that if he presented the "laws of design" from the major periods in European history, the students would be able to apply these laws "to new conditions" and "new forms or new modifications."[83] Warren encouraged the young men to see that "beautiful architectural forms are organic expressions of structural functions," a concept that Ruskin and Pugin had promoted.[84] Yet Warren was by no means committed exclusively to the Gothic Revival, and he, like Norton, found merit in the classical tradition. What they both detested was extravagant ornamentation, specifically the florid ornament associated with the French school. Indeed, by the turn of the twentieth century, the program at Harvard was recognized as an American school that distanced itself from the Beaux-Arts model.[85] On the other hand, Warren was well versed in École planning methods, which he had learned from Richardson, and he adopted this approach for the Harvard program.

In many aspects, the architecture courses at Harvard related to the Arts and Crafts movement as it developed in Boston. In Warren's final lecture on the ancient world, students learned how the "lavish ornament" of the Romans marked a departure from "Greek simplicity and refinement."[86] In a lecture on the Middle Ages, Warren praised the "absolute simplicity" that had produced the beauty of the French cathedral at Laon.[87] The call for simplicity was an ongoing theme. Warren regularly dedicated lecture time to medieval craftsmanship, such as stone sculpture, stained glass, and wrought iron, and he referred his students to the windows by Morris and Burne-Jones installed in 1882 in Boston's Trinity Church.[88] In classes on Gothic architecture in England, he emphasized Perpendicular churches and their "beautiful towers."[89]

A regard for "the people" was another recurring theme. When discussing the fifteenth-century English parish church, for example, Warren explained that it was governed primarily by "the people." In a heartfelt moment, Warren enthused, "The English parish church is the most beautiful building that Christianity ever produced."[90] When he turned to the Italian Renaissance, Warren again favored restrained designs, specifically from the fifteenth century, rather than the architecture of later periods.[91] As with the course on the Middle Ages, Warren warmed when he shifted his focus to England, describing the appeal of the English country house and the charm of Christopher Wren. Occasionally Warren touched on colonial American architecture, and he sometimes provided examples as the basis for design problems—an unusual approach at this time.[92] In 1899 Harvard's architecture students encountered another proponent of Boston's Arts and Crafts movement when Warren hired Denman Ross to teach the theory of design.[93] Ross's attention to abstract principles related directly to his and Walker's interests at the Museum of Fine Arts and the Museum School as well as the Society of Arts and Crafts.

Meanwhile, for the better part of the decade, Norton held forth at Harvard until he presented his last fine arts course in the spring of 1898. Through his teaching, Norton's grand objective was to ignite the student's imagination while disciplining the mind and character. In introductory notes on a syllabus, Norton wrote, "The true intellectual life and the moral life go hand in hand."[94] By studying the fine arts, he explained, we learn what we owe to the human race. These thoughts captured Norton's essential views—the motivation behind his teaching and writing—and they would be embraced and restated by the leaders of Boston's Arts and Crafts movement.

A third initiative that engaged Boston's architects during the 1890s was

FIG. 4.9 Charles
Bulfinch,
Massachusetts
State House,
Boston, 1795–98.

the battle to preserve the Massachusetts State House (1795–98), designed by Bulfinch (fig. 4.9). Whereas earlier preservation battles in the city and around the country had been undertaken to save buildings for their historical and political significance, this effort was different in that the State House was valued for its architecture and its architect. Also, the crusade to save the State House appears to mark the first time a group of architects formally led a preservation effort in the United States.[95] The future of the building did not seem to be an issue during the 1880s. It was clear that Massachusetts government needed more room, and the legislature approved an expansion to the Bulfinch building. By the early 1890s, an annex designed by Charles Brigham was nearing completion, but the decaying wood in the Bulfinch building, especially in the dome, raised questions about the wisdom of preservation. Arguments were made that the state would be better served if the old building were demolished and replaced with a structure of better-quality materials and fireproof construction. Another problem to emerge was that the Bulfinch building now seemed out of scale with Brigham's sizable annex that loomed behind it. In 1893 a state legislative committee voted to demolish the original building and erect a new structure based on Bulfinch's design but with larger proportions to harmonize with the addition.

PLATE I Cram and Ferguson, All Saints' Episcopal Church, Peterborough, NH, 1916–23.

PLATE I-A "Madonna and Child," stained glass by Charles Connick.

PLATE I-B Wood carving by Johannes Kirchmayer.

PLATE I-C Ironwork by Samuel Yellin.

PLATE 2 Warren, Smith, and Biscoe, New Church Theological School chapel, Cambridge, MA, 1899–1901, glass by Donald MacDonald.

PLATE 2-A Carved angel on reredos by Hugh Cairns.

PLATE 2-B Tile supplied by Henry Chapman Mercer.

PLATE 3 Cram, Goodhue, and Ferguson, Emmanuel Church, Newport, RI, 1900–1902.

PLATE 3-A Window over altar by Harry Goodhue.

PLATE 4-A R. Clipston Sturgis, Schwab house, New Haven, CT, 1895–96.

PLATE 4-B Newhall and Blevins, Burton Halls, Cambridge, MA, 1909.

PLATE 5 R. Clipston Sturgis, Perkins Institution for the Blind (Perkins School for the Blind), Watertown, MA, 1909–12, Howe Building.

PLATE 5-A Interior of Howe Building.

PLATE 5-B Concrete pier
with Grueby tile.

PLATE 6-A Andrews, Jaques, and Rantoul, Williams house (Connecticut Governor's Residence), Hartford, CT, 1909.

PLATE 6-B Lois L. Howe, Cornish house, Cambridge, MA, 1916.

PLATE 7   C. Howard Walker, Pine Cone, Tamworth, NH, 1891.

PLATE 7-B   Fireplace andiron.

PLATE 7-A Living room with trestle table.

PLATE 8 Charles D. Maginnis, Maginnis house, Brookline, MA, 1920.

PLATE 8-A Column between living room and library.

PLATE 8-B Living room window.

PLATE 8-C Interior
door hardware.

Early in 1894, the executive committee of the Boston Society of Architects rallied against the scheme. First they met with the legislative committee, and then they presented the situation to their members, who voted to take "the most energetic action" to preserve the exterior and restore the interior of the historic building.[96] Their support was surely colored by the memory of the John Hancock house, built by Hancock's uncle in the early eighteenth century, which had stood at the base of the State House until it was demolished after a struggle in 1863. Three decades later, in 1893, as the debate over the State House was under way, Massachusetts erected its state building at the World's Columbian Exposition in Chicago. Designed by Peabody, the state building was modeled after the Hancock house, rekindling interest in what was now widely recognized as a regrettable loss.[97] The architects spoke out to save the Bulfinch building, emphasizing its importance as the work of a distinguished American architect. They also presented the building as a landmark in American architectural history, pointing out that it had served as a model for state houses elsewhere in the country.

Early in 1896, the situation came to a head. At an April meeting of the Boston Society of Architects, Andrews called for and received support to print notices in the Boston papers, advocating for preservation of the State House.[98] Again the legislative committee voted for demolition and reconstruction, but in the end, it was the vote of the entire legislature that mattered, and its members voted for preservation. Andrews, Charles A. Cummings, and Arthur G. Everett were charged with the restoration, and the work was finished in time for a celebration of the building's centennial in January of 1898.[99] That month, when the Boston Society of Architects met, the members decided to fund a bronze tablet to be installed at the State House "to the memory of Charles Bulfinch, the architect of the building," specifying that it would include a bas-relief portrait.[100] Bulfinch's image would represent the importance of the architectural profession.

The architects' crusade to preserve the Massachusetts State House relates directly to the values promoted by England's leading Arts and Crafts theorists. By honoring a noble building from the past, the architects paid homage to Ruskin's Lamp of Memory. The Boston architects also appreciated the real and ongoing work involved in preserving England's monuments, led by Morris with the founding of the Society for the Protection of Ancient Buildings in 1877. Indeed, at an 1897 meeting of the Boston Society of Architects, Warren gave a report from their Committee on the Preservation of Peterborough Cathedral, an English monument.[101] Support for historic preservation would distinguish Boston's Arts and Crafts movement and the work of its architects from many of America's other Arts and Crafts proponents.

At the same time, preservation in Boston was unlike that in England, with Boston's focus on buildings from the colonial and federal periods rather than the Middle Ages, and as a result, the architects' enthusiasm for the Colonial Revival was reinforced. Current with English trends and generally eager to embrace them, the Boston architects also responded to the Neo-Georgians and their admiration of Wren. It was a logical step for the Bostonians to add Bulfinch to the pantheon of revered forefathers. In the 1890s, Boston architects were responding to a new direction in English taste—an aesthetic preference for lighter, finer forms. This preference became apparent in the applied arts as well as in architecture when the Society of Arts and Crafts was organized.

CHAPTER FIVE

Looking Backward: From Romanesque to Gothic Revival

As THE NINETEENTH CENTURY drew to a close, the new direction in architecture, based on the tenets of England's Arts and Crafts movement, gathered steam in Boston. Buildings began appearing in New England's cities and towns that demonstrated the architects' commitment to craftsmanship in their projects' ornament and in their quality of construction—English Arts and Crafts concepts transferred to the northeast corner of the United States. While exploring these ideas, the architects who assumed leading roles in the Society of Arts and Crafts gave a great deal of thought to their New England heritage. Restraint was admired. The architects reflected on the writings and persona of Emerson, the unpretentious Yankee; they also pondered Norton's call for simplicity and sincerity. On the whole, the buildings that the architects in this Boston-based circle designed were conservative stylistically. Indeed, for the most part, they may be described as backward looking. Many of their projects honored the English forebears of the Yankee population through Gothic Revival designs—designs that also responded to the academic orientation that characterized the culture of the region, including a love of history.

The Decline of Richardsonian Romanesque

After Henry Hobson Richardson died in 1886, his work continued to be published in the architectural press. At the same time, through the remaining years of the decade, Richardsonian Romanesque buildings were erected throughout the United States, although they often only vaguely captured Richardson's approach.[1] As one might expect, however, the projects designed by Andrews, Longfellow, and Warren during this transitional period closely reflected the architects' years of training under the master.

A superb example is Cambridge City Hall (1888–91) in Massachusetts, by Longfellow, Alden, and Harlow, constructed of light-pink quarry-faced

Milford granite and blocks of chocolate-brown Longmeadow sandstone
that accent the round window arches (fig. 5.1).[2] Dominating the building
is a tall square tower crowned by an attenuated pyramid, similar to Richardson's design for Albany City Hall (1880–83) in New York. As at Albany
City Hall and Richardson's Allegheny County Courthouse (1883–88) in
Pittsburgh, the Cambridge tower projects slightly from the main facade so
that it seems to erupt from the ground and push skyward. Yet the thrust
is held in check. A degree of control is achieved in the designs of both the

courthouse and Cambridge City Hall through their symmetry, the massing balanced around the central towers. In other ways, Cambridge City Hall seems to be heading in a new, calmer direction with its greater breadth, its horizontally laid courses of stone, and the suggestion of a frieze in the third story. Also notable is the balcony positioned over the building's main entrance, a Renaissance-inspired motif. Entering the front vestibule, the visitor encounters fluted pilasters, another classical element. Even at this time, Longfellow and his partners were moving away from the picturesque, irregular aspects of Richardson's work. On the other hand, Richardson's Arts and Crafts tendencies are carried forward in the carved capitals at the building's entrance, the ironwork decorating the doors, and the leaded glass over the paneled dado in the vestibule.

By the early 1890s, the new version of the Gothic Revival was attracting attention, but Romanesque designs continued to be built. One may reasonably wonder whether the clients, rather than the architects, were responsible for the persistent interest in the Romanesque styles. For example, we know that in 1891, when the Congregational Mount Vernon Church sought proposals for a new building in Boston's Back Bay, an entry by O. F. Smith was Richardsonian Romanesque in character, with heavy round arches, light masonry, and brownstone trim.[3] Walker also submitted a Romanesque design, suggesting that the architects were responding to a stated or inferred preference. The attachment on the part of this particular client may have been a holdover from the mid-nineteenth century, when Congregational leaders had endorsed erecting churches in the round-arched style.[4] But Walker's Romanesque differed from that of Richardson; his design was closer to the Norman churches of England (fig. 5.2).

Built between 1891 and 1892, the Mount Vernon Church was constructed with blocks of stone that were smaller than Richardson's and with walls that were more planar, while the round arches were constructed of smooth-faced voussoirs edged with fine geometric carving. A corner tower rises above Beacon Street and Massachusetts Avenue, detached from the main body of the church, a reprise of Richardson's Brattle Square Church (1870–72), a few blocks away. Yet Walker's tower has a more English character, with its pinnacles rising from the upper stage. The palette of the church also is different from that favored by Richardson. The church walls are constructed of Roxbury pudding stone, a conglomerate of browns and beige, and the trimmings are of light sand-colored freestone.[5] At the end of the decade, Hugh Cairns, an architectural sculptor and stone carver, advertised

that he had worked on the Mount Vernon Church.[6] Cairns would become
a founder of the Society of Arts and Crafts.

By the time Walker was hired to design a library in the town of
Hopedale, Massachusetts, in 1898, he and his fellow Boston architects generally preferred Gothic to Romanesque. Once again, the client probably
was responsible for the decision to erect a Romanesque building. In this
case, Walker was commissioned by a leading Hopedale citizen, Joseph Bancroft, who built the library at his own expense and then transferred it to
the town in 1899 (fig. 5.3).[7] Just a block away on the same street stands a
Richardsonian Romanesque town hall, dating from 1886 to 1887.[8] Bancroft
may have asked Walker to design a Romanesque library to harmonize with
the municipal building. Both structures were built with the light-pink gran-

FIG. 5.3 Walker
and Kimball,
Bancroft Memorial
Library, Hopedale,
MA, 1898.

FIG. 5.4 Bancroft
Memorial Library,
arches.

ite that had been quarried in the neighboring town of Milford, reinforcing
the visual connection between them. But the town hall alone was trimmed
with brown Longmeadow sandstone, which Walker would have considered
terribly passé.

In terms of style, the Bancroft Memorial Library alludes to English
Norman sources. Under a broad gable that establishes the entrance, wall

buttresses flank three large round arches defined by a few spare moldings (fig. 5.4). In *Theory of Mouldings* from 1926, Walker would write, "There is not more common fault in designing mouldings than that of making them excessive in quantity and scale." Restraint, he admonished, is a virtue.[9] Capping the piers that support the three arches are simple leaves, while to one side, columns with related foliate capitals divide a grouping of windows. The carving is minimal, yet it contributes to the craftsmanship that enhances the entrance. Ironwork adds another note of interest. Strap hinges decorate the double doors, an iron grille fills the light over the transom, and iron lanterns project from the piers that frame the doors. The windows are clear leaded glass. Passing through the entrance, the first-time visitor is surprised by a stunning hammer-beam roof. Pendants drop from the hammer beams, while the upper braces meet to produce a rhythm of round arches overhead. The way in which Walker let the structural components give expression to his interior was consistent with the emphasis on structure promoted by his fellow architects in the Society of Arts and Crafts, and followed the precepts of Ruskin and Pugin.

When Ralph Adams Cram published *Church Building* in 1901, he argued, "There is one style, and only one, that we have a right to: and that is Gothic as it was when all art was destroyed at the time of the Reformation."[10] To his mind, earlier English Gothic periods had already been perfected, and he didn't believe "Norman or Romanesque" held any promise for the modern age. Yet Cram eventually had a change of heart and designed several Romanesque-inspired chapels. All Saints' Episcopal Church in Peterborough, New Hampshire (1916–23), is an outstanding example (pl. 1).[11] Designed as if it were transitional in style, All Saints' has Gothic components: pointed arches, a rose window over the entrance, and an apsidal east end. But the church has the weight and sheer walls of the Romanesque, and its massing is modeled after St. Mary the Virgin, Iffley, Oxfordshire, a Norman church from about 1170. Like Iffley, the main facade of Peterborough is located at the building's gable end, and both churches are dominated by a large square tower that is the width of the nave and positioned over the crossing.

A wealthy woman, Mary Lyon Cheney Schofield, was responsible for erecting All Saints' Church. Her first husband was Charles Paine Cheney, with whom she had three children before he died of tuberculosis in 1897. Charles's father was Benjamin Pierce Cheney, a New Hampshire native who founded an express firm that merged into the American Express Company and produced a substantial financial legacy.[12] In building the Peter-

borough church, Mary sought to memorialize Charles. By this time she had
married again, and her second husband, William Henry Schofield, appears
to have influenced her ideas for All Saints' design. A Harvard professor of
literature, he had recently published *English Literature: From the Norman
Conquest to Chaucer*; in the preface, he thanked Charles Eliot Norton for his
assistance.[13] One may imagine that Schofield's literary pursuits had encouraged Mary's interest in Norman architecture. Further, her husband's col-
legial relationship with Norton may have heightened her appreciation for

the Arts and Crafts movement. Then again, Cram would have encouraged his clients to incorporate the work of leading craftsmen in his buildings—typically members of the Society of Arts and Crafts with whom he had developed ongoing relationships (fig. 5.5). Such was the case at All Saints' Church, where stained glass was provided by Charles Connick, carved wood by Johannes Kirchmayer, and ironwork by Samuel Yellin.[14]

Gothic Revival Churches

As in England, the architects in Boston who became leaders in the Arts and Crafts movement were eager to design Gothic Revival churches. This preference reflected their admiration for the Gothic churches of the Middle Ages and the embellishments by skilled craftsmen. For the architects working in New England, their enthusiasm for Gothic churches happily coincided with the growing popularity of the Episcopalian faith. Many of the young people who descended from the region's old guard were leaving the Congregational and Unitarian congregations to become Episcopalians. As new churches were built at the turn of the twentieth century, the parishioners favored English Gothic designs, in no small part because of their association with the Church of England. But as time went on, members of most Christian denominations became comfortable erecting Gothic houses of worship that were English in character. By the early twentieth century, a time when the upper and middle classes were prospering, churches of this type arose throughout New England.

No one did more to advance the popularity of the Gothic-style church than Cram, who was a prolific designer and writer. His first ecclesiastic commission was All Saints, Ashmont, an Episcopal church located in Dorchester, a streetcar suburb of Boston. It was soon recognized as a paradigm of the Arts and Crafts movement in New England (fig. 5.6). Designed and erected from 1891 through 1894 by the firm of Cram, Wentworth, and Goodhue, the building was based on English parish churches from the fifteenth century. Dominating the west facade is a commanding square tower with buttressed corners and a parapet that is battlemented, and over the entry porch is a large lancet window. Beyond the tower are high nave walls covered by a low-pitched roof, and to the rear is a deep chancel. Seam-faced Quincy granite, cut from exposed rock in the quarry, gives the building variation in color, ranging from gray to ochre to rusty orange. This particular granite would be a favorite in New England through the first half of the

FIG. 5.6 Cram, Wentworth, and Goodhue, All Saints Episcopal Church, Ashmont, Dorchester, MA, 1891–94.

twentieth century. Inside All Saints, the timber roof is exposed in the manner that was typical of medieval English churches. To serve a congregation that emphasized ritual over preaching, the seating plan was developed to include long aisles for processionals and communion.

Shortly after the design for the church was accepted, it was published in an 1892 issue of the *American Architect and Building News*.[15] Through the decades that followed, All Saints continued to receive attention for the way in which Cram and Bertram Goodhue worked with craftsmen to enhance the interior. Stained-glass windows were a priority, leaded diamonds having been installed for the short term. During this period, the pictorial art glass of John La Farge and Louis Comfort Tiffany was in vogue, but Cram and Goodhue considered it inappropriate, and set out to revive a medieval approach.[16] In 1896 Harry Goodhue, Bertram's brother and a future mem-

FIG. 5.7 All Saints Episcopal Church, Ashmont, chancel completed by carvers Johannes Kirchmayer and John Evans with altarpiece painted by George Hallowell.

ber of the Society of Arts and Crafts, designed a clerestory window for All Saints that was more architectural than pictorial, with Mary and the Christ child posed frontally and enframed.[17] The architects viewed this new direction favorably. On the other hand, Harry failed to capture the quality of the glass that characterized the work of medieval masters. His window was made from the opalescent glass for which La Farge and Tiffany had become known—a milky glass that Cram and Goodhue concluded was ugly.

Ten years later, Cram engaged the Englishman Christopher Whall to provide a window for All Saints. It would be Whall's first project in the United States and represented a significant development in the history of American stained glass.[18] By 1906 Whall was widely respected for the medieval qualities of his work and had collaborated with England's leading Arts and Crafts architects, including John D. Sedding, Edward S. Prior, and W. R. Lethaby.[19] Whall's window for All Saints proved influential, inspiring the young glassmaker Charles Connick, who would design the greatest number of windows for the Dorchester church. A future president of the Society of Arts and Crafts, Connick became a national leader in his field.

The chancel of All Saints was decorated by some of Boston's leading artisans (fig. 5.7). In September of 1900, an article in *Architectural Review* described the many craftsmen who had contributed to its embellishment.[20] A reredos erected in 1898 was conceived by the architects and executed in Caen stone by John Evans and his shop.[21] A year earlier, Evans had helped found the Society of Arts and Crafts. The focus of the reredos was to be an altarpiece, which the architects hoped would be painted by Edward Burne-Jones—yet another example of their orientation toward England and the individuals associated with the Arts and Crafts movement there.[22] When Burne-Jones died in 1898, the architects redirected their gaze toward home, turning to George Hallowell, an artist member of the society. Carved oak paneling, designed by Bertram Goodhue, was executed by Irving and Casson, with sculpture carved by Kirchmayer, another society member.

In the same 1900 issue of *Architectural Review*, an unsigned editorial praised the way the Society of Arts and Crafts was bringing together designers and workers.[23] This concept was repeated in the years that followed. In 1911 Montgomery Schuyler published an essay in *Architectural Record* about the firm of Cram, Goodhue, and Ferguson, singling out the Dorchester church for its refinement of decoration and praising the mutual understanding of its designers and craftsmen.[24] Cram promoted the Arts and Crafts movement in the magazine *Christian Art*, which he edited, and continued to champion the idea of the architect and craftsmen as allies in his 1936 autobiography.[25]

The revival of the fifteenth-century English parish church had a long run in New England. Over the course of four decades, from the 1890s through the 1920s, Boston's Arts and Crafts architects explored its potential. Although they offered numerous reasons to justify why this church type was preferable, they clearly were following the lead from England. Doing so was logical enough given that they considered Americans to be English. As Cram wrote, "The English is ours; for we two are one people, with one history and one blood."[26] After Sedding and George F. Bodley heightened interest in the Perpendicular-inspired church type, it migrated to New England, mainly through Henry Vaughan and the example of his chapel for St. Paul's School in New Hampshire. Warren and Sturgis, informed by their training in England, also were early advocates for emulating the late Gothic parish church. In lectures, articles, and books, this group of architects described how it embodied important values. Just as Warren told his students how the parish church belonged to "the people," pointing out that they governed it, Cram, too, praised it as "the guardian of the privileges of the people."[27] According to Cram, the English parish church was the center of the community, even the center of "civilization" itself. Its simplicity was another virtue, a quality to be duplicated. Walker wrote that the churches were direct products of their localities, "built of the material at hand," and "with a direct simplicity of treatment."[28]

Several of the architects traveled to England to study the Gothic churches, and then presented their findings when they returned home. Warren's "Notes on Wenlock Priory," published in the first issues of *Architectural Review* in 1891, was an early instance of this scholarly study. In 1897 Sturgis delivered a paper, accompanied by photographs, to the Boston Society of Architects on English parish churches.[29] A few years later, he published articles on Somerset towers and English rood screens.[30] Cram published books including *English Country Churches* in 1898, followed by *Church Building* in 1901 and *The Ruined Abbeys of Great Britain* in 1905.[31] Walker made his own study trip and documented it with *Parish Churches of England*, which came out in 1915.[32]

The image of the fifteenth-century church proved compelling for congregations erecting new buildings in the small towns of New England and in the Boston suburbs. In 1893 Cram's firm was invited to submit a design for the Second Congregational Church in Exeter, New Hampshire. For a house of worship serving this faith, Cram believed a Georgian style reflecting the region's colonial architecture made the most sense. To his mind, a Protestant church in a Gothic style would be "incongruous."[33] Nevertheless, when the congregation decided to engage the firm, the members de-

FIG. 5.8 Cram, Goodhue, and Ferguson, Second Congregational Church (Phillips Church), Exeter, NH, 1897–99.

termined that they wanted a Gothic church, and Cram complied (fig. 5.8).[34] Built from 1897 to 1899, the church has an L-plan with a square tower in the inner angle. Its walls are constructed with seam-faced granite, while its trimmings are light Nova Scotia sandstone. Inside, a cypress ceiling is supported by trusses that spring from stone corbels carved as angels. Paneling carved with a pattern of Gothic arches was supplied by Irving and Casson.[35]

A more diminutive building was designed by Sturgis for St. Peter's Episcopal Church in Lyndonville, Vermont, north of St. Johnsbury (fig. 5.9). Its plans were produced in 1890, and the church was consecrated a year later.[36] Limited by a modest budget, Sturgis specified brick rather than stone. A single lancet window served as the facade's organizing feature, while the interior derived its appeal from the trusses and brick walls that were left exposed. To add an element of ornament, a painted border created a frieze.[37]

In an essay for an 1899 architectural exhibition catalogue, Warren observed that much of the ecclesiastical work in the region reflected a study of medieval English parish churches and the influence of modern England "such as is found, perhaps, to the same extent, nowhere else in the United States."[38] Apropos of this comment, Warren designed the New Church Theological School chapel in Cambridge, Massachusetts (1899–1901), for his fellow Swedenborgians (fig. 5.10). The Cambridge chapel was to be small, like the church designed by Sturgis in Lyndonville, but a more substantial budget meant that the chapel could be constructed in stone and more elab-

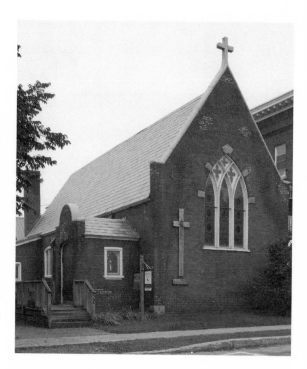

FIG. 5.9 R. Clipston Sturgis, St. Peter's Episcopal Church, Lyndonville, VT, 1898.

orately decorated (pl. 2).[39] All the artisans involved were associated with the Society of Arts and Crafts. Cairns, who had worked with Walker on the Mount Vernon Church, carved stone corbels with human heads for the entrance porch (fig. 5.11) and contributed angels for a reredos.[40] Irving and Casson supplied paneling and pews, and Henry Chapman Mercer supplied tile. The stained glass for the chancel was the result of a collaborative effort between Warren and Donald MacDonald and reflected their study of medieval grisaille glass—another early example of this historical approach pursued by the Boston designers.[41]

Stained glass was of particular interest to the architects at this time, and they were eager to find artisans who could capture the brilliance of medieval work. The window that Harry Goodhue produced for Emmanuel Church in Newport, Rhode Island, set a new standard.[42] Dating from 1900 to 1902, the church was designed by Cram, Goodhue, and Ferguson and was commissioned by the widow of John Nicholas Brown in his memory (pl. 3).[43] It was constructed of seam-faced granite with limestone trim. The exterior of the building is handsome but relatively plain, whereas the interior is sumptuous—a full-blown version of the parish church type. Stone columns supporting Gothic arches run the length of the nave, which is illuminated by clerestory windows. High walls carry beams that support a flat timber roof,

FIG. 5.10 Warren, Smith, and Biscoe, New Church Theological School chapel (Swedenborg Chapel), Cambridge, MA, 1899–1901.

FIG. 5.11 New Church Theological School chapel, corbel by Hugh Cairns.

resulting in a lofty space. Linenfold paneling was supplied by Irving and Casson, and the pavement features Mercer tile. The focus of the deep chancel is Goodhue's large stained-glass window. Unlike his earlier work for All Saints, Ashmont, both the design and the character of the glass itself were respectable revivals of the medieval windows that the architects admired.

After Warren and his partners were hired in 1904 by the Episcopal Church of the Epiphany in Winchester, near Boston, the firm guided its building and decoration over four decades (fig. 5.12).[44] For the memorial windows, the firm turned to Charles Eamer Kempe of London, whose work was indebted to his study of late medieval glass. Kempe had worked for Bodley—another example of the web connecting the Boston architects with English architects and artisans.[45] Yet the Boston architects also were committed to "mutually helpful relations" with the craftsmen who were their fellow members in the Society of Arts and Crafts. In 1908 Warren and his partner, Frank Patterson Smith, a member of the Winchester church, collaborated with Harry Goodhue in the creation of a memorial window. Illustrating this project in an ad for his workshop in an issue of *Christian Art*, Goodhue pitched his achievement: "No opalescent glass used in the making of Memorial Windows."[46]

Walker and Newhall also designed what might be considered typical examples of the turn-of-the-century New England church. In East Weymouth, south of Boston, Walker produced a Gothic Revival building for

FIG. 5.13 C. Howard Walker, Congregational Church, East Weymouth, MA, 1904–5.

Congregationalists that is extremely spare (fig. 5.13). Without stone sculpture or wood ornament, its exterior derives a degree of richness from the variegated coloration of its seam-faced granite walls. Dating from 1904 though 1905, the main feature of the building was a bell tower, buttressed at its corners and finished with battlements.[47] Stained wood trusses enhance the interior.

Newhall's firm, Newhall and Blevins, developed variations on this theme for the Third Congregational Church, Cambridge (1911; fig. 5.14), and Payson Park Congregational Church, in nearby Belmont (1915–19; fig. 5.15). Both churches were built with seam-faced granite and dominated by square towers. The Third Congregational Church was the more ambitious of the two projects, with a large lancet window in the tower above the doorway and elaborate hammer-beam trusses inside.[48] Faulkner Methodist Church in the Boston suburb of Malden, also by Newhall and Blevins, shares the massing and scale of the other churches, but it was built of neither granite nor brick (fig. 5.16). Dating from 1907, it was constructed with fieldstone walls, stucco, and half-timbering.[49] The budget was less than desirable. For Cram, building a church with these materials would not have been an option. In *Church Building* from 1901, he stated that rounded fieldstones "can never be used under any circumstance whatever." A wall must have "unity and coherency," he argued, and round stones "prevent these results."[50] If dressed stone was too expensive, brick could be employed. As for the con-

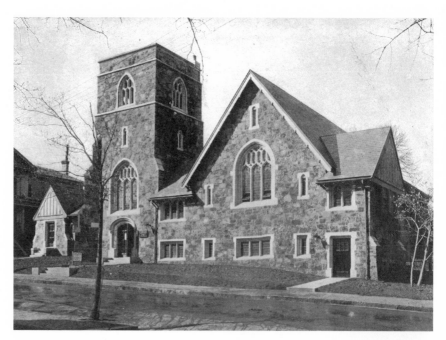

FIG. 5.14 Newhall and Blevins, Third Congregational Church, Cambridge, MA, 1911.

FIG. 5.15 Newhall and Blevins, Payson Park Congregational Church, Belmont, MA, 1915–19.

gregation that couldn't afford brick, Cram apparently would have advised its leaders to carry on with the fund-raising. The architects didn't agree on everything.

The enduring regard for the medieval parish church type is evident in

FIG. 5.16 Newhall
and Blevins,
Faulkner
Methodist Church
(Imani Temple),
Malden, MA, 1907.

the example of Christ the King Church in Rutland, Vermont, near Burling-ton, erected between 1928 and 1929 (fig. 5.17). Designed by Charles Magin-nis of Maginnis and Walsh, it was constructed of Vermont marble—"built of the material at hand," as Walker recommended. In an article published in *Architectural Forum* in 1917, Maginnis restated the point, writing that the village church "should be built, if possible, from materials of the local-ity."[51] Christ the King was planned so that its gable end fronts on the street and is entered through a porch. Buttresses alternate between small lancet windows along the nave walls, and a square bell tower is positioned on the church's north side. The exterior is minimally ornamented, yet the interior is finished with carved corbels, a deep chancel with a substantial reredos, and a large Gothic window in the eastern wall (fig. 5.18). In 1930, when Bos-ton celebrated the 300th anniversary of its founding with a major exhibition of fine arts and crafts, one of the Rutland church windows was displayed.[52] The stained glass was a collaborative effort between the architects and H. Wright Goodhue, Harry Goodhue's son.

Maginnis, like his architect colleagues, believed the village churches
built in England during the Middle Ages provided good models for American Roman Catholic churches such as Christ the King. In 1917 he wrote
that it would be hard to imagine "a rarer comity between architecture
and untrained nature than that exemplified in the little ivy-clad, Gothic
churches of some of the English counties." Although he accepted other historic sources for Catholic churches, he lauded the English churches for their
"repose and simplicity."[53] That Christ the King, like many of the parishes

FIG. 5.18 Christ the King Church, interior.

served by Maginnis and Walsh, was built by people of Irish descent didn't divert him. English churches, not Irish churches, were the topic of the time, and Cram was especially important to Maginnis's thinking. As members of the Society of Arts and Crafts, the architects worked closely together to promote the work of the craftsmen in churches and church furnishings, and in 1929, Maginnis wrote the introduction to a book on the work of Cram and Ferguson.[54] Typical of individuals who came from ethnic-minority backgrounds and succeeded in Boston at this time—Brandeis

FIG. 5.19 Ralph
Adams Cram, St.
George's School
chapel, Middletown,
RI, 1924–28.

FIG. 5.20 St. George's School
chapel, sculpture of St. George
by Joseph Coletti.

being another example—Maginnis was comfortable adopting the region's English heritage as his own.

In 1928, as work began in Vermont on Christ the King Church, the chapel at St. George's School in Middletown, Rhode Island, was consecrated with much fanfare (fig. 5.19). It cost more than $1 million and was commissioned by John Nicholas Brown Jr., whose mother had employed Cram, Goodhue, and Ferguson for the design of Emmanuel Church in Newport.[55] Brown had graduated from the Episcopal boarding school in 1918, and two years later, while a student at Harvard, he turned to Cram to build the chapel. In describing the experience, Cram recalled how Brown worked closely with him and his associates "in studying and determining the design in all its details."[56] At Harvard, Brown enrolled in a class on medieval sculpture taught by the renowned Arthur Kingsley Porter. In addition to inspiring his interest in medieval art, this class was where Brown met Joseph Coletti, the son of Italian immigrants.[57] Coletti had spent two years as an apprentice carver with John Evans when a series of fortunate events led to his studies at Harvard. Groundbreaking on the chapel took place in 1924, and two years later, Brown gave Coletti his first major commission to supply the building's most important ornamental sculpture (fig. 5.20).

St. George's chapel was built with Bedford, Indiana, limestone in the English Perpendicular style and is graced by a square tower crowned by pinnacles and pierced battlements. Slender columns in the nave rise to masonry vaults. Additional carving was undertaken by Harry Thomas Easton and his assistants, who were based in Indiana.[58] Originally from Cambridge, Massachusetts, Easton, like Coletti, had apprenticed under Evans. Another carver who worked on the chapel was Andrew Dreselly, who had trained under Kirchmayer. A second generation of carvers—offspring, so to speak, of the senior craftsmen in the Society of Arts and Crafts—was brought together by Brown and Cram. Yellin, a member of the society, supplied the ironwork.[59] When the chapel was consecrated, Daniel Berkeley Updike, by now one of the society's senior members, printed the program booklet.[60] Over the following decades, stained-glass windows were installed, the work of Wilbur H. Burnham and Joseph G. Reynolds, both of whom had trained under Harry Goodhue and both members of the society.[61] Thus St. George's School chapel may be seen as a late blossoming of the Arts and Crafts movement in New England.

Dwelling in the Medieval Manner

As with their ecclesiastic commissions, the architects' domestic work responded to English trends. Following the lead of designers such as Richard Norman Shaw, they admired the vernacular houses of the late Middle Ages and erected Tudor Revival residences around Boston at an early date. The architects who had trained in England were especially influential. John Hubbard Sturgis, Clipston's uncle, was such a man and designed one of the more splendid examples. The John E. Thayer house, built in 1886 in Lancaster, Massachusetts, was begun by the senior architect and finished by his nephew (fig. 5.21).[62] Irregularly massed, it was constructed with a stone first story and half-timbering and plaster on the second floor, all under a roof with multiple gables and tall chimneys. By the 1880s, Queen Anne houses with Tudor features had become common in Boston, but they were typically frame, shingled, and treated with applied wood trim that mimicked half-timbering. The Thayer house was recognized for being truer to its sources, designed in a style "suggesting English domestic work."[63]

In 1887 Walker designed a Tudor Revival house in Manchester, Massachusetts, for Edward Robinson, a curator and future director of the Museum of Fine Arts in Boston and the Metropolitan Museum of Art in New York (fig. 5.22). The picturesque pile of stone and half-timbering was built the following year.[64] Having apprenticed with John Hubbard Sturgis

FIG. 5.22 C. Howard Walker, Robinson house, Manchester, MA, 1887.

FIG. 5.23 Cram and Wentworth, Fellner house, Brookline, MA, 1891.

during the 1870s, Walker evidently continued to admire and learn from the buildings that emerged from the office of his onetime master. Cram, too, embraced this direction with a house for Eugene Fellner in Brookline (1891; fig. 5.23).[65] Instead of stone, the design as published in the *American Architect and Building News* was brick on the first story and half-timbered above. Typical of Tudor Revival houses, it was asymmetrical, its roof animated by tall chimneys and gables and dormers of different sizes. Like many English Arts and Crafts houses, its walls were constructed with groupings of vertical windows with small panes.

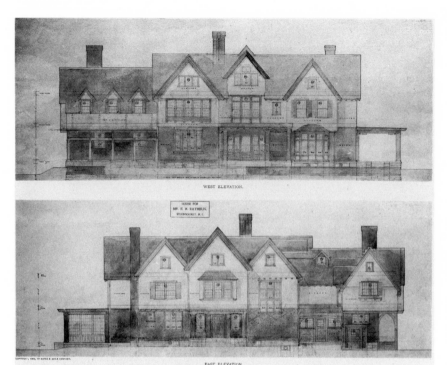

FIG. 5.24 Warren, Smith, and Biscoe, Annerslea, Rathbun house, Woonsocket, RI, 1902.

By the turn of the twentieth century, the architects' Tudor houses had become an established type while the Queen Anne Revival of the 1880s and 1890s had petered out. With silhouettes that were more controlled, the Tudor houses illustrated what the architects had in mind in calling for simplicity. A house for Yale professor John C. Schwab in New Haven (1895–96), designed by Clipston Sturgis, is balanced in its main elevation, although the fenestration of the two projecting bays does not match exactly and the entry porch and a turreted tower are off-center (pl. 4-a).[66] The ornament is not profuse but is well crafted, including carving in the bargeboard of the porch, leaded glass in the first-floor windows, and quatrefoil timbering on the tower. The first story of the house is seam-faced granite, while the rest is half-timbered and stuccoed. Sturgis regularly managed to attract clients for residential projects who had the means to build with durable materials. At an 1897 meeting of the Boston Society of Architects, Sturgis presented a paper titled "Our Wooden Suburbs."[67] Wood made him wince, whereas he advocated for building with brick and plaster. Building with stone, to be sure, was first choice.

The Edward H. Rathbun house, called Annerslea, designed by Warren and his partners in Woonsocket, Rhode Island (1902), is an even simpler

interpretation of the Tudor Revival residence (fig. 5.24).[68] Brick on the
first story and plastered above, it does not include any half-timbering, although wide bargeboards enhance its gables, typical of the revival. Leaded-glass windows with tiny panes are a related decorative feature. Having
been reared in England, Warren was especially fond of the English country
house. In a 1904 issue of *Architectural Review*, he recounted recent developments in English domestic architecture, extolling the virtues of its "quiet
and restrained beauty."[69] In the same issue, Andrews assessed "The Changing Styles of Country Houses," writing that "the glory of the country is the
heritage of England."[70] While observing that the French School was gaining
acceptance in the United States, Andrews encouraged his fellow American
architects to take their cues from the English.

Somewhat like a cousin of the Tudor Revival house was the country
house that drew upon the Jacobean period, bridging the Middle Ages and
the Northern Renaissance. These Jacobean-inspired houses were built of
masonry and usually featured parapets at their gable ends. They might include Tudor arches and leaded-glass casement windows as well as classical components such as columned porches. They were never widespread.
Sturgis designed an early example of the type for the Episcopal bishop of
Vermont, Arthur C. A. Hall, in 1894 (fig. 5.25).[71] Called Rock Point, the residence was built in Burlington overlooking Lake Champlain. Constructed
of red brick and trimmed with local stone, it was described as "designed on

FIG. 5.26 C. Howard
Walker, Hotel Ludlow,
Boston, 1888–89.

the quiet lines of an English country gentleman's house."[72] The exterior is
remarkably austere, especially for the date. Symmetrically massed, it derives
its interest from parapeted gables, a columned porch, and a carved shield
inset over the entrance. In his journal, Sturgis made note that the gables
would be coped with "special" brick, "made by hand"—an Arts and Crafts
approach.[73] Along with rooms for entertaining and rooms for students, the
residence includes a chapel and a library for which Sturgis developed the
decoration.[74] He even devised a bookplate for the bishop, reflecting the Arts
and Crafts interest in graphic design and printing. Not surprisingly, the im-
agery included a Perpendicular church tower along with a bishop's miter
and a tree.[75]

During the closing decades of the nineteenth century, apartment buildings became an attractive alternative to row houses in the city and single-family houses in the suburbs, and medieval sources offered possibilities
for treating these large structures. The Hotel Ludlow, built near Copley
Square in Boston's Back Bay (1888–89), was designed by Walker for Denman Ross (fig. 5.26).[76] A drawing of the project was displayed in the 1890
exhibition of the Boston Architectural Club.[77] Planned in a U, the building
had a court that opened onto the street, with the entrance located at the
interior of the court. Constructed of brick and six stories high, the Hotel
Ludlow was the essence of simplicity, devoid of ornament at the ground

FIG. 5.27 Cram, Goodhue, and Ferguson, Richmond Court, Brookline, MA, 1898.

level except at the doorway, where carved consoles supported a canopy. On the fifth floor, below an attic story, were Venetian arches: Gothic colonnettes framed the windows, while above them were roundels and larger embracing arches with voussoirs of alternating dark and light brick. Brackets carried overhanging eaves of a low-pitched roof. Although the design was restrained, it was decidedly Italian and medieval. Indeed, it suggested the influence of Ross's experiences with Norton, his ongoing reading of Ruskin, and especially his travels in Italy. In 1881 Ross had bought a watercolor from the English architect and designer Arthur H. Mackmurdo; the work focuses on three polychromed arches of Santa Maria Novella in Florence, and they could well have inspired the Ludlow's polychromed arches.[78]

Yet the attraction of English architecture soon won out. As with their churches and houses, the Boston architects preferred to mine England's late Middle Ages for sources they could apply to apartment buildings. An early and influential example is Richmond Court, an apartment designed by Cram, Goodhue, and Ferguson and built in Brookline, near Boston, in 1898 (fig. 5.27). *American Architect* reported that Richmond Court was "Elizabethan in style, and of the combination of materials generally used in original work of the period of the last of the Tudors, red brick and light limestone. The style has been scrupulously followed."[79] In its U-configured plan, the building was an outgrowth of the apartment buildings from the prior de-

cade. But its courtyard is larger than had been common and includes a garden and fountain at the center. Further, the building conveys the image of an English manor house, with the center entrance emphasized by a broken pediment and obelisks over the door, a large shield mortared into the third story, and finials decorating the parapet.[80] In the middle of the fountain stands a bronze nymph, sculpted by Lee Lawrie, who would work on many of the architects' projects, including the reredos at St. Thomas Church in Manhattan. Another artistic component of the apartment building is the elaborate wrought-iron gate, probably by Frederick Krasser, that screens the garden from the street.[81]

Newhall and his firm designed many of these Tudor-inspired apartment buildings in close proximity to Boston. Burton Halls (1909) is among the most distinguished of this type (pl. 4-b).[82] Located in Cambridge near Harvard Square, it was planned so that its court could be entered from the corner of the lot where two streets converge. Anchoring the entrance are a large planter and two arched brick gates (fig. 5.28). Angled bays at the front of the building rise to shaped Flemish gables, while the interior of the court is enlivened by tall chimneys, copper domes, and battlements. An escutcheon and leaded glass in the windows add another level of detail. Although the open area is not as large as at Richmond Court, it is wide enough to accommodate a narrow stretch of lawn and beds of shrubbery at the pe-

riphery. The presence of nature, even if minimal, was important to the Arts and Crafts way of living.

Gothic and Academic

Buildings that served educational purposes belonged to yet another major category of projects that the Boston architects deemed appropriate for their brand of the Gothic Revival. Included in this group were public school buildings and public libraries. But the most spectacular of all were the buildings erected on the campuses of private schools and colleges.

West Roxbury High School, Boston, designed by Andrews, Jaques, and Rantoul (1898–1901), is a representative schoolhouse (fig. 5.29).[83] Constructed in the "free Tudor style," as reported at the time of its dedication,

FIG. 5.30 Cram, Goodhue, and Ferguson, Hunt Library, Nashua, NH, 1901–3.

the red-brick and limestone building has a tower at one end and a projecting block at the other under a pyramidal roof.[84] The main entrance is through an ogee arch, and at the cornice is a molding with carved lion heads, shields, and foliate bosses. Although the carver has not been identified, Evans is a likely source given that he was supplying other ornamental work for the firm at this time.[85] Just a few years earlier, in 1894, the firm had designed Brookline High School patterned after the Romanesque of Richardson.[86] By turning to the Tudor Revival for the West Roxbury school building, Andrews and his partners were embracing a general trend in ecclesiastical and residential projects. The building's decorative components also give form to ideas Andrews promoted as a speaker for the Society of Arts and Crafts. In March of 1899, he lectured to the organization's members on "Craftsmanship in the Middle Ages."[87]

When Cram, Goodhue, and Ferguson won the commission for a public library in Nashua, New Hampshire, in 1901, a generous donation enabled them to indulge in designing the Tudor-style building with many Arts and

Crafts finishes (fig. 5.30).[88] From a distance, the library appears to be a sheer mass of red brick trimmed in limestone. Above the entrance is a hefty, square clock tower with buttresses at the corners, pointed-arch windows, and battlements. But as visitors approach the building, completed by 1903, they see that it benefits from a great deal of enrichment. Like the West Roxbury school building, the Nashua building is entered through an ogee arch. Carved Gothic niches flank the portal, which is surmounted by quatrefoils and shields. Inside the building, now a community center, patrons crossed under the tower through a double-height lobby that opened into the reference and reading room. In the manner of Cram's churches, the ceiling was finished in wood with visible structural beams, while casement windows were crafted with leaded diamonds and the walls paneled with fumed oak. The focus of the room is a fireplace enhanced by Mercer tiles set in a large surround and crowned by a carved wood overmantel. Wrought-iron light fixtures add another handcrafted element to the space. Montgomery Schuyler praised the Nashua library for the way the architects treated its "weight and mass" and lauded its detail as "familiar and domestic."[89]

Campus construction surged at the turn of the twentieth century, and England's Tudor and Jacobean periods provided a point of departure for many of the Boston architects' projects. The buildings soon became labeled "collegiate Gothic," although they drew upon the broader range of styles from the late Middle Ages through the Early Renaissance. Designing educational buildings along these lines suggested appealing connections to Oxford and Cambridge as well as to English values.[90] Cram admired the English residential college system for the way it molded character. Interestingly, one of the virtues that he believed this living arrangement would foster was "self-reliance," thereby adding an Emersonian allusion to a list that included "personal honour, clean living, fearlessness in action," and "obedience to law."[91]

Both Sturgis and Cram credited Philadelphia architects John Stewardson and Walter Cope with the rise of the collegiate Gothic through their work at Bryn Mawr College in the late 1880s and early 1890s.[92] Stewardson and Sturgis had been members of the same class at Harvard, and the time that Stewardson spent in Cambridge formed the basis of an enduring relationship between the two men as well as with other Boston architects. When Stewardson died in an accident in 1896, the Boston Society of Architects passed resolutions to honor him and his achievements, something not normally done for an architect from another part of the country.[93] A year

FIG. 5.31 Maginnis and Walsh, Gasson Hall, Boston College, Newton, MA, 1909–13.

later, the Boston Architectural Club welcomed Cope as a member of the committee organizing the show that would run alongside the city's first Arts and Crafts exhibition. In addition to the Philadelphia architects, Vaughan contributed to the development of collegiate Gothic. His Searles Science Building (1893–94) at Bowdoin College, Brunswick, Maine, was another example of the emerging trend.[94]

As collegiate Gothic took hold, several of the architects associated with the Society of Arts and Crafts designed soaring Perpendicular towers that dominated the campuses where they were constructed. The architects also worked closely with favorite artisans to finish the buildings with the hand-crafted ornament that the society promoted. In 1912 Cram reported on recent developments on American campuses, including the work of Maginnis and Walsh at Boston College, located in suburban Newton, and Sturgis at the Perkins Institution for the Blind in Watertown, also near Boston.[95]

In April of 1909, Maginnis and Walsh won a competition for a campus plan and the central academic building for Boston College (fig. 5.31).[96] Leaders of the school had concluded that the time had come to leave their tight quarters in the city's South End, where the Jesuits had been educating a mainly Irish Catholic student body since 1864, and they prepared to relocate to farmland in Newton. As an organizing concept, the architects proposed to plan the site by alluding to a cathedral, with cross axes suggesting a nave and transept arms. From the main gates, one would proceed down a long tree-lined drive toward the junction of the axes, where a Perpendicular bell tower would rise from the central academic building—the place where the crossing in a cathedral would be located. When additional buildings were erected, the 200-foot tower would crown the landscape. Thus inspired by the conceit of a cathedral, Maginnis and Walsh presented new possibilities for the Perpendicular tower as a unifying feature on the American campus. Excavation began in the fall of 1909, and two years later, Evans produced molds for the casting of concrete ornament.[97] Murals were painted by a Jesuit brother, Francis C. Schroen, and the building, renamed Gasson Hall, was opened in the spring of 1913.[98]

As it happened, Cram in 1909 was working on a scheme at Princeton for a collegiate Gothic complex to house the graduate students.[99] The most likely site for the project seemed to be land adjacent to the university campus. But between 1909 and 1910, a debate raged over whether a location that was removed from the campus might be preferable. In May of 1910, an alumnus left a bequest that supported a separate location on open land, and the issue was resolved. That summer, Cram worked out his design for the Graduate College, including a magnificent Perpendicular tower, for which Evans provided models.[100] As at Boston College, Princeton's Cleveland Tower was pivotal to the overall scheme. In 1911 Evans was again working on the project, this time overseeing the creation of its ornament, including heads.[101] Two years later, the first buildings were completed, oriented around Cram's 173-foot masterpiece.[102]

When the towers for the two campuses were being designed and built, Maginnis and Cram had been working closely together in the Society of Arts and Crafts. For the society's 1907 exhibition, Cram chaired the section devoted to ecclesiastical work and was assisted by three other members, including Maginnis. After the exhibition ended, the society established a permanent committee to promote the cause, which soon was christened Saint Dunstan's Guild. Now Maginnis was in charge, identified as the "warden," and Cram assisted him as "vice-warden."[103] Cram valued Maginnis as a leader and as a designer.[104]

FIG. 5.32 R. Clipston Sturgis, Perkins Institution for the Blind (Perkins School for the Blind), Watertown, MA, 1909–12.

The tower at Boston College also appears to have led Sturgis to envision an iconic tower for the Perkins Institution (fig. 5.32). In journal entries from August of 1909, Sturgis jotted notes that record his first meetings with representatives of the school to discuss a new campus. On one page, he sketched a pencil drawing of a Perpendicular tower, which became the focal point of the forty-acre site in Watertown.[105] A year earlier, Sturgis had designed a collegiate Gothic building to anchor a new campus for the Winsor School, a private day school for girls in Boston that was completed in 1910.[106] But the Perkins Institution commission was more ambitious. Sturgis saw the potential from the start, and one can appreciate how he was intrigued by the prospect of designing a signature tower of his own. Perkins had been founded in 1829 as the nation's first school for the blind, and it now was moving from two locations in Boston to a prominent setting overlooking the Charles River.[107] When it opened in 1912, the campus would include residences and a central building with a museum, library, auditorium, and chapel. Sturgis described the groups of housing for the upper-school students as "closes," comparing them to the Vicars' Close at Wells in England.[108] In additional references to Gothic England, the main building at Perkins was planned around two cloistered quadrangles, while the center of the building carried a 180-foot-tall bell tower with pinnacles and a lantern. A sketch of the tower was published in the December 4, 1912, issue of *American Architect*.[109]

To embellish the brick buildings, Sturgis turned to artisans from the Society of Arts and Crafts (pl. 5). Evans supplied the models for cast-concrete sculpture, including eagles that were positioned over the entrance to the main building.[110] Grueby tile designed by Addison Le Boutillier was embedded in walks and walls, fireplaces and fountains.[111] Even though the young people who would live on the campus could not see, the school's director thought the buildings should be beautiful to lift the spirits of the people who dedicated their lives to the children.[112]

If erecting an entirely new collegiate Gothic campus was not an option for most schools, the next best choice was to erect a large building of the favored type and to site it in a prominent location. This was the approach taken at Mount Holyoke College, established as a seminary in 1837 in South Hadley, Massachusetts, north of Springfield, for the education of women. Skinner Hall, designed by Putnam and Cox, was a Tudor Revival classroom building constructed in 1915 to preside over a large green (fig. 5.33).[113] Like Maginnis, William Putnam was a generation younger than many of the architects leading the Society of Arts and Crafts. Putnam and his partner, Allen H. Cox, probably were hired through Cox's local connections. Cox had been born and raised in the area, and the firm had already designed two fraternity houses at Amherst College when they received the Mount Holyoke commission.[114] Then, too, Sturgis may have recommended the firm.

By this time, he would have gotten to know Putnam through the Society of Arts and Crafts, and he may have remained in contact with his onetime client, Yale's John C. Schwab, who had become a Mount Holyoke trustee.[115]

In any case, Skinner Hall was built to the highest standard in terms of design, materials, and finishes. The facade overlooking the green reveals the architects' scholarly knowledge of English Tudor architecture, with a battlemented bay that quotes a similar entrance at Compton Wynyates house in Warwickshire. Yet the English manor is asymmetrical and irregular in its massing, whereas Skinner Hall is balanced, reflecting the early twentieth-century attraction to Jacobean order. Built of brick and trimmed with sandstone, it features carved seals of American and foreign women's colleges. Leaded casement windows sparkle with stained-glass medallions that represent the academic disciplines taught inside. Putnam and Cox would design four more collegiate Gothic buildings for Mount Holyoke, the last one erected in 1932.[116]

Both the craftsmen and the architects who banded together in the Society of Arts and Crafts contributed to the evolution of collegiate Gothic architecture in New England and beyond. Because ornament of the highest quality was integral to the success of these buildings, it is not surprising that craftsmen who joined the society were sought after by architects in cities besides Boston, especially architects practicing in the Northeast. For example, before the society was even founded, Evans was identified by New York's Charles C. Haight and then hired to take charge of the stone carving on Vanderbilt Hall, an early collegiate Gothic dormitory at Yale, built in 1894.[117] Connick's workshop produced stained glass for many campuses, including Marsh Chapel at Boston University and Houghton Chapel at Wellesley College, as well as Heinz Chapel and the Cathedral of Learning at the University of Pittsburgh.[118]

The Boston architects were influential, too. After they had demonstrated the appeal of seam-faced granite, quarried south of Boston, the material was selected for the collegiate Gothic buildings of Yale and the University of Michigan Law School. Through their towers, Maginnis, Cram, and Sturgis inspired other academic institutions to erect skyscraping Perpendicular landmarks. The architects' exemplars at Boston College, Princeton, and Perkins Institution were followed by Yale's 216-foot-tall Harkness tower (1917–21) designed by New York's James Gamble Rogers, and Wellesley's 182-foot-tall Galen Stone tower (1929–31) designed by Philadelphia's Charles Z. Klauder. The beauty of New England's collegiate Gothic buildings is due in no small part to the Boston architects and their craftsmen colleagues, Arts and Crafts collaborations for which they all deserve recognition.

CHAPTER SIX

Looking Backward:
Colonial Revival as Arts and Crafts

Even while the Boston architects were promoting the English Gothic Revival, they were looking back to the region's colonial past as a starting point for their designs. They viewed the early buildings as expressions of New England's heritage and respected them for their workmanship—the same Arts and Crafts values that lay behind the architects' admiration of the Gothic buildings of England. Yet when Colonial Revival architecture emerged in New England, it began with the design of houses, unlike the late nineteenth-century Gothic Revival, which began with the design of churches.

During the 1880s, several Colonial Revival residences were erected that would prove to be influential. Contributing to the trend were Charles McKim, with the Henry A. C. Taylor house in Newport and the John F. Andrew house in Boston's Back Bay; and Peabody and Stearns, with 246 Beacon Street in the Back Bay. Another early example of the revival is the house built in Cambridge in 1882 for Arthur Carey, who would become a founder and the second president of the Society of Arts and Crafts (fig. 6.1).[1] Designed by Sturgis and Brigham, the house was constructed at precisely the time when Clipston Sturgis was training in his uncle's office. An early admirer of colonial architecture, John Hubbard Sturgis had made measured drawings of the Hancock house before its demolition in 1863, and he revived some of its features for the Carey house, including the second-floor balcony and the broken-scroll pediment. Unlike the Hancock house, which was symmetrical, the Carey house is irregular in its massing and suggests the Queen Anne preference for variety. But most important, the house represented a direct response to Boston's colonial architecture on the part of the senior Sturgis and Carey, while it presented new possibilities for the younger Sturgis.

Boston's federal period architecture, especially the work of Charles Bulfinch, was equally compelling and provided another dimension for the

emerging Colonial Revival. In 1886 Waddy Longfellow was commissioned by his cousin Annie Longfellow Thorp, daughter of the poet, and her husband Joseph to design a house (fig. 6.2).[2] It was to be built on Brattle Street, Cambridge, a short distance away from the colonial era mansion where Annie was raised. The young architect and his clients envisioned a design

FIG. 6.3 Longfellow, Alden, and Harlow, Andrew house, Hingham, MA, 1890–91.

that would harmonize with the Georgian dwelling and the other historic houses on the street. In some respects, the Thorp house draws upon eighteenth-century sources—as in its massing under a gambrel roof and the twisted balusters and newel posts of the front hall staircase. In the fineness of its ornament, however, the Thorp house reflects the federal period. Columns supporting the front porch and inset in the second story are attenuated, while delicate swags decorate the portico. In the front parlor, pairs of thin columns flank a fireplace, and airy garlands on a frieze encircle the room. Overhead, the ceiling is coved in an ellipse, following the example in the dining room of the third house that Bulfinch designed for Harrison Gray Otis. When the Thorp house was finished in 1887, its exterior was painted a creamy yellow with white trim, a distinct break with the darker Victorian palette that had prevailed since the years after the Civil War.

A few years later, from 1890 to 1891, Longfellow and his partners designed a summer house in Hingham, south of Boston, for John F. Andrew and his wife, who had commissioned McKim to design their Back Bay town house (fig. 6.3).[3] The main elevation of the Hingham house was symmetrical and had a Palladian window centered on the second story, above which was a short attic story under a hip roof, similar to Bulfinch's first house for Otis. The porch of the Andrew house, however, was much larger than anything Bulfinch would have designed. No one would have mistaken the house as a product of the federal period.

FIG. 6.4 Shaw and Hunnewell, the Ridges, Bigelow house, Cohasset, MA, 1890.

For the most part during the early 1890s, Boston's architects were not at all rigid in their ideas about Colonial Revival houses, and they manipulated their sources freely. George Shaw and Henry Hunnewell took this approach with the Ridges, the summer residence of Albert S. Bigelow built in 1890 in Cohasset on Boston's South Shore (fig. 6.4).[4] Long and low, the first story of the house was constructed with stone that came from the site, another example of the preference for local building materials that was encouraged by Boston's and England's Arts and Crafts architects. With its shingled second story, the house could be categorized as Shingle Style.[5] At the center of the facade was a rounded central bay covered by a conical roof—an element that was essentially medieval. But the house was symmetrically organized, and its decorative features were derived from eighteenth and early nineteenth-century New England architecture. On the exterior, it had classical columns and dormers with semicircular windows centered in them, and inside it had a large staircase with the twisted newel posts that were becoming fashionable.

To enrich these residential projects, the architects turned to their artisan colleagues, especially for woodwork and plasterwork. In doing so, the architects and craftsmen hoped to revive the spirit of the colonial craftsman and his intuitive approach. Writing in 1899 in an essay titled "Architecture in New England," Langford Warren explained how colonial carpenters and masons learned about ornament from English publications and the occasional immigrant. "These forms they modified unconsciously and generally with right feeling for the material—wood—in which nearly all their architectural detail was executed," he wrote. Most detail, he added, was developed by the craftsman as he worked.[6] Warren went on to describe New England architecture of the nineteenth century. In his view, Bulfinch still adhered to "the earlier traditions." Notably, Warren argued that most of the architecture from the first twenty years of the century—that is to say, the federal period—could be classified as "Colonial" or "Georgian."[7] This assertion is important as an illustration of how Warren and his colleagues identified and justified broad parameters from the past for the region's Colonial Revival.

Two years later, Cram commented on the differences between the domestic architecture being built in New York City and in Boston. Much of the New York work, he believed, showed "a certain opulence and luxuriousness that verges too often on something that might almost be called vulgarity." On the other hand, he wrote that the domestic work in Boston sometimes adhered too closely to colonial precedent. All in all, however, Cram found it to be "fine in its effect of delicate and courtly reserve."[8] Over the coming decades, the Colonial Revival house found favor across the United States— even in the suburbs of New York. But while architects in other parts of the country were pursuing a variety of styles for their residential projects, the architects in Boston, especially those leading the Society of Arts and Crafts, were convinced that the colonial-inspired house was most appropriate for the region.

Between 1905 and 1906, Andrews built a Colonial Revival house in Brookline for himself and his family (fig. 6.5). Sheathed in clapboard, the house has a substantial porch with classical columns and a Palladian window on the rear elevation.[9] Yet unlike houses from the seventeenth and early eighteenth centuries, the Andrews house has a broad hip roof that flares at the ends and extends beyond the exterior walls. Many years earlier, Andrews would have encountered this roofline when he worked with Richardson, who used it in the design of the train station in North Easton, Massachusetts (1881–84), perhaps inspired by Japanese architecture.[10] The Andrews house was representative of the colonial houses that he and his colleagues were building at this time.

For clients with deeper pockets, the architects preferred to specify brick with stone trimmings. In 1909 Andrews, Jaques, and Rantoul were commissioned by Dr. George C. F. Williams to build a house in Hartford (pl. 6-a).[11]

FIG. 6.5 Robert Andrews, Andrews house, Brookline, MA, 1905–6.

It was purchased in 1943 by the state of Connecticut to serve as the governor's residence and now is regularly the setting for public events. Grand as it is, the Williams house closely resembles an even larger mansion, called La Rochelle, that the architects had designed in Bar Harbor, Maine, from 1901 to 1903.[12] Williams admired published images of the house and hired the Boston firm to build one like it for him. What was unusual about the Bar Harbor house was its high hipped roof, which gave it a distinct French accent. The concept seems to have come from the client, who was of French extraction.[13] In other respects, however, La Rochelle fit in with the Colonial Revival. Williams must have liked the prominent roof, for it was reproduced for his new home. Projecting pavilions at each end of the main facade have roofs that are hipped, and they flare at the ends. Otherwise, the exterior of the house is Georgian, built of brick with limestone trim, and symmetrically organized around a narrow stone temple front and a pediment that breaks through the eaves. Inside, the decorative features are light and fine, in the spirit of the federal period.

Residential work was something of a specialty for Lois Howe, who designed dozens of Colonial Revival houses. Howe's Skyfield, a summer house in Harrisville, New Hampshire, illustrates another interpretation of the revival (fig. 6.6).[14] Built for Mrs. Edward C. Jones of New Bedford, Massachusetts, in 1916, the house is a controlled composition informed by a scholarly study of New England's early architecture. Like many of her colleagues, Howe regularly measured and drew the architectural compo-

FIG. 6.6 Lois L. Howe, Skyfield, Jones house, Harrisville, NH, 1916.

nents of historic dwellings in the region, culminating in her 1913 publication with Constance Fuller of *Details of Old New England Houses*.[15] Skyfield is a symmetrical, broadly massed brick structure with tall chimneys, three small dormers, and hip-roofed pavilions that project at each end. The entrance is understated, with a fanlight and pediment over the door. In its kinship with designs by Christopher Wren, the house suggests the interest in him that was shared by the Boston architects and England's Neo-Georgians.[16] Inside Skyfield, Howe incorporated antique fireplace surrounds that came from Salem, Massachusetts.

Also in 1916, Howe designed a Colonial Revival house in Cambridge, Massachusetts, for Louis C. Cornish, a Unitarian minister (pl. 6-b).[17] It was unusual for its time in that it was based on the seventeenth-century dwellings of the Puritans and is considered the earliest revival in Cambridge from this period. Built with a profusion of gables and gabled dormers, the house has clapboarded walls that overhang and pendants that decorate the corners. Given that Skyfield contained architectural salvage from Salem, one may imagine that Howe was thinking of Salem's seventeenth-century houses when she designed the house in Cambridge. Whatever the inspiration, the fenestration of the Cornish residence is modern. Double-hung sash windows grouped in twos and threes provide a bright interior.

FIG. 6.7 Longfellow, Alden, and Harlow, Phillips Brooks House, Harvard University, Cambridge, MA, 1897–99.

Colonial on Campus

Just as Waddy Longfellow was in the vanguard in designing Colonial Revival houses, so too was he early to embrace this direction for the Harvard campus. Richardson, Longfellow's onetime employer, contributed to the trend with Sever Hall (1878–80), built with red brick and a pedimented entrance facing the street, as if acknowledging the college's colonial and federal survivors. Sever was followed by McKim's Johnston Gate (1889), which welcomed students and visitors to Harvard Yard with a Georgian

FIG. 6.8 Shaw and Hunnewell, Pierce Hall, Harvard University, Cambridge, MA, 1900.

design that harmonized with the buildings just beyond it.[18] Longfellow's Phillips Brooks House (1897–99) was the first fully developed Georgian Revival building for the Yard (fig. 6.7).[19] Conceived as a center for student religious societies and charitable organizations, it was constructed with red brick and stone trimmings. Longfellow adopted several features from the college's oldest buildings. Round-arched windows on the first story and oculus windows in gables are reminiscent of those at Harvard Hall, while each of two entrances is through a pavilion surmounted by a pediment, echoing the same approach at Hollis and Stoughton Halls. John Evans supplied the decorative stonework.[20] Inside, the building is enriched by oak paneling and an imposing staircase with a twisted newel post and balusters inspired by colonial precedents, including the stairway of the demolished Hancock house in Boston.

Just outside the Yard, Shaw and Hunnewell designed Pierce Hall, built in 1900 of red brick with limestone trimmings (fig. 6.8).[21] Erected for the instruction of mechanical, civil, and electrical engineering, Pierce is a grand version of the Colonial Revival. Indeed, its design is more indebted to English Georgian architecture than the modest buildings of colonial New England. Planned in an H, it has front and rear facades that terminate in projecting wings under hipped roofs—a favorite massing of

the period. When seen from a distance, Pierce Hall seems fairly severe. Yet when viewed at closer range, it exhibits a generous amount of carved stone, especially over the entrance porches, which was more than had been used on any other building at Harvard up to this time.

A new residential hall for the Women's College at Brown University, built of brick and limestone in 1910, could be considered a classic example of the Colonial Revival as it was adopted on New England campuses (fig. 6.9). Designed by Andrews, Jaques, and Rantoul, the dormitory, subsequently named Miller Hall, extends into the depth of the site. Hipped roofs cover wings at its ends. In an article published in a 1911 issue of *Architectural Record*, Montgomery Schuyler stated that the architects had "reverted to the inheritance of the institution" with good results.[22] Although it may appear to be generically Georgian, the building resembles other work by Andrews, Jaques, and Rantoul. Like the Williams house in Hartford, built a year earlier, the dormitory's main facade is balanced around a distinctively narrow pavilion that rises to a relatively small pediment.[23]

Even Cram, the impassioned advocate for the Gothic Revival, contributed to the spread of the Colonial Revival on campuses. It may be recalled that as far back as the early 1890s, he thought that a Congregational church should be Georgian in style—not Gothic—to acknowledge its Protestant origins. When he and his firm were hired to develop a master plan for Wheaton Seminary, now Wheaton College, in 1898, they envisioned Georgian buildings for the Norton, Massachusetts, site. In the decades that fol-

FIG. 6.10 Cram and Ferguson, Cole Memorial Chapel, Wheaton College, Norton, MA, 1915–17.

lowed, the firm designed Colonial Revival buildings for campuses including Wheaton, Williams College in Williamstown, Massachusetts, Phillips Exeter Academy in Exeter, New Hampshire, and Choate School in Wallingford, Connecticut.[24] The Wheaton chapel (1915–17) blends elements from Boston's earliest churches, giving it a familiar air (fig. 6.10). The porch and pediment are reminiscent of St. Paul's Cathedral, and the octagonal belfry suggests the one at the Old South Meeting House. According to Cram, the firm's Colonial Revival projects were mainly handled by Alexander Hoyle.[25] Nevertheless, Cram was fully committed to taking this path. In 1914, as chairman of the City Planning Board, he urged Boston's mayor to restore Faneuil Hall, pressing for the removal of paint from the brick and for painting the wood trim white.[26] Cram the Gothicist evidently was pleased with the Wheaton chapel when it was completed. The press coverage it received would have originated with the firm, and the project was documented extensively in a 1918 issue of *Architectural Review*, attributed to Cram and Ferguson.[27]

Boston's colonial past also provided a frame of reference for the design of a building that would house a new institution of higher education in the city. When Sturgis was commissioned in 1906 as architect for the Franklin Union, a polytechnic institute funded by a bequest from Benjamin Franklin, there was general agreement that a colonial style would recall the era when the school's benefactor lived (fig. 6.11).[28] What resulted, in fact, was

FIG. 6.11 Sturgis and Barton, Franklin Union (Benjamin Franklin Institute of Technology), Boston, 1906–8.

FIG. 6.12 Franklin Union, sculpture by John Evans.

not much like the humble structures of eighteenth-century Boston; rather, the design was more like a building from Georgian England, in keeping with the Colonial Revival. Limestone faces the first story, with the upper three stories of red brick. Over the main entrance and slightly recessed is a colonnade, while the side entrance to the school is surmounted by a large Palladian window. Where the building meets a street corner, a sculpted eagle spreads its wings, its back against the corner, with a kite, a key, and the letters B and F intertwined in the space under each wing (fig. 6.12). The sculpture came from Evans's workshop.[29] Known today as the Benjamin Franklin Institute of Technology, the school was erected in the city's South End to educate and train young men in one-year and two-year programs. Shortly after the building opened in 1908, it was illustrated in *Brickbuilder* and *Architectural Review*.[30] Readers were informed that the Franklin Union had "reserve and dignity" although "rather at the expense of variety and interest." Tellingly, it was described as a "distinctively 'Bostonese' design."[31]

Municipal Buildings and Libraries

Community leaders and architects shared the view that when civic buildings were erected, they should reflect the region's heritage. For town halls and city halls, a Colonial Revival image could evoke the long tradition of democratic governance in New England. Just when the Richardsonian Romanesque Cambridge City Hall was completed, Warren's town hall for Lincoln, Massachusetts (1891–92), presented a new approach (fig. 6.13).[32] By

FIG. 6.13 H. Langford Warren, Lincoln Town Hall (Bemis Hall), Lincoln, MA, 1891–92.

the late 1880s, Warren had established his office on Park Street in a house that had been designed by Bulfinch and was located across Beacon Street from Bulfinch's State House. This exposure to Bulfinch's work proved to be instructive. Warren's new municipal building for Lincoln, today Bemis Hall, was constructed of red brick and trimmed in white wood. Dominating the facade is a temple front, its pediment supported by narrow pilasters, while a cupola crowns its hip roof. Providing interest to the central hall are attenuated Corinthian columns and a staircase with twisted newel posts. According to a local newspaper report, the woodwork would be "cream white," recognizing the departure from the dark Victorian colors that were still in vogue.[33] In addition to the carved wood, the building was finished with leaded and bull's-eye glass, reminders of colonial craftsmanship.

Forty years after the building in Lincoln was finished, the Colonial Revival Blackburn Memorial Hall was dedicated in Walpole, Massachusetts, designed by Putnam and Cox (fig. 6.14).[34] It demonstrates the enduring appeal of the style. Built from 1929 to 1932, the civic auditorium is a brick rectangular building under a pitched roof. It rests on a high basement, defined by a cast stone water table, and a wide flight of stairs leads visitors to the entrance of the building. At each of its narrow ends are four Ionic columns that carry an entablature. Sited on the edge of a park planned by

FIG. 6.14 Putnam and Cox, Blackburn Memorial Hall, Walpole, MA, 1929–32.

John Nolen, the auditorium is visible from all four sides.[35] It is simple yet monumental.

Library buildings, too, were often given a Colonial Revival treatment. The William Fogg Library in Eliot, Maine (1906–7), was designed by Walker to be compatible with its rural setting (fig. 6.15).[36] Treated in the manner that had become favored for domestic projects, it has a sizable hip roof that flares at the corners and eaves that overhang. When construction began, citizens donated their stone walls, hauling the rock to the site, where the choicest specimens were selected for the new building. Granite for the foundation and trimmings was quarried locally. Having admired English churches "built of the material at hand," Walker would have felt that the fieldstone linked the new library to its locale and local history. Cram may have disliked the use of fieldstone, at least when he was writing *Church Building* in 1901, but Newhall would have been sympathetic, having found fieldstone acceptable for the Faulkner Methodist Church, Malden, built at the same time as the project in Maine. The bequest for the Fogg Library evidently did not allow for much embellishment. Four Ionic columns at the entrance and two columns inside are the prime decorative elements for what is a small building. Two fireplaces are finished with plain wood surrounds and mantel shelves, consistent with the simple finishes of rural New

England buildings. As critic of the Society of Arts and Crafts jury, Walker respected plain designs as long as the materials were good and the proportions harmonious.

How the architects interpreted the Colonial Revival for a small-town building could be quite different from how they approached a building for an urban setting, especially Boston. The Kirstein Memorial Library, located in the heart of the city, is an elegant federal revival design that explicitly recalls one of Boston's great architectural losses (fig. 6.16). Designed by Putnam and Cox, the facade of what was a business library closely approximates the central pavilion of Bulfinch's Tontine Crescent, a town house development from 1794 that was demolished in the late 1850s.[37] The red-brick building incorporates all the major elements of the Bulfinch design: the arch on the ground floor; a Palladian window framed by two-story columns and pilasters on the second and third levels; with a fanlight and a pediment at the top. When the library opened in 1930, the press explained the reason for the allusion.[38] In the rooms above the Tontine Crescent arch, some of the space was allocated to the Boston Library Society, the earliest collection of books available to the city's residents. The Kirstein Library thus suggested Boston's library tradition as well as a work of one of its great architects. Although often not obvious, the designs of Bulfinch provided ideas for a multitude of Colonial Revival buildings.

At Home in Historic Houses

Several of the architects and supporters who became active in the Society of Arts and Crafts bought colonial and federal houses for themselves. They had read and reread Ruskin, and they responded to his passion for England's medieval buildings by transforming it into a passion for the houses of early New England. The Society for the Protection of Ancient Buildings, established by Morris in 1877, also was galvanizing. In the Boston area,

FIG. 6.17 R. Clipston Sturgis, Martine Cottage, Portsmouth, NH, circa 1690 house renovated and expanded, 1890.

Charles Eliot Norton's fondness for old New England houses, including his eighteenth-century house in Ashfield, was widely known. The region's literary figures contributed to this interest, too. Emerson's love of the landscapes of early New England was taken to heart, as was the poetry of Henry Wadsworth Longfellow, replete with affectionate images of the region's colonial period.

In 1886 J. Templeman Coolidge Jr., an artist who would become a founder of the Society of Arts and Crafts, chairman of its jury, and president from 1933 to 1935, bought Wentworth Farm in Little Harbor, New Hampshire, outside Portsmouth.[39] The rambling colonial house that anchors the farm had been the setting for Longfellow's poem "Lady Wentworth" and was the subject of a drawing that Robert Swain Peabody published in 1877 in the *American Architect and Building News*.[40] Coolidge turned to Waddy Longfellow, who had just launched his practice, to oversee the restoration of the house and to expand a henhouse and barn, converting them into additional quarters for what would become a family compound along Sagamore Creek.[41] Within a few years, the area grew into a summer colony, including several residents who would play leading roles in the Society of Arts and Crafts. A year after buying Wentworth Farm, Coolidge sold forty acres to Arthur Carey, who promptly built a large summer home that Longfellow designed.[42] The property that Carey acquired included a diminutive colonial house, said to date from 1690, called Martine Cottage.

In 1890 Carey sold the little house to Clipston Sturgis and his family, thereby welcoming them into the summer retreat.[43] Martine Cottage was a one-story frame building with a pitched roof and dormers in the attic; a single window was positioned on either side of the center entrance. A large central chimney stack with three hearths served a kitchen, another comparably sized room, and a little room in the back. To create more living space, Sturgis elongated the house and added a wing to the rear (fig. 6.17). In 1903 he published an article in *House and Garden* about the Wentworth house and Martine Cottage. He encouraged his readers to see the "artistic value of restraint" in old New England houses and observed that in "simplicity of sentiment," the Wentworth house was like the much smaller cottage.[44] Sturgis wrote in the language of the Society of Arts and Crafts.

Langford Warren also was attracted to living in a colonial house. Shortly after his marriage in November of 1887, he and his wife moved into a mid- to late-eighteenth-century house in the Boston suburb of Newton.[45] It was a two-story wood structure, massed under a hip roof, with a door in the center and pairs of windows at each side on both stories. In 1889 the house was described and illustrated in *King's Handbook of Newton, Massachusetts* because of its historic interest.[46] Despite this distinction, Warren felt no qualms about making changes to the structure, just as Sturgis proceeded to modify and expand Martine Cottage. Warren added a porch with columns to one side of the house and an extension to the rear. On the main facade, he appears to have added a portico and inserted an oriel window above it.

Similarly, in 1906 Cram and his wife bought a federal house in Sudbury, west of Boston, which Cram enhanced and expanded. Dating from around 1815, the house is two stories high, sheathed in clapboard, and symmetrically planned around a center entrance. Cram added a balustrade to the shallow hip roof and installed trellises and a pair of wood benches to frame the front door. A second story was constructed over a group of sheds adjacent to the house, and a large new wing accommodated his library.[47] Named Whitehall, the Cram estate encompassed more than 100 acres. Eventually, the author of *Church Building* and architect of dozens of churches wanted his own place for worship. In 1914 Cram erected a simple chapel, incorporating fieldstone from the property—using the very material he had once scorned.[48] Always emphatic in his views, Cram was capable of changing his mind.

By the turn of the twentieth century, colonial and federal houses were attracting more and more interest, and Howe regularly was hired to update and enlarge them for clients. In 1898 she oversaw the expansion of an early nineteenth-century farmhouse in East Billerica, northwest of Boston, for Boston painter H. Winthrop Peirce and W. H. Smith. A sizable addition included a studio that was open to the second floor, with north-facing windows and a large fireplace.[49] In 1908 John C. Runkle bought a Brattle Street house in Cambridge, dating from about 1765, and moved it to a lot around the corner where Howe directed its reconstruction.[50] Often antique houses weren't wanted when they were occupying desirable lots, but they appealed to buyers who were willing to move and rebuild them. Between 1913 and 1915, Longfellow took on a similar project when he was retained by Eleanor Gray Tudor to oversee the relocation of a distinguished federal house, also in Cambridge, that dated from 1808.[51]

Historic Houses for Institutions

As the region's Yankee population prospered, its members occasionally purchased old houses, preferably with some historic association, to serve educational, social, and cultural institutions. In 1885, for example, a two-story house at the edge of Cambridge Common was acquired for the future Radcliffe College, at that time called the Harvard Annex, which had been established six years earlier for the education of women. The house, dating from 1806, was valued in part because it was constructed of brick—unusual for a Cambridge dwelling of this vintage.[52] Funding to rebuild and expand it came from one of the college's founders, Alice Longfellow, who engaged her cousin Waddy for the project. Between 1890 and 1893, Fay House gained new classrooms, a library, and a music room (fig. 6.18). A new staircase and new woodwork reflected the architect's understanding of high-style federal architecture and ornament. Assisting Waddy with the interior finishes was Sarah Whitman, an artist and founding member of the Society of Arts and Crafts. In describing the work on the building, the Boston press noted that the interior would be painted "sage green" with "cream white" woodwork. As it happened, this information was reported in November of 1891, coinciding with the announcement about the choice of "cream white" for the woodwork inside Warren's town hall in Lincoln—further evidence of the language, both visual and verbal, shared by the leaders in the Society of Arts and Crafts.[53]

Historic houses were readily adapted for use by private clubs. In 1882 the Country Club was founded in Brookline, the first organization of this

type in the country.[54] When the club was established, the members leased an 1802 farmhouse, buying the buildings and land five years later. Eventually the two-story clapboarded house was deemed too small, and in 1901, Andrews, Jaques, and Rantoul designed an addition (fig. 6.19). Two years later they oversaw a further expansion, which included a ballroom, a new dining room, a kitchen, and offices. The informal image of a farmhouse meshed with the concept of a place where suburban residents could gather to pursue equestrian sports, lawn tennis, and golf. As a gathering place for a group that included descendants of some of the region's earliest inhabitants, the antique house reinforced their sense of connection with the past.

In the Boston suburb of Winchester, a similar strategy was followed. Winchester Country Club was founded in 1897, and five years later, the members bought an early nineteenth-century farmhouse and land on the Arlington-Winchester line. In 1916 they commissioned Warren and Smith to restore the farmhouse, convert a barn into a social hall, and build locker rooms.[55] The rustic character of the barn was complemented by the addition of a massive brick fireplace and plastered walls with exposed framing timbers.

A historic house could also meet the needs of a city club. In 1901 the Graduate Club in New Haven, Connecticut, bought a federal period house on Elm Street overlooking the historic green. The club was founded in 1892

FIG. 6.19 Andrews, Jaques, and Rantoul, the Country Club, Brookline, MA, 1802 house renovated and expanded, 1901 and 1903.

FIG. 6.20 R. Clipston Sturgis, Graduate Club, New Haven, CT, 1799 house renovated and expanded, 1901–2.

by a group of young college graduates, who hired Sturgis to take charge of the remodeling and expansion of a house that had been built for Jonathan Mix in 1799 (fig. 6.20).[56] A two-story, clapboarded structure, it had pairs of windows on each side of a central door that was surmounted by a Palladian window. Sturgis preserved the small rooms of the original house, but

FIG. 6.21 Lois L. Howe, Concord Art Center for the Concord Art Association, Concord, MA, 1761 house remodeled, 1922–23.

he opened the rear to connect to a large brick addition. The new space on the main level accommodated a paneled social hall with a balcony and two fireplaces, and the second floor included a library, a boardroom, and guest rooms, all stylistically consistent with the historic house.

More extensive interventions were required to transform an old house into the Concord Art Center near Boston, but the aura of history that the building evoked was valued there, too. The Concord Art Association was established in 1917 through the leadership of Elizabeth Wentworth Roberts, a painter from a wealthy Philadelphia family. In 1922 she bought "an old colonial mansion" and engaged Howe to reconfigure it (fig. 6.21). Although not exactly a mansion, the John Ball house, built in 1761, was a generously sized dwelling adjacent to the town center. When the remodeling was finished in 1923, the rooms on the first floor became small galleries, and the doors and hardware were preserved. Upstairs, the interior walls were removed, and the space was opened into the attic, creating a large exhibition area. Howe also added steel to reinforce the building. To commemorate the achievement, the association published a booklet about the art center. Readers were encouraged to envision how the house had witnessed the Red Coats "as they marched by to meet the farmers at the Old North Bridge," a location where more recent ceremonies took place "in the shadow of the pine trees planted by Ralph Waldo Emerson."[57] By establishing themselves in the John Ball house, Roberts and the Concord Art Association members embraced not only local colonial history but also the town's reputation as the home of one of New England's most prominent intellectual figures of the nineteenth century.

Preserving Architectural Monuments

The desire to preserve the region's buildings of architectural and historical significance gained momentum at the turn of the twentieth century. For Boston's architects, the restoration of the Massachusetts State House between 1896 and 1898 was a major triumph, with Andrews contributing both to the preservation campaign and to the actual work. In the next two decades, several of the architects involved in Boston's Arts and Crafts movement devoted themselves to the cause of preservation. As usual, they stayed informed about the efforts of their English counterparts. In November of 1900, *Architectural Review* reported that C. R. Ashbee would be leaving his practice to further the work of the National Trust for Places of Historic Interest or Natural Beauty, which had been established in 1894.[58] Earlier that fall, Ashbee had embarked on a tour of the United States to promote the organization. Boston was on his itinerary, and his visit included a meeting with Norton and an address to the Society of Arts and Crafts.[59] Committed to various endeavors relating to preservation, Ashbee had founded the Survey of London to document monuments and encourage an appreciation for them. His personal agenda was far-reaching, and he advocated tirelessly for a range of issues relating to land use and social reform. Although he was frustrated by the people he met in Boston and Philadelphia, finding them to be self-satisfied, he also believed that in these two cities, "more work has been done in the direction we are aiming than in any others in America I have visited."[60]

Even if Bostonians were not as ambitious as Ashbee, the narrower focus on protecting the region's architectural heritage was taking hold. In 1910 William Sumner Appleton Jr., who had studied with both Norton and Denman Ross at Harvard, founded the Society for the Preservation of New England Antiquities.[61] Two years later, the preservation society's bulletin reported on "The Movement to Buy the Cooper-Austin House," located in Cambridge and dating to the mid-seventeenth century.[62] One of the five people who coordinated raising the funds to buy it was Howe, and it became the third house to be acquired by Appleton's organization.

By 1913 the Society for the Preservation of New England Antiquities listed Cram, Howe, Longfellow, and Ross as members.[63] Cram also would serve as a trustee, and the Boston Society of Architects joined as an institutional member.

In their private practices, Sturgis and Andrews were commissioned to restore several of the region's most important historic buildings. Between 1912 and 1914, Sturgis directed the work on Boston's Christ Church, better known as Old North Church (1722–24). Long pews were removed, and original box pews were reinstalled. Sturgis restored the chancel, which had been shortened; reopened the chancel windows; and added a new colonial-style wineglass pulpit and sounding board. When white paint was found beneath gray, the church trim was repainted white.[64] Between 1914 and 1917, Andrews, assisted by Sturgis and William Chapman, oversaw the construction of new wings on the Bulfinch State House. Over their objections, the legislature determined that the additions would be clad in white marble. Appleton was dismayed, fearing that the Bulfinch building would be veneered in marble to match. Although the State House was spared this indignity, the red brick was painted white.[65] The outcome was disappointing, but the expansion further assured the preservation of the original building.

In Hartford, another preservation effort addressed the old Connecticut State House, which opened in 1796 and is generally accepted as the work of Bulfinch. It had served as the state capitol until 1873, when a larger building was erected. Between 1918 and 1920, Andrews and H. Hilliard Smith of Hartford directed the restoration of the Old State House. In its bulletin, the Society for the Preservation of New England Antiquities reported that the work had been "excellently carried out."[66]

When the Society of Arts and Crafts was founded in June of 1897, not only was the restoration of the Massachusetts State House moving forward. That spring, the manuscript written by William Bradford, governor of the Plymouth colony, was delivered from London to Boston.[67] With much fanfare, on May 26, 1897, a joint convention of both houses was held in the Representatives' Chamber of the State House, where legislators and dignitaries heard orations about Bradford's chronicle and the valor of the pilgrims. The manuscript, written from 1620 to 1647, was enshrined in a bronze and glass case in the State House library, and an edited version was published that same year. The pride in the region's colonial heritage and history was thus refueled.

From Italy to Japan

In addition to designing Gothic Revival and Colonial Revival buildings, the architects in this circle pursued a limited number of other stylistic directions. One such direction was loosely classical, informed by the Italian Renaissance and marked by restraint. The vocabulary for these buildings also was mastered by the society's craftsmen. Typically, the Boston version of the Renaissance revival was adopted for august institutions such as banks. For Catholic churches, Maginnis recommended a Lombard Gothic—a style that seemed suitable for the many parishes that wanted to build with brick. And although never common, the architecture of Japan inspired a few projects, reflecting an early and serious investigation into Japanese art and architecture, both in Boston and in the Society of Arts and Crafts.

Writing in 1897 about developments in American design, Andrews observed that the most important recent buildings were in the "classic style," except for the Gothic churches.[68] Tall buildings, he continued, reflected the tendency toward classicism. Andrews also was cognizant of recent developments in the West—a reference to Chicago—where the architects were willing to "present the real facts of structural necessity in their naked simplicity." His position, however, was not that tall buildings in the East should emulate Chicago-style simplicity. Rather, he hoped to see an "intermingling" of the western "love of construction" with "the wider cultivation of the eastern seaboard."[69] Cultivation meant classicism. More specifically, Andrews advised that the architect's classical models should draw upon archaic periods. He believed that the later periods of all arts become artificial—an underlying theme in the fine arts courses taught by Norton.

What Andrews had in mind can be better appreciated through the example of the State Mutual Building, a ten-story structure in the commercial center of Boston that provided offices for the State Mutual Insurance Company, the State National Bank, and other businesses (fig. 6.22). Dating from 1902 to 1903, the building was designed by Andrews, Jaques, and Rantoul, and when it was completed, the partners moved their firm into the top floor.[70] At the street level, the facade features five large arches, the center arch framed by engaged Corinthian columns. Rusticated limestone activates the first two stories, whereas the office stories are plain and taut: mainly buff-colored Roman brick with flat courses of stone between levels of windows. The top floor, faced with stone, is decorated with foliated brackets that support a cornice and copper cresting. Thus the building "intermin-

FIG. 6.22 Andrews, Jaques, and Rantoul, State Mutual Building, Boston, 1902–3.

FIG. 6.23 State Mutual Building, capital by Hugh Cairns.

gles," as Andrews would have said, an urban facade from Quattrocento Italy with the austere ideal of modern Chicago. Hugh Cairns provided carved stone ornament (fig. 6.23), and Hecla Iron Works fabricated bronze doors and an elevator screen. Hecla Iron Works, like Cairns, participated in the activities of the Society of Arts and Crafts.[71]

Sturgis subscribed to a similar line of classicism. In 1919, when he was president of the Society of Arts and Crafts, he developed the plans for the Federal Reserve Bank of Boston (fig. 6.24). It also was a sober interpretation of Italian Renaissance architecture, intended to suggest "the great houses of Florence, Genoa and other North Italian cities."[72] Completed in 1922, it was built of rusticated granite on the ground floor and limestone on the main four stories. A bay at the center projects slightly to emphasize the entrance to the building, while the *piano nobile* is animated by arches alternating with spare pilasters. In the fashion of an Italian palazzo, the top of the bank is defined by a heavy cornice and balustrade. Although there is little ornament on the exterior, the interior was finished with columns, coffering, and swags, all supplied by Evans.[73]

For Maginnis, the question at the beginning of his career was how to apply the principles of Boston's Arts and Crafts movement to the design of

FIG. 6.24 R. Clipston
Sturgis, Federal
Reserve Bank of
Boston (Langham
Hotel), 1919–22.

Catholic churches. Most parish budgets were relatively small, and therefore the buildings were often constructed of brick rather than stone. When Maginnis received a commission to design St. Patrick's Church in Whitinsville, south of Worcester, Massachusetts, he found the solution to his problem in the Gothic churches of Lombardy (fig. 6.25). They were brick and they were simple. Dating from 1898, St. Patrick's was well received, a perspective of it illustrated in the catalogue of Boston's major architectural exhibition in 1899.[74] Two years later, Maginnis published "A Criticism of Catholic Architecture in the United States" in *Architectural Review*.[75] He was distressed by brick used in styles that had originated in stone, and by plastered ceilings that were intended to give the illusion of stone vaulting. Equally distasteful were churches decorated with simulated marble—popularized, he added, by "the cheap fanfare of the New York hotel." Maginnis, like Ruskin half a century earlier, argued for "the moral principle in architecture."[76] In future years, Maginnis returned to the Lombard Gothic style for brick churches while he also introduced a variant based on the Byzantine brick churches from Ravenna.

The plan of St. Patrick's Church is rectangular, terminating in an apse, with an octagonal chapel and a campanile to the rear. Red-brick walls are

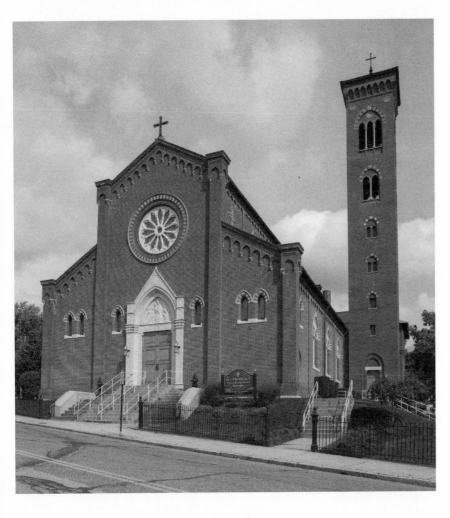

FIG. 6.25 Maginnis and Walsh, St. Patrick's Church, Whitinsville, MA, 1898.

accented by buff-colored brick on the Gothic arches and a rose window. Inside, the clerestory roof is left open, with the wood trusses visible, and the clerestory walls are supported by columns between the church nave and side aisles. As an economical way to provide sculpture, Maginnis regularly employed terra cotta. In the tympanum over the entrance is a relief of Mary and the Christ Child with Saints Patrick and Bridget, cast in terra cotta and probably modeled by Cairns. Stained-glass windows were designed by Harry Goodhue, and the stenciling inside was the work of L. Haberstroh and Son, a decorating firm that participated in the Society of Arts and Crafts exhibitions.[77]

The fascination with Japan, which swept Europe and the United States during the second half of the nineteenth century and contributed to the Aesthetic movement, took a scholarly turn in Boston in the late 1870s. In

1877 Edward S. Morse of Salem, Massachusetts, traveled to Japan to teach zoology in Tokyo. There he began collecting ceramics and pottery, eventually becoming an expert on the Japanese arts, including architecture. Through the efforts of Morse, Ernest F. Fenollosa, and William Sturgis Bigelow, Boston's Museum of Fine Arts acquired the nation's leading collection of Japanese art. In 1885 Morse published *Japanese Homes and Their Surroundings*.[78]

Three years later, Morse was back in Salem cataloging his collection, assisted by a young Japanese man named Bunkio Matsuki. By 1894 Matsuki was running a successful business selling Japanese wares in a Salem store and was married to a local woman. With the help of Andrews, Jaques, and Rantoul, the couple built a Japanese American house on a lot next door to Morse (fig. 6.26).[79] On the whole, it is a typical New England dwelling: two stories high, with double-hung sash windows, and sheathed in clapboard. But it has a gabled roof at the top that extends into a hip roof with overhanging eaves, following the Japanese manner. The main entrance is reached through a porch covered by a shed roof and protected by a panel that hangs like a *shoji* screen. On the second floor is a recessed balcony, a common feature in Japanese houses.

Probably by coincidence, in 1894 Cram was commissioned to design a Japanese-influenced house for Arthur M. Knapp and his wife in Fall River, Massachusetts (fig. 6.27).[80] A Unitarian minister, Knapp had lived in Japan and wanted a home that was reminiscent of its architecture. The Knapp house, like the Matsuki house, is conventionally American with its two-

story massing and double-hung windows. Like the Matsuki house, the
Knapp house has a roofline that is Japanese in character as well as a recessed
second-floor balcony. But the Knapp house is considerably more elaborate,
with a roof that is pierced by an eyebrow dormer and flares at the corners.
It also is ornamented with carved panels around the front door and on the
second floor under the windows and across the balcony. Through Knapp's
contacts, Cram pursued a commission to design a new Parliament for Japan, traveling there in January of 1898. The project fell through, but Cram's
involvement with Japanese architecture continued. Later that year, he designed a tea house for the rear of the Knapp house.

Although the Knapp house became the most recognized Japanese-style
residence to appear in New England, several other Japanese-inspired buildings were erected in and around the island colony of North Haven, Maine,
in Penobscot Bay, starting in the 1890s. A real estate developer there, J. Murray Howe, had become enthralled by Japan through his father-in-law, who
had traveled to Japan in 1855 and established a trading company. In developing the North Haven summer community, Howe incorporated Japanese architectural elements into several of his buildings, including the Hiroshima
guest house of 1896.[81] Howe's flights of fancy would have been known to the
Boston architect Edmund Wheelwright, who had been employed by Howe
and who also owned land on North Haven. Perhaps not coincidentally, in
July of 1896, Wheelwright published a design for a pagoda-like shelter and
duck house for Boston's Back Bay Fens in the *American Architect and Build-*

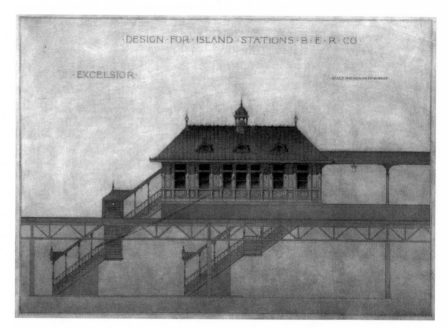

DESIGN·FOR·ISLAND·STATIONS·B·E·R·CO·

·EXCELSIOR·

FIG. 6.28 Alexander
W. Longfellow Jr.,
Boston Elevated
Railway Station,
competition entry,
1898.

ing News.[82] The draftsman was Maginnis, then working for the city under Wheelwright. The structures for the Fens were never built, but Wheelwright's flirtation with Japan presents further evidence of the fascination with the country among Boston architects.

Within a year after the Society of Arts and Crafts was founded, Cram, excited by his travels and new expertise, was publishing articles about Japanese architecture in *Architectural Record* and *Architectural Review*. In 1899 Morse lectured to the society on "The Industrial Arts of Japan," and Ross lent his Japanese and Chinese bronzes to the second Arts and Crafts exhibition. In the opening years of the new century, Cram and Morse lectured to the society about Japanese topics again. J. Templeman Coolidge wrote about Japanese wood carving in *Handicraft*, and Morse and Thomas Mott Shaw, George Shaw's architect son, sent their Japanese pottery and pewter jars to the 1907 Arts and Crafts exhibition.[83] To be sure, the architects involved in the society did not believe in reproducing Japanese houses and temples for New England; however, they were attracted to Japanese architectural forms, most notably the rooflines with flaring overhanging eaves. One such example is Longfellow's design for a Boston Elevated Railway station (1898; fig. 6.28). But as Cram wrote, what Japanese architecture offered above all were principles: lessons about a constructional approach to architecture, lessons about an appreciation for the qualities of natural wood, and—most closely aligned with the aesthetic interests of the Boston movement—lessons about conveying a sense of repose.[84]

Looking backward by building on history was fundamental for the leaders of Boston's Arts and Crafts movement. They had no sympathy for Art Nouveau. Writing in the January 1904 issue of *Architectural Review* about the new style, Walker declared that it was "socialism in art." Its followers belonged to a cult for whom "the art of the past" was dead.[85] To Walker, Art Nouveau designs were chaotic, dependent on fantasy and defiant of teaching. He conceded that in the applied arts, such as jewelry and ceramics, the forms could be successful, but for architecture, he said, Art Nouveau "violates constructive laws." Darmstadt's Peter Behrens, the Glasgow School, and England's M. H. Baillie Scott all were subjected to his criticism. Baillie Scott in particular was lambasted for "unmitigated puerility."[86]

In the same issue, Andrews and Warren paid tribute to English architecture, especially English country houses and parish churches. In taking their inspiration from English and English colonial sources, Boston's architects certainly had company across the United States. But the architects in Boston embraced those sources above all, while rejecting the many stylistic directions that proliferated at the turn of the century. Just as the styles that Walker categorized as "Art Nouveau" were to be avoided, so was French Beaux-Arts classicism. New York's manifestations were the cause of much consternation, its new buildings scorned for their love of display and magnificence. More than a little hopefully, the Boston architects wondered "whether there will not soon come a reaction, with a return to extreme simplicity in the city's art and architecture."[87] In the early years of the twentieth century, a return to simplicity—and its companion virtue, sincerity—seemed likely, if not inevitable.

CHAPTER SEVEN

Looking Forward:
Building for the Twentieth Century

Perhaps paradoxically, the architects who were most prominent in Boston's Society of Arts and Crafts could be described as both backward looking and forward looking. In their commitment to history and devotion to historic architectural styles, based mainly on English and regional colonial sources, they mirrored a wider culture. Indeed, during the years when the Arts and Crafts movement was in its ascendancy, a love of scholarship in the region contributed to solidifying Boston's position as the country's intellectual capital. By contrast, New York City glittered, having secured its position as the nation's commercial capital, and its architecture reflected this orientation.

The cultural distinctions between these two centers were observed by England's H. G. Wells when he published *The Future in America* in 1906.[1] Nevertheless, Boston was vibrant, too, and its architects were fully engaged with the modern age. The city was rumbling into the new century, the nation's first subway having opened there in 1897, the year when the Society of Arts and Crafts was founded. In many respects, buildings erected by the group's leading architects could be characterized as forward looking. Some of their designs were reductive in approach. The architects also experimented with new materials. And they assiduously examined the needs of modern society, devising functional plans and finishes.

Attentive to the exhortations of Norton and the writings of Morris, the architects were mindful of the miserable conditions afflicting the worker and the immigrant. They believed in the potential of their profession and that they could improve people's lives. In his autobiography, Cram described the architects' buoyant optimism during those years, recalling, "To us it was a golden age, with the promise of high fulfillment."[2] Sam Warren expressed a similar outlook when he wrote to Brandeis about forming a partnership. He hoped that as lawyers they might become involved with public work, telling his former classmate that "together we could make a more gallant fight."[3] Although the society rejected the socialism of Morris and the broad reform agenda of C. R. Ashbee, several of the architects were drawn to projects such as community centers and worker housing that were tinged with an Arts and Crafts ethos. Often the architects became allies with their wealthy friends and clients to erect buildings that would serve Progressive Era institutions and causes, focusing on the future.

A Reductive Approach

To the extent that they reflect historic precedents, the buildings designed by Boston's Arts and Crafts architects contrast strikingly with the work of the Prairie School architects, most notably Frank Lloyd Wright, and the work of the Californians such as the Greene brothers and Irving Gill. Yet in striving for simplicity, Boston's architects shared with the more stylistically innovative architects an interest in reducing their designs to fundamental shapes.

One sizable group of these buildings was shingled houses. Having flourished during the 1880s, the Shingle Style in New England continued to evolve through the turn of the century.[4] Some of the houses included classical ornament such as columns, urns, and swags, but others were completely lacking in ornament. Rather than columns, porches might be supported by squared posts and brackets or piers covered in shingles. The success of the designs depended solely on the expression of massing, shadow, and texture. Often these houses were erected in summer retreats.

One such destination grew around Lake Chocorua in Tamworth, New Hampshire, where several distinguished Bostonians including the Harvard psychologist William James spent their summers. Walker designed at least a half-dozen houses there, one of which was a home for his family. Howe also designed at least one house.[5] Shortly after buying property overlooking the lake in 1891, Walker and his wife built Pine Cone (pl. 7). Covered by a hipped roof, the house is shingled and sits on a fieldstone foundation. Rising from the foundation are fieldstone piers, which carry a porch roof that runs across the front of the house and wraps around one corner. Above the front entrance, on the second story, is a bay that encloses a sleeping porch. Like the main roof, the porch roof and sleeping-porch roof are hipped, creating a repetition of spreading pyramidal forms. Some of the Walker family's furnishings remain inside today, including a large wood trestle table and wrought-iron andirons, almost certainly made by members of the Society

FIG. 7.1 Alexander W. Longfellow Jr., the Graunkar, Brown house, Falmouth, ME, 1901.

of Arts and Crafts. They are simple in design and emphasize the materials from which they were fashioned, in keeping with the principles underlying the design of the house.

Writing in 1904, Walker stated that the best architecture, whatever the style or material, "should be so designed and proportioned that ornament need not be a part of it." He discussed how architecture is "primarily proportioned construction," adding that the "first duty" of any ornament is that it not deny or violate the expression of the building's construction. Especially on the exterior of buildings, Walker explained, broad surfaces generally "are best left plain."[6] He and his colleagues were committed to restraint and respected designs that were spare and unassuming.

Waddy Longfellow took a similar approach for residences in Maine, beginning in the late 1880s and continuing well into the twentieth century.[7] An especially fine example was the Graunkar (1901), built for Herbert J. Brown and his wife in Falmouth on a site overlooking Casco Bay (fig. 7.1).[8] The two-and-a-half-story house was asymmetrical, planned as a T positioned on its side, with the entrance located in the long axis and a perpendicular wing extending to the front and rear at one end. An overhanging roof with

FIG. 7.2 Andrews and Jaques, Perkins house, Beverly Farms, MA, 1888.

visible rafter tails added shadow and depth to the overall effect. The entire house was clad in shingles, the walls enlivened by patterns of windows divided by small panes. A pair of settle benches greeted the visitor at the entrance and, along with the shingles and windows, alluded to colonial New England architecture. But on the whole, the aesthetic success of the house was based on its massing and texture.

Like the shingled houses, houses finished in stucco were often fairly austere and may be considered protomodern. An early illustration of this development is the summer house designed in 1888 by Andrews and Jaques for Elizabeth W. Perkins on an oceanfront property in Beverly Farms, north of Boston (fig. 7.2).[9] Wide and low, the house has overhanging eaves with prominent rafter tails, while the second story jetties over the first story, supported by wood brackets. On one side of the entry elevation is a portion of a two-story octagon that dies into the rectangular end of the house. Notes of craftsmanship are provided by dark wood brackets supporting an entrance canopy and wrought-iron grilles covering two front windows.

Both Putnam and Maginnis built homes for their families in the suburb of Brookline, and both took a reductive approach in designing with stucco. The Putnam house (1910) is just one story, planned in a square with an open court at the center, recalling the courts of Greek and Roman houses (fig. 7.3).[10] At one corner of the square, a projecting rectangular mass contains the dining room, and another rectangular mass contains what was a sleeping loggia. A third corner opens into a portion of an octagon and is covered

PUTNAM & COX, ARCHITECTS, BOSTON, MASS.

HOUSE FOR MRS. WM. E. PUTNAM, JR. THE COURT IN WINTER

HOUSE FOR MRS. WM. E. PUTNAM, JR. THE LIVING ROOM

FIG. 7.3 William E. Putnam Jr., Putnam house, Brookline, MA, 1910.

by an octagonal roof, while triangular dormers animate the roof on all elevations. Simplified classical columns frame the front entrance, and similar columns are located on two sides of the interior court. Other than the plan, they are the only allusions to architectural precedent.

The Maginnis house (1920) similarly represents an abstract interpretation of earlier traditions, but in this case, it is reminiscent of English medieval houses and American seventeenth-century houses (pl. 8). An asymmetrical design includes a steeply pitched roof broken by cross-gables and dormers, covering broad expanses of wall. Emphasizing the front door are brackets that support a flat roof with an iron railing, the work of Frank Koralewsky.[11] Contrasting with the minimal decoration of the exterior, Arts and Crafts details enhance the Maginnis house interior, including iron hardware and stained and leaded glass. A carved wood column capital is dedicated on its faces to each of the family's four children.

Writing about American houses in 1920, Cram recognized that they were products of a diverse nation with regional and racial differences.[12] He noted, "At present the best we can hope for is increasing good taste, honesty, sincerity, and a fine interpretation of our chosen styles."[13] He admired colonial houses, illustrating several examples, but he also included a house by Wright and another "of the plains type" that he considered successful. Small American houses from the past decade showed the most promise—"a progressive getting away from the over-loaded luxuriance and a return to simple, colloquial modes and manners that are quite beyond all praise."[14] He argued for simplicity, underscoring the importance of "good composition and good workmanship."[15] Decrying Georgian mantels decorated with glued-on molded ornament and mechanically cut stone, he concluded by calling for good craftsmanship. Echoing the views of Ruskin, Morris, and Norton, Cram wrote that "it is the hand of man that counts."[16] Whether they were invoking the ideals of sincerity or handicraft, Cram and his colleagues may be considered backward looking, especially by 1920. But in their advocacy for simple designs, they were in accord with emerging modernists such as Wright.

Stucco, Concrete, and Steel

Much as the architects in this circle were committed to quality craftsmanship, they also were receptive to the potential of new building products. Stucco, which was common in Europe, attracted the architects' attention.

Yet in the example of the Elizabeth Perkins house, it may have been the client who proposed using the new material. Even though the house does not express an obvious style on the entrance facade, it opened on the ocean facade to a patio that was Moorish, tiled on the floor and walls, and oriented around a low tiled fountain. Choosing to build with stucco in 1888 was unusual, and perhaps Perkins thought the material would suggest a Mediterranean villa.

In 1907 Perkins lent historic objects to the Society of Arts and Crafts exhibition, and in 1911 she helped organize a decorative arts exhibition in Boston, lending dozens of her own treasures, including furniture, tile, and jewelry, mainly from the Middle Ages and Renaissance.[17] Many of the objects were Spanish, including a Gothic iron jewel box and dagger, sixteenth-century glass, and "Hispano-Mauresque" tiles.[18] It is also possible that the architects of the Perkins house, Andrews and Jaques, presented stucco as an option, intrigued by the way it had been used by a colleague. Between 1887 and 1888, Warren designed and built a stucco house for William B. Strong in Brookline. By this time, the three architects had become close friends, having worked together for Richardson, and they would have stayed abreast of each other's projects.[19]

By the early twentieth century, stucco houses had become more common, reflecting the interest among Boston architects in houses designed by English architects, who were using the material frequently.[20] In 1907 the architect Frank Chouteau Brown, a member of the Society of Arts and Crafts, wrote about "Exterior Plaster Construction" in a three-part series in *Architectural Review*. Significantly, Brown commented on the "comparatively recent introduction" of the material in the United States.[21] His observation leads one to better appreciate the innovative spirit of Andrews, Jaques, and Warren in designing stucco houses during the late 1880s.[22] Brown went on to state, "Of all the materials available for the exterior treatment and surfacing of the small or inexpensive dwelling, none other offers such attractive effects as are inexpensively obtained by the use of cement plaster."[23] Although cheaper than stone or brick, stucco was not, in fact, inexpensive, and Brown acknowledged that it cost more than clapboards or shingles. But stucco was more durable and required less maintenance than any wood cladding. Among the projects that Brown illustrated was a stucco house by Howe.

Building with reinforced concrete also attracted the architects. Yet whether the material would hold up, especially in New England, was far from certain. Between 1897 and 1900, Warren collaborated with Lewis J.

FIG. 7.4 Warren and Smith, Chadwick house, Winchester, MA, 1909.

Johnson and Ira N. Hollis, professors of engineering at Harvard, on the design of a gate and fence piers for Soldiers Field, the university's athletic grounds.[24] To give the concrete texture, a heavy aggregate was employed, and to provide color, brick trim was added. The experiment was judged a success and led Harvard to build a stadium of ferroconcrete, completed in 1903. Warren and his business partner, Frank Patterson Smith, applied the experience at Harvard to the design of a reinforced concrete house for Everett D. Chadwick in Winchester, Massachusetts (1909), that was Georgian Revival in style (fig. 7.4).[25] Like the gate and fence at Soldiers Field, the concrete of the Chadwick house was mixed with pebbles that became visible when the forms were removed and the surface brushed. Red brick accented the corners and window openings, and the house was enhanced by traditional Arts and Crafts elements such as Grueby tile, wrought iron, and leaded glass.

Andrews, Jaques, and Rantoul designed a concrete house, Rockledge,

FIG. 7.5 Andrews, Jaques, and Rantoul, Rockledge, Walker house, Gloucester, MA, 1910–12.

that was located in Gloucester, Massachusetts, perched on a granite point above the Atlantic Ocean. Rockledge was built as a summer retreat between 1910 and 1912 for James Harrington Walker of Detroit, whose fortune came from the Hiram Walker liquor company (fig. 7.5).[26] Prior to building the house, Walker and his wife had been remodeling an existing house on the site when it caught fire and burned. The decision to rebuild with reinforced concrete walls and floors thus was motivated by the loss and by the couple's desire for fireproof construction. Once the architects and the Walkers established that they would erect a house of concrete, they seem to have become enamored with the material. A concrete retaining wall was constructed to support grass terraces, and concrete columns were cast and installed for a pergola at the edge of a tennis court. Arts and Crafts enrichment is provided by wrought-iron balcony railings, tile paving, and carved stone columns and pilasters at the entry portico.

As the architects ventured into what was in essence new territory—the world of reinforced concrete—they began to theorize about how to design for it. In 1908 C. Howard Walker told readers of *American Architect* that the surfaces of reinforced concrete needed to be respected. If surfaces were to be ornamented, they "should be more generally ornamented than in stone buildings," the concrete evenly encrusted with glass, stone, or clay products.[27] Nevertheless, he considered plain surfaces more than acceptable while ornament could be concentrated at a building's openings and possibly at the cornice. Wrought-metal grilles and balconies as well as elaborate fenestration offered additional opportunities to embellish "a system of structure which is devoid of large piers, deep reveals and heavy shadows."[28] Walker concluded by asserting that an aesthetic treatment of concrete could be achieved without "strange and bizarre forms or detail."[29] Who the perpetrators of such forms were, he did not say, but it was clear that he was aiming a shot at the European architects who were experimenting with concrete to create more expressive designs.

Precast concrete, or "concrete stone," became a favorite building material for the architects mainly because it was more affordable than stone for their clients. Often it was combined with carved stone, especially early on. In drawings for West Roxbury High School in Boston (1898–1901), Andrews, Jaques, and Rantoul called for bosses of carved stone, while moldings for the Tudor Revival building were to be concrete.[30] By the early twentieth century, almost three dozen companies were producing artificial stone in Massachusetts alone.[31] The Boston firm of Emerson and Norris gained recognition for the quality of its stone, specified by Warren and Smith for a 1906 addition to Harvard's Gore Hall, the old college library built of Quincy granite. Sturgis turned to Emerson and Norris for cast stone when he oversaw the construction of the Perkins Institution for the Blind in Watertown (1909–12).[32]

When Cram published *Church Building* in 1901, he criticized imitation materials, including imitation stone, arguing for honesty.[33] But before the decade ended, Cram and his partners had found an attractive product made by the Economy Manufacturing Company of New Haven, Connecticut. There were several advantages of Economy's cast stone over real stone. Besides being cheaper, it was more impermeable than limestone, a long-favored natural material, and it also was more resistant to fire. For St. James Episcopal Church, a Gothic Revival building by Cram, Goodhue, and Ferguson in Woodstock, Vermont (1907–8), Economy provided all the concrete stone trim, including window tracery (fig. 7.6).[34]

The nineteenth-century concern about honesty had fallen by the wayside. Appearance was what the architects valued most, and the concrete

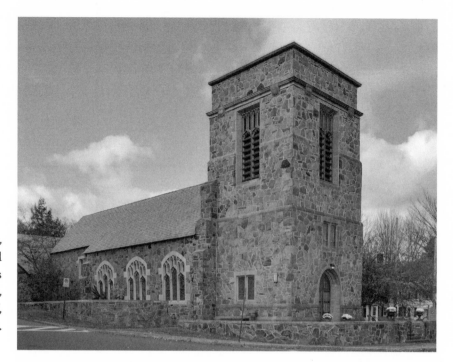

FIG. 7.6 Cram,
Goodhue, and
Ferguson, St. James
Episcopal Church,
Woodstock, VT,
1907–8.

stone made by Economy, mixed with a high percentage of aggregate, met with their approval. In addition to supplying concrete stone, Economy worked with the architects and the sculptor Lee Lawrie, who made models that then were cast. Early in his career, Lawrie had been commissioned by Cram and Goodhue to create the fountain sculpture for Richmond Court, the Gothic Revival apartment building in Brookline from 1898. With the possibility of incorporating modeled rather than carved work in the architects' buildings, sculpture became more affordable, a development that was welcomed.

Steel was problematic, especially for ecclesiastic projects. At the turn of the twentieth century, the architects championed building churches with load-bearing masonry walls and true vaults. Cram sharply criticized "false construction" in church design, explicitly stating that steel covered in stone should be avoided.[35] This view was shared by his colleagues. For example, when Warren, Smith, and Biscoe were awarded the commission to build the Gothic Revival Church of the Epiphany in the Boston suburb of Winchester, begun in 1904, they designed it with brick vaults over the side aisles. To construct the vaults, the masons needed to erect centering—arched wood forms—following the method that had been employed in the Middle Ages.[36]

But for other types of buildings, steel had much to offer, and for certain projects, it was virtually essential. By the early twentieth century, steel had become the standard way to frame an office building, such as the ten-story State Mutual Building in Boston (1902–3) designed by Andrews, Jaques, and Rantoul. More surprising, however, was the fact that Howe called for two steel I-beams to be embedded between the first and second stories of a Tudor-style house constructed in Newburyport, Massachusetts, for Anne M. Paul (1911–12).[37] In the prior century, constructing with steel and then concealing it would have been condemned. By this time, however, most of the architects had accepted the latest construction materials and practices, even if they sometimes struggled to reconcile their designs with their theories and principles.

Modern Demands, Modern Solutions

In planning their buildings, the architects took pride in meeting the demands of modern life. This interest extended to churches, the most traditional of buildings, which were integral to the Arts and Crafts movement in England and New England. Cram wrote that "when we build here in America, we are building for *now*, we are manifesting the living Church."[38] In an article published in 1900 about All Saints Church, Ashmont, in Dorchester, Massachusetts (1891–94), by Cram, Wentworth, and Goodhue, the author pointed out that although it was based on fifteenth-century churches, the plan was modern.[39] Because uninterrupted views of the altar and pulpit were considered desirable, a wide nave was adopted and the side aisles were treated as passages. Writing in 1901 about Catholic architecture in the United States, Maginnis reiterated Cram's view.[40] The designs had to meet modern conditions, he asserted, explaining how the relationship between the nave and aisles needed to be adjusted so that the congregation could see the chancel. To meet modern conditions, the architects also planned social halls, spacious kitchens, and classrooms for religious schools.

Houses were studied, too. Howe, for example, gave much thought to kitchens and pantries, offering the benefit of her experience in an article published in 1907.[41] In designing these rooms, she wanted them to be functional and convenient. At a time when the layout of cooking and serving areas was evolving, Howe's desire to provide sufficient counter space was practical and analytical. She didn't like it when upper cabinets were so deep or shelves so high that a "short woman" struggled. She wanted drawers that were big enough to store a turkey platter or hold tablecloths. Her suggestion for kitchen walls was especially forward looking. She advised using white paint, conceding that her view could seem "daring." But, she elaborated in the article, "there are enamel paints on the market which will wear well and wash like a china bowl, and look as clean as tiling." When building houses where servants would be employed, Howe encouraged providing comfortable spaces for them. If there were no servants' sitting room, she wrote, an alcove could suffice as a place to retire.[42]

Commissions to design town halls meshed with the architects' values. As seats of self-governance, they embodied ideals extolled by Ruskin and Norton. By the turn of the twentieth century, most communities in New England had erected municipal buildings, but many of them were frame and small. New town halls were constructed of brick or stone, were planned with spaces that served town meetings, and provided offices for an expanding number of boards and departments. Warren's Town Hall in Lincoln, Massachusetts (1891–92), established the type at an early date, with offices on the first floor and an assembly room on the second floor. Warren subsequently designed a town hall for Billerica, Massachusetts (1894–95), and the city hall for Concord, New Hampshire (1902–3).[43] In addition to designing the city hall for Cambridge, Longfellow in 1911 designed a town hall for Lancaster, Massachusetts, to complement a surviving 1817 church by Bulfinch.[44] Elsewhere in Greater Boston, Andrews, Jaques, and Rantoul were engaged to build Nahant Town Hall (1912), and Sturgis was retained to erect town halls for Arlington (1912) and Watertown (1931–32).

Public schools were another building category that the architects analyzed and designed in great numbers. Andrews, Sturgis, and Walker received commissions for schoolhouses early in their careers, and Cram, Longfellow, Maginnis, and Newhall also were hired for these projects. After the Massachusetts legislature established the Schoolhouse Commission in 1901 to oversee the design and construction of Boston's school buildings, Sturgis led a tour around the country to study educational facilities.[45] Both *Architectural Review* and *American Architect and Building News* reported on Boston's novel arrangement and the conclusions of the national study.[46] Red brick was recommended over the light brick being used in New York. In Washington, D.C., the schools were not fireproof, and in Chicago the schools had only fireproof corridors; however, fireproof construction was considered essential. Wood flooring in corridors was deemed undesirable, whereas terrazzo, cement, or rock asphalt were endorsed. Stairways, classrooms, and lavatories all were scrutinized. Plans were analyzed, and attention was given to lighting, ventilation, and sanitation.

The architects' interest in public school buildings brought together an Arts and Crafts concern for improving the lot of the working class, a Progressive Era faith in scientific study and professional expertise, and a deeply rooted commitment in Boston to public education. When West Roxbury High School, designed by Andrews, Jaques, and Rantoul, was dedicated in 1901, no less a person than Charles W. Eliot, president of Harvard, made time to appear as the guest speaker.[47] The Tudor-style building was planned and equipped to prepare students to excel in the colleges and universities of the twentieth century, with laboratories for physics and chemistry and even a roof platform for a telescope and the study of astronomy.

New Types for a New Century

To serve a growing class of businessmen and professionals, the architects—professionals themselves—focused on new building types. One of the new concepts that appealed to the architects was the apartment. In Boston it had emerged as an alternative to the row house, and many apartments were built in the Back Bay during the second half of the nineteenth century.[48] Yet many of the architects and their clients preferred greener settings, consistent with the Arts and Crafts appreciation of nature, even as they remained oriented toward the cities where they worked. By the end of the century, neighborhoods ringing the city, such as Brookline, Cambridge, and Dorchester, were places where apartment buildings were well suited. Richmond Court, built in 1898 by Cram, Goodhue, and Ferguson in Brookline, was a model not only for its design as an English manor house, but also for its interior plan in which rooms for entertaining were well buffered from the bedrooms by doors and hallways.[49] Cram and his wife fit the profile of the people who were drawn to such dwellings, and in fact, they lived in Richmond Court during the early years of their marriage.

Private clubs multiplied, attracting not only the wealthiest members of society but also successful members of a growing upper-middle class. Whether a country club or a city club, the clubhouse was in essence an expanded residence, planned with dining rooms, social rooms, and bedrooms to accommodate out-of-town members. In addition to Boston, the smaller cities of New England were locales where substantial club buildings were erected. In Hartford, Connecticut, for example, Andrews, Jaques, and Ran-

FIG. 7.7 Andrews, Jaques, and Rantoul, Hartford Club, Hartford, CT, 1901–4.

toul were commissioned to design a new home for the Hartford Club after it merged with the Colonial Club (fig. 7.7). Located on Prospect Street in the center of the city and dating from 1901 to 1904, the new building was Colonial Revival in style, constructed of red brick and trimmed in stone. Corinthian columns dominate a semicircular entrance porch, while carved stone and iron balconies enhance second-story windows. When the club-house opened, it was illustrated in the architectural press and described as a "very simple, dignified building," no doubt the tone that the architects and members had wished to exude.[50] The value of belonging to a club appealed to women, too. In 1912 Howe was hired by Boston's newly organized Business Women's Club to remodel the interior of an existing building on Beacon Hill to serve as the club's home.[51] In March of the following year, the *Boston Evening Transcript* reported that Dr. Anna Howard Shaw would be speaking to members and guests on "Equal Suffrage."[52] Clubhouses became centers for a spectrum of values, some certainly conservative, but others solidly progressive.

With their offices in Boston, the architects in this group confronted evolving ideas about buildings that were focused on commerce. In April of 1897, when the formation of a Society of Arts and Crafts was being debated, Norton had said he would support it if "advertising and commercialism" could be avoided. He went on to say that the group would need leaders who would not be enthralled by the big manufacturers.[53] To a limited degree, the architects shared a desire to maintain some detachment from such businesses. None of them pursued commissions for department stores, and many did not take on other large-scale commercial projects. Designing bank buildings was considered respectable, however, providing work for Sturgis, while insurance companies were identified as worthy, providing commissions for Cram. Both Andrews and Walker were comfortable designing Boston office buildings, framed in steel and clad in brick, along the lines of the State Mutual Building.[54]

The invention of the automobile apparently intrigued Andrews and his partners, who produced several buildings associated with the horseless carriages. In 1901 they designed an "auto house" for a Brookline client, an early example of a suburban garage.[55] At the end of the decade, Andrews, Jaques, and Rantoul were retained by the Peerless Motor Car Company of New England, a Cleveland-based manufacturer of luxury automobiles, to build a six-story sales and service building on Beacon Street just west of Massachusetts Avenue (fig. 7.8). When it opened in 1910, it was described as "an absolute fireproof building throughout," clad in red brick and carved limestone, with a "massive bronze and metal marquee" over the entrance.[56] Large glass windows on the ground floor displayed the cars in the showroom, which was handsomely finished in mahogany and complemented by matching mahogany furniture. A building for the sale and service of automobiles would seem antithetical to the Arts and Crafts values of Morris and Norton. Yet at this site, nineteenth-century craftsmanship and twentieth-century engineering commingled. In the building's upper stories, Peerless employed teams of workers to repair and overhaul the cars. Men worked as machinists, upholsterers, blacksmiths, and painters—not as assembly-line laborers, but as skilled artisans.

New modes of transportation intrigued many of the architects and provided opportunities for creativity. In the spring of 1896, the members of the Boston Society of Architects heard a talk about the subway that would be opening in the coming year.[57] In 1897, when the Boston Architectural Club presented its exhibition in conjunction with the exhibition sponsored by the Society of Arts and Crafts, nine drawings of subway entrances by Wheelwright and Haven were shown, and the catalogue included an illustration of one of these.[58] That same year, the Boston Elevated Railway Company announced a competition for a model station, attracting entries from eleven leading firms. Among them were Andrews, Jaques, and Rantoul; Shaw and

FIG. 7.8 Andrews, Jaques, and Rantoul, Peerless Motor Car Company (Barnes and Noble at Boston University), Boston, 1910.

Hunnewell; and Longfellow, who was proclaimed the winner in the spring of 1898.[59]

Longfellow's station design was framed in steel and featured a hipped roof covered in copper and ornamented by a lantern. On the sides of the building were copper panels that alternated with windows enhanced by diamond-patterned leaded glass. In isolation, the station was charming and elegant, consistent with the Arts and Crafts architecture of New England; in its purpose, serving the city's broad populace, it was consistent with Progressive Era objectives. Yet the fact that the elevated railway was about to darken the streets along its course would have distressed Norton as well as some of the architects in the society. Moreover, concerns arose about the power of the Boston Elevated Railway Company, resulting in heated political battles. In 1897 Brandeis played a leading role alongside fellow civic-minded business leaders who fought successfully to balance the interests of the public with the monopoly of the Boston Elevated Railway.[60] For the architects, who regularly invoked moral and aesthetic objectives, deciding what to make of this particular client would have required trying to reconcile conflicting values—or to ignore the project's harsher aspects.

Educational institutions, on the other hand, were clients that all of the architects could happily accept. In addition to designing public school buildings, they received major commissions from colleges and universities. Indeed, the growth of higher education in New England would come to define the region in the twentieth century. The architects built a variety of campus structures. They updated types that were well established, such as dormitories, classroom buildings, and libraries, and they developed new types.

Facilities for athletics belong to a category of buildings that emerged and evolved considerably on American campuses during the nineteenth century. At Harvard, Edward Clarke Cabot, the first president of the Boston Society of Architects, designed a gymnasium that was built in 1859, followed by the more substantial Hemenway Gymnasium of 1878 by Peabody and Stearns.[61] With funding from Arthur Carey, Harvard hired Longfellow to provide them with another building for sports. Erected in 1888, the Carey Athletic Building was a relatively simple rectangular block under a high hipped roof, providing an open, uninterrupted space indoors for play. After Harvard acquired Soldiers Field across the Charles River in Boston, Warren was hired to design another facility.[62] Designed in collaboration with Lewis J. Johnson, the civil engineering professor, the new Carey Cage was supported by steel trusses—the first steel-framed building for Harvard.

FIG. 7.9 Andrews, Jaques, and Rantoul, Athletics Building (Royall Tyler Theater), University of Vermont, Burlington, VT, 1901.

In 1901 Andrews, Jaques, and Rantoul designed an athletics facility for the University of Vermont in Burlington, sited to overlook the University Green and Lake Champlain (fig. 7.9).[63] The red-brick building with brownstone trim is Romanesque in style, an extremely conservative choice for the new century, but the design evidently was intended to harmonize with neighboring buildings in the row, including Richardson's Billings Library of 1885. The new facility was well equipped and up-to-date with a bowling alley, a shooting gallery, a running gallery, and a swimming tank.

Buildings for the study of the sciences and engineering posed greater challenges. For example, Shaw and Hunnewell's Pierce Hall at Harvard (1900) served courses in mechanical, civil, and electrical engineering. In addition to being fireproof, it had to support great weights. For flooring, concrete was poured to cover iron beams, while the interior walls were entirely brick, left exposed and simply painted. Engines and dynamos were, as was reported, "of the most modern patterns," and a blueprint room serviced two spacious drafting rooms.[64]

While campuses were expanding, residents in the suburbs and towns throughout New England were eager for opportunities to expand their knowledge, too, resulting in many commissions for small public libraries. Frequently the projects were funded through a gift or bequest by a local philanthropist. In New England, the idea of the library was intertwined

FIG. 7.10 Shaw and Hunnewell, Proctor House, McLean Hospital, Belmont, MA, 1893–95.

with the Emersonian faith in self-culture, dear to Norton as well as the architects. Domestic in scale and aura, these buildings provided visitors with comfortable seating around a fireplace, so that reading rooms were transformed into community living rooms. The Tudor Revival library designed by Cram, Goodhue, and Ferguson in Nashua, New Hampshire (1901–3), was a relatively lavish example of this development. Walker's Colonial Revival William Fogg Library in Eliot, Maine (1906–7), was much simpler, congruent with its country setting.[65]

The optimism that reflected both Emerson and the rise of America's Progressive Era infused Boston's Society of Arts and Crafts, and this same outlook inspired the region's leading citizens. During the nineteenth century, they had founded a variety of institutions to assist those in need, and at the turn of the new century, they raised the funds and hired the architects to build larger facilities. One such endeavor was the McLean Hospital, which began in Somerville in 1818 as an asylum run by Massachusetts General Hospital to treat the mentally ill.[66] Although private, both the hospital and asylum were sufficiently endowed to be able to accept the indigent. By the 1870s, the hospital concluded that the time had come to relocate the asylum to a more rural site. Guided by a report from Frederick Law Olmsted, the trustees bought 176 acres in Belmont in 1875, determining that they would build group houses that were domestic in scale. The decision to erect a cottage-style campus rather than a single sprawling building emerged at an early date for what would become a national trend in the following decade.

Construction didn't begin until the early 1890s, however. In 1895 the new campus opened, with the name changed to McLean Hospital. Shaw and Hunnewell designed four of the buildings: three residences and a women's gymnasium. Styles were deliberately varied so that the effect would seem less institutional and more like a suburban enclave. Proctor House (1893–95) was Jacobean, built of red brick with limestone trim and carved lions' heads in the gables of two projecting pavilions (fig. 7.10). On the other hand, Wyman House and Bowditch House (both 1894–95) were Colonial Revival in style, while the gym (1895–97) was Tudor Revival. In addition to accommodating athletic activities, the gym included an art room outfitted with plaster casts and original artwork. Both exercise and artistic expression were understood to offer therapeutic potential for the patients.

Much like McLean, the Perkins Institution, founded in Boston in 1829, had met with such success that it was able to relocate and build a new campus, opening in Watertown in 1912. Sturgis believed his plan was superior to that of the Pennsylvania Institution for the Instruction of the Blind, erected in Philadelphia and completed in 1899, designed by Cope and Stewardson.[67] In an article in *Brickbuilder*, Sturgis explained that in Pennsylvania, "the dormitory plan was adopted, and there the school departments as well as the living quarters were grouped under a single roof. Here the cottage system was adopted."[68] As at McLean, intimate living arrangements were identified as more progressive. In various and detailed ways, Sturgis and the administration created an environment that could be negotiated easily by the blind children. Raised tile was installed in the floors where corridors intersected, while stairs were positioned to run from the sides of corridors rather than at the ends.

Shortly after the new Perkins campus was completed, Andrews oversaw the design and construction of a campus for the Connecticut School for the Blind in Hartford, built between 1913 and 1917. The interest that the architects had in these projects was shared by their colleagues leading the Society of Arts and Crafts. In January of 1907, when the council was planning the tenth anniversary exhibition, the members voted that "the weavers working under the Committee for the Blind be invited to submit work for the Exhibition without membership."[69] When the exhibition opened, the catalogue listed seventeen exhibits in the Department of Textiles and Embroidery

entered by blind contributors, with a note explaining that they had created their own designs, only receiving assistance in choosing colors.[70]

Humane treatment and the care of animals was another cause that coalesced in Boston in the nineteenth century. In 1868 George T. Angell, an attorney, founded the Massachusetts Society for the Prevention of Cruelty to Animals, the second such society to be organized in the United States.[71] Joining him in incorporating the organization were two other men; one was Samuel G. Howe, director of the Perkins Institution. In the decades that followed, the MSPCA attracted support from the state's leading citizens, including Emerson, who served as a vice president from the time of the group's inception until 1872, when his wife carried on in this capacity.[72] After Angell's death in 1909, his successors raised the funds to honor his memory by erecting a veterinary hospital and offices. When Angell Memorial Hospital for Animals opened in Boston in 1915, it was the largest and best equipped building of its kind in the world.[73] Designed by Putnam with Putnam and Cox, it was Georgian Revival in style, constructed in red brick with stone trimmings (fig. 7.11). Today a Harvard Medical School building, it has a stately facade dominated by a portico with four colossal Ionic columns. Among the dignitaries who participated in the dedication were Mayor James Michael Curley and Abbott Lawrence Lowell, president of Harvard. For Putnam, the mission of this client was compelling, and he subsequently served on the MSPCA's board of directors.

Buildings to Serve the Urban Poor

The miserable living conditions of the urban poor, long a concern of the English Arts and Crafts movement, were addressed by several of the architects who applied their skills to designing buildings for this population. New England's tradition of social activism was an enduring one, and it reinforced their sensitivity. At a relatively early date, decent housing was recognized as a fundamental need—the cause that Norton took up in the 1850s, both in his writing and in raising money for model lodging houses.[74] In 1871 Sarah Whitman, who would sign on alongside Norton in founding the Society of Arts and Crafts, became a director of the newly organized Boston Cooperative Building Company, dedicated to providing acceptable rental housing for working-class residents.[75]

Longfellow was drawn into the Boston Cooperative Building Company in 1889 when he designed a group of eight dwellings that ringed an entire block in the city's South End.[76] Three stories in height, these simple brick buildings were planned to shelter one family per floor, with all three levels served by a single entrance. The most innovative feature of the project was the landscaped courtyard in the center of the block, resulting in better light and ventilation for the units and a green space for the residents' enjoyment. A few years later, an annual report commented, "A year never passes without some request for permission to inspect this estate, with a view to reproducing its main features elsewhere."[77] When the Society of Arts and Crafts was founded in 1897, Whitman was secretary of the Boston Cooperative Building Company, and Longfellow had joined the board of directors. In

December of that year, Longfellow described his model housing development at a meeting of the Boston Society of Architects.[78]

Another building type that the Boston Society of Architects examined in an 1897 meeting was the bathhouse, and architects in the Society of Arts and Crafts designed several such projects.[79] The city had just begun erecting these facilities to serve neighborhood residents at no charge. By the early twentieth century, bathhouses were combined with gymnasiums, all under one roof, to function as community centers. A model of this type was the North Bennet Street Bathhouse (1904–6), designed by Maginnis and his firm and located in Boston's teeming North End (fig. 7.12).[80] The red-brick Renaissance revival building was trimmed with terra cotta, a decorative material that Maginnis favored. Showers and dressing rooms were located on the first and second floors along with an infirmary and residence for the superintendent. Most of the second floor was dedicated to a two-story gymnasium, encircled by a running track at the third story—an arrangement that had become common in college facilities. The building was published

FIG. 7.13 Sturgis
and Barton,
South Bay Union,
Boston, 1901–3.

extensively, appearing in *American Architect*, *Architectural Review*, and *Brickbuilder*. In 1909 Newhall and Blevins were hired by the city to design a similar center for East Boston.[81] In addition to showers and a gymnasium with an upper-level running track, it included two "play rooms," a handball court, and a room for wrestling or fencing.

Of all the architects who were active in the Society of Arts and Crafts, Sturgis and Barton demonstrated the most pronounced interest in working for institutions that sought to better the lives of the downtrodden. Barton's travels in England and his encounter with Morris had focused his attention on society's oppressed.[82] When Barton joined Sturgis as a partner in 1902, Sturgis had been hired the year before to build a social center in Boston's South End, a neighborhood congested with factories and tenements.[83] The commission would have been especially appealing to Barton. Completed in 1903, the South Bay Union (fig. 7.13) was erected under the direction of the South End House, a social service organization. As Fiske Kimball explained in *Architectural Record*, unlike similar organizations that operated from extensive complexes, such as Hull House in Chicago, South End House strategically scattered buildings throughout various neighborhoods to reach more people in the community.[84] The South Bay Union included a lunch room, a kindergarten, club rooms, and an industrial school for boys and girls. Its largest space was an assembly hall that was conceived as an informal town hall that would "help the district achieve civic unity."[85] Consistent with this image, the building was Colonial Revival in style, constructed with red brick and light stone trimmings, with Tuscan columns flanking the entrance and an iron railing that ran along a shallow second-story balcony.

As work on the new center was under way, the leaders within the Society of Arts and Crafts contemplated how their organization might approach South End House to pursue their mutually shared objectives. Not coincidentally, Carey was the society's president during this period, and he hoped to promote Morris's socialistic approach. In the society's annual report of 1901, a plan was set forth to recruit craftsmen through South End House. Its leaders would assist, "identifying small shops which employ only a few men and thus more nearly approach the old system of production than do the larger shops where subdivision of labor is in force."[86] Already, South End House had undertaken training women in lace making, and the experiment was considered successful. When Carey resigned in exasperation from the Society of Arts and Crafts at the end of 1903 and Warren succeeded him as president, the two organizations went their separate ways. The society remained committed to promoting the craftsman, but the desire to link that goal with elevating the lives of immigrants and the poor dissipated with Carey's departure.

In the years that followed, Sturgis and Barton continued to be drawn to clients with service missions. Between 1906 and 1908, Sturgis and Barton oversaw the design and construction of the Franklin Union, also located in Boston's South End, dedicated to educating young men in the industrial arts.[87] As chairman of the city's Schoolhouse Commission, Sturgis pursued his personal interest in designing facilities that would enhance the education of the city's children. After Barton left the partnership in 1909, Sturgis continued to take on projects that aided the urban poor, designing the Elizabeth Peabody Settlement House (1912–13) in the city's West End. When it opened, it was believed to be "the best equipped building for settlement purposes this side of Chicago."[88]

After the outbreak of World War I, Sturgis became occupied with a new housing challenge. Suddenly the Allies were ordering massive quantities of munitions, leading to a rapid expansion of the factories in Bridgeport, Connecticut, along with the construction of new ones. An influx of workers overwhelmed the city, and the housing shortage was acute. Recognizing the

FIG. 7.14 R. Clipston
Sturgis, Seaside
Village house,
Bridgeport, CT,
1918–19.

problem, the Remington Arms Corporation erected more dwellings, but this effort was not sufficient. In 1916 a group of civic leaders formed the Bridgeport Housing Company and moved quickly to acquire tracts of land and build houses at a high standard yet reasonable cost.[89] What these leaders wanted to avoid was the construction of frame three-deckers, the housing type that had become the standard shelter for working-class New England. The Bridgeport Housing Company built garden apartments, two-family and single-family houses, mainly Colonial Revival in style, and brick.[90] Of the several architects who were employed, Sturgis was the most prominent. The effect that he created, wrote Sylvester Baxter in *Architectural Record*, "is that of a 'garden-city' development that resembles the English type, though in architecture it has a distinctively New England character."[91] Contours of the land were respected, outcroppings of ledge preserved, and clumps of trees retained. In 1917 Sturgis exhibited his residential designs in an exhibition jointly sponsored by the Society of Arts and Crafts and Boston's architectural organizations.[92]

As the demand for wartime housing persisted, both in Bridgeport and in other American industrial centers, Congress created the United States Housing Corporation, the first federal program to build public housing. Five different projects were planned for the Bridgeport area, and Sturgis was the architect directing them all (fig. 7.14).[93] For a development of three-story apartments, he grouped the buildings to create courts that, as Baxter observed, resembled college quadrangles. In another development consisting of detached houses, two-family houses, and four-family houses, the effect suggested to Baxter "an old-time New England village, like Marblehead or Ipswich."[94] Anyone familiar with those towns might have raised an eyebrow over the comparison, given that the old houses of Marblehead and Ipswich are frame and clad in shingles or clapboard. Nevertheless, the brick houses that Sturgis designed were varied in scale and massing, and he managed to avoid the monotony that is common in worker housing developments. When the war ended in 1918, the federal government put a halt to many of the projects that were scheduled to be built. But the projects in Bridgeport went forward, with all of the dwellings completed a year later and sold to working-class households.

A related phenomenon of the period was a desire to erect buildings where altruistic individuals could gather with others of a similar mind. Phillips Brooks House at Harvard, designed by Longfellow, served this purpose.[95] As early as 1890, Brooks, the rector of Trinity Church in Boston, had floated the idea of establishing such a center where students could organize charitable endeavors that they would pursue outside the university. From the beginning, Phillips Brooks House was expected to provide a meeting place for religious societies where all sects would be welcome. In 1897, a lot on the northwest corner of Harvard Yard was committed to this purpose, and in January of 1900, Phillips Brooks House was dedicated. It soon became a home for a wide variety of groups and social causes. Here in 1905 was where the Harvard Ethical Society heard Brandeis speak about "The Opportunity in the Law," calling for lawyers to use their training on behalf of "the people."[96]

The Boston City Club was equally welcoming to diverse members and ideas. Founded in 1904 by leading businessmen including Edward Filene and Brandeis, it was open to all, regardless of creed, and encouraged debate over the controversial issues of the period.[97] Extremely successful, the members hired Newhall and Blevins in 1913 to design an eight-story clubhouse that was constructed that year (fig. 7.15).[98] Located at the edge of Beacon Hill and adjacent to the center of the city, it was a federal-style building of stone and brick, its main elevation swelling gently in two shallow bays. Inserted in the cornerstone was a bronze tablet that described the club's mission to bring men together for the service of the city and "to destroy

FIG. 7.15 Newhall and Blevins, Boston City Club (Sawyer Building, Suffolk University), Boston, 1913.

the class, religious, and racial prejudices which exist when men don't know each other."[99] Soon after the clubhouse was finished, the Boston City Club claimed more than 4,000 members.

Reform through Law

Although the leaders of Boston's Society of Arts and Crafts flatly rejected the socialism of their English counterparts, they were reformers all the same. They were idealists in a Yankee mold and shared a Progressive Era outlook. Within other organizations and on their own, the architects advocated for changes, especially relating to the realms of building design and planning, and they saw the potential of law. To some degree, this orientation may have reflected their experiences in New England, where local laws have long been enacted by citizens who assemble to vote in town meetings. Several of the architects would have been influenced by contacts with colleagues at Harvard Law School, which was located in Austin Hall, designed by Richardson. And in their practices, the architects were advised by lawyers. In one such example, when Sturgis was working with the Museum of Fine Arts on its move from Copley Square to the Fenway, he and Barton consulted with Brandeis's firm on the acquisition of land.[100]

In the architects' projects and in their writing, law was venerated. At Longfellow's Cambridge City Hall, an inscription was carved over the entrance that reads in part, "If the laws are not enforced, the people are not well governed."[101] When Andrews, Jaques, and Rantoul designed the expansion of the county courthouse in Worcester, Massachusetts (1897–99), Andrews authored this inscription: "Obedience to Law Is Liberty."[102] Cram emphasized the importance of law in his publications. To his mind, the English monasteries of the Middle Ages were enlightened centers "of law, order, education, and mercy."[103] He also revered the English residential colleges, which he credited with shaping character and promoting a long list of virtues, among them being "obedience to law."[104] These particular words were used by Cram in 1912, and we may guess that he appropriated them from Andrews. Exactly what the two had in mind in calling for "obedience to law" is not at all clear, but they must have been thinking of some serious challenges of the period, ranging from corruption in government to urban crime.

Andrews and his colleagues became advocates for their views in the legislature and in the courts. As a representative of the Boston Society of Architects, Andrews had been a key player during the mid-1890s in pressing the state legislature to renovate and preserve Bulfinch's State House. By the late 1890s, the Boston Society of Architects became embroiled in a significant fight over building heights and urged the adoption of legal restrictions. From today's perspective, an outcry over a tall building might seem backward looking, but the cause was also about controlling development. The focus of so much concern was the construction of a ten-story apartment building called Westminster Chambers, which a syndicate began erecting in the summer of 1897 on a corner of Copley Square between Trinity Church and the Museum of Fine Arts.[105] At completion, it was to be 120 feet tall.

That October, the Boston Society of Architects charged its executive committee with promoting legislation that would restrict the height of buildings in the city.[106] Early in 1898, the lead editorial of the January 29 *American Architect* reported on the potential "disfigurement" of Copley Square by the apartment building, and a few days later, the Boston Society of Architects voted to support regulating the height of buildings in Copley Square.[107] The subject was introduced by Walker and the resolution offered by Andrews. No doubt the architects were concerned about the impact of the new apartment building on Trinity Church and the museum. Among those serving on the museum's board of trustees during this period were several of their colleagues in the Society of Arts and Crafts, including Carey, Norton, Ross, and Sam Warren.[108] Then again, those involved said virtually nothing about the fact that the new apartment was rising on a lot immediately next to the Hotel Ludlow, designed by Walker and owned by Ross. Brandeis, too, was drawn into the fray, arguing on behalf of the Copley Square Protective Committee.[109]

Meanwhile, Langford Warren reported to readers of *Architectural Review* that several new offices were rising in the heart of London, four to six stories high. They "make one sigh for the days before the elevator," he continued, "and grateful that its ravages have not been extensive as yet in the great cities of Europe."[110] This was a cause that struck a chord with C. R. Ashbee. When he published his 1901 report to the English National Trust after touring the United States, he expressed his wish to assist the architects in their campaign to restrict building heights.[111]

The Westminster Chambers battle unfolded over several years. In the state legislature, members voted a height restriction and then reversed themselves, after which the governor vetoed their reversal. Subsequently the state's Supreme Judicial Court upheld the restriction.[112] Finally, the developer appealed the decision to the United States Supreme Court, and in February of 1903, the justices upheld the Massachusetts decision.[113] That summer, the roof was lowered on Westminster Chambers, while the city of Boston paid the syndicate nearly $350,000 in damages. The case was of national significance as the Supreme Court's first ruling on restricting the height of buildings, validating a concept that would become integral to American planning.[114]

Yet if there was consensus among Boston's architects about controlling building heights in Copley Square, they were not of one mind about tall buildings in general. Warren, in publicly ruing the emergence of four-, five-, and six-story office buildings in London, positioned himself at one extreme. In his own practice, he never designed a building of this type.[115] Andrews, on the other hand, could oppose the height of Westminster Chambers in Copley Square but could accept tall buildings elsewhere—as in the center of the city, where he and his partners designed and built the ten-story State Mutual Building between 1902 and 1903, with space on the top floor for Andrews, Jaques, and Rantoul.

However they differed in the specifics of their views, the Boston architects believed in local and regional planning—an emerging field that brought together urban design and law. By the early twentieth century, the City Beautiful movement was inspiring municipalities across the country to undertake large-scale, government-funded projects constructing parks, tree-lined avenues, and civic centers. In Boston, the creation of a park system designed by Frederick Law Olmsted during the 1880s and 1890s led his successors to think boldly.[116] Ashbee especially admired the Boston-based Trustees of Public Reservations, a land trust chartered by the Massachusetts legislature in 1891 to save "beautiful and historic places."[117] Two years later, the work of this private organization was augmented by the creation of a Metropolitan Park Commission, both initiatives championed by Charles Eliot, the son of Harvard's president.

The interest in planning expanded to include more and more citizens. In 1904 the Metropolitan Improvement League was organized in Boston, with Walker serving as its president until 1912. Through a newsletter and appearances before government boards, Walker and his colleagues focused on projects such as the design of Copley Square, the Esplanade along the Charles River, and the Back Bay Fens.[118] In 1906 the Boston Society of Architects prepared a comprehensive study that outlined possibilities for the region.[119] Funding the report were eight organizations, representing business-oriented associations of realtors and builders as well groups such as the Metropolitan Improvement League. Seventeen architects were engaged in the endeavor, with Robert Swain Peabody serving as chairman, and Andrews, Cram, Longfellow, Maginnis, Sturgis, and Walker all participating.

In their report, the architects addressed functional and economic concerns, proposing ring roads and harbor redevelopment, and they presented ideas for aesthetic improvements. These included Walker's design for Copley Square and Cram's vision for building an island in the Charles River. The Boston Society of Architects did not endorse the proposals in the report, but expressed the hope that the concepts would spur further interest in planning for the region. The fact that Boston-1915, the exhibition held in 1909 that Brandeis helped organize, attracted more than 200,000 visitors demonstrated that an interest in thinking imaginatively about the growth of the city had become widespread. With Cram's appointment as the first chairman of the City Planning Board in 1914, the belief that architecture could contribute to government was validated.

In introducing their report on municipal improvements for Boston, the architects conveyed both their love for the city's history and their commitment to steering its growth. Readers were told,

> Our forefathers handed on to us an old-fashioned English city that was prosperous and convenient and of great beauty. Is it a better city in our hands, and are we preparing properly for its future? Old Boston is full of local charm that we all want to preserve, but how is it with the New Boston? These are the questions we have had to consider.[120]

With an Arts and Crafts orientation, infused by the spirit of Progressive Era New England, the architects were crusaders. They allied themselves with individuals, organizations, and institutions with ambitious—even audacious—aspirations. Several of the architects, most notably Barton, Sturgis, and Longfellow, embraced an Arts and Crafts concern for the immigrant and the urban poor, erecting buildings to address their needs. Several of the architects turned to the law, seeking to bring better design and wider vision to the process of building. They sought to foster a gentler version of the modern metropolis. At the same time, they sought to enhance New England's cities and towns with substantial, well-planned civic buildings, schools, churches, and houses that would endure for generations to come, long into the new century.

Epilogue: Confronting Modernism

Reading through the handwritten notes and typed carbon copies documenting the meetings and activities of the Society of Arts and Crafts, one cannot help but be impressed by the endless hours that the architects devoted to promoting an Arts and Crafts movement. Stepping back, one faces the challenge of evaluating the legacy of the eleven men and one woman. How meaningful was their participation in the society? How did they influence the architectural community in Boston? And to what extent did they contribute to the direction of architectural design elsewhere in the United States?

To begin with, it should be remembered that forty architects joined the Society of Arts and Crafts at one time or another during its first two decades.[1] In addition to the dozen who were most active, serving as officers and on the governing council, many more were sympathetic to the cause, paying dues, attending exhibitions and lectures, and employing the craftsmen. Among the prominent members of this group were Francis R. Allen, Frank Chouteau Brown, Bertram Goodhue, and Edmund Wheelwright. At a time when societies and clubs were proliferating—characteristic of the Progressive Era—architects in Boston prioritized joining the Boston Architectural Club and aspired to admission into the Boston Society of Architects. To become involved with additional groups meant committing money and time beyond the requisite membership in the two major professional organizations.

When the membership of other groups is analyzed, the fact that forty architects became members of the Society of Arts and Crafts is shown to be significant. By comparison, the Boston chapter of the Archaeological Institute of America attracted a smattering of architects, one of whom was Langford Warren.[2] This fact is noteworthy, considering that many members of the Society of Arts and Crafts signed on, no doubt in part because the Archaeological Institute of America was the progeny of Norton. In the early twentieth century, the roster of supporters included Carey, J. Templeman Coolidge Jr., Ross, and Sam Warren. Elizabeth W. Perkins, who had commissioned Andrews and Jaques to design her summer house in Beverly

Farms, Massachusetts, served on the Boston chapter's Committee on Membership, and they attracted a large and diverse group, including Mrs. Louis Brandeis.[3] Yet Andrews was not a member, nor was Walker—surprising, given that in the 1880s, Walker had journeyed to Assos, the first excavation sponsored by the institute. Apparently the architects concluded that the Society of Arts and Crafts was the organization that needed them more.

Expending time and dollars with these groups certainly was not necessary for an architect to develop a successful practice. The Society of Arts and Crafts never enticed Robert Swain Peabody to become a member. Richardson's successors, George F. Shepley, Charles H. Rutan, and Charles A. Coolidge, did not join either, even though their founder had contributed to the movement and their fellow alumni from Richardson's studio—Andrews, Longfellow, and Warren—held leadership positions in the society. Then again, for the most part, the partners and colleagues of the architects never felt obliged to participate—including Frank Patterson Smith, Warren's business partner; and George F. Newton, hired by Warren to teach design at Harvard. Nevertheless, these practitioners would have been sympathetic to Arts and Crafts objectives.

Looking beyond this group in an attempt to evaluate the architects' influence in New England, one struggles to establish a means of measurement. Although such an objective is elusive, one can page through local surveys and scholarly studies of the region's architecture and conclude that these architects' favored styles were embraced by the greater architectural community during this period. So, too, were the favored craftsmen, such as carvers Hugh Cairns, John Evans, and Johannes Kirchmayer; glass artist Charles J. Connick; and tile maker Henry Chapman Mercer.[4]

As opportunities for architects expanded at the end of the century across the United States, the architects from the Society of Arts and Crafts extended their reach.[5] Four of them opened offices in other states: Cram and Goodhue in New York City; Warren in Troy, New York; Longfellow with his partners in Pittsburgh; and Walker and his partners in Omaha. Andrews and Jaques established a favorable reputation in Colorado, where they landed substantial commissions, while Cram and Maginnis became designers of choice for major ecclesiastic and campus projects throughout the continent.[6] The architects also spread their influence by training a younger generation who often settled far from Boston. Before moving to Pasadena, California, the brothers Charles and Henry Greene worked for Andrews, Jaques, and Rantoul as well as Sturgis and Warren.[7] At the same time, the

Boston architects were not operating in a vacuum, and their ideas about architecture were intermingled with ideas that came from architects elsewhere in the country. The Boston group maintained especially close ties to several architects from Philadelphia, in particular John Stewardson, Walter Cope, Frank Miles Day, and Wilson Eyre, who shared a commitment to the English tradition with their colleagues to the north and were early proponents of the Gothic Revival and Colonial Revival.

In the story of Arts and Crafts architecture in New England, the denouement began in the late 1920s with the arrival of Modernism. At the turn of the century, when the architects in the Society of Arts and Crafts scorned the more innovative European trends such as Art Nouveau, the clientele in New England shared this resistance, eschewing the new stylistic directions. On the other hand, the early buildings of Frank Lloyd Wright were well received. In June of 1900, *Architectural Review* published a laudatory feature on his work, and in the same issue, Cram wrote of Wright, "Here is originality and unquestionable genius."[8] But by 1929, with Modernism making inroads, Cram had aligned himself with the opposition. In an issue of *House Beautiful*, Cram addressed the question, "Will This Modernism Last?"[9] Reflecting the popular view that a battle was under way, his essay forecasting that Modernism would have a short run was published alongside an essay that made the counterargument. To his mind, Modernism was fraught with distortions and artificiality. Even so, Cram found some good in the movement, praising its "honest" use of materials and "simple" schemes of form and furnishing—reiterating Arts and Crafts themes.[10]

When Cram published his autobiography in 1936, he devoted an entire chapter to Modernism.[11] It still struck him as a fad, "a matter of fashion."[12] Not wishing to be discounted as a reactionary, however, he acknowledged that it would be "irrational, perverse and misleading" to apply the forms of the past for modern building types such as a moving picture palace, a garage, a hangar, a skyscraper, or a cocktail bar, and he even recognized elements of courage and adventure driving the trend. Nevertheless, he saw "no reason why these attributes of Modernism should be expressed in horrid forms."[13] Singling out the apartment houses of Le Corbusier, Cram disparaged them as "a betrayal of trust, a vicious though unintentional assault on the basic principles of a sane and wholesome society."[14] Baffled yet not beaten, he wrote, "I suppose we have got to begin again—pick up something of the lost social tradition, something also of the lost architectural tradition."[15]

Walker took a public position against Modernism, too. When the American Institute of Architects convened in Washington, D.C., in the spring of 1930, he participated in a debate on style, with George Howe of Philadelphia taking the Modernists' side. The news story was covered in *Time* magazine.[16] Howe associated Modernism with imagination and courage, its architects working in a new style "to meet modern needs in the light of modern economic and engineering genius." Walker, described as "defending Conservatism," parried, "It has been reserved for the so-called Modernists to be irritated at any resemblance to anything that has calm, and to adore excess in every direction, to be shapeless, crude, eliminated in detail to nothingness, explosive in detail to chaos . . . creating sensation with the slapstick and the bludgeon."[17]

Within the Boston architectural community, Modernism was recognized as a potent assault on Arts and Crafts ideals. In the fall of 1930, the Boston Society of Architects sponsored a program titled "The Influence of Modern Architecture on the Position of the Historic Craftsman." Maginnis introduced the guest speakers, who included Walker, Connick, and Cairns, carrying the standard for their longtime cause. George H. Edgell, dean of the faculty of architecture at Harvard, also spoke. Uncowed by his companions, Edgell stated that he thought the historic craftsman was dead, adding rather sharply that not all of the craftsmen of the Middle Ages were good.[18] A year later, Edgell campaigned to build a modernist wing for Robinson Hall, the Georgian Revival building designed by Charles McKim for Harvard's architecture program.[19] Cram objected vehemently, but because of the Great Depression, leading to a decline in student enrollment and lack of funds, the plan was squashed.

If the aging architects rejected the severe forms of what had become identified as the International Style, they were open to Art Deco with its more complex massing and potential for ornament. In 1897 Art Deco designs might have been condemned for "specious originality," as spelled out in the mission statement drafted by Norton for the Society of Arts and Crafts. By the late 1920s and early 1930s, however, several of the architects flirted with the new style, based on geometric forms and patterns. Cram's firm partnered with James A. Wetmore in designing the Art Deco Post Office and Federal Building (1929–31) in Boston's Post Office Square.[20] South of Boston in Hull, Putnam and Cox designed the Mary Jeanette Murray Bathhouse, an Art Deco structure on Nantasket Beach (1930; fig. E.1). Low-slung with curving walls and glass block, it includes two large relief panels set in the walls, ornamented with abstractions of cod, starfish, and crabs.[21]

FIG. E.I Putnam and Cox, Murray Bathhouse, Hull, MA, 1930.

For his own house in Brookline, Maginnis finished a third-floor retreat for his teenaged children in an Art Deco scheme of saturated reds, golds, and blues.[22] At one end of the room, a fireplace was built with an onyx surround, and a mural dominated by turquoise and pink was painted with flowers and flamingos.

By the mid-1940s, it was clear that Modernism was not going to fade away. Only Lois Howe, Maginnis, Putnam, and Sturgis remained to witness its triumph. Still energetic, Maginnis articulated his concern. In a lecture titled "The Crisis in Architecture," he addressed the National Institute of Arts and Letters in New York City in 1945.[23] More than anything, Maginnis was disconcerted by the "aggressive Modernist with the conscience of a Puritan or a Trappist monk who refuses to make a sinful compromise with beauty." He rejected the thesis that beauty is an automatic product of function, and he was distressed by the onset of "universal monotony, so that modernity at Moscow looks like modernity at Indianapolis." In Modernism he found "a harsh and defiant emptiness." While recognizing that the old veneration of the styles of the European past was no longer acceptable, he called for a respect for the artistic principles "which today are as precious and valid as they ever were."[24] Having served as president of the American Institute of Architects from 1937 to 1939, Maginnis did not hesitate to speak out.

In the early 1950s, Sturgis also voiced his objections to Modernism, focusing on new buildings at Harvard. But the fact that he had served as president of the American Institute of Architects many decades earlier, from 1914 to 1915, would have made him less influential than Maginnis. Now in his nineties, Sturgis was something of a relic. In 1950 and again in 1951, he submitted letters to the *Harvard Alumni Bulletin* to vent his displeasure with the university's stark new buildings, including the 1949 Graduate Center designed by Walter Gropius and his firm.[25] "No possible stretch of the imagination can see any sign of beauty in these structures," wrote Sturgis. "There is no excuse for such absolute disregard of Harvard's traditional right to have buildings that are at once functional, and, above all, beautiful."[26] The elderly man's plea faintly echoed the words of Morris, who had long ago called for the useful and the beautiful in all aspects of design. But to no avail.

Today we can evaluate the Arts and Crafts architecture in New England as a chapter of the region's and the nation's architectural history. By focusing on the work of the architects who were most actively engaged in the Society of Arts and Crafts, we can appreciate how their buildings, whether Gothic Revival or Colonial Revival, were unified by shared ideas. In general, the Boston movement was especially close to the movement that emerged in England through the work of Ruskin and Morris, transmitted by Norton and Richardson, and developed through regular contact by the Boston architects with their English counterparts.

Norton, the first president of the Society of Arts and Crafts, must be recognized for his central role as theorist and advocate. Like Ruskin, he believed that as one sharpens one's aesthetic acuity, one gains a more heightened perception of the world in general, including an ability to see social ills. Like Ruskin and Morris, Norton crusaded against industry, cheap goods, materialism, and commercialism. He believed the degradation experienced by those laboring in industry was connected to the degradation of goods consumed in the modern economy. By reviving the role of the craftsman, he hoped to restore dignity to labor. As an educator and historian at Harvard, Norton established fertile ground for an Arts and Crafts movement based in Boston, a movement that would emphasize the region's history and heritage.

Emerson supplied a Yankee cast to the region's movement. His personal simplicity and lack of pretense meshed with Arts and Crafts ideals. Also, his love of New England and its ordinary places was similar to the respect Ruskin and Morris had for England's Gothic and vernacular architecture. Emerson's validation of Yankee culture paralleled English nationalism and reinforced the regionalism that was an aspect of New England's Arts and Crafts architecture. At the same time, the excoriating writings of Ruskin and Morris, along with the despair voiced by Norton, were not well aligned with the views held by most of the leadership in the Society of Arts of Crafts. Emerson's optimism and hope for America better fit their mind-set. Emerson's belief in the potential of the individual and his emphasis on self-reliance were appreciated by the leaders of the society in Boston, who rejected Morris's socialistic agenda.

As working professionals, the architects in the Society of Arts and Crafts believed in capitalism and saw the benefits of a modern, industrial society. Contemporaries with Brandeis, they were pragmatic as well as re-form-minded. They were ambitious, too, seeing their causes as national in scope.

The values that formed the basis of Norton's Arts and Crafts outlook were simplicity and sincerity, sobriety and restraint—ideals that he promoted for handicraft, the fine arts, and life itself. They were ideals that also would have appealed to Emerson and Brandeis. They became the distinguishing values that guided the Arts and Crafts architecture in New England.

In 1893, when Andrews addressed the Boston Architectural Club, we may recall that he quoted Emerson before urging his fellow architects not to set their art on a high pedestal, "to bar the public out." Rather, he hoped the architects would produce work that "coming people shall love and maintain for the beneficence there is in it."[27] In evaluating these century-old buildings as functioning places of bricks and mortar, stone, stucco, and timber, we may conclude that Andrews's hopes have been realized. Visiting Walker's small-town libraries in Hopedale, Massachusetts, and Eliot, Maine, we find them bustling with patrons, the hearts of their communities. Churches by Cram and his partners, such as All Saints, Ashmont, in the Dorchester area of Boston, and by Maginnis, such as Christ the King in Rutland, Vermont, serve parishioners who take enormous pride in their houses of worship. At Harvard, students from around the globe fill Longfellow's beautifully maintained Phillips Brooks House with energy and idealism, dedicating their time to a range of social causes. Sturgis's worker housing in and around Bridgeport, Connecticut, continues to provide satisfying shelter for people of limited means.

If one were to choose a single project to represent the Arts and Crafts architecture of New England, it might well be Perkins School for the Blind

FIG. E.2 R. Clipston Sturgis, Howe Building, Perkins Institution for the Blind
(Perkins School for the Blind), Watertown, MA, 1909–12. Sculpture by John Evans.

in Watertown, Massachusetts (fig. E.2). Designed by Sturgis and based on Gothic models, its brick buildings resemble English Arts and Crafts architecture, enhanced by sculpture, tile, and carved wood—handcrafted ornament that Ruskin would have appreciated. The school's central administration and classroom building is especially memorable. Above the entrance, sculpted eagles perch on the parapet against the sky as if they are about to soar, and a Perpendicular tower rises overhead, a declaration of confidence and conviction. Addressing all of those who see, the art and architecture at Perkins proclaim that in this place, visually impaired children can learn to read, write, and enter society. Simple and sincere: the buildings at the Perkins School assert the optimism of the Arts and Crafts architects, their craftsmen collaborators, and their fellow advocates who lived and labored in New England during the Progressive Era.

Notes

Introduction: Grappling with Modernity

1. Samuel Eliot Morison, intro. to *Of Plymouth Plantation, 1627–1647*, by William Bradford, New York: Modern Library, 1952, pp. xxvii-xl.
2. *The Monument to Robert Gould Shaw: Its Inception, Completion and Unveiling, 1865–1897*, Boston and New York: Houghton Mifflin, 1897.
3. Ibid., p. 78.
4. Williams v. Parker, decided Feb. 23, 1903.
5. Lewis Mumford, *The Brown Decades: A Study of the Arts in America, 1865–1895*, New York: Dover, 1971 (orig. pub. 1931).
6. It should be added that the Colonial Revival was well under way by the time of the Centennial Exposition in Philadelphia. See Vincent J. Scully, *The Shingle Style and the Stick Style*, rev. ed., New Haven, CT, and London: Yale University Press, 1971 (orig. pub. 1955), pp. 19–33.
7. John Greenleaf Whittier, "To Faneuil Hall" (1844), *The Poetical Works of John Greenleaf Whittier*, Boston and New York: Houghton Mifflin, 1892, p. 56.
8. Alan Trachtenberg, *The Incorporation of America: Culture and Society in the Gilded Age*, New York: Hill and Wang, 1982, p. 7.
9. Trachtenberg observes that "the rhetoric of success continued to hail the self-made man as the paragon of free labor, even as the virtues of that fictive character grew less and less relevant. Thus, incorporation engendered a cultural paradox," p. 84. See also Michael McGerr, *A Fierce Discontent: The Rise and Fall of the Progressive Movement in America, 1870–1920*, New York: Free Press, 2003, p. 56.
10. Trachtenberg, p. 144.
11. Lawrence W. Kennedy, *Planning the City upon a Hill: Boston Since 1630*, Amherst: University of Massachusetts Press, 1992, pp. 103–4.
12. Douglass Shand-Tucci, *Built in Boston: City and Suburb, 1800–2000*, rev. ed., Amherst: University of Massachusetts Press, 2000 (orig. pub. 1978), pp. 101–30.
13. Robert Wiebe, *The Search for Order, 1877–1920*, New York: Hill and Wang, 1967, p. 45. See also Philip Dray, *There Is Power in a Union: The Epic Story of Labor in America*, New York: Doubleday, 2010.
14. Thomas J. Schlereth, *Victorian America: Transformations in Everyday Life, 1876–1915*, New York: Harper Perennial, 1992 (orig. pub. 1991), p. 53. See also Wiebe, p. 45, who notes that in 1886 Cleveland gave the first presidential statement on the subject of labor.
15. McGerr, pp. 119–20. He also discusses the handicrafts movement, pp. 133–34.
16. On the Progressive movement, see Trachtenberg, especially pp. 154–55. I am treating progressivism as a broad movement rather than the political effort that formed a party in 1912 to support Theodore Roosevelt's campaign for president.
17. Wiebe, p. 112.
18. Schlereth writes that in 1890, 202,963 students attended public high schools, rising to 1,851,965 students in 1920, p. 247. See also McGerr, p. 110, and Wiebe, pp. 118–21.
19. Schlereth, p. 260.

20. Schlereth, pp. 209–41. Benjamin Franklin Keith, a Boston showman, "fashioned the vaudeville that appealed to a family audience," p. 230.

21. Ibid., pp. 146–47.

22. Ibid., pp. 84, 164.

23. For a different view, see T. J. Jackson Lears, who discusses Norton, Adams, and the Boston Society of Arts and Crafts in *No Place of Grace: Antimodernism and the Transformation of American Culture, 1880–1920*, 2nd ed., Chicago and London: University of Chicago Press, 1994 (orig. pub. 1981). See ch. 2, "The Figure of the Artisan: Arts and Crafts Ideology," pp. 59–96.

24. Douglass Shand-Tucci, *Boston Bohemia 1881–1900: Ralph Adams Cram, Life and Architecture*, Amherst: University of Massachusetts Press, 1995; Shand-Tucci, *Ralph Adams Cram: An Architect's Four Quests*, Amherst: University of Massachusetts Press, 2005; Ethan Anthony, *Architecture of Ralph Adams Cram and His Office*, New York: W. W. Norton, 2007; Doris Cole and Karen Cord Taylor, *The Lady Architects: Lois Lilley Howe, Eleanor Manning, and Mary Almy*, ed. Sylvia Moore, New York: Midmarch Arts Press, 1990; Margaret Henderson Floyd, *Architecture After Richardson: Regionalism Before Modernism—Longfellow, Alden, and Harlow in Boston and Pittsburgh*, Chicago: University of Chicago Press with the Pittsburgh History and Landmarks Foundation, 1994; and Maureen Meister, *Architecture and the Arts and Crafts Movement in Boston: Harvard's H. Langford Warren*, Hanover, NH: University Press of New England, 2003.

25. *Inspiring Reform: Boston's Arts and Crafts Movement*, exhibition catalogue (hereafter ex. cat.), Marilee Boyd Meyer, consulting curator, Wellesley, MA: Davis Museum and Cultural Center, Wellesley College, 1997; and Beverly K. Brandt, *The Craftsman and the Critic: Defining Usefulness and Beauty in Arts and Crafts-Era Boston*, Amherst: University of Massachusetts Press, 2009.

1. DRAMATIS PERSONAE: TWELVE ARCHITECT-LEADERS

1. The origins and early history of the Society of Arts and Crafts, Boston, are addressed in *Inspiring Reform: Boston's Arts and Crafts Movement*, ex. cat., Marilee Boyd Meyer, consulting curator, Wellesley, MA: Davis Museum and Cultural Center, Wellesley College, 1997; and Beverly K. Brandt, *The Craftsman and the Critic: Defining Usefulness and Beauty in Arts and Crafts-Era Boston*, Amherst: University of Massachusetts Press, 2009. See also Maureen Meister, *Architecture and the Arts and Crafts Movement in Boston: Harvard's H. Langford Warren*, Hanover, NH: University Press of New England, 2003, pp. 84–101.

2. See Papers of the Society of Arts and Crafts, Boston, Archives of American Art, Smithsonian Institution, microfilm reel 319, frame 705 (hereafter cited as SACB Archives, AAA/SI reel: frame). Denman Ross also was among those who signed.

3. *Boston Sunday Globe*, Mar. 21, 1897. Also on microfilm, SACB Archives, AAA/SI 322: 188.

4. William D. Austin, "A History of the Boston Society of Architects in the 19th Century," 3 vols., manuscript, 1942, Boston Athenaeum, vol. 2, ch. 15, p. 17.

5. Ibid., vol. 3, ch. 16, p. 26.

6. The exhibition catalogues are available in the Fine Arts Dept. of the Boston Public Library. For example, see *Catalogue of the First Annual Exhibition of the Boston Architectural Club*, Boston: Boston Architectural Club, 1890.

7. See *Exhibition by the Boston Architectural Club*, Boston: Boston Architectural Club, 1897. For the cover of the catalogue, see SACB Archives, AAA/SI 322: 194.

8. The meetings were covered in the Boston newspapers, and many of the articles may be found on microfilm, SACB Archives, AAA/SI 322: 216–25.

9. Some surviving records identify twenty-one charter members, but other records list twenty-four members. In addition to those mentioned, the Society of Arts and Crafts founders who are consistently identified are Julia de Wolf Addison, J. Templeman Coolidge Jr., Morris Gray, Barton P. Jenks, George P. Kendrick, and Sarah Wyman Whitman. The three additional people identified as founders, mainly in later recollections and documents, are Ralph Adams Cram, Bertram G. Goodhue, and Sarah Choate Sears. See SACB Archives, AAA/SI 300: 6–7; and AAA/SI 316: 660. In a Sept. 23, 1933, article in the *Boston Evening Transcript*, Henry Lewis Johnson lists twenty-four founders, including Cram, Goodhue, and Sears. See SACB Archives, AAA/SI 322: 292–93. Brandt has concluded that twenty-one individuals were charter members. She discusses them in *The Craftsman and the Critic*, pp. 57–68.

10. SACB Archives, AAA/SI 316: 342. Brandt provides an extensive discussion of the jury of the Society of Arts and Crafts, pp. 141–84.

11. SACB Archives, AAA/SI 300: 628.

12. After reporting on bylaw revisions at the Jan. 7, 1898, meeting of the Boston Society of Architects, Austin noted that "the Society has, almost annually, been making changes in the By-Laws, and probably will continue to do so." See Austin, vol. 3, ch. 17, p. 19.

13. "Visitors with Note Books," *Boston Herald*, Apr. 9, 1897. Also on microfilm, SACB Archives, AAA/SI 322: 210.

14. Warren's remarks were reprinted as "Our Work and Prospects," *Handicraft*, vol. 2, no. 9 (Dec. 1903), p. 185.

15. The relationship of architects with the Society of Arts and Crafts is discussed in Beverly Brandt, "The Essential Link: Boston Architects and the Society of Arts and Crafts, 1897–1917," *Tiller*, vol. 2, no. 1 (Sept.–Oct. 1983). She identified thirty-nine architect members. The fortieth architect was Theodore H. Skinner, whose name appears in the list of members in the 1899 Society of Arts and Crafts exhibition catalogue.

16. In addition to the twelve architects discussed as leaders, the following architects were members of the society for a year or more from 1897 through 1917: Francis R. Allen, Henry F. Bigelow, Frank C. Brown, Francis Chandler, Frank E. Cleveland, Charles K. Cummings, Hartley Dennett, Godfrey Downer, Henry H. Dwight, J. Henry Eames, Frank W. Ferguson, George P. Fernald, Richard A. Fisher, Bertram G. Goodhue, William R. Greeley, Alexander E. Hoyle, George Hunt Ingraham, Herbert Jaques, Addison LeBoutillier, Joseph P. Loud, Guy Lowell, Edward Nichols, Frederick Reed, Theodore H. Skinner, W. Dana Swan, Edmund Sylvester, Bertrand E. Taylor, and Edmund Wheelwright. The sources for these names are the 1899 exhibition catalogue and the society's annual reports from 1899 forward.

17. The annual reports of the Society of Arts and Crafts lists of officers, council members, and committee members.

18. Robert D. Andrews obituary, *American Art Annual*, vol. 26, 1929, p. 383. For his time with Peabody, see Robert D. Andrews, "Conditions of Architectural Practice Thirty Years and More Ago," *Architectural Review*, new series vol. 5, no. 11 (Nov. 1917), p. 237.

19. See the tribute to Robert D. Andrews by C. Howard Walker, May 6, 1929, Massachusetts Historical Society, Boston, Tavern Club Records, carton 1, "Andrews, Robert"

folder. See also Robert D. Andrews obituary, *Boston Society of Architects Bulletin*, vol. 14, no. 7 (Oct. 1928), p. 3, which mentions that after his studies at Massachusetts Institute of Technology, Andrews entered the office of Cummings and Sears.

20. Austin, vol. 3, ch. 16, p. 26. See also Walker tribute.

21. George Edward Barton, "Henry Vaughan," obituary, *Journal of the American Institute of Architects*, vol. 5, 1917, pp. 518–19. "Personal," *Brochure Series of Architectural Illustration*, vol. 1, no. 7 (July 1895).

22. "Personal," *Brochure Series*.

23. "Consolation House," *Trained Nurse and Hospital Review*, vol. 52, no. 6 (June 1914), p. 360. Barton's wife described Morris as her husband's "old master," but she doesn't say how Barton was engaged. See Isabel G. Newton, "Consolation House," reprint from *Trained Nurse and Hospital Review* (Dec. 1917), p. 2.

24. The partnership was announced under "Architects' Removals, Etc.," *American Architect and Building News*, vol. 77, no. 1385 (July 12, 1902), p. x.

25. Barton recommended Cockerell to Boston Public Library trustee Henry Bowditch. Early in 1900, Barton contacted Cockerell, who replied in a letter in May expressing his interest in serving as an agent for the library. Barton then forwarded the letter to Bowditch. See letter from Sydney Cockerell to George Edward Barton, May 30, 1900, forwarded by Barton to Henry Bowditch, Nov. 1900, Rare Books, Boston Public Library, MS Eng 147.

26. William P. Stoneman, "'Variously Employed': The Pre-Fitzwilliam Career of Sydney Carlyle Cockerell," in *Transactions of the Cambridge Bibliographical Society*, vol. 13, no. 4 (2010 for 2007), pp. 350–56.

27. "'Pipe of Desire' at Metropolitan," *New York Times*, Mar. 19, 1910. The libretto was published in 1905 and printed by Daniel Berkeley Updike and the Merrymount Press.

28. For more on Barton, see Virginia Anne Metaxas Quiroga, *Occupational Therapy: The First Thirty Years, 1900–1930*, Bethesda, MD: American Occupational Therapy Association, 1995, pp. 116–25. See also Kathleen Barker Schwartz, "Reclaiming Our Heritage: Connecting the *Founding Vision* to the *Centennial Vision*," *American Journal of Occupational Therapy*, vol. 63, no. 6 (Nov./Dec. 2009), pp. 681–90.

29. In a letter to a fellow founder, Barton wrote that he had been the first secretary of the Society of Arts and Crafts and remembered "how easily things slipped out of the hands of the ones who alone were fitted to control its policies." Evidently his sympathies had been with Arthur Carey and a more socialistic direction for the Arts and Crafts organization. See letter from Barton to William Rush Dunton Jr., Dec. 26, 1916, Wilma L. West Archives, American Occupational Therapy Association, Bethesda, MD.

30. Quiroga, p. 125.

31. Barton collaborated with George G. Will of Boston in their entry that won the Shattuck Prize. See *American Architect and Building News*, vol. 62, no. 1196 (Nov. 26, 1898), pp. 73–74. Barton published "Port Sunlight. A Model English Village" in *Architectural Review*, vol. 6, no. 5 (May 1899), pp. 62–66.

32. Archival records indicate that Cram was not a charter member of the Society of Arts and Crafts; however, at a meeting of the council on Apr. 30, 1925, surviving charter members of the society were voted "honorary members," and Cram was included in this group. See SACB Archives, AAA/SI 316: 276. In 1933, Cram was identified as a charter member by Henry Lewis Johnson, suggesting that Cram (along with Bertram

Goodhue and Sarah Choate Sears) joined the organization soon after it was launched and was later considered a founder.

33. For a short overview of Cram's career, see Richard Guy Wilson, "Ralph Adams Cram: Dreamer of the Medieval," in *Medievalism in American Culture*, eds. Bernard Rosenthal and Paul E. Szarmach, Binghamton, NY: Medieval and Renaissance Texts and Studies, vol. 55, 1989, pp. 193–214. The most extensive studies of Cram's career are Douglass Shand-Tucci, *Boston Bohemia 1881–1900: Ralph Adams Cram, Life and Architecture*, Amherst: University of Massachusetts Press, 1995; and Shand-Tucci, *Ralph Adams Cram: An Architect's Four Quests*, Amherst: University of Massachusetts Press, 2005. See also Ethan Anthony, *Architecture of Ralph Adams Cram and His Office*, New York: W. W. Norton, 2007.

34. Montgomery Schuyler, "The Works of Cram, Goodhue, and Ferguson," *Architectural Record*, vol. 29, no. 1 (Jan. 1911), pp. 45–50.

35. "Cram on Tech Faculty," *Boston Evening Transcript*, June 27, 1914. See also Ralph Adams Cram, *My Life in Architecture*, Boston: Little, Brown, 1936, pp. 200–217. Cram served as "senior professor" while a chairman was appointed to handle administrative duties.

36. Howe wrote a short record of her life for her fiftieth reunion at MIT. See "Lois Lilley Howe, MIT '90," 1940, copy in Vertical Files for Architects, Historic New England Library and Archives, Boston. An entry for her also appears in *American Architects Directory*, ed. George S. Koyl, New York: R. R. Bowker for the American Institute of Architects, 1955. For overviews of Howe and her firm, see Doris Cole and Karen Cord Taylor, *The Lady Architects: Lois Lilley Howe, Eleanor Manning, and Mary Almy, 1893–1937*, ed. Sylvia Moore, New York: Midmarch Arts Press, 1990; and Sarah Allaback, *The First Women Architects*, Urbana and Chicago: University of Illinois Press, 2008, pp. 104–17.

37. The MIT Office of the Registrar records that Howe was a student from the fall of 1888 through the spring of 1890, and that she also studied there during the spring term of 1899.

38. Louise Blanchard Bethune became the first female member of the American Institute of Architects in 1888.

39. Measured drawings by Howe and Manning are included in the Historic New England Library and Archives and in the Howe, Manning and Almy Papers, MC9, Institute Archives and Special Collections, MIT.

40. Lois L. Howe and Constance Fuller, *Details From Old New England Houses*, New York: Architectural Book Publishing, 1913; and Howe, *An Architectural Monograph: The Colonel Robert Means House at Amherst, New Hampshire*, White Pines Series of Architectural Monographs, New York: R. F. Whitehead, 1927.

41. The first female fellow of the American Institute of Architects was Louise Blanchard Bethune, who received the designation along with the entire membership of the Western Association of Architects when they joined the institute in 1889. Theodate Pope Riddle was the second fellow, elected in 1926.

42. The work of the firm is well documented by extensive holdings in the Institute Archives and Special Collections, MIT.

43. For highlights of Longfellow's career, see *Who's Who in New England*, Chicago: A. N. Marquis, 1909; and *Who Was Who in America, 1897–1942*, vol. 1, Chicago: Marquis Who's Who, 1943. See also tributes by C. Howard Walker and J. Templeman Coolidge

Jr., Tavern Club Records, carton 4, A. W. Longfellow folder, Massachusetts Historical Society. Archival records on Longfellow are located at the Longfellow House–Washington's Headquarters National Historic Site, Cambridge, MA. The authoritative study of Longfellow's career is Margaret Henderson Floyd's *Architecture After Richardson: Regionalism Before Modernism—Longfellow, Alden, and Harlow in Boston and Pittsburgh*, Chicago: University of Chicago Press with Pittsburgh History and Landmarks Foundation, 1994.

44. See Roland Cosgrove, "Charles D. Maginnis Elected to Membership in Academy of Design," *Boston Traveler*, Mar. 11, 1941; and Robert P. Walsh, "Biographical and Bibliographical Notes," *Liturgical Arts*, vol. 23, no. 4 (Aug. 1955), pp. 154–55. Milda B. Richardson provides additional information in "Chancel Remodeling: Charles D. Maginnis (Maginnis & Walsh)," *The Makers of Trinity Church in the City of Boston*, ed. James F. O'Gorman, Amherst and Boston: University of Massachusetts Press, 2004, pp. 175–94.

45. The fact that Maginnis worked for Peabody and Stearns is noted in a tribute to him written by Daniel Sargent, Tavern Club Records, carton 5, Charles D. Maginnis folder, Massachusetts Historical Society.

46. Annie Robinson, *Peabody and Stearns: Country Houses and Seaside Cottages*, New York: W. W. Norton, 2010, p. 18.

47. Charles D. Maginnis, *Pen Drawing*, Boston: Bates and Guild, 1898.

48. "Artists to Pay New Honor to Architect Maginnis," *Boston Herald*, Nov. 29, 1948.

49. Archives from the firm are maintained as the Maginnis and Walsh Collection in the Fine Arts Dept., Boston Public Library.

50. Charles D. Maginnis, "Catholic Church Architecture," *Architectural Forum*, vol. 27, no. 2 (Aug. 1917), pp. 33–38.

51. For more on the work at Trinity Church, see Richardson, "Chancel Remodeling."

52. Two obituaries for Newhall are on file in the Boston Architectural College Archives, Record Group 035: Boston Architectural Club, Louis C. Newhall folder and Clippings 1892–1925 folder. Sources are not noted.

53. Louis C. Newhall, *The Minor Chateaux and Manor Houses of France*, New York: Architectural Book Publishing, 1914.

54. Unsigned carbon copy tributes to Newhall, one dated Oct. 3, 1933, titled "Louis C. Newhall Memorial Meeting," Boston Architectural College Archives, Record Group 035: Boston Architectural Club, Newhall Memorial 1933 folder.

55. The opening of the clubhouse is described in "Greet 1911 in New Home," *Boston Post*, Jan. 2, 1911.

56. Patricia J. Fanning, *Through an Uncommon Lens: The Life and Photography of F. Holland Day*, Amherst: University of Massachusetts Press, 2008, pp. 161–64, 185.

57. One of Putnam's classmates was William Sumner Appleton Jr., who would found the Society for the Preservation of New England Antiquities in 1910.

58. Putnam contributed regularly to the Harvard College Class of 1896 reports, Harvard University Archives, HUD 296.25. See reports for 1901, 1906, 1911, 1916, 1921.

59. "Young Men Win Bid. Putnam & Cox Chosen to Build New Athenaeum," *Boston Herald*, May 27, 1902. Copy at Harvard University Archives, HUG 300, Putnam, William E., Jr.

60. "W. E. Putnam, Architect, Dies," *Boston Herald*, Aug. 5, 1947. Copy at Harvard University Archives, HUG 300, Putnam, William E., Jr.

61. Shaw also is listed as a member of the society's first jury, appointed in 1900, in May

R. Spain, *The Society of Arts and Crafts, 1897–1924*, Boston and New York: Society of Arts and Crafts, 1924, p. 16. Spain's short history, including her list of jurors, is available on microfilm, SACB Archives, AAA/SI 319: 342. Yet the surviving records of the jury never identify Shaw as a jury member. Brandt, in *The Craftsman and the Critic*, does not include Shaw in Appendix A, "Members of the SACB Jury, 1900–1917," p. 293.

62. "Geo. R. Shaw; Was Designer of Pierce Hall," *Boston Evening Transcript*, Jan. 16, 1937; "George R. Shaw, Architect, Dead," *Boston Herald*, Jan. 16, 1937. Copies at Harvard University Archives, HUG 300, Shaw, George Russell. See also submissions from George Russell Shaw in the Harvard College class of 1869 reports of 1884, 1894, 1901, 1908, Harvard University Archives, HUD 269.

63. The registrar at MIT reports that George Shaw also studied there from 1883 to 1884.

64. Harvard College class of 1869, report of 1908, submission from Robert Gould Shaw, Harvard University Archives, HUD 269.

65. Shaw's thirty-four pocket notebooks, including architectural sketches and notes, may be examined on microfilm. See George Russell Shaw Papers, Archives of American Art, Smithsonian Institution, reels 1120–21.

66. George Russell Shaw, *Knots: Useful and Ornamental*, Boston and New York: Houghton Mifflin, 1924. Reissued by Dover as *Practical and Ornamental Knots*.

67. George Russell Shaw's most important work was *The Genus Pinus*, Cambridge, MA: Riverside Press, 1914.

68. The exhibit was displayed in the Hunnewell Building at the Arnold Arboretum, Boston, but has since been transferred to the Harvard University Herbaria in Cambridge. Shaw's botanical studies are maintained in the Archives of the Arnold Arboretum of Harvard University, Boston, "Papers of George Russell Shaw, 1890s–1930s," II A-1, GRS. George's brother Robert Shaw amassed an extensive collection relating to the history of the theater, which he donated to Harvard in 1915, establishing the Harvard Theater Collection.

69. Thomas Mott Shaw also designed Colonial Revival buildings for Brown University.

70. "Noted Building Designer Dead: Clipston Sturgis Famed Throughout Country," *Boston Herald*, May 9, 1951. Copy at Harvard University Archives, HUG 300, Sturgis, Richard Clipston. See also submissions by Sturgis in Richard Herndon, ed., *Boston of To-Day*, Boston: Post Publishing, 1892, p. 413; in the Harvard College class of 1881 report from 1906, Harvard University Archives, HUD 281.25A; and in *Who's Who in America, 1924–1925*, vol. 13, Chicago: A. N. Marquis, 1925.

71. See "City School-Houses. A Review of the Recent Reports of the Board of School-House Commissioners of Boston, Mass.," *Architectural Review*, vol. 11, no. 6 (June 1904), pp. 161–66; "Boston Public School Buildings," *American Architect and Building News*, vol. 93, no. 1671 (Jan. 4, 1908), pp. 1–4; and R. Clipston Sturgis, "The Schoolhouse Problem," *The Architectural Quarterly of Harvard University*, vol. 2, no. 2 (Dec. 1913), pp. 36–63.

72. R. Clipston Sturgis, "English Gardens," in *European and Japanese Gardens*, ed. Glenn Brown, Philadelphia: Henry T. Coates, 1902; and Sturgis, "Sir Christopher Wren," *Journal of the American Institute of Architects*, vol. 11, no. 3 (1923).

73. Goody, Marvin E., and Robert P. Walsh, eds., *Boston Society of Architects: The First Hundred Years, 1867–1967*, Boston: Boston Society of Architects, pp. 79–80.

74. Sturgis's architectural notebooks and day books, documenting more than 500 of his projects, are at the Boston Athenaeum, Mss. L378.

75. In 1922 the society reported that it had nearly 1,100 members. See SACB Archives, AAA/SI 316: 350.

76. Walker's role as critic of the jury is discussed by Brandt, *The Craftsman and the Critic*, pp. 167–77.

77. "C. H. Walker, 79, Architect, Dies," *Boston Herald*, Apr. 13, 1936; "C. Howard Walker, Architect, Is Dead. Internationally Known as an Authority in Profession and Other Fine Arts," *New York Times*, Apr. 13, 1936. See also entries on Walker in Herndon, ed., *Boston of To-Day*, p. 431; and *Who Was Who in America*, vol. 1, 1897–1942, Chicago: Marquis Who's Who, 1943.

78. Walker's sketchbooks from the expedition and his travels may be examined on microfilm, C. Howard Walker Papers, 1877–1936, Archives of American Art, Smithsonian Institution, reel 1049.

79. C. Howard Walker, *Parish Churches of England*, Boston and New York: Rogers and Manson, 1915; Walker, "Some Old Houses on the Southern Coast of Maine," *White Pine Series of Architectural Monographs*, vol. 4, no. 2 (Apr. 1918), pp. 2–14.

80. George C. Nimmons, ed., *The Significance of the Fine Arts*, Boston: Marshall Jones, 1923; and Walker, *Theory of Mouldings*, Cleveland: J. H. Jansen, 1926, reissued with a foreword by Richard Sammons, New York: W. W. Norton, 2007.

81. "C. Howard Walker, Architect, Is Dead."

82. "Recent Deaths. Professor H. Langford Warren," *Boston Transcript*, June 27, 1917; Ralph Adams Cram, "Letters to the Editor. Masters in Architecture—Langford Warren, Henry Vaughan," *Boston Evening Transcript*, July 2, 1917; R. Clipston Sturgis, "Herbert Langford Warren," obituary, *Journal of the American Institute of Architects*, vol. 5, no. 7 (July 1917), p. 352–53; John Taylor Boyd, "Notes and Comments: Professor H. Langford Warren," *Architectural Record*, vol. 42, no. 6 (Dec. 1917), pp. 588–91; and Charles A. Coolidge, "Herbert Langford Warren (1857–1917)," *Proceedings of the American Academy of Arts and Sciences*, vol. 68 (Dec. 1933), pp. 689–91. See also "Faculty of Architecture. Minute on the Life and Services of Dean Herbert Langford Warren," *Harvard University Gazette*, Dec. 1, 1917, p. 45. Copy on file at Harvard University Archives, HUG 1875.80. James Sturgis Pray is named as author of the tribute in a note on the clipping. See also Meister, *Architecture and the Arts and Crafts Movement in Boston*.

83. For Sturgis, Warren wrote an entry on the architecture of Provence and Languedoc. For Edmund Buckley, ed., *The Fine Arts: A Course of University Lessons on Sculpture, Painting, Architecture, and Decoration*, Chicago: International Art Association, 1900, Warren contributed the chapter titled "Architecture: Renaissance and Modern," pp. 190–234.

84. H. Langford Warren, *The Foundations of Classic Architecture*, intro. by Fiske Kimball, New York: Macmillan, 1919.

85. On Warren's early career, see the entry in Herndon, ed., *Boston of To-Day*, p. 437.

2. Arts and Crafts Advocates, Arts and Crafts Architects

1. A concise introduction to the Arts and Crafts movement may be found in Elizabeth Cumming and Wendy Kaplan, *The Arts and Crafts Movement*, rev. ed., London: Thames and Hudson, 2004 (orig. pub. 1991). See also Wendy Kaplan, *The Arts and Crafts Movement in Europe and America: Design for the Modern World*, ex. cat., Los Angeles and New York: Los Angeles County Museum of Art and Thames and Hud-

son, 2004; Karen Livingstone and Linda Parry, *International Arts and Crafts*, ex. cat., London: V & A Publications, 2005; Isabelle Anscombe and Charlotte Gere, *Arts and Crafts in Britain and America*, New York: Van Nostrand Reinhold, 1978; and Gillian Naylor, *The Arts and Crafts Movement: A Study of Its Sources, Ideals and Influence on Design Theory*, Cambridge, MA: MIT Press, 1971.

Two important exhibition catalogues that address the American Arts and Crafts movement are Wendy Kaplan, ed., *"The Art That Is Life": The Arts and Crafts Movement in America, 1875–1920*, ex. cat., Boston: Museum of Fine Arts and Bulfinch Press, 1987; and Robert Judson Clark, ed., *The Arts and Crafts Movement in America, 1876–1916*, ex. cat., Princeton, NJ: Princeton University, 1972.

2. A. W. N. Pugin, *Contrasts: Or, a Parallel between the Noble Edifices of the Fourteenth and Fifteenth Centuries, and Similar Buildings of the Present Day, Shewing the Present Decay of Taste*, London: the author, 1836; and Pugin, *The True Principles of Pointed or Christian Architecture*, London: J. Weale, 1841. See also Paul Atterbury, ed., *A.W.N. Pugin: Master of Gothic Revival*, ex. cat., New York and New Haven, CT: Bard Graduate Center and Yale University Press, 1995; and Rosemary Hill, *God's Architect: Pugin and the Building of Romantic Britain*, New Haven, CT: Yale University Press, 2009 (orig. pub. 2007).

3. Atterbury, p. 314.

4. Michael Fisher, *Hardman of Birmingham: Goldsmith and Glasspainter*, Ashbourne, England: Landmark Publishing, 2008.

5. John Ruskin, *Modern Painters*, 2nd ed., vol. 3 (part IV, "Of Many Things"), London: Smith, Elder, 1867 (orig. pub. 1856), ch. 3, "Of the Real Nature of Greatness of Style," pp. 24–44.

6. Ibid., p. 36.

7. John Ruskin, *The Seven Lamps of Architecture*, London: Smith, Elder, 1849. See also Michael Brooks, *John Ruskin and Victorian Architecture*, London: Thames and Hudson, 1989 (orig. pub. 1987).

8. Ruskin, *The Seven Lamps of Architecture*, pp. 186–87. In his 1857 address to the Architectural Association, Ruskin also condemned the architect who feels "its being incumbent upon him to invent a 'new style' worthy of modern civilization in general, and of England in particular." See Lecture IV, "The Influence of Imagination in Architecture," no. 101, in Ruskin, *The Two Paths*, Opington and London: George Allen, 1900 (orig. pub. 1859), p. 137.

9. John Ruskin, *The Stones of Venice*, vol. 2, London: Smith, Elder, 1853, pp. 151–231.

10. Ibid., p. 171.

11. Owen Jones, *The Grammar of Ornament*, London: Day, 1856.

12. See Stephen Calloway and Lynn Federle Orr, eds., *The Cult of Beauty: The Aesthetic Movement, 1860–1900*, ex. cat., London: V & A Publications, 2011. See also Elizabeth Aslin, *The Aesthetic Movement*, New York: Praeger, 1969; and Doreen Bolger Burke et al., *In Pursuit of Beauty: Americans and the Aesthetic Movement*, New York: Metropolitan Museum of Art and Rizzoli, 1986.

13. Cumming in Cumming and Kaplan, pp. 14–21.

14. Morris's lecture appeared in the Dec. 8, 1877, issue of *The Architect*. A year later, it was issued as a pamphlet, "The Decorative Arts: Their Relation to Modern Life and Progress," London: 1878; reprinted as "The Lesser Arts," May Morris, ed., *Collected Works of William Morris*, London: Longmans, Green, 1915, XXII, pp. 3–28. See also Peter Stansky, *Redesigning the World: William Morris, the 1880s, and the Arts and Crafts*, Palo

Alto, CA: Society for the Promotion of Science and Scholarship, 1996 (orig. pub. 1985), pp. 57–59.

15. Stansky, p. 52–56.
16. William Morris, "The Aims of Art," London: Office of "the Commonweal," 1887.
17. Morris published these ideas in "The Revival of Handicraft," *Fortnightly Review*, vol. 1 (Nov. 1888), pp. 603–10. Excerpted in Stansky, pp. 64–66.
18. Morris first presented this material in an 1889 lecture for the Arts and Crafts Exhibition Society and then published it in *Gothic Architecture*, London: 1893. See Stansky, pp. 235–38.
19. See Cumming in Cumming and Kaplan, pp. 17–28, and Anscombe and Gere for summaries about English guild activities. See also Stansky.
20. Fiona MacCarthy, *The Simple Life: C. R. Ashbee in the Cotswolds*, London: Lund Humphries, 1981; and Alan Crawford, *C. R. Ashbee: Architect, Designer, and Romantic Socialist*, New Haven, CT: Yale University Press, 1985.
21. The stylistic diversity of the Arts and Crafts movement and its unifying themes are addressed in Wendy Kaplan, *The Arts and Crafts Movement in Europe and America*, and in the introduction by Karen Livingstone and Linda Parry in *International Arts and Crafts*. On Arts and Crafts architecture in Britain, see Elizabeth Cumming, "Architecture in Britain" pp. 31–65, in Cumming and Kaplan; and Peter Davey, *Arts and Crafts Architecture*, London: Phaidon, 1995 (orig. pub. 1980).
22. See Michael J. Lewis, *The Gothic Revival*, London: Thames and Hudson, 2002, for an overview of the revival in Europe and North America. On Strawberry Hill, see pp. 23–33.
23. Davey, pp. 13–18, discusses Pugin's work as a precursor to Arts and Crafts architecture.
24. Lewis, pp. 90–98.
25. Davey, pp. 19–21; Lewis, pp. 108–19, 142–44.
26. Cumming in Cumming and Kaplan, p. 15.
27. Andrew Saint, *Richard Norman Shaw*, New Haven, CT, and London: Yale University Press, 1976. See also Davey, pp. 46–50; and Cumming in Cumming and Kaplan, pp. 34–36.
28. See Margaret Richardson, *The Craft Architects*, New York: Rizzoli in association with the Royal Institute of British Architects, 1983, pp. 23–57.
29. Sheila Kirk, *Philip Webb: Pioneer of Arts and Crafts Architecture*, Chichester, West Sussex, UK: Wiley Academy, 2005. See also Davey, pp. 39–46.
30. Kirk, pp. 83, 89.
31. Ibid., p. 6.
32. On Webb's country houses, see Kirk, pp. 104–64.
33. Ibid., pp. 86–88. See also Kirk's discussion of Smeaton Manor, Great Smeaton, North Yorkshire (1876–79), in which Webb responded to the English classical tradition, pp. 129–31.
34. Richardson, p. 113.
35. Ibid.
36. Richardson, pp. 113–21.
37. William Morgan, *The Almighty Wall: The Architecture of Henry Vaughan*, New York and Cambridge, MA: Architectural History Foundation and MIT Press, 1983, pp. 15–16. See also Lewis, pp. 172–79.

38. Godfrey Rubens, *William Richard Lethaby, His Life and Work*, London: Architectural Press, 1986. See also Davey, pp. 65–77; and Stansky, pp. 132–40.

39. Anscombe and Gere, pp. 48, 144.

40. Richardson, pp. 32–33.

41. Now demolished, the Hurst is illustrated in Sir Lawrence Weaver, *Small Country Houses of To-Day*, vol. 1, London: Country Life and George Newnes, 1922. See also Davey, p. 68; and Richardson, p. 48.

42. W. R. Lethaby, *Architecture, Mysticism and Myth*, 2nd ed., London: Percival, 1892 (orig. pub. 1891), p. 8.

43. See Richardson, p. 102.

44. Ibid., p. 104.

45. T. Raffles Davison, *Modern Homes: Selected Examples of Dwelling Houses*, London: George Bell and Sons, 1909, pp. 20–21. See also Stuart Durant, *C. F. A. Voysey*, London: Academy, 1992, pp. 34–37; and Davey, p. 93.

46. C. F. A. Voysey, "Ideas in Things," in Durant, p. 114, reprinted from T. Raffles Davison, ed., *The Arts Connected with Building*, London: B. T. Batsford, 1909.

47. Voysey in Durant, p. 118.

48. "The English Home," *British Architect*, vol. 75, 1911, p. 69, quoted in Davey, p. 99.

49. See Cumming in Cumming and Kaplan, p. 55.

50. Davey makes this observation, writing that "most Arts and Crafts architects were torn between Ruskinian savageness and changefulness . . . and an attempt to achieve fidelity to place: one of the reasons for the rise of Neo-Georgian architecture," p. 140.

51. Davey, pp. 112, 168.

52. Davison, pp. 175–80; Davey, p. 102. Newton condemned the "freak architecture," specifically the "New Art" on the Continent, in his introduction to *A Book of Country Houses*, London: B. T. Batsford, 1903.

53. Robert D. Andrews, "The Future of American Architecture," *Boston Architectural Club Exhibition Catalogue*, ex. cat., Boston: Boston Architectural Club, 1904, p. 11.

54. See C. Howard Walker, "L'Art Nouveau," *Architectural Review* (this and subsequent references are to the Boston-based periodical), vol. 9, no. 1 (Jan. 1904), pp. 13–20. He writes that "where there is no canon of taste, there is a chaos of interpretations," p. 13.

55. For example, see H. Langford Warren, "The Influence of France upon American Architecture," *American Architect and Building News*, vol. 66, no. 1248 (Nov. 25, 1899), pp. 67–68.

56. On the Society of Arts and Crafts, Boston, see Marilee Boyd Meyer, consulting curator, *Inspiring Reform: Boston's Arts and Crafts Movement*, Wellesley, MA: Davis Museum and Cultural Center, Wellesley College, 1997. See also Beverly K. Brandt, *The Craftsman and the Critic: Defining Usefulness and Beauty in Arts and Crafts-Era Boston*, Amherst: University of Massachusetts Press, 2009; and Maureen Meister, *Architecture and the Arts and Crafts Movement in Boston: Harvard's H. Langford Warren*, Hanover, NH: University Press of New England, 2003, pp. 84–101.

57. Henry Lewis Johnson, "Another Boston 'First,'" *Boston Evening Transcript*, Sept. 23, 1933.

58. Leslie M. Freudenheim, *Building with Nature: Inspiration for the Arts and Crafts Home*, Salt Lake City, UT: Gibbs Smith, 2005, pp. 69–71. See also Richard Guy Wilson, "'Divine Excellence': The Arts and Crafts Life in California," in Kenneth R. Trapp, ed., *The*

Arts and Crafts Movement in California: Living the Good Life, New York: Abbeville, 1993, p. 18.

59. Clark notes the creation of the Minneapolis Chalk and Chisel Club in his "Chronology," p. xiv. See also James Massey and Shirley Maxwell, *Arts and Crafts Design in America*, San Francisco: Chronicle, 1998, p. 166.

60. Wendy Kaplan quotes Margaret Whiting, one of the Deerfield society's founders, in "America: The Quest for Democratic Design," *The Arts and Crafts Movement in Europe and America*, p. 255.

61. On the Arts and Crafts movement in Chicago, see Judith A. Barter and Monica Obniski, "Chicago: A Bridge to the Future," in *Apostles of Beauty: Arts and Crafts from Britain to Chicago*, Judith A. Barter, ed., Chicago and New Haven, CT: Art Institute of Chicago and Yale University Press, 2009, pp. 151–88.

62. Ibid., p. 158.

63. Ibid., pp. 158, 176.

64. On Hubbard and Roycroft, see Marie Via and Marjorie Searl, eds., *Head, Heart, and Hand: Elbert Hubbard and the Roycrofters*, Rochester, NY: University of Rochester Press, 1994. See also Brandon K. Ruud, "'To Promote and to Extend the Principles Established by Morris': Elbert Hubbard, Gustav Stickley, and the Redefinition of American Arts and Crafts," in *Apostles of Beauty*, pp. 83–118.

65. Jack Quinan, "Elbert Hubbard's Roycroft," in *Head, Heart, and Hand*, pp. 1–19.

66. Ibid., p. 7. Quinan observes that it is not known whether Hubbard met Morris during this visit, p. 17, n. 5.

67. Ibid., p. 11.

68. William Ayres, ed., *A Poor Sort of Heaven, A Good Sort of Earth: The Rose Valley Arts and Crafts Experiment*, ex. cat., Brandywine River Museum, Chadds Ford, PA, 1983.

69. William Ayres, "Intersections: Place, People, and Ideology," in *A Poor Sort of Heaven, A Good Sort of Earth*, p. 13.

70. Ibid., p. 20.

71. Nancy E. Green, ed., *Byrdcliffe: An American Arts and Crafts Colony*, ex. cat., Herbert F. Johnson Museum of Art, Cornell University, Ithaca, NY, 2004.

72. Tom Wolf, "Byrdcliffe's History," in *Byrdcliffe*, pp. 16–35.

73. Wolf, "Art at Byrdcliffe," in *Byrdcliffe*, pp. 97–98.

74. See Ruud, "'To Promote and to Extend the Principles Established by Morris.'" See also David Cathers, *Gustav Stickley*, London: Phaidon, 2003.

75. On Craftsman Farms, see Mark A. Hewitt, *Gustav Stickley's Craftsman Farms: The Quest for an Arts and Crafts Utopia*, Syracuse, NY: Syracuse, 2001; and *Gustav Stickley—His Craft: A Daily Vision and a Dream*, Parsippany, NJ: Craftsman Farms Foundation, 1992.

76. Eileen Boris, *Art and Labor: Ruskin, Morris, and the Craftsman Ideal in America*, Philadelphia: Temple University Press, 1986, pp. 32–33.

77. Meister, p. 99.

78. See Leland Roth, *A Concise History of American Architecture*, New York: Icon, 1980 (orig. pub. 1979), pp. 128–38.

79. Ibid., p. 128.

80. Lewis, pp. 119–20.

81. The English carvers were Robert Ellin and John Kitson. At Brattle Square Church, Evans directed a team in carving the sculpture created by Auguste Bartholdi. In his subsequent work, Evans developed his own designs in collaboration with the architects.

See Ann Clifford, "John Evans (1847–1923) and Architectural Sculpture in Boston," unpublished MA thesis, Tufts University, 1992.

82. Richard Guy Wilson, "American Arts and Crafts Architecture: Radical though Dedicated to the Cause Conservative," in Kaplan, ed., "*The Art That Is Life*," pp. 109–12.

83. The Arts and Crafts movement in American architecture is examined by Wendy Kaplan, "Regionalism in American Architecture," in Cumming and Kaplan, pp. 107–42; Wilson, "American Arts and Crafts Architecture," pp. 101–31; and Davey, pp. 193–217. See also Massey and Maxwell, *Arts and Crafts Design in America*, which presents a sampling of Arts and Crafts buildings throughout the United States. Kaplan includes her views on Arts and Crafts architecture in America in "America: The Quest for Democratic Design," Kaplan, ed., *The Arts and Crafts Movement in Europe and America*. Richard Guy Wilson expands his analysis in his introduction to *From Architecture to Object: Masterworks of the American Arts and Crafts Movement*, New York: Dutton in association with Hirschl and Adler Galleries, 1989, pp. 11–21.

84. Wilson discusses these two directions in American architecture in "American Arts and Crafts Architecture," p. 105, and in *From Architecture to Object*, p. 13.

85. H. Langford Warren, "The Year's Architecture," in *Catalogue of the Architectural Exhibition*, ex. cat., Boston: Boston Architectural Club and Boston Society of Architects, 1899, p. 17.

86. Vaughan's contribution was the Chapel of St. Peter and St. Paul, St. Paul's School, Concord, NH (1886–94), discussed in Morgan, *The Almighty Wall*, pp. 89–100. Cope and Stewardson introduced this new collegiate Gothic at Bryn Mawr College during the 1880s. See Lewis, *The Gothic Revival*, pp. 185–86.

87. Warren, "The Year's Architecture," p. 18.

88. In "The Year's Architecture," p. 18, Warren comments on Boston's Colonial Revival. On Philadelphia's Arts and Crafts architecture, see Jane Perkins Claney, "The New Simplicity: Domestic Architecture of Philadelphia's Main Line, 1900–1920," *Tiller*, vol. 2, no. 6 [1984], pp. 42–85.

89. Claney, p. 43.

90. In describing trends in Boston in his 1899 essay "The Year's Architecture," Warren writes, "The recent revival of Georgian work in England and the renewed study of the work of Wren, Hawksmoor, and Gibbs has not been without its influence," p. 18.

91. Ibid., p. 17.

92. Architectural Notebooks of Richard Clipston Sturgis, Boston Athenaeum, series 2, no. 39, May 1907–Oct. 1907. Undated draft letter.

93. Richard Oliver, *Bertram Grosvenor Goodhue*, New York and Cambridge, MA: Architectural History Foundation and MIT Press, 1983. See also Romy Wyllie, *Bertram Goodhue: His Life and Residential Architecture*, New York: W. W. Norton, 2007.

94. See Ray Stubblebine, *Stickley's Craftsman Homes: Plans, Drawings, Photographs*, Layton, UT: Gibbs Smith, 2002.

95. C. R. Ashbee, *A Report by Mr. C. R. Ashbee to the Council of the National Trust for Places of Historic Interest and Natural Beauty, on His Visit to the United States*, London: Essex House Press, 1901.

96. H. Allen Brooks, *Frank Lloyd Wright and the Prairie School*, New York: Braziller, 1984.

97. Quoted in Anscombe and Gere, p. 36.

98. Wilson Eyre, "The Development of American Dwelling Architecture during the Last Thirty Years," *Architectural Review*, new series vol. 5, no. 11 (Nov. 1917), p. 243.

99. Charles Keeler, *The Simple Home*, Santa Barbara, CA: Peregrine Smith, 1979 (orig. pub. 1904). For a discussion of the concept of the simple home, including the influence of Charles Wagner's *The Simple Life* of 1901, see Cheryl Robertson, "House and Home in the Arts and Crafts Era: Reforms for Simpler Living," in Kaplan, ed., "*The Art That Is Life*," pp. 336–57.

100. Edward R. Bosley and Anne E. Mallek, eds., *A New and Native Beauty: The Art and Craft of Greene and Greene*, ex. cat., London and Pasadena, CA: Merrell and the Gamble House, 2008. In particular, see the essay by Bruce Smith, "Sunlight and Elsewhere: Finding California in the Work of Greene and Greene," pp. 59–81.

101. Cram did not mention the Greenes by name, but he clearly was referring to them and their work. See Ralph Adams Cram, "The Promise of American House Building," in Richardson Wright, ed., *Low-Cost Suburban Homes*, New York: Robert M. McBride, 1920, pp. 29–30.

102. Oliver, pp. 108–19.

103. Kaplan in Cumming and Kaplan, pp. 127–29.

3. An Intellectual Stew: Emerson, Norton, Brandeis

1. See Philip F. Gura, *American Transcendentalism: A History*, New York: Hill and Wang, 2007, pp. 8, 289.

2. Alexander Wadsworth Longfellow Papers, box 3, 1882 Diary (no. 2), entry on Sunday, Apr. 30, 1882. Longfellow House–Washington's Headquarters National Historic Site, Cambridge, MA.

3. In 1826 Sampson Reed published a treatise, "Observations on the Growth of the Mind," that Emerson greatly admired and that led to his study of Swedenborg. See Gura, pp. 59–64. See also John McAleer, *Ralph Waldo Emerson: Days of Encounter*, Boston: Little, Brown, 1984, pp. 84–85.

4. McAleer, p. 85.

5. Douglass Shand-Tucci, *Boston Bohemia 1881–1900: Ralph Adams Cram, Life and Architecture*, Amherst: University of Massachusetts Press, 1995, p. 6.

6. Douglass Shand-Tucci, *Ralph Adams Cram: An Architect's Four Quests*, Amherst: University of Massachusetts Press, 2005, p. 321.

7. Shand-Tucci, *Boston Bohemia*, p. 32. In a third stage, when he was still in his early twenties, Cram wrote that he had turned to Buddhism.

8. Shand-Tucci presents his own ideas about how Emerson's writings would have resonated with Cram. See *Ralph Adams Cram: An Architect's Four Quests*, pp. 321–22.

9. Caroline Healey Dall, *Transcendentalism in New England: A Lecture*, Boston: Roberts Brothers, 1897; and Thomas Wentworth Higginson, *Cheerful Yesterdays*, Boston: Houghton Mifflin, 1898.

10. See "Address of Charles Eliot Norton" in *The Centenary of the Birth of Ralph Waldo Emerson as Observed in Concord*, May 25, 1903, Concord, MA: Social Circle in Concord, 1903, pp. 45–58.

11. The editors of *Handicraft* did not provide the sources of the Emerson quotes.

12. *Handicraft*, vol. 1, no. 10 (Jan. 1903).

13. See Emerson's "Art," from *Essays* (first series), in Joel Porte, ed., *Ralph Waldo Emerson: Essays and Lectures*, New York: Library of America, 1983, p. 439.

14. First published by William Morris in "The Beauty of Life," *Labour and Pleasure versus*

Labour and Sorrow, Birmingham, England: Cund Bros, 1880; republished in Morris, *Hopes and Fears for Art*, London: Ellis and White, 1882.

15. *Handicraft*, vol. 2, no. 1 (Apr. 1903). From Emerson's "Beauty," *The Conduct of Life*, in Porte, ed., pp. 1103–4.

16. *Handicraft*, vol. 2, no. 2 (May 1903). From Emerson's "Considerations by the Way," *The Conduct of Life*, in Porte, ed., p. 1090.

17. *Handicraft*, vol. 2, no. 5 (Aug. 1903). From Emerson's "Considerations by the Way," in Porte, ed., p. 1086.

18. *Handicraft*, vol. 2, no. 7 (Oct. 1903). From Emerson's "Art," in Porte, ed., p. 431.

19. *Handicraft*, vol. 2, no. 9 (Dec. 1903). From Emerson's "Art," in Porte, ed., pp. 431–32.

20. *Handicraft*, vol. 2, no. 8 (Nov. 1903). From Emerson's "Self-Reliance," *Essays* (first series), in Porte, ed., p. 279.

21. Ibid., p. 278.

22. Ibid.

23. Ibid.

24. Sarah Whitman, "Stained Glass," *Handicraft*, vol. 2, no. 6 (Sept. 1903), p. 131.

25. Frederic Allen Whiting, "What the Arts and Crafts Movement Has Accomplished," *Handicraft*, vol. 3, no. 3 (June 1910), p. 97.

26. Emerson, "Beauty," in Porte, ed., pp. 1103–4. At the conclusion of "Considerations by the Way," Emerson repeats his belief in the importance of loving "what is simple and beautiful," in Porte, ed., p. 1096.

27. Emerson, "Beauty," in Porte, ed., p. 1112.

28. Emerson, *Nature*, first published anonymously in 1836, in Porte, ed., p. 10.

29. Emerson, "Considerations by the Way," in Porte, ed., p. 1090.

30. Emerson, "Self-Reliance," in Porte, ed., p. 275.

31. Emerson, *English Traits*, published in 1856, in Porte, ed., pp. 763–936.

32. Ibid., p. 935.

33. Ralph Waldo Emerson, "Progress of Culture," delivered as a lecture July 18, 1867, *Letters and Social Aims*, rev. ed., Boston: James R. Osgood, 1876, pp. 172–73. See also Kathleen Verduin, "Medievalism and the Mind of Emerson," in Bernard Rosenthal and Paul E. Szarmach, eds., *Medievalism in American Culture*, Binghamton, NY: Medieval and Renaissance Texts and Studies, 1989, pp. 129–50.

34. Thoreau translated passages from the *Lotus Sutra*, discussed by Lawrence Buell, *Emerson*, Cambridge, MA, and London: Belknap Press of Harvard University Press, 2003, p. 172.

35. For example, see Emerson, "Self-Reliance," in Porte, ed., p. 275.

36. For Emerson's comments on travel, see "Self-Reliance," in Porte, ed., pp. 277–78; and "Considerations by the Way," in Porte, pp. 1090–91.

37. Although Emerson abandoned the Unitarian church, he remained interested in various religious traditions, including Eastern religions. See Buell, pp. 158–98.

38. Emerson, "Art," in Porte, ed., p. 440.

39. Emerson, "Progress of Culture," p. 168.

40. Emerson, "Considerations by the Way," in Porte, ed., p. 1089.

41. Among those who emphasized social reform were Orestes Brownson, George Ripley, and Theodore Parker, discussed by Gura in *American Transcendentalism*.

42. For Emerson's friendship with Carlyle, see McAleer, *Ralph Waldo Emerson*; and Robert D. Richardson Jr., *Emerson: The Mind on Fire*, Berkeley: University of California, 1995.

43. Ruskin called Emerson a great teacher while also criticizing him in Letter 12, "Dicta-torship," Mar. 20, 1867, *Time and Tide, by Weare and Tyne*, New York: John Wiley and Son, 1869 (orig. pub. 1867), p. 74. Ruskin also wrote that next to Carlyle, "for my own immediate help and teaching, I nearly always look to Emerson," E. T. Cook and Alex-ander Wedderburn, eds., *Works of John Ruskin*, vol. 17, London: George Allen, 1905, p. 477.

44. W. Holman Hunt, *Pre-Raphaelitism and the Pre-Raphaelite Brotherhood*, vol. 1, New York: Macmillan, 1905, p. 159.

45. See Walter Crane, *An Artist's Reminiscences*, New York: Macmillan, 1907, pp. 78–79. In 1891 Crane and his wife visited Concord and Emerson's son, p. 369. In 1896 and 1900, Ashbee traveled to Concord and visited Emerson family members. See Alan Crawford, *C. R. Ashbee: Architect, Designer, and Romantic Socialist*, New Haven, CT: Yale Univer-sity Press, 1985, p. 69; and Felicity Ashbee, *Janet Ashbee*, Syracuse, NY: Syracuse Uni-versity, 2002, p. 54. See also *A Report by Mr. C. R. Ashbee to the Council of the National Trust for Places of Historic Interest and Natural Beauty*, London: Essex House, 1901, p. 12. Morris stands out for having written virtually nothing about Emerson, which seems odd in light of the fact that so many of those close to Morris read the American's work.

46. "The Arts and Crafts," *Boston Daily Advertiser*, Apr. 30, 1897. Also on microfilm, SACB Archives, AAA/SI 322: 224.

47. Spain, May R., *The Society of Arts and Crafts, 1897–1924*, Boston and New York: Society of Arts and Crafts, 1924, pp. 10–11. Also on microfilm, SACB Archives, AAA/SI 319: 492–510.

48. "Encouraging Applied Art. Permanent Society Formed, with Many Members," *Boston Herald*, May 14, 1897. Also on microfilm, SACB Archives, AAA/SI 322: 225.

49. Spain, p. 11.

50. William D. Austin, "A History of the Boston Society of Architects in the 19th Century," 3 vols., manuscript, 1942, Boston Athenaeum, vol. 2, ch. 13, pp. 4, 6.

51. Records of the Tavern Club, including files on individual members, are held by the Massachusetts Historical Society, Boston.

52. "Letters from Europe Written by H. Langford Warren," bound volume of photocopies, Frances Loeb Library, Special Collections, Harvard University, May 1, 1893.

53. Kermit Vanderbilt, *Charles Eliot Norton: Apostle of Culture in a Democracy*, Cambridge, MA: Belknap Press of Harvard University Press, 1959, p. 21. See also James Turner, *The Liberal Education of Charles Eliot Norton*, Baltimore: Johns Hopkins University Press, 1999, p. 28; and Linda Dowling, *Charles Eliot Norton: The Art of Reform in Nine-teenth-Century America*, Hanover, NH: University of New Hampshire Press, 2007, pp. 99–100.

54. Sara Norton and M. A. DeWolfe Howe, eds., *Letters of Charles Eliot Norton*, vol. 1, Boston and New York: Houghton Mifflin, 1913, pp. 26–27.

55. [Charles Eliot Norton], "Dwellings and Schools for the Poor," *North American Review*, vol. 74, no. 155 (Apr. 1852), pp. 464–89.

56. For a discussion of Norton's model lodging-house project, see Vanderbilt, pp. 39–43. See also his letter of Feb. 7, 1860, to Elizabeth Gaskell, in *Letters of Charles Eliot Norton*, pp. 204–6, and [Charles Eliot Norton], "Model Lodging-Houses in Boston," *Atlantic Monthly*, vol. 5, no. 6 (June 1860), pp. 673–80.

57. See *Boston Directory*, Boston: Geo. Adams, 1855, p. 400. See also Vanderbilt, p. 47.

58. Norton met Ruskin when they attended the same party in London in 1850, but it was

not until 1855 that they had any meaningful interchange. See Vanderbilt, p. 36, and Turner, p. 90. On the 1855 meeting, see Turner, pp. 126–27; and Dowling, pp. 27–28.

59. Ruskin's influence on Norton is discussed by Dowling, pp. 13–21.

60. Charles Eliot Norton, "The Manchester Exhibition," *Atlantic Monthly*, vol. 1, no. 1 (Nov. 1857), pp. 33–46.

61. Charles Eliot Norton, *Notes of Travel and Study in Italy*, Boston: Ticknor and Fields, 1859. See also Dowling, pp. 33–36.

62. Vanderbilt, p. 63; Turner, p. 137; and Dowling, p. 19.

63. See the letter from Rossetti to Norton, no. 154, Jan. 9, 1862, in William Michael Rossetti, ed., *Ruskin, Rossetti, Preraphaelitism*, London: George Allen, 1899, pp. 296–307.

64. Norton and Howe, eds., *Letters of Charles Eliot Norton*, vol. 1, pp. 309–10. See also pp. 341–48.

65. Norton and Howe, eds., *Letters of Charles Eliot Norton*, vol. 2, pp. 285–86.

66. Gura describes the theological debate, pp. 21–45. He writes that Emerson broke with Unitarianism because he believed the literal "meaning of scriptural language was not as important as its more symbolic function," pp. 43–44. The Divinity School Address and its aftermath also are discussed by McAleer, pp. 245–66.

67. Turner, p. 111; and Dowling, p. 101.

68. Norton and Howe, eds., *Letters of Charles Eliot Norton*, vol. 1, pp. 185–86; and Turner, pp. 164–65.

69. Norton and Howe, eds., *Letters of Charles Eliot Norton*, vol. 1, p. 215.

70. "Address of Charles Eliot Norton," *The Centenary of the Birth of Ralph Waldo Emerson*, p. 51.

71. Norton and Howe, eds., *Letters of Charles Eliot Norton*, vol. 1, p. 399.

72. Ibid., p. 415.

73. Ibid., p. 503.

74. Ibid., p. 506. See also Vanderbilt, pp. 112–16; and Dowling, p. 134.

75. Norton and Howe, eds., *Letters of Charles Eliot Norton*, vol. 2, p. 132.

76. On Norton's career at Harvard, see Vanderbilt, pp. 119–41; and Turner, pp. 253–75.

77. Turner, p. 253.

78. Ibid., p. 256.

79. Vanderbilt, p. 141. In the 1874–75 academic year, Norton was hired as "Lecturer on the History of the Fine Arts as Connected with Literature." From 1875 until his retirement in 1898, he was "Professor of the History of Art." See the entry on Charles Eliot Norton in *Historical Register of Harvard University, 1636–1936*, Cambridge, MA: Harvard University, 1937, "Officers of Government and Instruction, 1637–1936," copy at Harvard University Archives.

80. Vanderbilt, pp. 126–32; and Turner, pp. 262–63, 302. See also "Fine Arts III, 1895–1896," notes taken by Arthur Rindge Wendell, Harvard University Archives, HUC 8895.328A, box 648.

81. Norton and Howe, eds., *Letters of Charles Eliot Norton*, vol. 2, pp. 133–34. On Norton and aestheticism, see Dowling, pp. 137–43. See also T. J. Jackson Lears, *No Place of Grace: Antimodernism and the Transformation of American Culture, 1880–1920*, Chicago and London: University of Chicago Press, 2nd ed., 1994 (orig. pub. 1981), pp. 243–47.

82. For example, see Norton's letter to Ruskin of Feb. 10, 1874, in Norton and Howe, eds., *Letters of Charles Eliot Norton*, vol. 2, pp. 34–35; and his letter to Ruskin of Mar. 18, 1874, p. 40. In addition to Ruskin, Norton was influenced by the philosopher John Stuart

Mill, who in 1867, as rector of St. Andrews University, gave an important address on the value of education in the fine arts. See Dowling, pp. 134–36.

83. Charles Eliot Norton, *Historical Studies of Church Building in the Middle Ages: Venice, Siena, Florence*, New York: Harper and Brothers, 1880.

84. Norton and Howe, eds., *Letters of Charles Eliot Norton*, vol. 1, pp. 269–72.

85. Ibid., p. 270.

86. Charles Eliot Norton, "The Lack of Old Homes in America," *Scribner's Magazine*, vol. 5 (May 1889), pp. 636–40.

87. Charles Eliot Norton, review of *The Oxford Museum* by Henry W. Acland and John Ruskin, *Atlantic Monthly*, vol. 4 (Dec. 1859), pp. 767–70.

88. Charles Eliot Norton, "The Fine Arts. The Harvard and Yale Memorial Buildings," *Nation*, vol. 5 (July 11, 1867), pp. 34–35. Norton was writing about an engraving of Memorial Hall that had just been issued. The building would be completed in 1878.

89. See "Fine Arts III, 1895–1896," Wendell notes, p. 11.

90. Charles Eliot Norton, "A Criticism of Harvard Architecture Made to the Board of Overseers," *Harvard Graduates Magazine*, vol. 12, no. 47 (Mar. 1904), pp. 359–62.

91. Guy Lowell's new lecture hall was subsequently named the Lowell Lecture Hall. See letter from Charles Eliot Norton to Charles W. Eliot, Apr. 25, 1904, Harvard University Archives, UAI.5.150, box 235, Charles Eliot Norton folder.

92. Robert D. Andrews refers to Norton's criticism in "The Compensation of Architects," *Architectural Review*, vol. 1, no. 3 (Feb. 1, 1892), p. 19.

93. Austin, vol. 3, ch. 16, p. 29.

94. See also Maureen Meister, "An 'Uncommonly Good' Design: H. Langford Warren's 1906 Drawings for a Proposed Press at Harvard," *Harvard Library Bulletin*, vol. 16, no. 4 (winter 2005), pp. 45–65.

95. Letter from Charles Eliot Norton to Charles W. Eliot, Mar. 2, 1906, Harvard University Archives, UAI.5.150, box 235, Charles Eliot Norton folder.

96. Letter from Charles Eliot Norton to Charles W. Eliot, Mar. 6, 1906, Harvard University Archives, UAI.5.150, box 235, Charles Eliot Norton folder.

97. The drawings are preserved in Special Collections, Frances Loeb Library, Harvard Graduate School of Design.

98. For the mission statement, see SACB Archives, AAA/SI 300: 9. It also appears in Spain, pp. 11–12, who credits Norton as the author.

99. "Aim of the Society of Arts and Crafts," *Boston Evening Transcript*, Mar. 15, 1898; and SACB Archives, AAA/SI 322: 200.

100. Charles Eliot Norton, ed., *The Correspondence of Thomas Carlyle and Ralph Waldo Emerson*, 2 vols., Boston: James R. Osgood, 1883.

101. Charles Eliot Norton, ed., *Letters from Ralph Waldo Emerson to a Friend, 1838–1853*, Boston: Houghton Mifflin, 1899. The friend was Samuel Ward.

102. The meeting was held on Nov. 17, 1898. See Charles Eliot Norton, "The Craftsman as Artist," *Architectural Review*, vol. 5, no. 8 (Dec. 10, 1898), pp. 81–82.

103. Norton, "The Manchester Exhibition," pp. 36–38. By 1872, if not earlier, Norton was using the words "simplicity" and "sincerity" together. See his journal entry describing Ernest Renan who, Norton believed, was lacking in both, in Norton and Howe, eds., *Letters of Charles Eliot Norton*, vol. 1, p. 417.

104. Norton, "The Manchester Exhibition," p. 43.

105. Emerson, "The Progress of Culture."

106. Charles Eliot Norton, "The Prospects of Architecture as a Fine Art in the United States," *Technology Architectural Review*, vol. 2, no. 4 (Aug. 3, 1889), p. 19.

107. Norton, "The Craftsman as Artist," p. 82.

108. H. L. W. [H. Langford Warren], "Current Periodicals," *Architectural Review*, vol. 5, no. 8 (Dec. 10, 1898), p. 87.

109. Norton, "The Craftsman as Artist," p. 82.

110. Melvin I. Urofsky, *Louis D. Brandeis: A Life*, New York: Pantheon, 2009, pp. 3–24. See also Allon Gal, *Brandeis of Boston*, Cambridge, MA: Harvard University Press, 1980.

111. On Brandeis and his years at Harvard Law School, see Urofsky, pp. 25–45.

112. Melvin I. Urofsky and David W. Levy, eds., *Letters of Louis D. Brandeis*, vols. 1–5, Albany, NY: State University of New York Press, 1971–78. On Brandeis's 1878 encounter with Longfellow, along with Oliver Wendell Holmes Sr. and probably John Singer Sargent, see vol. 1, pp. 23–25. On his 1878 meeting Emerson, see vol. 1, p. 13, n. 11; and vol. 1, pp. 92–93.

113. See Martin Green, *The Mount Vernon Street Warrens: A Boston Story, 1860–1910*, New York: Charles Scribner's Sons, 1989.

114. On Denman Ross, see Marie Frank, *Denman Ross and American Design Theory*, Hanover, NH: University Press of New England, 2011; and Marie Frank, "The Theory of Pure Design and American Architectural Education in the Early Twentieth Century," *Journal of the Society of Architectural Historians*, vol. 67, no. 2 (June 2008), pp. 248–73.

115. Urofsky and Levy, eds., *Letters of Louis D. Brandeis*, vol. 1, pp. 15–17, 19–21.

116. Ibid., p. 16.

117. Brandeis describes his admiration of Emerson in Urofsky and Levy, eds., *Letters of Louis D. Brandeis*, vol. 1, p. 12.

118. On the distinctive values of the region at this time, see Van Wyck Brooks, *New England: Indian Summer, 1865–1915*, New York: E. P. Dutton, 1940.

119. Brandeis first boarded on Joy St., then bought a house at 114 Mount Vernon St. He and his wife later moved to a larger house on Otis Pl. See Urofsky, pp. 48, 112, 115.

120. Urofsky and Levy, eds., *Letters of Louis D. Brandeis*, vol. 1, p. 112.

121. Urofsky, p. 81.

122. Austin, vol. 2, ch. 14, pp. 5–7; vol. 2, ch. 15, p. 2; and vol. 3, app. II, p. 4. Brandeis appears to have handled the incorporation at no cost, but this is not clear.

123. Ibid., vol. 2, ch. 13, p. 16.

124. Robert Wiebe discusses how, at the end of the century, professionals became interested in supporting other professionals. See Wiebe, *The Search for Order, 1877–1920*, New York: Hill and Wang, 1967, especially p. 128.

125. Austin, vol. 2, ch. 15, p. 1.

126. Urofsky and Levy, eds., *Letters of Louis D. Brandeis*, vol. 1, p. 60.

127. Holmes and his evolving concept of the law are discussed by Urofsky, p. 76; and Wiebe, p. 150. See also Eric F. Goldman, *Rendezvous with Destiny: A History of Modern American Reform*, New York: Vintage, 1955 (orig. pub. 1952), pp. 102–24; and Louis Menand, *The Metaphysical Club: A Story of Ideas in America*, New York: Farrar, Straus and Giroux, 2001, pp. 343–47.

128. Menand explores these ideas throughout *The Metaphysical Club*.

129. See Frank, "The Theory of Pure Design."

130. "Arts and Crafts Exhibit. Movement to Hold One Early in April Takes Definite Shape," *Boston Globe*, Jan. 5, 1897; and SACB Archives, AAA/SI 322: 166.

131. Spain, pp. 6–7. Sam Warren's wife was one of the exhibition's supporters.

132. "The Arts and Crafts Exhibition," *Boston Herald*, Apr. 7, 1897; and SACB Archives, AAA/SI 322: 209.

133. On Dec. 16, 1898, a month after Norton lectured to the Society of Arts and Crafts, Ross lectured on "Design" to the society. See SACB Archives, AAA/SI 319: 735. This was followed by Ross publishing "The Arts and Crafts: A Diagnosis" in *Handicraft*, vol. 1, no. 10 (Jan. 1903), pp. 229–43. In 1906 the society announced that Ross would give twelve lectures on "Theory of Design" on Saturday afternoons, especially for teachers, but with designers and artists welcome. See SACB Archives, AAA/SI 319: 470.

134. Denman Ross, *A Theory of Pure Design: Harmony, Balance, Rhythm with Illustrations and Diagrams*, Boston: Houghton Mifflin, 1907.

135. Urofsky and Levy, eds., *Letters of Louis D. Brandeis*, vol. 1, pp. 163–64. The petition was submitted by Henry Lee Higginson on behalf of the Public School Association.

136. Untitled newspaper articles from 1902 about the Schoolhouse Commission are at Harvard University Archives, HUG 300, 1881, in the file on R. Clipston Sturgis. See also "Boston Public School Buildings," *American Architect and Building News*, vol. 93, no. 1671 (Jan. 4, 1908).

137. See Guido Goldman, *A History of the Germanic Museum at Harvard University*, Cambridge, MA: Minda de Gunzburg Center for European Studies, Harvard University, [1989], p. 5. See also Gal, pp. 5–6, 79.

138. Goldman, pp. 22–31.

139. The museum trustees hired Sturgis in 1903, and he, Warren, and other trustees then traveled to Europe to study museum construction and installation. See Harvard University Archives, HUD 281.25A, *Twenty-fifth Anniversary Report of the Secretary of the Class of 1881 of Harvard College*, 1906.

140. The Boston City Club Collection is preserved at the Boston Public Library. See also Gal, p. 171.

141. Illustrations of the Boston City Club by Newhall and Blevins, 1913, appear in *American Architect*, vol. 107, no. 2048 (Mar. 24, 1915). The building is now owned by Suffolk University.

142. See SACB Archives, AAA/SI 300: 179–182; 316: 561; 316: 578. The outcome of the effort is described by Henry Lewis Johnson, "Another Boston 'First,'" *Boston Evening Transcript*, Sept. 23, 1933, also available on microfilm, SACB Archives, AAA/SI 322: 292–93.

143. In 1894, the Boston Society of Architects took an active role in lobbying the legislature to preserve and restore the State House. See Austin, vol. 2, ch. 15, pp. 17–18. The battle continued into 1896, with a successful outcome, Austin, vol. 3, ch. 16, pp. 40–43. On the effort to promote building-height restrictions between 1897 and 1898, see Austin, vol. 3, ch. 17, pp. 15, 22.

144. Urofsky, p. 132.

145. Michael Holleran, *Boston's "Changeful Times": Origins of Preservation and Planning in America*, Baltimore: Johns Hopkins University Press, 1998, pp. 187–89, 246.

146. Urofsky and Levy, eds., *Letters of Louis D. Brandeis*, vol. 4, pp. 93–94. See also Holleran, pp. 179–80; and p. 310, n. 45.

147. Urofsky and Levy, eds., *Letters of Louis D. Brandeis*, vol. 1, p. 334.

148. Ibid., vol. 2, pp. 236–37, 294–95, 379. See also James M. Lindgren, *Preserving Historic*

New England: Preservation, Progressivism, and the Remaking of Memory, New York: Oxford University Press, 1995, pp. 45–46; and Lawrence W. Kennedy, *Planning the City upon a Hill: Boston Since 1630*, Amherst: University of Massachusetts Press, 1992, pp. 123–24.

149. Brandeis was listed as one of sixteen directors of the Boston-1915 group. See *"1915" Boston Exposition Official Catalogue and the Boston-1915 Yearbook*, ex. cat., Boston: Boston-1915, 1909.

150. Untitled editorial, *American Architect and Building News*, vol. 63, no. 1206 (Feb. 4, 1899).

151. See letters from H. Langford Warren and Arthur Carey, SACB Archives, AAA/SI 300: 416–19.

152. H. Langford Warren, "Our Work and Prospects," *Handicraft*, vol. 2, no. 9 (Dec. 1903), pp. 179–202.

153. Brandeis is quoted in Urofsky, p. 203.

154. Urofsky, pp. 155–80.

155. Ibid., pp. 212–27.

156. This point is made about Brandeis by Richard Hofstadter in *The Age of Reform: From Bryan to F.D.R.*, New York: Vintage, 1955, p. 264.

157. Urofsky, p. 122. Urofsky writes that one such friend and ally was Henry Lee Higginson, p. 372.

158. Green, p. 207.

159. Urofsky, p. 445.

160. Urofsky and Levy, eds., *Letters of Louis D. Brandeis*, vol. 4, p. 192, n. 1.

161. Ibid., vol. 5, p. 295. Another admired friend was Ephraim Emerton, who had encouraged Brandeis to attend Harvard. Emerton became a member of the Harvard faculty. The third friend Brandeis admired was Walter Child who, according to Brandeis, studied art history and orchids.

4. AN ARTS AND CRAFTS MOVEMENT EMERGES IN NEW ENGLAND

1. Caroline Shillaber, *Massachusetts Institute of Technology, School of Architecture and Planning, 1861–1961: A Hundred Year Chronicle*, Cambridge, MA: MIT, 1963, pp. 4–28.

2. Keith N. Morgan and Richard Cheek, "History in the Service of Design: American Architect-Historians, 1870–1940," in Elisabeth Blair MacDougall, ed., *The Architectural Historian in America*, Washington, D.C.: National Gallery of Art, 1990, pp. 62–63.

3. William B. Rhoads, "The Discovery of America's Architectural Past, 1874–1914," in *The Architectural Historian in America*, pp. 23–24. See illustrations of two student drawings, one of the Park Street Church and the other of the Hollis Street Church, p. 24.

4. William D. Austin, "A History of the Boston Society of Architects in the 19th Century," 3 vols., manuscript, 1942, Boston Athenaeum.

5. Austin, vol. 1, ch. 5, p. 15.

6. Austin, vol. 2, ch. 9, pp. 7–8.

7. Ibid., p. 14.

8. Austin, vol. 1, ch. 7, pp. 17–19.

9. The art collector Isabella Stewart Gardner was among the Bostonians who attended Norton's classes. See James Turner, *The Liberal Education of Charles Eliot Norton*, Baltimore: Johns Hopkins University Press, 1999, pp. 268–69.

10. Ibid., pp. 277–80.

11. H. Winthrop Peirce, *The History of the School of the Museum of Fine Arts, Boston, 1877–1927*, Boston: Museum of Fine Arts, 1930.

12. Mary N. Woods, "History in the Early American Architectural Journals," in *The Architectural Historian in America*, pp. 77–89.

13. Two authoritative monographs are James F. O'Gorman, *Living Architecture: A Biography of H. H. Richardson*, New York: Simon and Schuster, 1997; and Margaret Henderson Floyd, *Henry Hobson Richardson: A Genius for Architecture*, New York: Monacelli Press, 1997. See also Jeffrey Karl Ochsner, *H. H. Richardson: Complete Architectural Works*, Cambridge, MA: MIT Press, 1984 (orig. pub. 1982); and Maureen Meister, ed., *H. H. Richardson: The Architect, His Peers, and Their Era*, Cambridge, MA: MIT Press, 1999.

14. "H. H. Richardson," *Sanitary Engineer*, vol. 13, no. 23 (May 6, 1886), p. 537. Although unsigned, the tribute was probably written by H. Langford Warren, employed at the time by the magazine.

15. Floyd, *Henry Hobson Richardson*, p. 211.

16. See "Narrative of a Practice" in Annie Robinson, *Peabody and Stearns: Country Houses and Seaside Cottages*, New York: W. W. Norton, 2010, pp. 18–31.

17. Robert Swain Peabody, "Early Reminiscences," unpublished manuscript, Wheaton Holden Collection, box 2, John Hay Library, Brown University. Also quoted in Robinson, p. 24.

18. See Rhoads, pp. 23–26; and Robinson, pp. 34–35. See also William E. Barry, *Pen Sketches of Old Houses*, Boston: James R. Osgood, [1874]; Robert Swain Peabody, "Georgian Houses of New England," *American Architect and Building News*, vol. 2, no. 95 (Oct. 20, 1877); and Arthur Little, *Early New England Interiors*, Boston: A. Williams, 1878.

19. Austin, vol. 2, ch. 9, p. 8.

20. Robinson, pp. 42–45. The house burned in 1892 and was replaced by the better-known "cottage," designed by Richard Morris Hunt.

21. See Leland M. Roth, *McKim, Mead and White, Architects*, New York: Harper and Row, 1983; and Richard Guy Wilson, *McKim, Mead and White, Architects*, New York: Rizzoli, 1983.

22. Roth, p. 19; and Robinson, p. 24.

23. Roth, p. 29. James R. Osgood of Boston was publisher. See Woods, pp. 81–83.

24. Charles Moore, *The Life and Times of Charles Follen McKim*, Boston: Houghton Mifflin, 1929, p. 41.

25. Richardson's influence is discussed in Jeffrey Karl Ochsner and Dennis Alan Andersen, *Distant Corner: Seattle Architects and the Legacy of H. H. Richardson*, Seattle: University of Washington Press, 2003, pp. 90–141.

26. Lindsay Leard-Coolidge, "William Morris and Nineteenth-Century Boston," in Peter Faulkner and Peter Preston, eds., *William Morris: Centenary Essays*, Exeter, UK: University of Exeter Press, 1999, pp. 160–61.

27. Mary Alice Malloy, "Richardson's Web: A Client's Assessment of the Architect's Home and Studio," *Journal of the Society of Architectural Historians*, vol. 54, no. 1 (Mar. 1995), pp. 8–23.

28. See James F. O'Gorman, *H. H. Richardson and His Office—Selected Drawings*, Boston: David R. Godine, 1974; and O'Gorman, "Documentation: An 1886 Inventory of H.

H. Richardson's Library, and Other Gleanings from Probate," *Journal of the Society of Architectural Historians*, vol. 41, no. 2 (May 1982), pp. 150–55.

29. "H. H. Richardson," *Sanitary Engineer*, May 6, 1886.

30. See James F. O'Gorman, *H. H. Richardson: Architectural Forms for an American Society*, Chicago: University of Chicago Press, 1987.

31. Robinson, pp. 50–53. Another influential mansion to be erected in Newport at this time was Wakehurst, built for James Van Alen. The concept was set forth in 1882 by Charles Eamer Kempe, an Englishman who had studied with George F. Bodley and established a leading stained-glass studio, and the house was built from 1884 to 1887.

32. Surviving glass is in the collection of the Delaware Art Museum.

33. Austin, vol. 2, ch. 10, pp. 1–13. See also Turner, p. 279.

34. Walker's sketches from the Assos expedition may be examined on microfilm. See C. Howard Walker Papers, AAA/SI 1049: 665–733.

35. Austin, vol. 2, ch. 12, pp. 3–4; vol. 2, ch. 13, p. 13.

36. Peirce, pp. 63–64.

37. Ibid., p. 64.

38. Austin, vol. 2, ch. 13, p. 6.

39. Margaret Henderson Floyd, *Architectural Education and Boston: Centennial Publication of the Boston Architectural Center, 1889–1989*, Boston: Boston Architectural Center, 1989, pp. 40–45. The club evolved from the Architectural Association of Boston, founded in 1883.

40. "The Rotch Scholars," *Brochure Series of Architectural Illustration*, vol. 1, no. 1 (Jan. 1895), pp. 13–15.

41. Floyd, *Architectural Education and Boston*, p. 41.

42. Roth, pp. 96–97.

43. See Bainbridge Bunting, *Houses of Boston's Back Bay: An Architectural History, 1840–1917*, Belknap Press of Harvard University Press, 1967, pp. 292–94. See also Roth, pp. 97–98.

44. Bunting, p. 45.

45. Ibid., pp. 315, 318.

46. Ibid., pp. 295–99. Bunting writes that "these designs appear so advanced that one might assume that they date from the twentieth century," p. 295.

47. Ralph Adams Cram, *Church Building: A Study of the Principles of Architecture in Their Relation to the Church*, Boston: Small, Maynard, 1901, p. 220.

48. Ibid., pp. 219–20.

49. Ibid.

50. William Morgan discusses the St. Paul's chapel at length in *The Almighty Wall: The Architecture of Henry Vaughan*, New York and Cambridge, MA: Architectural History Foundation and MIT Press, 1983, pp. 89–100.

51. Ralph Adams Cram, *My Life in Architecture*, Boston: Little, Brown, 1936, p. 36.

52. Also, St. Peter's was designed over an extended period of time, 1886–90, 1890–92, and 1905–8, lessening its influence. See Roth, pp. 103–4.

53. See Robinson, p. 47. The design for the church dates from 1889, when the cornerstone was laid. The church was consecrated in 1892.

54. "Personal," *Brochure Series of Architectural Illustration*, vol. 1, no. 7 (July 1895).

55. "Consolation House," *Trained Nurse and Hospital Review*, vol. 52, no. 6 (June 1914), p. 360.

56. Editors' note in Frank C. Sharp and Jan Marsh, eds., *Collected Letters of Jane Morris*, Woodbridge, UK: Boydell Press, 2012, p. 251, n. 1, citing William Morris's Day Diary, May 19, 1896, British Library.

57. *Architectural Review* was an outgrowth of *Technology Architectural Review*, published for the MIT Architectural Society between 1887 and 1890 to showcase the designs of the students. See Henry D. Bates, "The 'Inside Story' of the Founding of 'The Architectural Review,'" *Architectural Review*, new series vol. 5, no. 11 (Nov. 1917), pp. 255–56.

58. From 1891 through 1898, *Architectural Review* was published eight times a year. In 1899, it was issued monthly. Publication was suspended from May 1910 through Dec. 1911, when a so-called new series began. Publication continued through 1921.

59. *Architectural Review* did not regularly identify its editors. The roles of Walker and Cram were announced in an ad for the *Review* in *Catalogue of the Architectural Exhibition Held in the New Public Library Building*, ex. cat., Boston Society of Architects and Boston Architectural Club, Boston, 1891. At the end of 1893, a notice appeared in the periodical's advertising supplement stating that with the first issue of vol. 3, Andrews would assume charge of the editorial department, assisted by Walker. See "The Architectural Review. Publishers' Announcement," *Architectural Review*, vol. 2, no. 8 (Nov. 1893), supp., p. ii. I have not been able to determine when Andrews stepped down as editor; however, in the Apr. 1898 issue, vol. 5, no. 3, an unsigned editorial describes a memory of Richardson's thumbnail sketches, suggesting that Andrews was the writer and still served as editor. In an ad in an undated supplement of 1906, p. vii, it was announced that Henry H. Saylor was leaving the editorship.

60. Austin, vol. 2, ch. 15, pp. 20–22. Warren reported for the committee on the *American Architect* in 1897, 1898, and 1899, Austin, vol. 3, ch. 17, pp. 1, 19, 35.

61. H. Langford Warren, "Notes on Wenlock Priory," *Architectural Review*, vol. 1, no. 1 (Nov. 1891), pp. 1–4. The second part appeared in vol. 1, no. 6 (June 1892).

62. Ralph Adams Cram, "John D. Sedding. Some Considerations of his Life and Genius," *Architectural Review*, vol. 1, no. 2 (Dec. 1891), pp. 9–11. Given that Sedding's chief assistant was Henry Wilson, who became the first editor of the London *Architectural Review* in 1896, one may imagine that the Boston magazine inspired the English periodical.

63. Ibid., pp. 9, 10.

64. H. Langford Warren, "The Use and Abuse of Precedent," *Architectural Review*, vol. 2, no. 2 (Feb. 1893), p. 13.

65. C. Howard Walker, "Notes on the Sculpture and Architecture at the Columbian Exposition," *Architectural Review*, vol. 1, no. 5 (May 1892), p. 39.

66. Cram, "John D. Sedding," p. 11.

67. Warren, "The Use and Abuse of Precedent," pp. 11–15. Part 2 appeared in *Architectural Review*, vol. 2, no. 3 (Apr. 1893), pp. 21–25.

68. Robert D. Andrews, "The Broadest Use of Precedent," *Architectural Review*, vol. 2, no. 4 (May 1893), p. 32.

69. Ibid., p. 36.

70. Ibid., p. 35.

71. Robert D. Andrews, "President's Address to the Boston Architectural Club," *Architectural Review*, vol. 2, no. 8 (Nov. 1893), pp. 63–65.

72. Andrews eliminated a few words but did not change Emerson's meaning. In his essay, "The American Scholar," delivered in 1837, Emerson said, "I embrace the common, I

explore and sit at the feet of the familiar, the low." See Joel Porte, ed., *Ralph Waldo Emerson: Essays and Lectures*, New York: Library of America, 1983, pp. 68–69.

73. Andrews, "President's Address," pp. 64, 65.

74. Emerson was quoted again in an unsigned tribute, probably written by Andrews, after the death of Arthur Rotch. See *Architectural Review*, vol. 3, no. 3 (July 1894), p. 17.

75. Melvin I. Urofsky, *Louis D. Brandeis: A Life*, New York: Pantheon, 2009, p. 203. In his lecture on May 4, 1905, Brandeis stated, "We hear much of the 'corporation lawyer,' and far too little of the 'people's lawyer,'" pp. 3–24.

76. Ralph Adams Cram, "The Interior Decoration of Churches," *Architectural Review*, vol. 4, no. 7 (Nov. 1897), pp. 50–53; and Cram, "Good and Bad Modern Gothic," *Architectural Review*, vol. 6, no. 10 (Oct. 1899), pp. 115–19.

77. R. Clipston Sturgis, "The Garden as an Adjunct to Architecture," *Architectural Review*, vol. 5, no. 3 (Apr. 1898), pp. 21–24; and R.C.S., review of Walter Crane's *The Bases of Design*, *Architectural Review*, vol. 5, no. 7 (Oct. 1898), pp. 68–69.

78. Charles Eliot Norton, "The Craftsman as Artist," *Architectural Review*, vol. 5, no. 8 (Dec. 1898), pp. 81–82.

79. On the founding of the Harvard architectural program, see Maureen Meister, *Architecture and the Arts and Crafts Movement in Boston: Harvard's H. Langford Warren*, Hanover, NH: University Press of New England, 2003, pp. 56–83.

80. In addition to Norton, Ware, Peabody, and Andrews, Warren was endorsed for the position by Charles H. Moore, Arthur Rotch, and Edward Clarke Cabot. See "Letters from Europe Written by H. Langford Warren," bound volume of photocopies, Frances Loeb Library, Special Collections, Harvard University, May 1, 1893.

81. See John Ruskin, *The Study of Architecture*, New York: John B. Alden, 1885. The essay was first read before the Royal Institute of British Architects, May 15, 1865. He stated, "My wish would be to see the profession of the architect united, not with that of the engineer, but of the sculptor," p. 147. See also Charles Eliot Norton, "The Prospects of Architecture as a Fine Art in the United States," *Technology Architectural Review*, vol. 2, no. 4 (Aug. 3, 1889), p. 19.

82. Cynthia D. Fleming, "Instructors and Courses in the Museum School," in Trevor J. Fairbrother, *The Bostonians: Painters of an Elegant Age, 1870–1930*, ex. cat., Boston: Museum of Fine Arts, 1986, p. 233.

83. H. Langford Warren, "Architectural Education at Harvard University," *Harvard Engineering Journal*, vol. 1, no. 2 (June 1902), p. 79.

84. H. Langford Warren, "The Department of Architecture of Harvard University," *Architectural Record*, vol. 22, no. 1 (July 1907), p. 138.

85. Untitled editorial, *American Architect and Building News*, vol. 55, no. 1101 (Jan. 30, 1897), p. 49. See also H. Langford Warren, "The Influence of France upon American Architecture," *American Architect and Building News*, vol. 66, no. 1248 (Nov. 25, 1899), pp. 67–68.

86. Roger Bigelow Merriman, "Notes in Architecture 1a, 1896–97," Harvard University Archives, HUC 8896.305.1a, box 654, June 2, 1897.

87. C. Howard Walker, "History of Architecture," notes of lectures given by H. Langford Warren, Special Collections, Frances Loeb Library, Harvard University, Rare NA200. W252, vol. 2, p. 66. Walker's two volumes of typed notes contain his bookplate.

88. Ibid., pp. 86–87.

89. Ibid., pp. 177–78.

90. Ibid., pp. 179–80.

91. Little documentation survives for this third course taught by Warren. The best record of his teaching is H. Langford Warren, "Architecture: Renaissance and Modern," in Edmund Buckley, ed., *The Fine Arts: A Course of University Lessons on Sculpture, Painting, Architecture, and Decoration, in Both Their Principles and History*, Chicago: International Art Association, 1900, pp. 190–234.

92. John Taylor Boyd, "Notes and Comments: Professor H. Langford Warren," *Architectural Record*, vol. 42, no. 6 (Dec. 1917), p. 589.

93. On Denman Ross and his teaching at Harvard, see Marie Frank, *Denman Ross and American Design Theory*, Hanover, NH: University Press of New England, 2011.

94. "Fine Arts IV—Syllabus No. 1. Roman and Mediaeval Art," Harvard University Archives, HUC 8893.128.4, box 618.

95. The significance of the battle over the Massachusetts State House is discussed by Michael Holleran in *Boston's "Changeful Times": Origins of Preservation and Planning in America*, Baltimore: Johns Hopkins University Press, 1998, pp. 135–50.

96. Austin, vol. 2, ch. 15, pp. 17–18.

97. See Robinson, pp. 30–31.

98. Austin, vol. 3, ch. 16, p. 40.

99. *Centennial of the Bulfinch State House. Exercises Before the Massachusetts Legislature*, Boston, Jan. 11, 1898.

100. Austin, vol. 3, ch. 17, p. 20.

101. Ibid., p. 4.

5. Looking Backward: From Romanesque to Gothic Revival

1. On the afterlife of Richardson's Romanesque, see Jeffrey Karl Ochsner, "Seeing Richardson in His Time: The Problem of the Romanesque Revival," in Maureen Meister, ed., *H. H. Richardson: The Architect, His Peers, and Their Era*, Cambridge, MA: MIT Press, pp. 102–45. See also Ochsner and Dennis Alan Andersen, *Distant Corner: Seattle Architects and the Legacy of H. H. Richardson*, Seattle: University of Washington Press, 2003, especially ch. 4, 5, 7, 8.

2. Cambridge City Hall is discussed in Margaret Henderson Floyd, *Architecture After Richardson: Regionalism Before Modernism—Longfellow, Alden, and Harlow in Boston and Pittsburgh*, Chicago and Pittsburgh: University of Chicago Press in association with Pittsburgh History and Landmarks Foundation, 1994, pp. 61–63.

3. "Unsuccessful Design for the Mt. Vernon Church," O. F. Smith, illustration in *American Architect and Building News*, vol. 34, no. 824 (Oct. 10, 1891).

4. See *A Book of Plans for Churches and Parsonages. Published under the direction of the Central Committee appointed by the General Congregational Convention. October 1852.* New York: 1853.

5. See Robert B. Rettig, "Mount Vernon Church: Historic Preservation Statement," Boston Landmarks Commission, Jan. 24, 1972, Boston Public Library, U.S. Government Documents. After much of the church was destroyed in a fire, its walls and tower were incorporated into a design by Graham Gund for Church Court Condominiums, 1983.

6. The advertisement by Hugh Cairns appears in *Catalogue of the Architectural Exhibition, Boston Architectural Club and Boston Society of Architects*, ex. cat., Boston: Boston Architectural Club and Boston Society of Architects, 1899, p. 168.

7. National Register of Historic Places nomination for the library, prepared by Kathleen Kelly Broomer, 1998.

8. Hopedale Town Hall was designed by Fred Swasey with funding from George Draper.

9. C. Howard Walker, *Theory of Mouldings*, New York and London: W. W. Norton, 2007 (orig. pub. 1926), p. 2. The book was based on a series of articles called "The Theory of Mouldings" that appeared in *Architectural Review* from June 1899 (vol. 6, no. 6) through Jan. 1900 (vol. 7, no. 1).

10. Ralph Adams Cram, *Church Building: A Study of the Principles of Architecture in Their Relation to the Church*, Boston: Small, Maynard, 1901, p. 43.

11. Another example of Cram's Romanesque work is St. Elizabeth Chapel, built on his property in Sudbury, MA, 1914. See Douglass Shand-Tucci, *Ralph Adams Cram: An Architect's Four Quests*, Amherst: University of Massachusetts Press, 2005, pp. 173–209. See also Harold Donaldson Eberlein, "All Saints' Church, Peterborough, New Hampshire," *Architectural Record*, vol. 58 (Sept. 1925), pp. 278–88.

12. For the Cheney family relationships, see Charles Henry Pope, *The Cheney Genealogy*, Boston: C. H. Pope, 1897, entry 790 for Benjamin Pierce Cheney, pp. 505–8; and entry 923 for Charles Paine Cheney, pp. 541–43.

13. William Henry Schofield, *English Literature: From the Norman Conquest to Chaucer*, New York: Macmillan, 1906. Schofield thanks Norton in his preface, pp. ix–x. Schofield established Harvard's Department of Comparative Literature in 1906.

14. Joan Jessop Brewster, *The Stained Glass of All Saints'*, Peterborough, NH: All Saints' Parish Church, 2001.

15. *American Architect and Building News*, vol. 37, no. 868 (Aug. 13, 1892). Douglass Shand-Tucci deserves credit for stimulating a renewed appreciation for this landmark. Most influential is his discussion in *Built in Boston: City and Suburb, 1800–2000*, rev. ed., Amherst: University of Massachusetts Press, 1999 (orig. pub. 1978), pp. 155–81.

16. Ralph Adams Cram, *My Life in Architecture*, Boston: Little, Brown, 1936, pp. 191–93.

17. The window by Harry Goodhue attracted special interest and was described by Robert Brown in "All Saints Church, Dorchester, Mass.," *Architectural Review*, vol. 7, no. 9 (Sept. 1900), p. 103. See also Albert M. Tannler, "Harry Eldredge Goodhue: Pioneer of American Stained Glass," *Stained Glass Quarterly*, vol. 99, no. 1 (spring 2004), p. 55.

18. Peter Cormack, *The Stained Glass Work of Christopher Whall (1849–1924)*, Boston: Charles J. Connick Stained Glass Foundation and Boston Public Library, 1999, p. 42.

19. Ibid., pp. 13, 15, 35, 38.

20. Brown, "All Saints Church, Dorchester, Mass."

21. The reredos also is described by Edward Everett Hale in "Picturesque Massachusetts," *Picturesque and Architectural New England*, vol. 2, Boston: D. H. Hurd, 1899, pp. 86–87. Both Brown and Hale credit Evans with the execution while identifying Domingo Mora as the artisan who modeled the fifteen statues.

22. In "All Saints Church, Dorchester, Mass.," Brown writes that the architects intended to ask Burne-Jones to paint the altarpiece, p. 104.

23. Unsigned editorial, *Architectural Review*, vol. 7, no. 9 (Sept. 1900), p. 107.

24. Montgomery Schuyler, "The Works of Cram, Goodhue, and Ferguson," *Architectural Record*, vol. 29, no. 1 (Jan. 1911), entire issue.

25. See Cram's editorial in *Christian Art*, vol. 3, no. 1 (Apr. 1908), pp. 50–52. In Cram's *My Life in Architecture*, see ch. 11, "Allies in Art," pp. 185–99.

26. Cram, *Church Building*, p. 190.

27. C. Howard Walker, "History of Architecture," transcribed notes from lectures by H. Langford Warren, Special Collections, Frances Loeb Library, Harvard University, Rare NA200.W252, vol. 2, pp. 179–80; and Cram, *Church Building*, p. 33.

28. C. Howard Walker, *Parish Churches of England*, Boston and New York: Rogers and Manson, 1905, [p. 1].

29. H. Langford Warren, "Notes on Wenlock Priory," *Architectural Review*, vol. 1, no. 1 (Nov. 1891), pp. 1–4; and second part, vol. 1, no. 6 (June 1892), pp. 49–51. William D. Austin, "A History of the Boston Society of Architects in the 19th Century," 3 vols., manuscript, 1942, Boston Athenaeum, vol. 3, ch. 17, p. 16.

30. R. Clipston Sturgis, "Three Somerset Towers and Some Others," *Architectural Review*, vol. 7, no. 2 (Feb. 1900), pp. 13–16; and Sturgis, "Notes on Some English Rood Screens," *Architectural Review*, vol. 8, no. 12 (Dec. 1901), pp. 135–38.

31. Ralph Adams Cram, *English Country Churches*, Boston: Bates and Guild, 1898; Cram, *Church Building*; and Cram, *The Ruined Abbeys of Great Britain*, New York: J. Pott, 1905.

32. Walker, *Parish Churches of England*.

33. Cram, *My Life in Architecture*, p. 96.

34. See Ethan Anthony, *The Architecture of Ralph Adams Cram and His Office*, New York: W. W. Norton, 2007, p. 19. Renamed the Phillips Church in 1897, the building was acquired by Phillips Exeter Academy in 1922.

35. Illustrations of the church appeared in *American Architect and Building News*, vol. 75, no. 1368 (Mar. 15, 1902). The carved corbels were almost certainly the work of John Evans, although this has not been confirmed. The source of the woodwork is identified in an ad by Irving and Casson in *Architectural Review*, vol. 12, no. 12 (Dec. 1905), p. xii.

36. For Sturgis's role at the Lyndonville, VT, church, see Architectural Notebooks of Richard Clipston Sturgis, Boston Athenaeum, series 1, no. 18, entry following Mar. 15, 1898.

37. The *Echo*, a newsletter published in Burlington by the Episcopal Diocese of Vermont, Jan. 15, 1899.

38. H. Langford Warren, "The Year's Architecture," in *Catalogue of the Architectural Exhibition, Boston Architectural Club and Boston Society of Architects*, 1899, p. 18.

39. The design for the New Church Theological School chapel was published extensively, and attributed to Warren's firm of Warren, Smith, and Biscoe. For example, see *American Architect and Building News*, vol. 65, no. 1231 (July 29, 1899).

40. Cairns is identified as the source of the carving in *Catalogue of the Architectural Exhibition, Boston Architectural Club*, ex. cat., Boston: Boston Architectural Club, 1902, no. 303.

41. Irving and Casson identified their work for the chapel in their ad in *Architectural Review*, vol. 12, no. 12 (Dec. 1905), p. xii. The Mercer tiles may be identified by the patterns. For more information on attributions for the craftsmen who contributed to the chapel, see Maureen Meister, *Architecture and the Arts and Crafts Movement in Boston: Harvard's H. Langford Warren*, Hanover, NH: University Press of New England, 2003, pp. 195–96, n. 36–43.

42. The importance of Goodhue's Brown memorial window for Emmanuel Church, Newport, RI, is discussed by Tannler in "Harry Eldredge Goodhue," p. 55.

43. For a summary of research on Emmanuel Church, see the National Register of Historic Places nomination prepared by William McKenzie Woodward in 1995 and accepted in 1996.

44. The Church of the Epiphany, originally a project of Warren, Smith, and Biscoe, was illustrated extensively in the architectural press, beginning with *American Architect and*

Building News, vol. 86, no. 1509 (Nov. 26, 1904). The later stages of work were directed solely by Frank Patterson Smith. Records documenting the decoration of the church are in the Historic New England Library and Archives, Boston.

45. On Kempe, see Margaret Stavridi, *Master of Glass: Charles Eamer Kempe, 1837–1907, and the Work of His Firm in Stained Glass and Church Decoration*, Hatfield, Hertfordshire, UK: John Taylor Book Ventures for the Kempe Society, 1988.

46. An advertisement for Harry Goodhue's workshop appears in *Christian Art*, vol. 3, no. 6 (Sept. 1908), p. iv, and illustrates the window for the Church of the Epiphany, Winchester, MA.

47. The upper portion of the tower has been removed. The South Shore Historical Society postcard collection for East Weymouth, MA, includes a card that shows the church with the original tower.

48. Most of the Third Congregational Church was demolished after a fire during the 1970s, although the tower was preserved as the entrance to a new apartment building. For photographs and plans of the church, see *American Architect*, vol. 102, no. 1911 (Aug. 7, 1912).

49. Faulkner Church, Malden, MA, was illustrated in Walter Scott Athearn's *The Malden Survey*, New York: Interchurch World Movement of North America, 1920, p. 28.

50. Cram, *Church Building*, pp. 22–25.

51. Charles D. Maginnis, "Catholic Church Architecture," *Architectural Forum*, vol. 27, no. 2 (Aug. 1917), p. 35.

52. *Boston Tercentenary Fine Arts and Crafts Exhibition*, ex. cat., Boston, 1930, p. 19.

53. Maginnis, "Catholic Church Architecture," p. 34.

54. Charles D. Maginnis, intro. to *The Work of Cram and Ferguson, Architects*, New York: Pencil Points, 1929.

55. See John G. Doll, *Heart of the Hilltop*, Newport, RI: St. George's School, 2003. The building of the chapel is also discussed by Shand-Tucci in *Ralph Adams Cram*, pp. 235–37.

56. Cram, *My Life in Architecture*, p. 244.

57. See Alan Priest, intro. to *The Sculpture of Joseph Coletti*, New York: Macmillan, 1968.

58. For other carvers besides Coletti, see Doll, pp. 33–35.

59. Ibid., pp. 36–39.

60. "The Form of Consecration of St. George's Chapel," St. George's School, Apr. 23, 1928. Printed by D. B. Updike of Merrymount Press. A copy of the booklet is held by the Gilbert Y. Taverner Archives, St. George's School, Middletown, RI.

61. Doll, pp. 142, 238–39.

62. The Thayer house was illustrated in *American Architect and Building News*, vol. 24, no. 659 (Aug. 11, 1888), Imperial edition. It was described by Hale in "Picturesque Massachusetts," pp. 91–92.

63. Hale, p. 91.

64. Photographs of the Edward Robinson house, no longer standing, are in the Historic New England Library and Archives, Boston, Soule Art Company collection. Robinson and Walker had both participated in the expedition to Assos between 1881 and 1883. See Austin, vol. 2, ch. 10. When the house was built, Robinson was curator of classical antiquities at the Museum of Fine Arts, Boston. From 1902 to 1905, he served as its director, and from 1910 to 1931, he was director of the Metropolitan Museum of Art in New York City.

65. A design for the Eugene Fellner house was illustrated in *American Architect and Building News*, vol. 39, no. 898 (Mar. 11, 1893). A second scheme, rendered in watercolor, was offered to Fellner. The house has been demolished. See Douglass Shand-Tucci, *Boston Bohemia 1881–1900: Ralph Adams Cram, Life and Architecture*, Amherst: University of Massachusetts Press, 1995, pp. 97, 100. See also Anthony, p. 17.

66. The John C. Schwab house was published as a design of Sturgis and Cabot and illustrated in *American Architect and Building News*, vol. 53, no. 1080 (Sept. 5, 1896). It also is documented in Architectural Notebooks of Richard Clipston Sturgis, series 1, nos. 9–11, June 1895–Apr. 1896.

67. Austin, vol. 3, ch. 17, p. 4.

68. The Edward H. Rathbun house was published in the *Architectural Review*, vol. 9, no. 4 (Apr. 1902), attributed to Warren, Smith, and Biscoe. Rathbun's wife, Anna Wilkinson, was a Reed and may have been related to Warren's wife, Catharine Reed.

69. H. Langford Warren, "Recent Domestic Architecture in England," *Architectural Review*, vol. 11, no. 1 (Jan. 1904), p. 5.

70. Robert D. Andrews, "The Changing Styles of Country Houses," *Architectural Review*, vol. 11, no. 1 (Jan. 1904), p. 2.

71. Sturgis documented his work on the residence for the Episcopal bishop of Vermont, Arthur C. A. Hall, in Architectural Notebooks of Richard Clipston Sturgis, series 1, nos. 6–8, Mar. 1894–Dec. 1894.

72. "New Home for the Bishop of Vermont. Erected in Burlington by the Generosity of the Wells Family," *New York Times*, Jan. 31, 1895.

73. Architectural Notebooks of Richard Clipston Sturgis, series 1, no. 7, June 29, 1894.

74. Ibid., no. 8, Sept.–Dec. 1894. Sturgis listed Davenport as supplying furnishings, evidently A. H. Davenport of Cambridge. Sturgis also mentioned that work was being done by "Ross's man" and Ross himself, probably a reference to William F. Ross, who would establish a shop in Cambridge and specialize in ecclesiastical furnishings.

75. Ibid., Sept. 1894.

76. The Hotel Ludlow has been demolished, but photographs of it are in the Print Dept., Boston Public Library, filed under "Hotels." One of them is labeled "Hotel Boylston," with "Hotel Ludlow" given as the alternative title. See also Walker's sketch of the building, available on microfilm of his notebooks, C. Howard Walker Papers, 1877–1936, AAA/SI 1049, second series: 104.

77. "The Exhibition of the Boston Architectural Club," *American Architect and Building News*, vol. 28, no. 756 (June 21, 1890).

78. Marie Frank, *Denman Ross and American Design Theory*, Hanover, NH: University Press of New England, 2011, pp. 18–52. Frank mentions construction of the Hotel Ludlow, p. 21, and illustrates the watercolor by Mackmurdo, fig. 1.2.

79. Excerpt from text accompanying illustrations of Richmond Court in *American Architect and Building News*, vol. 63, no. 1212 (Mar. 18, 1899), p. 88. The text appears to have been submitted by the architects because it borrows directly from a longer essay about Richmond Court in a printed prospectus, "The Richmond Court Apartments," 1898, preserved by the Brookline Preservation Commission, MA. Additional illustrations appeared in *American Architect*, vol. 66, no. 1243 (Oct. 21, 1899). The apartment building was illustrated in *Architectural Review*, vol. 6, no. 11 (Nov. 1899); and *Brickbuilder*, vol. 9, no. 5 (May 1900).

80. In *My Life in Architecture*, Cram describes Richmond Court as "the first attempt to

camouflage an apartment house through the counterfeit presentment of a great Tudor mansion," p. 101. He and his wife lived in Richmond Court during their first years of marriage.

81. Frederick Krasser was responsible for some of the finest ironwork produced in late nineteenth-century Boston, including the iron for the Harvard fence. He is discussed in the entry on Frank L. Koralewsky, who worked for him, in *Inspiring Reform: Boston's Arts and Crafts Movement*, ex. cat., Marilee Boyd Meyer, consulting curator, Wellesley, MA: Davis Museum and Cultural Center, Wellesley College, 1997, p. 219.

82. An exterior photograph and the plan of Burton Halls, credited to Newhall and Blevins, were illustrated in *American Architect*, vol. 96, no. 1774 (Dec. 22, 1909). The same issue included illustrations and plans of two other Tudor apartment buildings in Cambridge by Newhall and Blevins: Washington Court and Bromley Court. The exterior photograph of Burton Halls also appeared in *Architectural Review*, vol. 17, no. 1 (Jan. 1910). *Architectural Record* published "Tendencies in Apartment House Design" by Frank Chouteau Brown from 1921 to 1922, in which several complexes by Newhall and Blevins are featured. See part VI, vol. 50, no. 6 (Dec. 1921) for Linnean Hall and Remington Gables, both Cambridge; part VII, vol. 51, no. 1 (Jan. 1922) for Agassiz Apartments, Cambridge, and Babcock Halls, Brookline; and part X, vol. 51, no. 4 (Apr. 1922) for Lexington and Concord Halls, Mather Court, and Wadsworth Chambers, all Cambridge.

83. West Roxbury High School, later renamed Jamaica Plain High School, is now a condominium building called Sumner Hill House. It was published in *Architectural Review*, vol. 5, no. 6 (Sept. 10, 1898) and *Inland Architect and News Record*, vol. 40, no. 6 (Jan. 1903).

84. "Handsome West Roxbury High School Building on Elm St., Jamaica Plain, Dedicated," *Boston Globe*, Nov. 23, 1901. Andrews spoke at the Nov. 22 dedication, indicating that he was its designer. The building was planned to accommodate an addition, which was constructed in the late 1920s, so that the projecting block is now in the middle of the main elevation.

85. See John Evans Collection, Fine Arts Dept., Boston Public Library, "Sketchbook/Record Book 1898–99."

86. The Brookline Preservation Commission maintains archival records, including images, of the high school.

87. See SACB Archives, AAA/SI 322: 228

88. The Nashua, NH, Public Library was renamed the Hunt Memorial Library, honoring the large donation from the family of John M. Hunt. Today the Hunt Memorial Building is a community center. The library was illustrated in *Brickbuilder*, vol. 10, no. 11 (Nov. 1901) and *Architectural Review*, vol. 8, no. 12 (Dec. 1901).

89. Schuyler, p. 24.

90. Ralph Adams Cram, "American University Architecture," in *The Ministry of Art*, Boston and New York: Houghton Mifflin, 1914, pp. 169–211. Cram's essay first appeared as "Recent University Architecture in the United States," *Journal of the Royal Institute of British Architects*, May 25, 1912, pp. 497–518. Collegiate Gothic architecture in America and Cram's promotion of it are discussed by Peter Fergusson, "A New Vision: Collegiate Gothic," in *The Landscape and Architecture of Wellesley College*, Wellesley, MA: Wellesley College, 2000, ch. 7.

91. Cram, "American University Architecture, p. 170.

92. Sturgis praised the Bryn Mawr work in his tribute to Stewardson, *Twenty-fifth Anni-*

versary *Report of the Secretary of the Class of 1881 of Harvard College*, Cambridge, MA, 1906, pp. 203–4. Cram credited Cope and Stewardson for their role in introducing collegiate Gothic in "American University Architecture," p. 193. On Nov. 1, 1930, a letter from Sturgis was published in the *New Yorker* stating that it was not Cram but Stewardson, Cope, and Frank Miles Day "who started English Collegiate Gothic." A copy of the letter is in the folder for R. Clipston Sturgis, Tavern Club Records, carton 6, Massachusetts Historical Society, Boston.

93. Austin, vol. 3, ch. 16, p. 35.

94. William Morgan, *The Almighty Wall: The Architecture of Henry Vaughan*, Cambridge, MA: Architectural History Foundation and MIT Press, 1983, pp. 105–7.

95. Cram, "American University Architecture," pp. 186–96, 202–3.

96. For a history of Boston College's move to the Newton campus, see David R. Dunigan, *A History of Boston College*, Milwaukee: Bruce Publishing, 1947, especially pp. 180–205. See also Donna M. Cassidy, "The Collegiate Gothic Designs of Maginnis and Walsh," in *Studies in Medievalism*, vol. 3, no. 2 (fall 1990), pp. 153–85.

97. John Evans Collection, Fine Arts Dept., Boston Public Library, "Sketchbook/Record Book 1910–14," May 10, 1911.

98. Dunigan, p. 199. The Recitation Building, later named Gasson Hall, was illustrated in *American Architect*, vol. 105, no. 1986 (Jan. 14, 1914).

99. On the planning of and the battle over the location for Princeton's Graduate College, see Willard Thorp, Minor Myers Jr., and Jeremiah Stanton Finch, *The Princeton Graduate School: A History*, Princeton, NJ: Association of Princeton Graduate Alumni, 2000 (orig. pub. 1978), ch. 5, "The Struggle," pp. 107–58. Cram's preliminary plan for the Graduate College was published in his article titled "Princeton Architecture," *American Architect*, vol. 96, no. 1752 (July 21, 1909). For recent studies on Cram's work at Princeton, see Johanna G. Seasonwein, *Princeton and the Gothic Revival, 1870–1930*, ex. cat., Princeton, NJ: Princeton University Art Museum, 2012; and W. Barksdale Maynard, *Princeton: America's Campus*, University Park, PA: Pennsylvania State University Press, 2012.

100. Thorp, Meyers, and Finch, p. 161. John Evans Collection, Fine Arts Dept., Boston Public Library, "Sketchbook/Record Book 1910–14," Aug. 15, 1910. It seems that the models of two towers were made to show two alternative designs.

101. John Evans Collection, "Sketchbook/Record Book 1910–14," Aug. 24, 1911.

102. Cram states explicitly that he designed Cleveland Tower, in *My Life in Architecture*, p. 121. Princeton's Holder Memorial Tower, a Perpendicular design by Frank Miles Day and Brothers, also would have influenced Cram. It was 140 feet high and dated from 1908 to 1910. It did not play a central role in organizing the campus plan, however; that position was retained by Nassau Hall, the first building erected at Princeton.

103. On the 1907 exhibition, see SACB Archives, AAA/SI 320: 61; and on Saint Dunstan's Guild, see *Society of Arts and Crafts Twelfth Annual Report*, 1909, SACB Archives, AAA/SI 318: 660.

104. A few years later, Cram expressed further admiration for the Boston College campus. See Ralph Adams Cram, "The New Boston College," *American Architect*, vol. 119, no. 2370 (June 8, 1921).

105. Architectural Notebooks of Richard Clipston Sturgis, series 3, no. 44, Aug. 20, 1909. Entries for the Perkins project appear regularly through series 3, nos. 45, 46.

106. For the first entry on the Winsor School commission, see Architectural Notebooks of

Richard Clipston Sturgis, series 2, no. 40, Jan. 17, 1908. The school opened at the new campus in 1910. It was illustrated in *American Architect*, vol. 98, no. 1826 (Dec. 21, 1910).

107. R. Clipston Sturgis, "Perkins Institution and Massachusetts School for the Blind at Watertown, Massachusetts," *Brickbuilder*, vol. 22, no. 7 (July 1913), pp. 154–58.

108. Ibid., p. 155.

109. *American Architect*, vol. 102, no. 1928 (Dec. 4, 1912).

110. See Day Book of Richard Clipston Sturgis, July 1910–Jan. 1912, Feb. 11, 1911, in which Sturgis notes that he visited Evans, who "has many models started" for Perkins. In the day books, Sturgis recorded his time, whereas he used the notebooks to record design ideas and information. See also the John Evans Collection, Fine Arts Dept., Boston Public Library, "Job Book" listing for the Perkins Institution in 1910.

111. See Susan J. Montgomery, *The Ceramics of William H. Grueby*, Lambertville, NJ: Arts and Crafts Quarterly Press, 1993, p. 68.

112. Electus D. Litchfield discusses this point about Perkins in "Country House Architecture in the East," *Architectural Record*, vol. 40, no. 4 (Oct. 1916), p. 358.

113. *Report of the President, 1913–1916*; and *Report of the Treasurer, 1915–1916*, South Hadley, MA: Mount Holyoke College, Nov. 1916. President Mary E. Wooley records that Skinner Hall opened in Sept. 1915, and she describes the building, pp. 19–20. See also "New Equipment," unsigned typescript, Dec. 2, 1915, Mount Holyoke College Archives and Special Collections, RG 7094.6, folder 1.

114. Putnam and Cox would design seven fraternity houses for Amherst College. Prior to the firm's work at Mount Holyoke, Cox had been hired to build Psi Upsilon (1911–12) and Phi Delta Theta (1913). See Stanley King, *"The Consecrated Eminence": The Story of the Campus and Buildings of Amherst College*, Amherst, MA: Amherst College, 1951. Putnam was the senior partner of the firm, and given the scale of the Skinner Hall commission, it seems likely that both partners were involved with it. In *Report of the President*, Wooley credits the building to the firm, not just to Cox.

115. See *Report of the President*, p. 4, for a tribute to John C. Schwab, who died Jan. 12, 1916. Schwab had served as a Mount Holyoke trustee since 1908, and he probably was responsible for the college appointing Sturgis as the supervising architect in 1915.

116. After Skinner Hall opened, Putnam and Cox designed four more substantial brick buildings in the collegiate Gothic style for the campus. Two were dormitories: Hillside (later named the Mandelles) and Rockefeller (both 1923). Two were academic buildings: Clapp (1922–24) and the New Physics Building (1932; later named Shattuck). The firm also designed the Outing Club cabin (1929), which does not survive.

117. "Mr. John Evans, Modeler and Carver," *Architectural Record*, Great American Architects' Series, no. 3 (July 1896), p. 117.

118. Orin E. Skinner, *Stained Glass Tours: Boston*, Boston: Connick Foundation, [2012] (orig. pub. 1965); and Albert M. Tannler, *Charles J. Connick: His Education and His Windows in and near Pittsburgh*, Pittsburgh: Pittsburgh History and Landmarks Foundation, 2008, pp. 106–28.

6. LOOKING BACKWARD: COLONIAL REVIVAL AS ARTS AND CRAFTS

1. Margaret Henderson Floyd, *Architecture After Richardson: Regionalism before Modernism—Longfellow, Alden, and Harlow in Boston and Pittsburgh*, Chicago and Pittsburgh: University of Chicago Press in association with the Pittsburgh History and Landmarks

Foundation, 1994, pp. 99–100. See also Douglass Shand-Tucci, *Built in Boston: City and Suburb, 1800–2000*, rev. ed., Amherst: University of Massachusetts Press, 1999 (orig. pub. 1978), pp. 70–71.

2. Floyd, pp. 103–9. Photographs of the Thorp house from the time of the Thorps's residency are in the Historic New England Library and Archives, Boston.

3. Ibid., pp. 111–14. The house was published in *American Architect and Building News*, vol. 24, no. 874 (Sept. 24, 1892). It has been demolished.

4. The Bigelow house is described and illustrated by Edwin M. Bacon in "Picturesque Estates and Country Seats," in *Picturesque and Architectural New England*, vol. 1, Boston: D. H. Hurd, 1899, pp. 74–76. The house has been demolished.

5. Vincent J. Scully, *The Shingle Style and the Stick Style*, rev. ed., New Haven, CT, and London: Yale University Press, 1971 (orig. pub. 1955).

6. H. Langford Warren, "Architecture in New England," in *Picturesque and Architectural New England*, vol. 1, p. 19.

7. Ibid., p. 31.

8. Ralph Adams Cram, "Current Periodicals," *Architectural Review*, vol. 8, no. 9 (Sept. 1901), p. 108.

9. The house was photographed and documented by the Brookline Historical Commission and is listed on the National Register of Historic Places. The house has since been altered.

10. This is not to say that Richardson introduced this roofline, but he contributed to the interest in it.

11. The George C. F. Williams house is listed on the National Register of Historic Places as a contributing building to the Prospect Avenue Historic District, Hartford.

12. La Rochelle was published as "House at Bar Harbor, Maine," *Architectural Review*, vol. 9, no. 11 (Nov. 1902). It then was featured in an article by I. Howland Jones, "'La Rochelle': A Summer Home at Bar Harbor, Maine," in *House and Garden*, vol. 7, no. 5 (May 1905), pp. 246–50.

13. The house was built for George S. Bowdoin, a partner in the Morgan bank.

14. On Skyfield, see the National Register of Historic Places nomination for the Beech Hill Summer Home Historic District, Harrisville, NH, prepared by Lucinda A. Brockway, Jan. 14, 1988. See also William Morgan, *Monadnock Summer: The Architectural Legacy of Dublin, New Hampshire*, Jaffrey, NH: David R. Godine, 2011, p. 99.

15. Howe kept extensive records of measured drawings of historic houses she visited throughout New England. Many of them survive at MIT, Institute Archives and Special Collections, Howe, Manning, and Almy Papers, box 9. See also Lois L. Howe and Constance Fuller, *Details From Old New England Houses*, New York: Architectural Book Publishing, 1913.

16. In his essay "The Year's Architecture," H. Langford Warren described the "renewed study of the work of Wren, Hawksmoor, and Gibbs" in England that had been influencing buildings in the region. See *Catalogue of the Architectural Exhibition, Boston Architectural Club and Boston Society of Architects*, 1899, p. 18.

17. The house is discussed briefly in Doris Cole and Karen C. Taylor, *The Lady Architects: Lois Lilley Howe, Eleanor Manning, and Mary Almy: 1893–1937*, New York: Midmarch Arts, 1990, p. 35.

18. On the Harvard campus, see Bainbridge Bunting, *Harvard: An Architectural History*,

completed and edited by Margaret Henderson Floyd, Cambridge, MA: Belknap Press of Harvard University Press, 1985.

19. Phillips Brooks House is discussed by Bunting, pp. 80–82; and Floyd, pp. 398–401. See also Harvard University Archives, HUB 1687.2, box 26, "Phillips Brooks House." It should be pointed out that in 1893, Conant and Perkins Halls were built in Colonial Revival styles, designed by Shepley, Rutan, and Coolidge, Richardson's successor firm.

20. John Evans Collection, Fine Arts Dept., Boston Public Library, "Sketchbook/Record Book 1898–99," Sept. 28, 1898.

21. Bunting, p. 105. See also Harvard University Archives, HUB 1692.2, box 1.

22. Montgomery Schuyler, "Architecture of American Colleges. VII. Brown, Bowdoin, Trinity, and Wesleyan," *Architectural Record*, vol. 29, no. 2 (Feb. 1911), p. 148.

23. Evans seems to have played a part in the ornament of two gateposts and probably provided other carved work on the project. See John Evans Collection, "Sketchbook/Record Book 1910–1914," June 27, 1910.

24. Douglass Shand-Tucci, *Ralph Adams Cram: An Architect's Four Quests*, Amherst: University of Massachusetts Press, 2005, pp. 11–17.

25. Ralph Adams Cram, *My Life in Architecture*, Boston: Little, Brown, 1936, p. 237.

26. "Restoring Faneuil Hall. Ralph Adams Cram, Chairman of the City Planning Board, Would Use Methods Similar to Those on Old South Meeting House," *Boston Evening Transcript*, Nov. 9, 1914.

27. "Recent American Churches," *Architectural Review*, new series vol. 6, no. 1 (Jan. 1918).

28. "Franklin Union New Building. Plan Decided upon by Fund Managers," *Boston Globe*, Oct. 20, 1906. See also "Franklin Union Schools Will Begin in October," *Boston Globe*, Aug. 21, 1908. Preliminary work that Sturgis did on the Franklin Union is documented in Architectural Notebooks of Richard Clipston Sturgis, Boston Athenaeum, series 2, no. 35, Apr.–July 1906. The press reported that Sturgis was hired for the project, but it was managed by the firm of Sturgis and Barton.

29. In research for a lecture delivered Apr. 9, 2011, Timothy T. Orwig learned from Franklin Union records that Evans was paid as a subcontractor for carving.

30. *Brickbuilder*, vol. 17, no. 11 (Nov. 1908); and "Current Periodicals," *Architectural Review*, vol. 15, no. 12 (Dec. 1908).

31. "Current Periodicals," *Architectural Review*, vol. 15, no. 12 (Dec. 1908), p. 190.

32. See *An Account of the Celebration by the Town of Lincoln, Mass., of the 150th Anniversary of Its Incorporation*, Lincoln, MA: Town of Lincoln, 1904, including the frontispiece illustration; and Margaret Mutchler Martin, *Inheritance: Lincoln's Public Buildings in the Historic District*, Lincoln, MA: Lincoln Historical Society, 1987, pp. 52–58. The town hall was listed in *Catalogue of the Architectural Exhibition Held in the New Public Library Building*, ex. cat., Boston: Boston Society of Architects and Boston Architectural Club, 1891, no. 331.

33. "Lincoln's New Town Hall," *Boston Herald*, Nov. 6, 1891, p. 5.

34. For Blackburn Memorial Hall, Walpole, MA, see the inventory form prepared by Kathleen Kelly Broomer, May 2008, rev. June 2008, filed with the Massachusetts Historical Commission.

35. The siting for Blackburn Hall follows the recommendation of John Nolen in his 1923 plan for Walpole's Memorial Park. See John Nolen, *New Towns for Old*, Boston: Marshall Jones, 1927, p. 46.

36. See "Dedication of William Fogg Memorial Library at Eliot—Address by Ex-Mayor Baxter of Portland," *Portland Press*, May 23, 1907; and Gail Willis Libby, "The History of Libraries in Eliot," unpublished manuscript, 1957; both William Fogg Library, Eliot, Maine, History of the Fogg Library collection, binder 7.

37. See the inventory form, unsigned, submitted by the Boston Landmarks Commission, June 1980, filed with the Massachusetts Historical Commission.

38. "Kirstein Memorial Library Is Opened," *Boston Globe*, May 8, 1930.

39. J. Templeman Coolidge Jr. is profiled in Beverly K. Brandt, *The Craftsman and the Critic: Defining Usefulness and Beauty in Arts and Crafts-Era Boston*, Amherst: University of Massachusetts Press, 2009, pp. 60–61; see also pp. 64, 67–68. His role as chairman of the society's jury is documented in SACB Archives, AAA/SI 316: 2.

40. Henry Wadsworth Longfellow's "The Poet's Tale: Lady Wentworth" first appeared in 1863 in *Tales of a Wayside Inn*. Robert Swain Peabody's drawing of the Wentworth house was published in *American Architect and Building News*, vol. 2, no. 93 (Oct. 6, 1877). In the eighteenth century, the house was the home of Benning Wentworth, first governor of New Hampshire.

41. Floyd discusses how Coolidge and Longfellow developed the Wentworth Farm property, pp. 85–90.

42. See "Creek Farm: The Arthur Astor Carey Summer Home," on file with the New Hampshire Division of Historical Resources, Concord, NH. Longfellow's design for the Carey house was published in *American Architect and Building News*, vol. 23, no. 647 (May 12, 1888).

43. R. Clipston Sturgis, "Two Old New England Houses," *House and Garden*, vol. 4, no. 1 (July 1903), pp. 20–27; and Sturgis, "A New World House in an Old World Garden," *Country Life* (Garden City, NY), vol. 43, no. 5 (Mar. 1923), pp. 68–70. Sturgis also recorded his work on Martine Cottage in Architectural Notebooks of Richard Clipston Sturgis, series 1, no. 2, Jan.–July 1892; series 1, no. 3, July 1892–Apr. 1893; and series 1, no. 16, June 1897.

44. Sturgis, "Two Old New England Houses," pp. 21, 25.

45. Winifred B. Warren, "Recollections of My Early Childhood. Our Home in Waban," written after 1969, unpublished manuscript, original copy owned by James William Stoutamire of Tallahassee, FL. See also Aleca Sullivan, "Landmark Report," Apr. 30, 1997, at the Jackson Homestead, Newton Historical Society Archives, Newton, MA; and Maureen Meister, *Architecture and the Arts and Crafts Movement in Boston: Harvard's H. Langford Warren*, Hanover, NH: University Press of New England, 2003, pp. 26–28.

46. M. F. Sweetser, *King's Handbook of Newton, Massachusetts*, Boston: Moses King, 1889, pp. 232, 242.

47. The changes that Cram made to the house are mentioned in captions that accompany two illustrations of it in Julian Buckly, "Architecture in Massachusetts During the Latter Part of the 18th Century," White Pine series of Architectural Monographs, vol. 2, no. 2 (Apr. 1916).

48. Cram, *My Life in Architecture*, pp. 229–35. Both the house and the chapel are contributing buildings in the Old Sudbury Historic District, listed on the National Register of Historic Places, July 14, 1976.

49. Howe, Manning, and Almy Papers, MIT Archives, box 2, folder 60, July 15, 1898.

50. Howe, Manning, and Almy Papers, MIT Archives, box 9, folder 578, Clients R. The folder includes photographs taken before and after the house was moved.

51. Floyd, p. 384. See also Howe and Fuller, *Details From Old New England Houses*. Called the Larches, the house is documented by the Cambridge, MA, Historical Commission.

52. Floyd, pp. 115–17.

53. F. B. W., "All About the Annex. Its Relations to Harvard University. Sketch of Its Beginning and Growth—What Fay House Is Like—How the Students Amuse Themselves," *Boston Evening Transcript*, Nov. 14, 1891.

54. For the Country Club, Brookline, which includes the William Spooner house, see the inventory form prepared by Leslie Larkin, Mar. 1980, filed with Massachusetts Historical Commission. See also Elmer Osgood Cappers, *The Centennial History of the Country Club, 1882–1982*, Brookline, MA: Country Club, 1981. The expansion under Andrews, Jaques, and Rantoul would have been led by Herbert Jaques, an active member of the club and its president from 1912 until his death on Dec. 21, 1916. Jaques joined the Society of Arts and Crafts in 1908 and remained a member for the rest of his life.

55. Most of the work on the Winchester Country Club project would have been done by Warren's partner, Frank Patterson Smith, who was a Winchester resident. Photographs and plans for the work on the club are preserved in Historic New England's Library and Archives, Boston. See also Meister, pp. 139–45.

56. See Architectural Notebooks of Richard Clipston Sturgis, series 2, no. 26, entries dated Nov. 26, 1901, and Dec. 28, 1901; and series 2, no. 27, Feb. 26, 1902. Entries between Sept. 1900 and Feb. 1902 also record meetings that Sturgis held with Theodore Salisbury Woolsey, professor of international law in the Yale Law School, for renovations to his house at 250 Church St., built by his father, Yale president Theodore Dwight Woolsey.

57. Howe, Manning, and Almy Papers, MIT Archives, box 9, folder 567, Clients C. *Concord Art Association: History of the Art Centre and the Permanent Collection*, Concord, MA: Concord Art Association, [1924].

58. "The National Trust," *Architectural Review*, vol. 7, no. 11 (Nov. 1900). The English National Trust was modeled after two Massachusetts groups: the Trustees of Public Reservations, chartered in 1891, and the Metropolitan Park Commission, serving the Boston region, established in 1893. See Michael Holleran, *Boston's "Changeful Times": Origins of Preservation and Planning in America*, Baltimore: Johns Hopkins University Press, 1998, pp. 132–33.

59. C. R. Ashbee, *A Report by Mr. C. R. Ashbee to the Council of the National Trust for Places of Historic Interest and Natural Beauty, on His Visit to the United States*, London: Essex House Press, 1901. See also James M. Lindgren, *Preserving Historic New England: Preservation, Progressivism, and the Remaking of Memory*, New York: Oxford University Press, 1995, p. 54.

60. Ashbee, p. 22.

61. Lindgren, pp. 15–25.

62. "The Movement to Buy the Cooper-Austin House," *Bulletin of the Society for the Preservation of New England Antiquities*, vol. 3, no. 1 (Mar. 1912), pp. 9–11. The house was believed to date from 1657, but today the accepted date is 1681.

63. *Bulletin of the Society for the Preservation of New England Antiquities*, vol. 4, no. 1 (Aug. 1913), pp. 33–36.

64. "The Restoration of Christ Church, Boston," *Bulletin of the Society for the Preservation of New England Antiquities*, vol. 3, no. 3 (Feb. 1913), pp. 5–8.

65. "Bulfinch Front, State House, Boston," *Bulletin of the Society for the Preservation of New England Antiquities*, vol. 6, no. 1 (Apr. 1915), pp. 16–17. See also Lindgren, p. 109; Hol-

leran, pp. 163, 233; and William D. Austin, "A History of the Boston Society of Architects in the 19th Century," 3 vols., manuscript, 1942, Boston Athenaeum, vol. 1, ch. 2, pp. 38–39.

66. "Old State House, Hartford, Conn.," *Old-Time New England*, vol. 11, no. 1 (July 1920), p. 23.

67. Samuel Eliot Morison, intro. to *Of Plymouth Plantation, 1620–1647* by William Bradford, New York: Modern Library, 1952, pp. xxiii–xliii.

68. Robert D. Andrews, "The Tendency of American Design as Exemplified in Recent Buildings," *Architectural Review*, vol. 4, no. 8 (Dec. 1, 1897), p. 64.

69. Ibid., p. 65.

70. See the inventory form prepared by the Boston Landmarks Commission, June 1980, filed with the Massachusetts Historical Commission. The State Mutual Building was published in *Brickbuilder*, vol. 13, no. 3 (Mar. 1904); and vol. 14, no. 7 (July 1905).

71. Hugh Cairns listed his work on the State Mutual Building in an advertisement that appeared in *Catalogue: Boston Architectural Club Exhibition*, Boston, 1904, p. 140. Metalwork for the building is illustrated in *Hecla Iron Works from 1876 to 1908*, Brooklyn, NY: Hecla, 1908, in the collection of the New York Public Library. Hecla, based in Brooklyn, also had offices in Boston. Hecla's work was exhibited in the 1899 Society of Arts and Crafts Exhibition, SACB Archives, AAA/SI 319: 746.

72. *Fifth Annual Report of the Federal Reserve Bank of Boston for the Year Ended Dec. 31, 1919*, Boston: Federal Reserve Bank, 1920, p. 23. The bank was illustrated in *Architectural Forum*, vol. 48, no. 6 (June 1928, part 1). See also the inventory form prepared by the Boston Landmarks Commission, June 1980, filed with the Massachusetts Historical Commission.

73. John Evans Collection, "Sketchbook/Record Book 1920–1924," Jan.–Aug. 1921.

74. *Catalogue of the Architectural Exhibition, Boston Architectural Club and Boston Society of Architects*, 1899, p. 97.

75. Charles D. Maginnis, "A Criticism of Catholic Architecture in the United States," *Architectural Review*, vol. 8, no. 10 (Oct. 1901), pp. 111–15. An illustration of St. Patrick's appears on p. 115. St. Patrick's was featured in *Architectural Review*, vol. 6, no. 11 (Nov. 1899); it was illustrated again and a plan published in *Architectural Review*, vol. 12, no. 10 (Oct. 1905). See also Roland Cosgrove, "Charles D. Maginnis Elected to Membership in Academy of Design," *Boston Traveler*, Mar. 11, 1941.

76. Maginnis, "A Criticism," p. 114.

77. The New Jersey Terra-Cotta Company announced its contract for St. Patrick's in *Brickbuilder*, vol. 7, no. 1 (Jan. 1898), p. 22. Cairns listed his work for two projects by Maginnis, Walsh, and Sullivan, one of which was a panel in terra cotta, in the 1899 exhibition catalogue of the Society of Arts and Crafts. The client for the terra-cotta panel is not specified. See SACB Archives, AAA/SI 319: 740. Also in 1899, Goodhue exhibited a photograph of a stained-glass window in St. Patrick's that he designed and Horace J. Phipps and Co. executed. See SACB Archives, AAA/SI 319: 748. Work for St. Patrick's is listed in an advertisement by L. Haberstroh and Son, *Donahoe's Magazine*, vol. 53, no. 6 (June 1905), p. 662. The firm exhibited in the 1897 and 1899 exhibitions of the Society of Arts and Crafts.

78. Edward S. Morse, *Japanese Homes and Their Surroundings*, intro. by Clay Lancaster, New York: Dover, 1961 (orig. pub. 1885 by University Press; 1886 by Ticknor). Margaret Henderson Floyd discusses how Morse's lectures appear to have influenced Richardson

in *Henry Hobson Richardson: A Genius for Architecture*, New York: Monacelli, 1997, pp. 189–200.

79. See Frederic A. Sharf, ed., *"A Pleasing Novelty": Bunkio Matsuki and the Japan Craze in Victorian Salem*, ex. cat., Peabody Essex Museum, Salem, MA, 1993.

80. "An Oriental Home," *Boston Herald*, Feb. 17, 1895. See also Cram's "An Architectural Experiment," *Architectural Record*, vol. 8, no. 1 (July–Sept. 1898), pp. 82–91; and Charles Edward Hooper, *The Country House*, New York: Doubleday and Page, 1905. Douglass Shand-Tucci discusses the Knapp house in *Boston Bohemia 1881–1900: Ralph Adams Cram, Life and Architecture*, Amherst: University of Massachusetts Press, 1995, pp. 403–10.

81. Roger G. Reed, *Summering on the Thoroughfare: The Architecture of North Haven, 1885–1945*, Portland, ME: Maine Citizens for Historic Preservation, 1993, pp. 30–41. Another summer enclave inspired by Japanese architecture, Pine Tree Point Camp, was built in the Adirondacks for Frederick W. Vanderbilt and his wife in 1894. See William Hosley, *The Japan Idea: Art and Life in Victorian America*, ex. cat., Wadsworth Atheneum, Hartford, CT, 1990, p. 107.

82. "Shelter and Duck House Proposed for Back Bay Fens," illustration with caption crediting Edmund Wheelwright as architect, in *American Architect and Building News*, July 11, 1896, vol. 53, no. 1072.

83. Cram, "An Architectural Experiment"; Cram, "The Early Architecture of Japan," *Architectural Review*, vol. 5, no. 6 (Sept. 10, 1898), pp. 54–57; and Cram, "The Later Architecture of Japan," *Architectural Review*, vol. 5, no. 8 (Dec. 10, 1898), pp. 77–80. Cram also published *Impressions of Japanese Architecture and the Allied Arts*, New York: Baker and Taylor, 1905. On Morse's 1899 lecture, see SACB Archives, AAA/SI 316: 352; and AAA/SI 322: 228. The loan by Ross is listed in *Exhibition Catalogue of the Society of Arts and Crafts*, Boston, 1899, SACB Archives, AAA/SI 319: 756. For Cram's 1902 lecture, see SACB Archives, AAA/SI 316: 496; and for Morse's 1904 lecture, see SACB Archives, AAA/SI 316: 551. J. Templeman Coolidge Jr. published "A Few Considerations of Japanese Wood-Carving," *Handicraft*, vol. 2, no. 3 (June 1903), pp. 49–57. For the loan of Japanese pottery and pewter jars, see *Exhibition Catalogue of the Society of Arts and Crafts*, Boston, 1907, SACB Archives, AAA/SI 320: 112–19.

84. Cram, "The Later Architecture of Japan," p. 80.

85. C. Howard Walker, "L'Art Nouveau," *Architectural Review*, vol. 11, no. 1 (Jan. 1904), p. 13.

86. Ibid., pp. 13, 19.

87. "A Bachelor Apartment in the Ansonia, New York," *Architectural Review*, vol. 12, no. 5 (May 1905), p. 125.

7. LOOKING FORWARD: BUILDING FOR THE TWENTIETH CENTURY

1. H. G. Wells, *The Future in America: A Search after Realities*, New York and London: Harper and Brothers, 1906.

2. Ralph Adams Cram, *My Life in Architecture*, Boston: Little, Brown, 1936, p. 6.

3. Melvin I. Urofsky, *Louis D. Brandeis: A Life*, New York: Pantheon, 2009, p. 42.

4. See Vincent J. Scully Jr., *The Shingle Style and the Stick Style*, rev. ed., New Haven, CT: Yale University Press, 1971 (orig. pub. 1955), pp. 155–64.

5. See the National Register nomination for Chocorua Lake Basin Historic District, prepared by Elizabeth Durfee Hengen with James Bowditch, accepted June 9, 2005. See

also Bryant F. Tolles Jr., *Summer Cottages in the White Mountains*, Hanover, NH: University Press of New England, 2000.

6. C. Howard Walker, "The Decorative Treatment of Architecture," *Architectural Review*, vol. 11, no. 3 (Mar. 1904), p. 125.

7. On the Maine houses, see Margaret Henderson Floyd, *Architecture After Richardson: Regionalism before Modernism—Longfellow, Alden, and Harlow in Boston and Pittsburgh*, Chicago and Pittsburgh: University of Chicago Press in association with Pittsburgh History and Landmarks Foundation, 1994, pp. 411–35.

8. See the survey form by Janet Roberts for the Maine Historic Preservation Commission, Oct. 20, 1992; and Floyd, pp. 433–36.

9. The house was illustrated in *Engineering and Building Record*, vol. 18, no. 16 (Sept. 15, 1888). See also Maureen Meister, *Architecture and the Arts and Crafts Movement in Boston: Harvard's H. Langford Warren*, Hanover, NH: University Press of New England, 2003, pp. 44–47.

10. *American Country Houses of Today*, preface by Frank Miles Day, New York: Architectural Book Publishing, 1912, pp. 146–49.

11. See the survey form by Carla Benka for the Brookline Preservation Commission, MA, Apr. 1980. The current owners of the house learned from Elizabeth Maginnis, daughter of the architect, that Koralewsky provided the iron. The woodwork was supplied by Irving and Casson.

12. Ralph Adams Cram, "The Promise of American House Building," in Richardson Wright, ed., *Low-Cost Suburban Homes*, New York: Robert M. McBride, 1920, pp. 31–41.

13. Ibid., p. 35.

14. Ibid., pp. 32, 37.

15. Ibid., p. 40.

16. Ibid., p. 41.

17. *Exhibition of the Society of Arts and Crafts*, ex. cat., Boston, 1907. The catalogue may be read in AAA/SI 320: 112–19. Loans made by Perkins are listed in *Retrospective Exhibition of the Decorative Arts*, ex. cat., Boston: Copley Society, 1911.

18. *Retrospective Exhibition of the Decorative Arts*.

19. On the Strong house, see Meister, pp. 44–47.

20. For example, see H. Langford Warren, "Recent Domestic Architecture in England," *Architectural Review*, vol. 11, no. 1 (Jan. 1904), pp. 5–12.

21. *Architectural Review* vol. 14, no. 1 (Jan. 1907), p. 1.

22. Frank Chouteau Brown, "Exterior Plaster Construction," part I, *Architectural Review*, vol. 14, no. 1 (Jan. 1907), pp. 1–8. This article included illustrations of a stucco house for Mrs. A. A. Burrage, 1904, Brookline, MA, designed by Lois L. Howe. Part II by Brown appeared in Feb. 1907, and part III ran in Oct. 1907.

23. *Architectural Review*, vol. 14, no. 1 (Jan. 1907), p. 1.

24. Ira N. Hollis, "Origin of the Harvard Stadium," *Harvard Engineering Journal*, vol. 3, no. 2 (June 1904), p. 100.

25. The Everett D. Chadwick house was illustrated in *American Architect*, vol. 105, no. 1985 (Jan. 7, 1914); and *Architectural Review*, new series vol. 3, no. 2 (Feb. 1914), pp. 30–31. Plans for the house are held by Historic New England Library and Archives, Boston. See also Meister, pp. 126–31.

26. "The Picturesque Walker House. At Magnolia Replaces One Burned Two Years Ago," *Gloucester Times*, May 23, 1912.

27. C. Howard Walker, "The Artistic Use of Steel and Reinforced Concrete," *American Architect*, vol. 93, no. 1673 (Jan. 18, 1908), p. 25.

28. Ibid.

29. Ibid., p. 26.

30. See plates for West Roxbury High School by Andrews, Jaques, and Rantoul in *Architectural Review*, vol. 5, no. 6 (Sept. 10, 1898).

31. See *A Directory of Massachusetts Manufactures*, Boston: Commonwealth of Massachusetts, 1913, under "Artificial Stone," with thirty-one companies listed.

32. See the advertisement in *Boston Architectural Club Exhibition*, ex. cat., Boston: Boston Architectural Club, 1907, p. 49. The firm of Emerson and Norris identified the Perkins Institution as one of its customers in an advertisement in *Current Architecture. Joint Exhibition: Architecture, Landscape Architecture, and the Allied Arts*, ex. cat., Boston: Boston Society of Architects, Boston Architectural Club, Society of Landscape Architects, and Society of Arts and Crafts, 1916, p. 220. The firm of Maginnis and Walsh also is identified as a customer.

33. Ralph Adams Cram, *Church Building: A Study of the Principles of Architecture in Their Relation to the Church*, Boston: Small, Maynard, 1901, p. 85.

34. See the advertisement for Economy Manufacturing Company in *Christian Art*, vol. 4, no. 2 (Nov. 1908), p. iv, listing the company's work for St. James, Woodstock, VT. See also *Some Examples of the Recent Use of Concrete Stone*, New Haven, CT: Economy Manufacturing, 1907, including work by Lee Lawrie.

35. Cram, *Church Building*, p. 84.

36. Photographs showing the construction of the vaults of Church of the Epiphany, Winchester, MA, are in the collection of Historic New England Library and Archives, Boston.

37. For the Anne M. Paul house, see the Howe, Manning, and Almy Papers, box 2, folders 80, 81, 94; and box 9, folder 574, at Institute Archives and Special Collections, MIT, Cambridge, MA.

38. Cram, *Church Building*, p. 13.

39. Robert Brown, "All Saints Church, Dorchester, Mass.," *Architectural Review*, vol. 7, no. 9 (Sept. 1900), p. 102.

40. Charles D. Maginnis, "A Criticism of Catholic Architecture in the United States," *Architectural Review*, vol. 8, no. 10 (Oct. 1901), p. 113.

41. Lois L. Howe, "Serving-Pantries in Small Houses," *Architectural Review*, vol. 14, no. 3 (Mar. 1907), pp. 31–33.

42. Ibid., p. 33.

43. Meister, pp. 48–52, 118–21.

44. Floyd, pp. 392–93.

45. See untitled *Boston Post* clipping, Apr. 9, 1902, in Harvard University Archives, Cambridge, MA, HUG 300, 1881, "Richard Clipston Sturgis."

46. "City School-Houses. A Review of the Recent Reports of the Board of School-House Commissioners of Boston, Mass.," *Architectural Review*, vol. 11, no. 6 (June 1904), pp. 161–66; and "Boston Public School Buildings," *American Architect and Building News*, vol. 93, no. 1671 (Jan. 4, 1908), pp. 1–4. Both articles are unsigned. *Architectural Review* illustrates buildings and plans designed by Longfellow; Maginnis, Walsh, and Sullivan; Andrews, Jaques, and Rantoul; and Cram, Goodhue, and Ferguson. The article in *American Architect* includes illustrations of the Mather School, Dorchester, by Cram,

Goodhue, and Ferguson; and the Oliver Wendell Holmes School, Dorchester, by Longfellow.

47. "Handsome West Roxbury High School Building on Elm St., Jamaica Plain, Dedicated," *Boston Globe*, Nov. 23, 1901.

48. On apartment buildings in Boston, see Douglass Shand-Tucci, *Built in Boston: City and Suburb, 1800–2000*, rev. ed., Amherst: University of Massachusetts Press, 1999 (orig. pub. 1978), pp. 101–30.

49. "The Richmond Court Apartments," 1898, a prospectus held by the Brookline Preservation Commission, MA.

50. *Architectural Review*, vol. 11, no. 3 (Mar. 1904), p. 133. See also *Brickbuilder*, vol. 13, no. 2 (Feb. 1904).

51. For records documenting Howe's work for the Business Women's Club, Boston, see Howe, Manning, and Almy Papers, MC9, box 2, folder 83, 1912, MIT Archives.

52. "Business Women's Club," *Boston Evening Transcript*, Mar. 22, 1913.

53. "The Arts and Crafts," *Boston Advertiser*, Apr. 30, 1897, SACB Archives, AAA/SI 322: 224.

54. Among the Boston office buildings designed by Walker were the Niles Building (1915) and the Oliver Ditson Building (1918).

55. The "auto house" of 1901 was erected to accompany a house at 15 Circuit Rd., Brookline, MA, by Andrews, Jaques, and Rantoul (1898), its building permit granted to Herbert Jaques. It is the oldest documented garage in Brookline. See Roger G. Reed and Greer Hardwicke, *Carriage House to Auto House: A Guide to Brookline's Transportation Buildings to 1940*, Brookline, MA: Brookline Preservation Commission, 2002.

56. "Massachusetts: Boston," *Automobile Topics*, vol. 20, no. 22 (Sept. 3, 1910), pp. 1481–82. See also "Service for Peerless Owners. This Company's Interest in a Car Continues Long After It Is Sold," *Boston Evening Transcript*, Apr. 15, 1911.

57. William D. Austin, "A History of the Boston Society of Architects in the 19th Century," 3 vols., manuscript, 1942, Boston Athenaeum, vol. 3, ch. 16, p. 37.

58. *Special Exhibition. Boston Architectural Club*, ex. cat., Boston: Boston Architectural Club, 1897, pp. 35, 145.

59. Floyd, pp. 361–71.

60. Urofsky, pp. 133–40.

61. Bainbridge Bunting, *Harvard: An Architectural History*, completed and edited by Margaret Henderson Floyd, Cambridge, MA: Belknap Press of Harvard University Press, 1985, pp. 96–101.

62. Meister, pp. 133–37.

63. Today called the Royall Tyler Theater, the gymnasium is documented in files of the University of Vermont Library, Special Collections, Burlington, VT.

64. "Harvard's Engineering Home," *Boston Evening Transcript*, Nov. 1, 1901. This article, another newspaper article without a source identified, and a 1902 pamphlet about Harvard's Division of Engineering are at Harvard University Archives, HUB 1692.2, box 1.

65. Walker also designed the Baxter Memorial Library, Gorham, ME, 1908, and the Sharon, MA, Public Library, 1914.

66. Plans for the new McLean campus appear in *79th Annual Report of the Trustees of Massachusetts General Hospital and McLean Hospital*, 1892, Boston: 1893. See also S. B. Sutton, *Crossroads in Psychiatry: A History of the McLean Hospital*, Washington, D.C.:

American Psychiatric Press, 1986; and "McLean Hospital National Register District," nomination to the National Register of Historic Places, prepared by Candace Jenkins and Shary Page Berg with Edward Zimmer, accepted Jan. 23, 2003. For a broader context, see Carla Yanni, *The Architecture of Madness: Insane Asylums in the United States*, Minneapolis: University of Minnesota Press, 2007.

67. R. Clipston Sturgis, "Perkins Institution and Massachusetts School for the Blind at Watertown, Massachusetts," *Brickbuilder*, vol. 22, no. 7 (July 1913), pp. 154–58.

68. Ibid., p. 154.

69. SACB Archives, AAA/SI 316: 059.

70. *Exhibition of the Society of Arts and Crafts*, ex. cat., Boston: 1907, entries 1383–99. See also SACB Archives, AAA/SI 320: 100.

71. The American Society for the Prevention of Cruelty to Animals was founded in New York City in 1866. On the Massachusetts society, see George Thorndike Angell, *Autobiographical Sketches and Personal Recollections*, Boston: American Humane Education Society, [1892].

72. "Officers of the Society," *Our Dumb Animals*, vol. 1, no. 1 (June 2, 1868), and succeeding issues. Emerson was one of several dozen vice presidents, and in this role he endorsed the organization but did not actively serve it.

73. Francis H. Rowley, "Angell Memorial Animals' Hospital and Headquarters for Our Two Societies," *Our Dumb Animals*, vol. 44, no. 8 (Jan. 1912), pp. 117–18; "Angell Hospital for Animals," *Boston Globe*, Dec. 13, 1914; "Angell Memorial Hospital," *Boston Medical and Surgical Journal*, vol. 172, no. 3 (Jan. 21, 1915), pp. 117–18; and "Angell Memorial Hospital for Animals," *Humane Advocate*, vol. 10, no. 6 (Apr. 1915), pp. 756–57. See also "W. E. Putnam, Architect, Dies. Designed Angell Animal Hospital," *Boston Herald*, Aug. 5, 1947. In 1974 Angell Memorial Hospital relocated, and the building was bought by Harvard Medical School.

74. Discussed in ch. 3.

75. Sarah Whitman's involvement is documented in the annual reports of the Boston Cooperative Building Company.

76. Floyd illustrates and discusses this project by Longfellow, p. 377. She does not discuss an earlier commission that appears to have gone to C. Howard Walker. In the Architects File at the Boston Public Library, Fine Arts Dept., a card under Walker's name identifies him as the architect of a house built for the cooperative in the South End in 1886. The company's 1887 report confirms that a "double house" was built in the prior year at that location.

77. *28th Annual Report of the Boston Cooperative Building Company*, Boston: Barta Press, 1899, p. 12. In 1899 Longfellow was engaged again to build a similar group of brick houses in Roxbury, built in 1900. See *29th Annual Report of the Boston Cooperative Building Company*, Boston: Barta Press, 1900, p. 12.

78. Austin, vol. 3, ch. 17, p. 18.

79. Ibid., p. 6. Presentations were made on Mar. 5, 1897, covering bathhouses of Europe, Brookline bathhouses, and the "new free baths" for the city of Boston. Prior to this date, Sturgis designed at least one bathhouse for a city park. See Architectural Notebooks of Richard Clipston Sturgis, Boston Athenaeum, series 1, no. 13, Sept. 4, 1896.

80. "North End Bath-house for the City of Boston," illustration with caption crediting Maginnis, Walsh, and Sullivan as architects, *American Architect and Building News*, vol. 86, no. 1508 (Nov. 19, 1904); *Architectural Review*, vol. 11, no. 12 (Dec. 1904), p. 254; *Brick-*

builder, vol. 17, no. 11 (Nov. 1908); and *Architectural Review*, vol. 15, no. 12 (Dec. 1908), p. 190.

81. "Proposed Gymnasium and Public Baths, Paris Street, East Boston," illustration with caption crediting Newhall and Blevins as architects, *Brickbuilder*, vol. 18, no. 6 (June 1909); and "New Municipal Gymnasium, East Boston, Mass.," illustration with caption crediting Newhall and Blevins as architects, *American Architect and Building News*, vol. 99, no. 1846 (May 10, 1911).

82. "Consolation House," *Trained Nurse and Hospital Review*, vol. 52, no. 6 (June 1914), p. 360.

83. See Architectural Notebooks of Richard Clipston Sturgis, series 2, no. 26, entries from Dec. 1901, for South End House. When completed, the South Bay Union, identified as "South Bay Mission House," was illustrated in *Brickbuilder*, vol. 12, no. 5 (May 1903), attributed solely to Sturgis. It also was illustrated in *Architectural Review*, vol. 10, no. 6 (June 1903). In 1895 Sturgis designed a Brighton tenement, recorded in Architectural Notebooks of Richard Clipston Sturgis, series 1, no. 9, Mar. 1895. A year later, he met with Theodore Monroe Davis to discuss plans for a Workingman's Club in Newport, RI. It is not clear whether the project was realized. See Architectural Notebooks of Richard Clipston Sturgis, series 1, no. 12, Apr. 29, 1896.

84. Fiske Kimball, "The Social Center. Part II. Philanthropic Enterprises," *Architectural Record*, vol. 45, no. 6 (June 1919), pp. 531–33.

85. Ibid., p. 532.

86. *Society of Arts and Crafts, Annual Report*, Boston: n.p., 1901.

87. Discussed in ch. 6.

88. "School and College—Elizabeth Peabody House," *Boston Evening Transcript*, Apr. 11, 1913.

89. Sylvester Baxter, "The Government's Housing at Bridgeport, Connecticut," *Architectural Record*, vol. 45, no. 2 (Feb. 1919), pp. 123–41. See also "A Successful Housing Achievement: Houses for Industrial Workers Built by the Bridgeport Housing Company"; and Ralph E. Winslow, "The Workingman's Home from the Workingman's Point of View," both in *House Beautiful*, vol. 43, no. 5 (Apr. 1918), pp. 265–69. And see Harry I. Shumway, "Some Homes in Lordship Manor," *House Beautiful*, vol. 44, no. 4 (Sept. 1918), pp. 200–201, 215.

90. See the National Register of Historic Places nomination, "Wartime Emergency Housing in Bridgeport, Conn., 1916–1920," prepared by Steven Bedford and Nora Lucas, approved Aug. 9, 1990.

91. Baxter, p. 131. Sturgis recorded his meetings for the Bridgeport housing projects in Architectural Notebooks of Richard Clipston Sturgis, series 4, nos. 65–67, May 1917–Mar. 1918 entries. Although Barton had left Sturgis by this time, he also had been interested in worker housing, having published "Port Sunlight. A Model English Village" in *Architectural Review*, vol. 6, no. 5 (May 1899), pp. 62–66.

92. *Joint Exhibition: Boston Society of Architects, Boston Architectural Club, Boston Society of Landscape Architects, Society of Arts and Crafts*, ex. cat., Boston: Boston Society of Architects, Boston Architectural Club, Boston Society of Landscape Architects, Society of Arts and Crafts, 1917.

93. Frederick Law Olmsted Jr. led the town planning at a national level, and Arthur Shurtleff planned the Bridgeport developments for which Sturgis was the architect. See John Nolen, *New Towns for Old*, Boston: Marshall Jones, 1927, pp. 95, 98.

94. Baxter, p. 140.

95. See folder "Phillips Brooks House," Harvard University Archives, HUB 1687.2, box 26.

96. Urofsky, p. 203.

97. "Boston City Club Collection," Special Collections, Boston Public Library. See also "Discussion on Insurance. Louis Brandeis and Others Speak at the Boston City Club," *Boston Evening Transcript*, Dec. 28, 1906.

98. Illustrations of the City Club appeared in *American Architect*, vol. 107, no. 2048 (Mar. 24, 1915) and *Brickbuilder*, vol. 24, no. 3 (Mar. 1915). The building was located next to the Boston Architectural Club, where Newhall was serving as president. Today the Boston City Club building is owned by Suffolk University.

99. Edwin M. Bacon, *The Book of Boston: Fifty Years' Recollections of the New England Metropolis*, Boston: Book of Boston, 1916, pp. 122–23.

100. Richard Clipston Sturgis Day Books, Boston Athenaeum, box 5, Day Book for Oct. 1903–June 1904. Note that these books are different from the Sturgis notebooks.

101. "The New City Hall," *Cambridge Chronicle*, Feb. 25, 1888. The inscription was requested by the donor.

102. "Andrews, Robert Day," in *Who Was Who in America*, vol. 1, 1897–1942, Chicago: Marquis Who's Who, 1943.

103. Ralph Adams Cram, *The Ruined Abbeys of Great Britain*, New York: James Pott, 1905, p. 3.

104. Ralph Adams Cram, "American University Architecture," in Cram, *The Ministry of Art*, Boston and New York: Houghton Mifflin, 1914, p. 170. Originally published as "Recent University Architecture in the United States," *Journal of the Royal Institute of British Architects*, May 25, 1912, pp. 497–518.

105. Michael Holleran, *Boston's "Changeful Times": Origins of Preservation and Planning in America*, Baltimore: Johns Hopkins University Press, 1998, pp. 173–82.

106. Austin, vol. 3, ch. 17, p. 15.

107. Lead editorial (untitled), *American Architect and Building News*, vol. 59, no. 1153 (Jan. 29, 1898); Austin, vol. 3, ch. 17, p. 22. The vote was taken Feb. 4, 1898.

108. For the trustees, see the annual reports of the Museum of Fine Arts. The legislation and litigation over Westminster Chambers were noted in *Twenty-third Annual Report for the Year Ending Dec. 31, 1898*, Trustees of the Museum of Fine Arts, Boston, 1899, p. 8.

109. Holleran, p. 180; and p. 310, n. 45.

110. H. L. W. [H. Langford Warren], "Current Periodicals," *Architectural Review*, vol. 5, no. 7 (Oct. 20, 1898), p. 75.

111. C. R. Ashbee, *A Report by Mr. C. R. Ashbee to the Council of the National Trust for Places of Historic Interest and Natural Beauty, on His Visit to the United States*, London: Essex House, 1901, p. 7. See also Holleran, p. 165.

112. "Boston Building Too High," *New York Times*, Mar. 14, 1901.

113. Williams v. Parker, decided Feb. 23, 1903.

114. Holleran, pp. 180–81.

115. See Meister, pp. 158–62.

116. Lawrence W. Kennedy, *Planning the City upon a Hill: Boston Since 1630*, Amherst: University of Massachusetts Press, 1992, pp. 88–94.

117. Holleran, pp. 129–34.

118. In June 1906, Walker and the Metropolitan Improvement League presented Walker's

plan to the mayor of Boston for rebuilding Copley Square, "Betterment of Copley Square," *Proceedings of Boston City Council,* 1907, pp. 26–27. See also Kennedy, p. 116.

119. *Report Made to the Boston Society of Architects by the Committee on Municipal Improvement,* Boston, 1907. The study was completed Dec. 1, 1906.

120. *Report Made to the Boston Society of Architects,* p. 1.

Epilogue: Confronting Modernism

1. Discussed in ch. 1.

2. *American Journal of Archaeology,* Supplement to Vol. 7, 24th Annual Report, 1902–1903, 1903. For members of the Boston group, see pp. 50–57. In addition to Langford Warren, architects Frank (Francis) W. Chandler and W. P. P. Longfellow are listed. The Boston Society of Architects also subscribed to a life membership.

3. Ibid., p. 51.

4. The most comprehensive survey to date is Keith N. Morgan, ed., *Buildings of Massachusetts: Metropolitan Boston,* Charlottesville, VA: University of Virginia Press for the Society of Architectural Historians, 2009. These craftsmen all appear in this volume. See also Douglass Shand-Tucci, *Built in Boston: City and Suburb, 1800–2000,* Amherst: University of Massachusetts Press, rev. 1999 (orig. pub. 1978).

5. On the influence of the Society of Arts and Crafts across the nation, see Beverly K. Brandt, *The Craftsman and the Critic: Defining Usefulness and Beauty in Arts and Crafts-Era Boston,* Amherst: University of Massachusetts Press, 2009, pp. 225–74.

6. Records of both architects' firms are at the Boston Public Library.

7. Edward R. Bosley, *Greene and Greene,* London: Phaidon, 2000, pp. 16–21.

8. Robert C. Spencer Jr., "The Work of Frank Lloyd Wright," *Architectural Review,* new series vol. 7, no. 6 (June 1900), pp. 61–72. In the same issue, see R. A. C. [Ralph Adams Cram], "Current Periodicals," p. 75.

9. Ralph Adams Cram, "Will This Modernism Last? No. Not in Itself, but It Will Leave an Influence for Good," *House Beautiful,* vol. 65, no. 1 (Jan. 19, 1929), pp. 45, 88. An MIT-trained Chicago architect, Thomas E. Tallmadge, wrote an opposing article.

10. Ibid., p. 88.

11. Ralph Adams Cram, *My Life in Architecture,* Boston: Little, Brown, 1936, pp. 259–83.

12. Ibid., p. 264.

13. Ibid., pp. 267–68.

14. Ibid., p. 272.

15. Ibid., p. 274.

16. "Architects in Washington," *Time,* vol. 15, no. 22 (June 2, 1930).

17. Ibid.

18. "Minutes of the Regular Meeting," *Bulletin of the Boston Society of Architects,* vol. 16, no. 6 (Oct. 1930), pp. 2–3.

19. Anthony Alofsin, *The Struggle for Modernism: Architecture, Landscape Architecture, and City Planning at Harvard,* New York: W. W. Norton, 2002, pp. 76–79. The proposed addition was designed by John Humphreys.

20. Shand-Tucci, pp. 221–23.

21. One of the plaques identifies Putnam and Cox as the architects.

22. Elizabeth Maginnis told the current owners of the house that the playroom decoration

was done in the 1930s by the Rambusch Studios when the firm oversaw the decoration of the nearby Coolidge Corner Theatre.

23. Charles D. Maginnis, "The Crisis in Architecture," an address to the National Institute of Arts and Letters, New York, Nov. 28, 1945, in Robert P. Walsh and Andrew W. Roberts, eds., *Charles Donagh Maginnis, FAIA: A Selection of His Essays and Addresses*, New Haven, CT: n.p., 1956, pp. 11–21.

24. Ibid., pp. 18, 19, 20, 21.

25. See Bainbridge Bunting, *Harvard: An Architectural History*, completed and edited by Margaret Henderson Floyd, Cambridge, MA: Belknap Press of Harvard University Press, 1985, pp. 228–29.

26. Letter from R. Clipston Sturgis, *Harvard Alumni Bulletin*, vol. 53, no. 13 (Apr. 7, 1951), pp. 530–31. See also a letter from Sturgis in *Harvard Alumni Bulletin*, vol. 53, no. 2 (Oct. 14, 1950), pp. 55, 81.

27. Robert D. Andrews, "President's Address to the Boston Architectural Club," *Architectural Review*, vol. 2, no. 8 (Nov. 15, 1893), pp. 64, 63.

Illustration Credits

Figure 1.1 Courtesy of the Trustees of the Boston Public Library, Arts Dept.

Figure 1.2 Courtesy of the Massachusetts Historical Society. From the Tavern Club Records.

Figure 1.3 Courtesy of the Massachusetts Historical Society. From the Tavern Club Records.

Figure 1.4 Library of Congress, Prints and Photographs Division.

Figure 1.5 Courtesy of the MIT Museum.

Figure 1.6 Courtesy of the National Park Service, Longfellow House-Washington's Headquarters National Historic Site.

Figure 1.7 John J. Burns Library, Boston College. Francis W. Sweeney, SJ, Humanities Series Director's Records, MS2002–37, box 62, folder 58.

Figure 1.8 Courtesy of the Boston Architectural College Archives, Boston, MA. RG 035, Boston Architectural Club Papers (1883–1944). Image ca. 1900.

Figure 1.9 Harvard University Archives, HUD 296.25, Putnam.

Figure 1.10 Arnold Arboretum Horticultural Library of Harvard University. © President and Fellows of Harvard College. Arnold Arboretum Archives.

Figure 1.11 *Brickbuilder*, Jan. 1915.

Figure 1.12 Harvard University Archives, HUP Walker, Charles Howard (1).

Figure 1.13 James William Stoutamire collection.

Figure 2.1 Margaret Henderson Floyd Collection, Tufts University.

Figure 2.2 The Landmark Trust.

Figure 2.3 Margaret Henderson Floyd Collection, Tufts University.

Figure 2.4 *Building News*, March 31, 1871.

Figure 2.5 © National Trust Images/Andreas von Einsiedel.

Figure 2.6 Peter Humpidge.

Figure 2.7 Courtesy of the Trustees of the Boston Public Library, Arts Dept. From Sir Lawrence Weaver, *Small Country Houses of To-Day*, 3rd ed., London: Country Life and George Newnes, 1922.

Figure 2.8 T. Raffles Davison, *Modern Homes*, London: George Bell and Sons, 1909.

Figure 2.9 *Architectural Review*, "Modern English Country Houses," June 1909.

Figure 2.10 Courtesy of Historic New England.

Figure 2.11 *American Architect and Building News*, Nov. 24, 1894.

Figure 2.12 Courtesy of the Trustees of the Boston Public Library.

Figure 2.13 Courtesy of the Trustees of the Boston Public Library, Arts Dept. From the *Craftsman*, June 1904.

Figure 2.14 Courtesy of the Frank Lloyd Wright Preservation Trust.

Figure 2.15 Greene and Greene Archives, The Gamble House, University of Southern California.

Figure 2.16 Library of Congress, Prints and Photographs Division.

Figure 3.1 Courtesy of the Concord Free Public Library, Concord, MA.

Figure 3.2 Harvard University Archives, HUP Norton, Charles Eliot (25b).

Figure 3.3 Courtesy of the Frances Loeb Library, Harvard Graduate School of Design.

Figure 3.4 Library of Congress, Prints and Photographs Division.

Figure 4.1 H. Langford Warren and Edward Everett Hale, *Picturesque and Architectural New England*, Boston: D. H. Hurd, 1889.

Figure 4.2 Brown Digital Repository. From G. W. Sheldon, *Artistic Country-Seats*, New York: D. Appleton, 1886–87.

Figure 4.3 Courtesy of the Trustees of the Boston Public Library, Arts Dept. From Sheldon, *Artistic Country-Seats*.

Figure 4.4 David Feigenbaum.

Figure 4.5 David Feigenbaum.

Figure 4.6 Courtesy of Historic New England.

Figure 4.7 David Feigenbaum.

Figure 4.8 David Feigenbaum.

Figure 4.9 Warren and Hale, *Picturesque and Architectural New England*.

Figure 5.1 David Feigenbaum.

Figure 5.2 Science, Industry and Business Library, The New York Public Library, Astor, Lenox, and Tilden Foundations. From *Photographs of Buildings Covered with Warren's Anchor Brand Natural Asphalt Roofing*, c. 1900.

Figure 5.3 David Feigenbaum.

Figure 5.4 David Feigenbaum.

Figure 5.5 David Feigenbaum.

Figure 5.6 David Feigenbaum.

Figure 5.7 David Feigenbaum.

Figure 5.8 David Feigenbaum.

Figure 5.9 David Feigenbaum.

Figure 5.10 David Feigenbaum.

Figure 5.11 David Feigenbaum.

Figure 5.12 David Feigenbaum.

Figure 5.13 William and Elaine Pepe Postcard Collection, South Shore Historical Society.

Figure 5.14 *American Architect and Building News*, Aug. 7, 1912.

Figure 5.15 David Feigenbaum.

Figure 5.16 David Feigenbaum.

Figure 5.17 David Feigenbaum.

Figure 5.18 David Feigenbaum.

Figure 5.19 David Feigenbaum.

Figure 5.20 David Feigenbaum.

Figure 5.21 Warren and Hale, *Picturesque and Architectural New England*.

Figure 5.22 Courtesy of Historic New England.

Figure 5.23 *American Architect and Building News*, March 11, 1893.

Figure 5.24 *Architectural Review*, April 1902.

Figure 5.25 David Feigenbaum.

Figure 5.26 Courtesy of the Trustees of the Boston Public Library.

Figure 5.27 David Feigenbaum.

Figure 5.28 Photography Collection, Miriam and Ira D. Wallach Division of Art, Prints, and Photographs, The New York Public Library, Astor, Lenox, and Tilden Foundations. From *The Pageant of America Collection*.

Figure 5.29 David Feigenbaum.

Figure 5.30 David Feigenbaum.

Figure 5.31 David Feigenbaum.

Figure 5.32 Courtesy of Perkins School for the Blind Archives.

Figure 5.33 Author.

Figure 6.1 David Feigenbaum.

Figure 6.2 David Feigenbaum.

Figure 6.3 *American Architect and Building News*, Sept. 24, 1892.

Figure 6.4 Warren and Hale, *Picturesque and Architectural New England*.

Figure 6.5 Brookline Preservation Commission.

Figure 6.6 David Feigenbaum.

Figure 6.7 David Feigenbaum.

Figure 6.8 David Feigenbaum.

Figure 6.9 Author's collection.

Figure 6.10 David Feigenbaum.

Figure 6.11 David Feigenbaum.

Figure 6.12 David Feigenbaum.

Figure 6.13 *An Account of the Celebration by the Town of Lincoln, Mass., of the 150th Anniversary of Its Incorporation*, 1904.

Figure 6.14 David Feigenbaum.

Figure 6.15 Author.

Figure 6.16 Courtesy of the Trustees of the Boston Public Library.

Figure 6.17 Courtesy of the Trustees of the Boston Public Library, Arts Dept. From *House and Garden*, July 1903.

Figure 6.18 The Schlesinger Library, Radcliffe Institute, Harvard University.

Figure 6.19 Author's collection.

Figure 6.20 David Feigenbaum.

Figure 6.21 David Feigenbaum.

Figure 6.22 David Feigenbaum.

Figure 6.23 David Feigenbaum.

Figure 6.24 Courtesy of Harvard College Library, Widener Harvard Depository HG2613. B74 F42. From *6th Annual Report of the Federal Reserve Bank of Boston for the Year Ended Dec. 31, 1920*.

Figure 6.25 David Feigenbaum.

Figure 6.26 Author.

Figure 6.27 David Feigenbaum.

Figure 6.28 Courtesy of Historic New England.

Figure 7.1 H. Martyn Payson collection.

Figure 7.2 David Feigenbaum.

Figure 7.3 *American Country Houses of Today*, preface by Frank Miles Day, New York: Architectural Book Publishing, 1912.

Figure 7.4 David Feigenbaum.

Figure 7.5 David Feigenbaum.

Figure 7.6 David Feigenbaum.

Figure 7.7 *Brickbuilder*, Feb. 1904.

Figure 7.8 David Feigenbaum.

Figure 7.9 David Feigenbaum.

Figure 7.10 David Feigenbaum.

Figure 7.11 Courtesy of the Trustees of the Boston Public Library.

Figure 7.12 David Feigenbaum.
Figure 7.13 *Architectural Record*, June 1919.
Figure 7.14 David Feigenbaum.
Figure 7.15 Courtesy of the Trustees of the Boston Public Library.
Figure E.1 David Feigenbaum.
Figure E.2 David Feigenbaum.
Plates: All by David Feigenbaum.

Index

Generously Donated by the Goodwyn Institute

MEMPHIS LIBRARY FOUNDATION

GREEN MATTERS™

Making Good Choices About
BIODEGRADABILITY

JUDY MONROE PETERSON

rosen publishing's
rosen
central

New York

To Laura and Steve, friends of the environment

Published in 2010 by The Rosen Publishing Group, Inc.
29 East 21st Street, New York, NY 10010

Library of Congress Cataloging-in-Publication Data

Peterson, Judy Monroe.
Making good choices about biodegradability / Judy Monroe Peterson.—1st ed.
    p. cm.—(Green matters)
Includes bibliographical references and index.
ISBN-13: 978-1-4358-5313-3 (library binding)
ISBN-13: 978-1-4358-5608-0 (pbk)
ISBN-13: 978-1-4358-5609-7 (6 pack)
1. Biodegradation—Juvenile literature. I. Title.
QH530.5.P47 2009
640—dc22

                                                                                      2009001045

Manufactured in Malaysia

CONTENTS

INTRODUCTION

All animals—even you—and plants are part of the earth's life cycle. When animals and plants die, their remains are naturally recycled back into the soil or seabed. Bacteria break down remains, or wastes, into substances that are usable by living beings. Without these bacteria, the wastes of living beings would not complete the life cycle. Instead, the earth would be covered with mountains of dead animals and plants from millions of years. Living animals and plants could not get the nutrients they need from the air, water, or soil. In addition, the earth could not sustain its great numbers and varieties of animals and plants.

Wastes that biodegrade, or break down, come from plants and animals. Biodegradability is the ability of substances to be broken down into simpler substances by bacteria. Substances that are capable of biodegrading are called bioactive. Bread, vegetables, and fruits break down to become simple sugars. Other materials, like leftover hot dogs, break down into carbon, oxygen, and water. Not all substances are bioactive. Most plastics, for example, are not bioactive. Biodegradation occurs aerobically (with the aid of oxygen) or anaerobically (without oxygen). Under aerobic conditions, oxygen helps break molecules apart, and substances break down much faster.

People around the world use great numbers of nonbiodegradable (incapable of breaking down) products, including plastics, medicines, and pesticides. Plastics are used to make cars, airplanes, medical equipment, cookware, and many other products. Medicines, such as antibiotics, help people fight off diseases caused by harmful bacteria.

Substances like plastic that don't biodegrade are mostly synthetic, or man-made. Since 1945, scientists have made more than eighty

thousand chemical compounds, with more than seven hundred new compounds introduced each year. For many years, scientists and other people seldom considered how these nonbiodegradable products would affect the environment. As a result, environmental problems have often been discovered only after a chemical has been used for some time. Today, scientists know that most man-made chemical compounds are nonbiodegradable. In addition, some of these substances are poisonous to people and other living creatures.

Man-made products that don't biodegrade have an impact on the environment. The process of biodegradation is key to the earth's life cycle. Life on earth as you know it would not exist without this process. Nonbiodegradable substances do not complete the earth's life cycle and never provide nutrients for living organisms. Bacteria that break down plant and animal waste don't recognize synthetic substances. As a result, nonbioactive substances enter the air, water, or soil without breaking down into simpler substances. You may see that plastic and other nonbiodegradable materials might rip, split, or fall apart over time. Whether large or small, man-made products continue to be nonbiodegradable.

Products that don't degrade are typically made from oil (petroleum), a fossil fuel. Other fossil fuels include coal and natural gas. These fuels were created from living organisms through processes that took millions of years. Companies use enormous amounts of oil and electricity to make and transport plastics and other nonbioactive products. The vast amounts of oil needed for nonbiodegradable products are using up the supplies of fossil fuels. Supplies of fossil fuels are limited and becoming more difficult to find. The burning of fossil fuels creates electricity but also damages the environment. Burning fossil fuels for electrical energy and transport produces greenhouse gases. These gases are causing the earth's climate to change, which is affecting ecosystems all over.

If unchecked, the production and use of substances that don't biodegrade could have huge effects on life on earth. Substances made from oil are in things that you, your family, and others commonly use or eat, including laundry detergents, clothes, cosmetics, computers, and chocolate bars. Instead of oil, much of the material that is used to make plastics and other products should come from biodegradable sources, such as corn and other plants. Products made from biodegradable sources become part of the earth's life cycle. Much of the energy needed to make products should not come from sources that are fossil fuels but from renewable sources, such as the wind and sun.

Living more sustainably, or "living green," means that you take actions, such as choosing and using biodegradable products, which will reduce your impact on the environment. People around the world are making changes in their lives to be more planet-friendly. Companies are changing their products and how they make them to be more environmentally friendly. Governments and other organizations are setting biodegradability standards for manufacturing. Any change, small or large, will influence environmental sustainability in positive ways.

You, your family, and your friends can make planet-friendly changes in all aspects of your lives. Changes at home are a good way to start. You can also change what you buy and throw away, and take other actions to live sustainably.

CHAPTER ①

At Home

By keeping biodegradability in mind, you and your family can live green at home in many ways. One way is to use eco-friendly products to control pests in the yard and garden. Read the labels of household and outdoor products. Look for any ingredient ending in "-ene" or "-ol," or with "phenol" or "glycol" in its name. Avoid using these products because they contain nonbiodegradable ingredients. Using eco-friendly products in and around your home can also be good for your health. Regular paints, cleaners, glues, and finishes can release small amounts of poisons throughout your home. These poisons can be harmful to your family's health and the health of your pets.

GREENER CLEANING

Many cleaners sold in stores leave kitchens, bathrooms, and other rooms sparkling with a "clean" odor. According to the Clean Water Fund, the average American uses 40 pounds (18.2 kilograms) of chemical

Green Works is the first natural cleaner made by a major company. All Green Works cleaners are made from plant-based oils and are biodegradable. The plastic bottles are recyclable.

cleaners in the home every year. Some people use an all-purpose, or general purpose, cleaner. Others prefer different cleaners for specific chores in the home. A family might stock a cabinet or shelf with cleaners for dishes, countertops, the stovetop, sinks, or the oven. They might tackle tubs, showers, windows, mirrors, furniture, carpets, or floors with other cleaning products. To clean and produce a gloss on metal pots and pans, some people apply polishes.

The sparkle, gloss, and smell come from the nonbiodegradable substances in most cleaners. These substances are synthetic chemicals made from fossil fuels that damage the environment. For example, cleaning products in spray cans release greenhouse gases into the home, which then move into the atmosphere. You breathe in the greenhouse gases and absorb them through your skin. In addition, many cleaners that are made from fossil fuels can irritate or burn people's skin and are poisonous if children swallow them.

The U.S. Environmental Protection Agency (EPA) regulates chemicals that might be a risk to the environment. The U.S. Consumer Product Safety Commission (CSPSC) oversees the safety of household cleaning products. These agencies, however, have not determined the risk or safety of most cleaners. By law, chemical companies must put storage and first-aid information on the labels of their products. The law does not require them to list the chemicals and other substances in their products. Sometimes, companies put "color" or "fragrance"—or other terms like "fresh scent," "mountain scent," or "clean smelling"— on their product labels. They never explain that these are terms for nonbiodegradable chemicals.

As a first step, you and your family can reduce your use of non-biodegradable cleaners. Check the labels of cleaners for words like "Danger," "Poison," "Warning," or "Caution." These signal words alert people that the chemicals in the cleaners often don't biodegrade and are poisonous to living organisms. Instead, use cleaners that are labeled biodegradable and don't have synthetic fragrances or dyes. Biodegradable cleaners are made from plant-based oils and natural minerals, such as calcite and feldspar. Say no to air fresheners and sprays, and open windows to let in fresh air. Flowers, sweetgrass, pinecones, or conifer branches bring natural plant odors indoors. Later, the plants can be composted.

Before synthetic products became available, people used natural cleaners. Homemade cleaners readily biodegrade, are easy to make, and save money. You and your family can make cleaners with earth-friendly ingredients, including vinegar, baking soda, hydrogen peroxide, plant-based oils, and castile soap or another vegetable-based soap. Books and Web sites discuss how to make natural cleaners for the home. Remember to use biodegradable scrubbers like natural sea sponges

The loofah plant is a climbing vine with long, green fruits. As the fruits age, they become dry and straw-colored. The fruits can then be used like a natural sponge.

and loofahs, gourd-like plants. If you use cellulose sponges, be sure they are biodegradable and made of wood from renewable tree farms.

ECO-LAUNDRY

About 35 billion pounds (15,875,732,950 kg) of clothes, bed linens, towels, and other things are washed every year in the United States.

Many families use stain removers and detergents made from fossil fuels to clean and add fragrance to laundry. Dryer liquids and sheets coat laundry with fragrances and other chemicals that make the family wash feel soft and free of wrinkles. Like many household cleaners, most stain removers, detergents, and dryer liquids and sheets contain large numbers of nonbiodegradable chemicals.

Eco-laundry detergents and fabric softeners are made from plants that readily biodegrade, such as plant seeds, citrus fruits, vegetable oils, and other natural oils, like coconut oil. Some products may have natural minerals, such as sodium silicate, baking soda, or sodium. You can make your own stain remover by mixing baking soda or cornstarch with cold water to form a paste. Gently rub the paste on the stain, and then pop the clothing into the laundry. Hydrogen peroxide, available at many stores, can remove stains, too.

You and your family can make laundry soap by using biodegradable liquid soap or detergent, baking or washing soda, and vinegar. To whiten clothes, tablecloths, and other things, add natural ingredients like lemon juice, oxygen bleach, or a mix of washing soda and hydrogen peroxide to the wash. Look in books and on Web sites for laundry cleaner recipes that use natural ingredients. Another natural cleaner for laundry is soapnuts, the dried fruit of the soapberry tree. The soap-like substance in the fruit works like laundry soap.

BIODEGRADABLE PRODUCTS IN BEDROOMS

Besides sleeping, many teens spend a lot of time in their bedrooms doing schoolwork, talking to friends, listening to music, and playing video games. Making some changes can result in more eco-friendly bedrooms. If you are getting a different bedroom floor, perhaps your family can use biodegradable wool carpeting or flooring from sustainable wood or bamboo. Plants that are sustainable grow very quickly and require much less energy from fossil fuels to harvest and produce things that people need or want.

Look at your mattress. Companies often treat mattresses with chemicals made from fossil fuels to retard (slow down) fire and resist water, stains, and wrinkles. Untreated, organic cotton or wool mattresses that biodegrade are better for the environment—and for sleepers.

Use organic cotton, organic wool, hemp, organic bamboo, or wild silk sheets, pillowcases, mattress pads, and comforters instead of standard bedding that is treated with fabric finishes. These chemical finishes help repel stains and wrinkles but are nonbiodegradable. Sleep on pillows made from organic cotton, organic wool, organic bamboo, or kapok, which are the seedpods from kapok trees. Be sure to use kapok from sustainable trees.

To store bedding, clothes, books, and other items, use furniture and containers made from plants that are sustainable. A variety of plants are made into chairs, tables, baskets, ottomans with storage space, and chests. Some of these plants include abaca (also called bacbac), rush, seagrass, vetiver root, rattan, and bamboo. See if the furniture was made with eco-friendly glues or finishes.

When it's time for a change, many teens paint the walls of their bedrooms. An open can of paint or a newly painted bedroom has a certain odor. That smell comes from the many synthetic chemicals that are in standard paints. To lessen the impact to the environment, use paints that are water-based instead of oil-based. You can also use eco-paints. In contrast to standard paints, eco-paints don't contain synthetic plastics and other nonbiodegradable chemicals. Instead, they are made of biodegradable substances, such as linseed oil, citrus oils plant, tree resins, waxes, and china clay (clay that occurs naturally), making them better products for the environment. Insulation in the walls and around windows in bedrooms and other rooms helps keep heat indoors during cold months.

If your family is adding insulation, ask if it can be biodegradable. One kind of biodegradable insulation is made from mushrooms spores. Wool fiber and hemp are other types of biodegradable insulation.

The blue-colored insulation in these walls is made from worn-out blue jeans that were recycled. Called denim insulation, this cotton material uses less energy to make than standard insulation and can also be recycled.

LAWNS AND GARDENS

Some families enjoy having a green lawn. They might also care for flowers, shrubs, and trees in their yards. To get lush growth, some people put synthetic pesticides and fertilizers on or near their green living plantings. Others hire lawn services that spray an array of chemicals on the grass. In both cases, many of the products used to treat pests and fertilize plants contain chemicals that are nonbiodegradable.

Chemical lawn services may put up warning signs on a lawn after spraying to warn people that the lawn has been treated. However,

Desert plants grow well in hot, dry climates. Plants such as cacti store water because they have no leaves. Other desert plants grow long roots to reach available water.

dogs and cats track the chemicals inside the house. Children who can't read yet might play on the treated lawn, absorbing chemicals through their skin and bringing them into the house on their footwear. Nonbiodegradable chemicals that kill pests also affect wild animals and beneficial insects.

Ask your family to find out what products the lawn service company sprays with and how often they service lawns. If the pesticides and fertilizers are nonbiodegradable, have your parents ask if the service can change to natural products. Or switch to a natural lawn care service, if available. Consider planting native plants and natural grasses that require fewer, if any, pesticides and fertilizers than standard lawn grasses. Some families have replaced their lawn with an eco-lawn

LIVING GREEN WITH PETS

According to the American Veterinary Medical Association, Americans share their homes with 154 million dogs and cats. Living green with dogs or cats means reading labels. Check that the pet food meets the American Association of Feed Control Officials (AAFCO) standards for balanced nutrition for dogs or cats. However, pet foods that meet this standard may not be eco-friendly. Some foods contain nonbiodegradable chemicals, such as pesticides, colors, and flavors. Look for the words "natural" or "organic" on the labels. Be aware that companies don't need to follow any laws for natural or organic pet food. Other steps to take include using organic canvas (cotton) for pet leashes or collars. Standard cat litter contains many synthetic chemicals. Instead, try litters that don't have fragrance or color and are made from biodegradable paper, wood, corn, or green tea leaves. Bathe your pet with an eco-friendly shampoo, and clean up after dogs with biodegradable bags.

mix of natural grasses, clovers, wildflowers, and herbs. Eco-lawns need less spraying and fertilizing than standard lawn grasses. As a bonus, these lawns don't require much water or mowing, which saves natural resources.

A growing number of families are raising their own vegetables and fruits. You and your family can try organic gardening by using natural products to feed plants and control pests. However, avoid gardening products that are made from fossil fuels. You can use biodegradable garden pots made from bamboo, paper, rice, corn, wheat, or peat.

MYTHS AND FACTS
MYTHS AND FACTS
MYTHS
FACTS
MYTHS AND
FACTS
MYTHS AND
MYTHS AND
FACTS
MYTHS AN
FACT

MYTH: Most of the biodegradable waste generated in the United States is composted.

FACT: In the United States, the great majority of solid waste goes to land-fills. Some is burned in incinerators, or large furnaces. Only a small percentage of solid waste is composted or recycled.

MYTH: Because the ocean is vast, it can absorb the trash that people throw into it. Trash sinks to the bottom of the ocean and does not create problems for the environment.

FACT: The ocean currents bring trash together in concentrated areas. This action creates large floating islands of trash, especially plastic, that never biodegrade. Floating trash islands in the sea are constantly growing larger.

MYTH: It is a good idea to burn trash that cannot biodegrade.

FACT: Burning nonbiodegradable trash, such as plastic, releases poisonous chemicals into the air. Some poisons attach to raindrops, which then spread across the earth. When the rain falls from the sky, the poisons go into the groundwater and soil. Other poisons are left in the ashes, which are sometimes dumped on the ground or into water.

CHAPTER ②

Shopping

You and your family can be eco-friendly when you shop. One way is to buy organic foods in place of standard foods. Organic foods are grown without chemical fertilizers or pesticides. Another way is to buy different kinds of biodegradable clothing, such as shirts, pants, and sleepwear. While shopping, say no to plastic bags that don't biodegrade. Bring your own reusable bags, preferably made from biodegradable materials like organic cotton. Look for biodegradable bags made from cornstarch, vegetable oil, and other renewable resources. Instead of buying a CD, you can download software online. Plastic CDs do not biodegrade. When eating out, buy food and beverages at restaurants that practice green policies. Support these restaurants whenever possible because they are doing the same eco-friendly things that many families are doing in their homes.

ORGANIC FOODS

Many of the foods in grocery

Laws in some states and cities ban the use of shopping bags that are plastic. As a result, many consumers bring reusable bags when shopping.

stores contain added chemicals. In the United States, most grains, vegetables, and fruits are grown on huge farms called factory farms. To manage their crops efficiently, most factory farmers rely on synthetic fertilizers (plant food) and pesticides that do not biodegrade. The pesticides go into the air, water, and soil and remain on many of the vegetables, fruits, and grains that people eat. In addition, Americans eat a lot of produce (vegetables and fruits) that is grown in other countries. Much of the produce is raised on farms that use pesticides. Produce and other foods that are transported across borders generally require extra pesticides to keep from being eaten by pests.

Meat, eggs, and dairy foods like milk come from animals that are given non-biodegradable drugs to stop them from getting sick. Other drugs quickly increase the size of the animals. Much of the meat, dairy foods, and eggs in grocery stores and supermarkets contain these man-made drugs. Chemicals known as additives are often added to processed foods like crackers, snacks, breads, cold cereals, and deli meats. Additives help food stay fresh longer and add color, flavor, and scent. However, additives do not biodegrade.

You and your family can buy and eat vegetables, fruits, grains, meats, eggs, and dairy foods that are

Foods must meet specific guidelines to be certified USDA Organic. However, some farmers choose not to go through the long and costly process of becoming certified organic.

organic. The U.S. Department of Agriculture (USDA) certifies that organic produce, meats, dairy products, and eggs meet specific guidelines. For example, synthetic pesticides and fertilizers cannot be used to grow certified organic foods. Check for the "USDA Organic" seal on foods. Families can buy organic foods in many grocery stores, super-markets, health food stores, farmer's markets, food co-ops, and other stores.

Read food labels before buying. Some products may contain a mixture of organic and standard ingredients. Foods labeled "natural"

The strawberries and asparagus at this stand were harvested early in the morning. Local produce saves on fuel for transporting and also tastes good because it is fresh and in season.

may be free of synthetic chemicals. However, no national standards define what natural foods are. Natural foods are minimally processed, which means they remain as close as possible to their whole, original form. You usually will not find white sugar, corn syrup, white flour, margarine, and synthetic food colors or flavors in natural foods. Maple syrup and raw honey are used in natural foods instead of white sugar or corn syrup, for example.

Families can be eco-friendly by buying and eating less meat. More energy from fossil fuels is required to raise a pound of meat than a pound of grain. Farmers must grow grain to feed animals, and then the animals are processed into meat for consumers. Finally, the meat

BUYING PERSONAL GROOMING PRODUCTS

Personal grooming products include shampoos, conditioners, liquid and bar soaps, cleansers, moisturizers, deodorants, and more. Made in factories from fossil fuels, most of these products do not biodegrade. Try to buy eco-friendly products that don't have synthetic chemicals, including fragrances, preservatives, colors, and detergents. Instead, choose all organic ingredients. If you can't find organics, carefully read the list of ingredients. The shorter the list of ingredients, the better the product is, especially if the product contains natural and herb extracts, minerals, and oils. Also, look for biodegradable toothbrushes that are made from cotton. Some biodegrade in a year.

is transported to stores. All of these steps require a lot of energy from fossil fuels. It is more energy efficient for people to eat the grains, which also results in fewer greenhouse gases.

Buy local foods. Local produce requires fewer pesticides and fuel for transporting. You can find local produce at grocery stores, super-markets, food co-ops, and farmer's markets. At farmer's markets, ask farmers how their produce was grown. They may grow organic vegetables and fruits, but the produce may not be certified as organic. Perhaps your family can go to local farms that sell pick-your-own berries, apples, and other produce. Some of these farms also sell organic produce.

Families can join a community supported agriculture (CSA) group. A CSA is a group of people that pledge to support farm partners in return for a share of the farms' harvest. After paying a fee, CSA members receive a box of fresh vegetables and fruits from the farms every week. The produce changes with the growing season. If your family decides to join a CSA, ask if the produce is grown organically.

ECO-FASHION

Clothing is made from synthetic fibers, natural fibers, or both kinds of fibers. Synthetic fibers, such as polyester and nylon, are made by the chemical processing of oil (petroleum). Natural fibers come from silk, cotton, bamboo, trees, corn, and other plants. Sheep, alpaca, and other animals provide natural fibers. Prized for their fiber, alpaca are herd animals that are originally from South America.

The threads and fabrics used to make clothing go through many processing steps, including spinning, dyeing, weaving, cleaning, and sizing. Huge amounts of energy, water, and chemicals are required to process, produce, package, and transport clothes made from synthetic fibers or natural fibers.

You may think that natural fibers in clothing may seem like a good way to be eco-friendly. However, farmers use large amounts of synthetic pesticides to grow cotton and produce wool. Chemicals like dyes and bleaches are often added to cotton and wool during the processing steps. Clothes that are labeled as permanent press, easy care, no wrinkle, no ironing, or crease resistant have chemical finishes. The synthetic chemicals that are used to make clothes with natural fabrics are nonbiodegradable.

Sometimes, clothes labeled "natural" include fabrics made from rayon, lyocell, or acetate. The term "natural" has no national standards, which means the clothing may not be eco-friendly. Rayon, lyocell, and acetate are made from cellulose, a plant fiber that comes from trees. The processing of cellulose into threads and fabrics requires many chemicals, and most of the cellulose from the trees is thrown away during processing.

To be eco-friendly, you and your family can buy clothes made from plants or wools that are sustainable, organic, and readily biodegrade. Check for labels that list organic cotton, organic wool, bamboo, hemp, or linen—a fabric made from the flax plant. In addition, check the label for organic certification by a state agency or an organization independent of the maker of the fabric. Organic cotton is used for many kinds of everyday, work, and sports clothes. Bamboo, hemp, and linen are hardy plants, grow quickly, and don't require pesticides.

Most dyes for clothes are made from oil. Look for low-impact colorings when buying clothes, or buy organic clothing that is not dyed. Cotton grows in shades of natural, blue, green, brown, and purple. Minerals and irons found in the earth are used to dye fabrics red, yellow, orange, and other colors. Fiber from sheep and alpaca come in more than a dozen natural colors and can be blended to produce other colors. You can find earth-friendly clothes at malls, at local stores, or on the Web. Some of the clothing store chains sell organic clothes and underwear. For rainy weather, people can buy umbrellas made from renewable bamboo, which biodegrades in one to two years.

Another way to go green is to buy fewer clothes. Then, less energy is used to produce and transport clothing, which reduces the amount of nonbiodegradable products and greenhouse gases that go into the environment. You can also buy used clothes at secondhand or thrift shops, at yard sales, or on the Web. Try swapping clothes with family members and friends. You will be helping the earth—and saving money!

EATING OUT

Many people eat in restaurants or buy food and beverages that they consume in the car, at sports events, at work, and so on. Students can buy meals, snacks, and beverages at school. Vending machines at malls, schools, and other places stock soda, juice, water, chips, and candy. Making some small changes can help make eating out more eco-friendly.

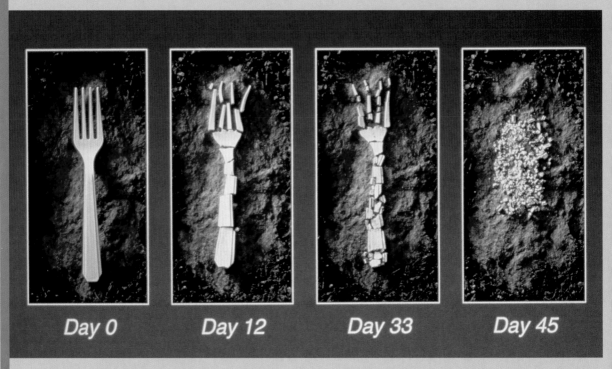

Day 0   Day 12   Day 33   Day 45

Companies are developing plant-based products that will biodegrade when they are no longer needed. This fork, which is made from corn, decomposes in forty-five days.

You can choose to eat at restaurants offering organic, natural, and local foods. Some restaurant owners and chefs grow and use their own organic vegetables and herbs. Find out if biodegradable utensils, dishes, cups, and takeout containers like bowls, cups, and boxes are used. Biodegradable straws made from paper are available. Be sure that chopsticks are made from a sustainable plant like bamboo. Use containers that restaurants provide to recycle biodegradable tableware and food scraps. You can also ask if the containers are made from biodegradable plants, such as corn, and if the restaurant disposes of food scraps by composting.

People can encourage restaurants to provide tableware and takeout containers that are environmentally friendly. Some cities have passed laws about the use of takeout containers that are nonbiodegradable. According to the organization Earth911, more than one hundred cities have banned restaurants and supermarkets from using takeout cups, containers, and other dishes made of polystyrene foam. Often called foam, this plastic is formed into small beads, which are then made into a variety of disposable (throwaway) containers. Most cities banning foam takeout containers require biodegradable containers for food and beverages.

Visit local eateries. Eating locally reduces the production of non-biodegradable substances and greenhouse gases by decreasing the energy needed for transportation. Local restaurants can offer a variety of interesting and tasty foods. In addition, local businesses help create jobs, which helps the community.

CHAPTER ③

Getting Rid of Waste

Families get rid of two kinds of waste: solid waste and wastewater. Solid wastes, or trash, are non-liquid materials that people commonly use and then throw away. This garbage ranges from packaging, food scraps, and grass clippings to old computers, sofas, and clothes. Packaging includes plastic wrap, milk cartons, cereal boxes, and cardboard. Wastewater, also called gray water or sewage, is water from the tap, toilet, shower, tub, and washing machine.

SOLID WASTE

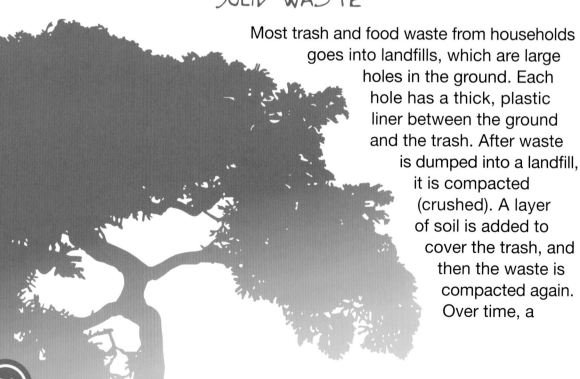

Most trash and food waste from households goes into landfills, which are large holes in the ground. Each hole has a thick, plastic liner between the ground and the trash. After waste is dumped into a landfill, it is compacted (crushed). A layer of soil is added to cover the trash, and then the waste is compacted again. Over time, a landfill forms into a large hill with layers of waste and soil. Landfills are carefully designed to prevent waste from mixing with soil and water in the ground and to reduce odors as the waste decomposes (breaks down). Some of the waste in landfills decomposes slowly, forming greenhouse gases that go into the atmosphere. Substances that are not biodegradable can leak into the water and soil.

Since 1960, the amount of solid waste generated by Americans has steadily increased. Although the population has also grown during this time to about three hundred million in 2008, the amount of solid waste produced per person has increased. In 2006, according to the EPA, paper and cardboard made up about 37 percent of the solid waste in the United States. Other solid waste categories were yard waste at 12 percent, food waste at 11 percent, and plastics at 11 percent. Metals were the next largest group, followed by glass, wood, clothes, rubber, leather, and other wastes. In 2007, the EPA estimated that Americans generated about 254 million tons (230 million metric tons) of trash.

Most materials that make up solid waste are either biodegradable or recyclable. However, most plastics don't biodegrade. In addition, plastics are more difficult to recycle than paper, yard, food, glass, wood, clothes, leather, and other wastes. One problem is that many kinds of plastic exist. Another problem is that different plastics remelt at different temperatures. Remelting is the first step in recycling processes.

THE 3R'S

Most goods that families buy and bring home end up as garbage sooner or later. Materials and energy are needed to make, transport, and get rid of belongings that people no longer want. Trash contains substances that don't biodegrade—or substances that could biodegrade if they were composted. To reduce the amount of trash dumped into landfills, you and your family can follow the 3 R's: reduce, reuse, and recycle. To "reduce" means to use less of something. Reducing leaves less trash for reusing and recycling. To "reuse" means to use something again,

The Citarum River is heavily polluted with plastics, chemicals, and human waste. People no longer fish in the river because all the fish have died. The dirty river supplies water to millions of people in Indonesia.

and to "recycle" means to prepare waste for reuse.

Reducing is more important waste management than reusing or recycling. Buying less saves natural resources and reduces the amount of nonbiodegradable substances that are used to make and transport things. For example, try not to buy disposable, or throwaway, products. Encourage your family to use products that are long lasting, for example, using china instead of paper plates. Instead of paper towels, clean up spills with washable cloths.

Families can reuse and repair objects and equipment around the home. Clean, empty egg cartons, plastic containers, and glass jars can be reused as storage containers, for example. You can reuse scrap paper before recycling it. Your family might repair tools, machines, and appliances instead of buying new products. For instance, metal tools with screws generally can be fixed. Quality clothes made from organic fabrics typically last a long time and don't come apart when washed. Books and Web sites provide many ideas for reusing every-day things and explain how to make household repairs.

The man in this photo shows some of the trash that he saved for one year. He wanted to make people aware of how much trash one person produces in a year.

REDUCING AND REUSING PACKAGING

According to the EPA, Americans throw away about 14 million tons (13 million metric tons) of packaging every year. Packaging is anything wrapped around or attached to a product. The main packaging materials are paper, cardboard, glass, aluminum, steel, wood, and plastics. Making and transporting packaging uses enormous amounts of fossil fuels and water, and it produces a variety of nonbiodegradable materials.

Some packaging is useful. It protects foods, such as peanut butter or jam, from damage and spoiling during shipment, and it helps make products easier to handle. Packaging can provide important information. You and your family read labels to learn how to prepare food or find the correct dosage of a medicine. Many products, though, come with a lot of packaging. For example, new televisions and clock radios are often packed in boxes, plastic bags, and plastic foam. If you look at a boxed, frozen meal, note that it has a paper box, a foil or plastic tray that holds the meal, and plastic wrap that covers the food. Families can buy products with less packaging. They can buy foods like cereals in large, rather than single-serving, containers. By going to the bulk food sections of stores, consumers can put the amounts that they want into containers. Cookies, chips, and other foods come in biodegradable bags that can be composted later.

Look for detergents and cleaners in ultra or concentrated forms because these containers are smaller than the regular products. Use bar soaps instead of liquid wash to save packaging. Cut back on wrapping waste by putting gifts in reusable bags or baskets. Tie gifts with biodegradable ribbons of raffia, a natural fiber. Some shipping stores will accept foam packing peanuts from households to reuse when sending packages.

RECYCLING AND COMPOSTING

The amount of energy needed to change recyclable materials into new products is often smaller than using new materials. However, energy is still required to transport, sort, and process recycled materials to make new products. Nonbiodegradable chemicals are still used and produced during the recycling process. Recycling, though, is a good and important idea. Many communities provide recycling programs. People sort their recyclable waste into different groups: glass, metals (aluminum and steel), most paper, and plastics. Trucks pick up the

To study how paper and plastic bags decompose, scientists placed both bags in a compost pile of leaves. This scientist is comparing the biodegradability of each bag.

sorted recyclables from households along street curbs, or people bring their recyclables to a central site (drop-off center).

Some recycling programs accept most plastics, while other programs take only certain kinds of plastics. Different kinds of plastic require different recycling processes. The plastics identification code of numbers 1 to 7 reveals the kinds of plastic. The codes are usually stamped on the bottom of containers.

Number 7 plastics include bioplastics, which are plastics made from biodegradable plants. Corn is the most commonly used plant in biomaterials that are made into plastic. Some disposable tableware comes from potatoes. You and your family can buy an ever-growing number of products made from bioplastics, including gift cards, clothes, water bottles, and food containers. Scientists are developing new bioplastics from vegetable oils, sugar cane, sugar beets, wheat, rice, soybeans, sweet potatoes, switchgrasses (grasses that are used to feed farm animals), and cassavas (roots that are eaten).

Most bioplastics can't be tossed into compost piles at home. Bioplastics require the high temperatures that a large, industrial compost site provides. Some companies are working to make bioplastics that can be composted at home, right along with food or yard waste. Other companies are developing bioplastics that will decompose at sea in the salty water.

Products made from bioplastics assure a decreased need for fossil fuels, but they are not the total answer to slow the growth of global warming. As bioplastics are made, carbon dioxide is released into the air, which contributes to global warming. The crops needed to make biomaterials require land and water to grow. In addition, recycling biomaterials can be a problem. Plastics with recycling codes 1 through 6 can be recycled into other products. Code 7 products include bio- plastics and all other plastics that don't fit into codes 1 to 6. Most recycling sites send code 7 plastics to landfills. The plastics industry developed the seven codes for plastics. In time, perhaps another code

CHAPTER ④

In Your Community and Beyond

Living green means to have a sustainable lifestyle at home, in the community, and in the larger world. You and your family can follow eco-friendly steps when you are in the community. For example, you can use biodegradable plates, cups, and cutlery when you go on picnics. If you camp in local, state, or national parks, use washing and cleaning products that are biodegradable. Use biodegradable bags to collect and recycle waste. When fishing in lakes or rivers, use biodegradable bait instead of plastic bait. When fish eat plastic, they cannot digest it or bring it back up from the stomach and out the mouth. The plastic stays in their stomachs, and the fish may die if they eat too much of it.

You can take other green steps. Be part of community, business, or other programs that safely dispose of products containing nonbiodegradable materials. Learn about the eco-labeling of products and how you might invest in living green. You can write letters

Fish eat plastic bait, which does not decompose in their stomachs. The plastic bait can kill fish and the water animals that eat the fish. People who fish should use biodegradable bait.

to the editors of local newspapers and decision makers about biodegradable issues and solutions.

COMMUNITY, BUSINESS, AND OTHER PROGRAMS

Many communities offer green programs for their residents. Take part in eco-programs that are offered in your area.

Every year in the United States, pet dogs produce millions of pounds of waste. Most dog waste goes to landfills. Some businesses provide a new service to dog owners. People get biodegradable bags for dog waste from these companies. When the bags are full, the owners return them, and the businesses compost the bags and waste or send everything to sites that can do the composting. Remember that dog or cat waste should not go into home compost piles because they don't get hot enough to kill microorganisms that could cause diseases.

The county solid waste center may provide a central compost site. Some centers also have compost drop-off sites throughout a city or an area. Families can bring yard waste in biodegradable bags to these sites. A growing number of communities have industrial compost sites. Bacteria are used to quickly biodegrade plant, meat, and dairy waste. Food scraps come from grocery stores, nursing homes, hospitals, colleges, and other organizations in the community. In turn, the sites sell the rich compost to the community.

Communities may have hazardous waste and drug take-back programs. Hazardous, or harmful, material is in some household products like antifreeze, batteries, paint, fluorescent bulbs and tubes, and more. Improper disposal of these products can harm groundwater, cause fires, and injure people and animals. Through a community program, residents can bring hazardous materials to a central site for safe disposal. In drug take-back programs, residents can give unwanted medicine to local pharmacies or take it to a central location in the community for proper disposal.

In this photo, people are bringing unwanted medicine to a drop-off site. The site then safely discards the medicine.

BIOREMEDIATION

Bioremediation is the process of using bacteria and other microorganisms to treat chemical leaks or spills on soil or in groundwater. Bacteria and other microorganisms constantly break down dead plants and animals in soil and water. If oil or other chemicals spill into an area, some natural microorganisms would die. Others would live and eat the chemical. Bioremediation provides fertilizer, oxygen, and other substances to the chemical-eating organisms. The added materials cause the microorganisms to grow rapidly, and, in turn, the microorganisms break down the spilled chemical quickly.

The raised areas pictured here are bacteria, and they are eating drops of oil. The bacteria will take six hours to eat all the oil.

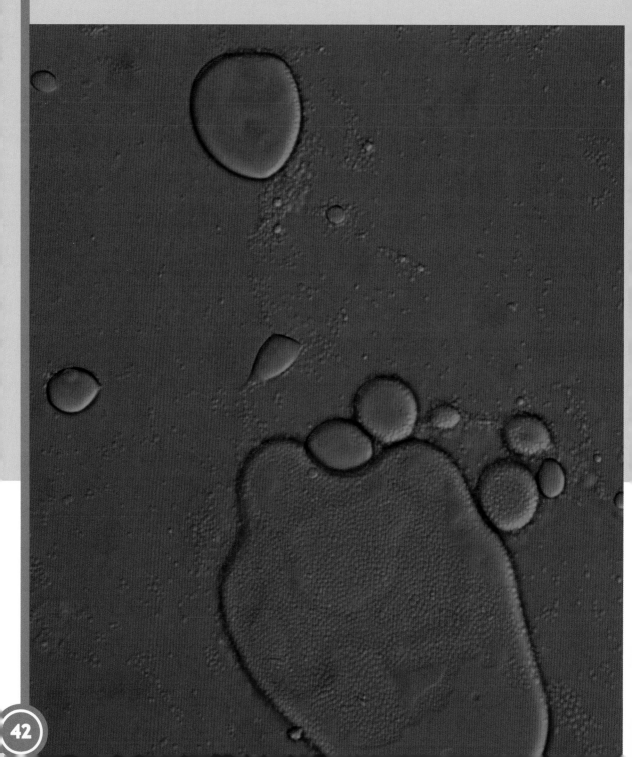

Bioremediation is often used to clean up oil spills on land or water. However, bioremediation may not work on chemicals that are poisonous to most microorganisms. Some metals and salts, such as sodium chloride (table salt), kill most bacteria. Bioremediation works on oil and other chemicals at the location where they were spilled. Large amounts of soil or water don't need to be dug up or pumped out of the ground to be treated.

To decrease the risk of future spills, all families should use less oil, as well as electricity and gas, which are made from oil. If less oil is required in the United States, not as much oil needs to be transported. You and your family can help by buying fewer products that are not needed. Walk, use a bicycle, or take the bus instead of traveling by car whenever possible. Have your family bring oil or oily waste to a hazardous waste site for disposal instead of dumping it in the garbage or sewer. If an oil spill occurs in your area, ask if you can help in the cleanup work.

INVESTING GREEN

Investing in stocks, bonds, or mutual funds is an opportunity to earn more money than you might in a savings account in a bank. Some people are investing in earth-friendly companies. You can invest in stocks, bonds, or mutual funds at any age, but your parent or guardian is the owner of your investment until you become eighteen years old. Eco-companies might be involved in developing bioplastics or renewable energy, growing organic foods, or using sustainable plants to make clothes. Some green companies use biodegradable packing peanuts, inks, and cleaning products.

One way to invest is to buy the stocks of a green company. Stocks are an investment in the ownership of a company. If the value of the stock goes up, the company pays you money when you sell the stock. A company might also pay you dividends, which are the part of

ONE COMMUNITY'S ECO-PROGRAM

The Western Lake Superior Sanitary District (WLSSD) in Duluth, Minnesota, provides free Waste Free Party Kits for weddings, family reunions, large parties, and other events. A kit contains big bins lined with biodegradable bags and signs that tell the kind of waste that goes into each bin. During the Waste Free event, people use biodegradable plates, bowls, cups, and other tableware made from corn, sugar cane, and potatoes. They throw their food scraps and other biodegradable waste into the labeled bins. Afterward, everything goes to the WLSSD site, and all waste from the event is composted at the industrial compost site.

the company's profit that it pays to its stockholders. If the company does poorly, a family might lose some or all of its investment.

Eco-friendly mutual funds are another option for investing. A mutual fund is a pool of money run by trained professionals. The professionals invest in a mix of stocks and other items. Every mutual fund has a different level of risk and opportunities to earn money.

A great way to learn about investing is to join investment clubs, which are offered in many high schools and colleges. A teacher supervises as students invest real or virtual (make-believe) money. Parents or guardians must sign a partnership agreement so that students under the age of eighteen can invest real money. An adult must also place the orders to buy and sell stocks. Whether using real or virtual money, students themselves research companies, decide what stocks to buy, and track their stocks' performance.

Some companies are making packaging materials that biodegrade. The white and tan packaging pebbles in these bags are biodegradable.

GREENWASHING AND ECO-LABELING

Buying and using earth-friendly products is one way to make a difference for the earth. However, some companies claim to follow green practices but really don't. "Greenwashing" is the practice of making a company or its products appear to be eco-friendly. Before buying from a company, determine if its products, services, and way of doing business are really green. Read labels and study any green claims.

Some companies put words such as "biodegradable," "eco," "natural," "environmentally friendly," "eco-friendly," or "nontoxic" (not poisonous) on their labels and packaging. Federal or state governments don't regulate the use of these words, and usually the words don't mean anything. The word "recyclable" on a label or package only means that you can recycle a product or packaging. The word "recycled" indicates that a company used recycled materials to make the product or package.

Some companies use packaging with soft, clean colors for a natural look. However, pink roses on a jug of laundry cleaner may not mean the soap is made from flowers. Read the ingredient label. You may discover that the laundry soap has man-made fragrance so that it only smells like roses. Be sure that you and your family look carefully at the labels of bio-based plastics. Some are totally made from biodegradable plants. Others come from a mix of petroleum and materials from plants, and these products don't biodegrade.

Look at product labels to find information about the green claims made by a company. If this information is not on the label, see if the company's Web address or phone number is listed. The company's Web site may have more information about its products. If you have any questions about green claims, call or e-mail the company. If you can't find any way to contact the company, the product may not be eco-friendly.

Check for certification by trustworthy organizations on products or their packaging. Recall from chapter 2 that foods meeting the U.S. Department of Agriculture standards for organic content can display the "USDA Organic" seal. Another federal program, called Energy Star, helps protect the environment by certifying products that use energy efficiently. Some products in this program include battery chargers, TVs, computers, laptops, printers, and more. Products that meet the standards carry the Energy Star logo.

The Canadian government started the EcoLogo program in 1988. Today, EcoLogo certifies products worldwide. Products that meet its strict standards display the EcoLogo logo. Green Seal is the largest eco-labeling organization in the United States and certifies many kinds of consumer products. A product must meet strict environmental standards to carry the Green Seal label. Look for the Forest Stewardship Council (FSC) logo on wood and paper products to certify that the wood came from well-managed forests. Products with the FSC logo are available worldwide.

BECOME ACTIVE

It's important to make changes in your own life. You can help other people and organizations make eco-friendly choices by sharing your knowledge about green matters and biodegradability. You can express your opinions about biodegradability issues, influence other people, and help create change. Start by writing an article for your school newspaper, or write a letter to your local newspaper or state represen- tatives. Describe a biodegradability issue and a solution. For example, you might ask that local schools serve lunch using biodegradable dishes, forks, knives, and spoons. Organize students to encourage local schools to send their biodegradable waste to an industrial compost site, start their own compost pile, create organic gardens for students, and buy foods for school lunches from local farms.

Man-made products that don't biodegrade have a direct effect on the environment. All the nonbiodegradable substances that people have ever made, used, and thrown away are still on the earth. By making small changes, you can reduce your use of nonbiodegradable substances. All changes, small and large, will add up to some very big changes that will help the planet and all of the living beings on it.

GLOSSARY

additive A chemical added to something to change or improve it in some way. Companies may add additives to help foods stay fresh longer or to change the color, flavor, texture, or scent.

biodegradability The ability of substances to be broken down into simpler substances by bacteria.

biodegrade Breaking down of substances into simpler substances by bacteria.

bioplastics Plastics that are made from plants that biodegrade.

bioremediation Using bacteria and other microorganisms to treat chemical leaks or spills on soil or in groundwater.

compost A mixture of decaying organic matter, such as food scraps and dead leaves, that is used to fertilize gardens.

consumer A user or buyer of a product.

farmer's market A market where farmers sell produce, meat, and other products directly to consumers.

fossil fuel Any material that is based on former life and can be burned, including oil, natural gas, and coal.

global warming An increase in the average temperature of the earth's atmosphere that causes changes in climate.

green The color associated with the environmental movement. People sometimes refer to becoming more earth-friendly as "living green."

greenhouse gas Any of the gases that absorb sunlight in the atmosphere and thus contribute to global warming.

greenwashing The practice of making a company or its products appear to be eco-friendly.

landfill A large hole in the ground in which a community's solid waste, or trash, is dumped. Landfills are carefully designed to prevent waste from mixing with soil and water in the ground and to reduce odors as the waste decomposes.

organic From a living organism; regarding food, something that is grown without chemical fertilizers or pesticides. Natural fertilizers and pesticides can be used on produce that is grown organically.

packaging The container and wrapping in which a product is sold.

peat Dead plant tissues that have partially decomposed in water.

pesticide A chemical that is used to kill weeds or animal pests. A natural pesticide is made from a natural product that has undergone only a little processing.

polystyrene foam A plastic, often called foam, that is formed into small beads that are then made into a variety of throwaway containers.

recycle To prepare waste materials for reuse.

reduce To lower the amount used of a certain material.

reuse To use again.

solid waste Trash; materials that people use and then throw away.

sustainable Able to continue with minimal effects on the environment. A level of consumption that can be supplied by the environment without overtaxing it.

synthetic Man-made.

wastewater Water that has been used and that goes down the drain in homes.

FOR MORE INFORMATION

EcoLogo Program
c/o TerraChoice Environmental Marketing
171 Nepean Street, Suite 400
Ottawa, ON K2P 0B4
Canada
(800) 478-0399
Web site: http://www.ecologo.org
EcoLogo certifies that the products and services bearing its logo
meet strict environmental standards. Search the EcoBuyer
Database on its Web site to find certified green products and
services worldwide.

Environmental Working Group
1436 U Street NW, Suite 100
Washington, DC 20009
(202) 667-6982
Web site: http://www.ewg.org
The Environmental Working Group works to protect public health and
the environment. Its Web site offers useful databases to consumers on personal, household, and food items, and more.

Friends of the Earth
1717 Massachusetts Avenue, Suite 600
Washington, DC 20036
(877) 843-8687
Web site: http://www.foe.org
This organization protects the earth by working on environmental
issues such as global warming, climate change, pollution,
and more.

Keep America Beautiful
1010 Washington Boulevard
Stamford, CT 06901
(203) 659-3000
Web site: http://www.kab.org
This nonprofit organization works with people on the issue of litter
    prevention and on ways to reduce, reuse, recycle, and properly
    manage waste materials.

Kids for Saving Earth
37955 Bridge Road
North Branch, MN 55056
(763) 559-1234
Web site: http://www.kidsforsavingearth.org
This organization educates children to protect the earth's environ-
    ment and provides action-oriented materials to kids, families,
    groups, and schools.

National Fish and Wildlife Foundation National Office
1133 Fifteenth Street NW, Suite 1100
Washington, DC 20005
(202) 857-0162
Web site: http://www.nfwf.org
Founded by Congress in 1984, the National Fish and Wildlife
    Foundation works to protect and restore the natural resources
    of the United States.

Natural Resources Defense Council
40 West 20th Street

New York, NY 10011
(212) 727-2700
Web site: http://www.nrdc.org
This organization works to safeguard the living organisms on the earth
    and the natural systems on which all life depends. It focuses on
    curbing global warming, moving the United States beyond oil,
    and reducing or getting rid of dangerous chemicals.

NSF International
P.O. Box 130140
789 North Dixboro Road
Ann Arbor, MI 48113-0140
(800) NSF-MARK (673-6275)
Web site: http://nsf.org
This organization develops standards, certifies products, and informs
    individuals and companies about the health and safety of food,
    water, and indoor air, and the protection of the environment.

Organic Consumers Association
6771 South Silver Hill Drive
Finland, MN 55603
(218) 226-4164
Web site: http://organicconsumers.org
This organization offers information and resources related to organic
    food, organic clothes, organic personal care products, and envi-
    ronmental sustainability. It also campaigns for health and justice.

Post Carbon Institute
6971 Sebastopol Avenue

Sebastopol, CA 95472
(800) 590-7734
Web site: http://www.postcarbon.org
The Post Carbon Institute provides research and education on issues
    relating to the need to reduce energy consumption.

Social Investment Forum
910 Seventeenth Street NW, Suite 1000
Washington, DC 20006
(202) 872-5361
Web site: http://www.socialinvest.org
This national association works to advance the concept, practice, and
    growth of socially and environmentally responsible investing.

U.S. Environmental Protection Agency (EPA)
Ariel Rios Building
1200 Pennsylvania Avenue NW
Washington, DC 20460
(202) 272-0167
Web site: http://www.epa.gov
The EPA protects human health and the environment. This agency
    leads the nation's environmental science, research, and educa-
    tion efforts.

Worldwatch Institute
1776 Massachusetts Avenue NW
Washington, DC 20036
(202) 452-1999
Web site: http://www.worldwatch.org

This institute develops information and strategies about climate change, energy consumption, and population growth.

Zero Waste Alliance
One World Trade Center
121 SW Salmon Street, Suite 210
Portland, OR 97204
(503) 279-9383
Web site: http://www.zerowaste.org
The Zero Waste Alliance partners with universities, governments, businesses, and other organizations to develop, promote, and apply more efficient ways of dealing with wastes.

WEB SITES

Due to the changing nature of Internet links, Rosen Publishing has developed an online list of Web sites related to the subject of this book. This site is updated regularly. Please use this link to access the list:

http://www.rosenlinks.com/gre/biod

FOR FURTHER READING

Amsel, Sherry. *Everything Kids' Environment Book: Learn How You Can Help the Environment by Getting Involved at School, at Home, or at Play*. Cincinnati, OH: Adams Media, 2007.

Amsel, Sherry. *365 Ways to Live Green for Kids: Saving the Environment at Home, School, or at Play—Every Day!* Cincinnati, OH: Adams Media, 2009.

Brezina, Corona. *Climate Change* (In the News). New York, NY: Rosen Publishing Group, 2007.

Burns, Loree Griffin. *Tracking Trash: Flotsam, Jetsam, and the Science of Ocean Motion*. Boston, MA: Houghton Mifflin, 2007.

Cherry, Lynne. *How We Know What We Know About Our Changing Climate: Scientists and Kids Explore Global Warming*. Nevada City, CA: Dawn Publications, 2008.

David, Laurie, and Cambria Gordon. *Down-to-Earth Guide to Global Warming*. New York, NY: Orchard Books, 2007.

Fardone, John. *Oil*. New York, NY: DK Children, 2007.

Gershon, John. *Journey for the Planet: A Kid's Five-Week Adventure to Create an Earth-Friendly Life*. Woodstock, NY: Empowerment Institute, 2007.

Hall, Julie, and Sarah Lane. *A Hot Planet Needs Cool Kids: Understanding Climate Change and What You Can Do About It*. Bainbridge Island, WA: Green Goat Books, 2007.

Langholz, Jeffrey, and Kelly Turner. *You Can Prevent Global Warming (and Save Money!)*. Kansas City, MO: Andrews McMell Publishing, 2008.

Martin, Laura. *Recycled Crafts Box*. North Adams, MA: Storey Publishing, 2004.

Mckay, Kim, and Jenny Bonnin. *True Green Kids: 100 Things You Can Do to Save the Planet*. Washington, DC: National Geographic Children's Books, 2008.

MySpace Community and Jeca Taudte. *MySpace/OurPlanet: Change Is Possible*. New York, NY: Harper Teen, 2008.

Nagle, Jeanne M. *Living Green* (In the News). New York, NY: Rosen Publishing, 2009.

Povey, Karen. *Energy Alternatives*. Clifton Park, NY: Lucent Books, 2007.

Rothschild, David. *Earth Matters*. New York, NY: DK Children, 2008.

Sivertsen, Linda, and Tosh Sivertsen. *Generation Green: The Ultimate Teen Guide to Living an Eco-Friendly Life*. New York, NY: Simon Pulse, 2008.

Thornhill, Jan. *This Is My Planet: The Kid's Guide to Global Warming*. Toronto, Canada: Maple Tree Press, 2007.

Woodward, John. *Climate Change*. New York, NY: DK Children, 2008.

Yarrow, Joanna. *How to Reduce Your Carbon Footprint: 365 Simple Ways to Save Energy, Resources, and Money*. San Francisco, CA: Chronicle Books, 2008.

BIBLIOGRAPHY

American Veterinary Medical Association. "Market Research Statistics."
U.S. Pet Ownership & Demographics Sourcebook (2007 Edition),
2008. Retrieved September 10, 2008 (http://www.avma.org/
reference/marketstats/sourcebook.asp).

Becker, Jeff (engineer, bio-compatible and bio-based products,
Minnesota Technical Assistance Program, University of Minnesota),
in discussion with the author, September 2008.

Brangien, Davis, and Katharine Wroth. *Wake Up and Smell the Planet*.
Seattle, WA: Skipstone, 2007.

Burnham, Chad. "Styrofoam Bans: Here to Stay?" June 23, 2008.
Retrieved September 20, 2008 (http://earth911.org/blog/2008/
06/23/stroyfoam-bans-here-to-stay).

Bush, Laura. "Marine Debris Takes a Grim Toll on Wildlife." National
Oceanic and Atmospheric Administration, National Ocean
Service Office, September 19, 2007. Retrieved September 6,
2008 (http://response.restoration.noaa.gov/topic_subtopic_
entry.php?RECORD_KEY(entry_subtopic_topic)=entry_
id,subtopic_id,topic_id&entry_id(entry_subtopic_topic)=
683&subtopic_id(entry_subtopic_topic)=31&topic_id(entry_
subtopic_topic)=3).

Clark, Duncan, and Richie Unterberger. *The Rough Guide to Shopping
with a Conscience*. New York, NY: Penguin Group, 2007.

Clean Up the World. "Waste in the Environment." 2008. Retrieved
September 19, 2008 (http://www.cleanuptheworld.org/PDF/en/
waste_in_the_environment.pdf).

Cleveland, Cutler J. "Exxon Valdez Oil Spill." August 26, 2008.
Retrieved September 26, 2008 (http://www.eoearth.org/article/
Exxon_Valdez_oil_spill).

Cornell University and Penn State University. "Bioremediation." 2006. Retrieved September 25, 2008 (http://ei.cornell.edu/biodeg/bioremed).

Dow Chemical Company. "What Is Styrofoam?" 2008. Retrieved September 20, 2008 (http://building.dow.com/styrofoam/what.htm).

Earth911. "Additional Benefits of Compost." 2008. Retrieved September 23, 2008 (http://earth911.org/composting/benefits-of-using-compost/additional-benefits-of-compost).

Earth911. "Facts About Cleaning Products." 2008. Retrieved September 10, 2008 (http://earth911.org/household-items/facts-about-cleaning-products).

E/The Environmental Magazine editors. Green Living: The EMagazine Handbook for Living Lightly on the Earth. New York, NY: Penguin Group, 2005.

Earth Action Network. Green Living: The EMagazine Handbook for Living Lightly on the Earth. New York, NY: Plume Book, 2005.

Erwin, Lewis, and L. Hall Healy. Packaging and Solid Waste: Management Strategies. New York, NY: American Management Association, 1990.

Greenwalt, Liz. "Green Certification." 2008. Retrieved September 28, 2008 (http://www.cleanlink.com/SM/article.asp?id=5821).

Grosvenor, Michael. Sustainable Living for Dummies. Milton, Australia: Wiley Publishing, 2007.

Horn, Greg. Living Green: A Practical Guide to Simple Sustainability. Topanga, CA: Freedom Press, 2006.

Little, Ken. Socially Responsible Investing. New York, NY: Penguin Group, 2008.

Loux, René. *Easy Green Living: The Ultimate Guide to Simple, Eco-Friendly Choices for You and Your Home*. Emmaus, PA: Rodale, 2008.

MacEachern, Diane. *Big Green Purse: Use Your Spending Power to Create a Cleaner, Greener World*. New York, NY: Penguin Group, 2008.

Matthews, A. J. (environmental program coordinator, Western Lake Superior Sanitary District, Duluth, MN), in discussion with the author, September 2008.

McKay, Kim, and Jenny Bonnin. *True Green: 100 Everyday Ways You Can Contribute to a Healthier Planet*. Washington, DC: National Geographic, 2006.

Minnesota Pollution Control Agency. "Pharmaceutical Waste: Disposing of Unwanted Medications." April 2008. Retrieved September 2, 2008 (http://www.pca.state.mn.us/oea/hhw/pharmaceuticals.cfm).

National Oceanic and Atmospheric Administration. "What's the Story on Oil Spills?" June 24, 2007. Retrieved September 24, 2008 (http://response.restoration.noaa.gov/topic_subtopic_entry. php?RECORD_KEY%28entry_subtopic_topic%29=entry_ id,subtopic_id,topic_id&entry_id(entry_subtopic_topic)= 184&subtopic_id(entry_subtopic_topic)=8&topic_id(entry_ subtopic_topic)=1).

Newton, David E. *Chemistry of the Environment*. New York, NY: Facts On File, 2007.

Pasko, Jessica M. "Mushrooms Are Eco-Friendly Insulation." *USAToday*, June 25, 2007. Retrieved October 6, 2008. (http:// www.usatoday.com/tech/products/environment/2007-06-25- mushroom-insulation_N.htm).

Rogers, Elizabeth, and Thomas M. Kostigen. *The Green Book: The Everyday Guide to Saving the Planet One Simple Step at a Time*. New York, NY: Three Rivers Press, 2007.

Schoff, Jill Potvin. *Green Up Your Cleanup*. Upper Saddle River, NJ: Creative Homeowner, 2008.

Selke, Susan E. *Packaging and the Environment: Alternatives, Trends, and Solutions*. Lancaster, PA: Technomic Publishing Company, 1994.

Springen, Karen. "In the Yard, Taking Care of Business." *Newsweek*, Volume 151, Issue 7, February 18, 2008, p. 18.

Steffen, Alex, ed. *World Changing: A User's Guide for the 21st Century*. New York, NY: Abrams, 2006.

Trask, Crissy. *It's Easy Being Green: A Handbook for Earth-Friendly Living*. Salt Lake City, UT: Gibbs Smith Publisher, 2006.

Uldrich, Jack. *Green Investing*. Avon, MA: Adams Media, 2008.

U.S. Department of Agriculture. "Organic Labeling and Marketing Information." Agriculture Marketing Service, April 2008. Retrieved August 28, 2008 (http://www.ams.usda.gov/AMSv1.0/getfile?dDocName=STELDEV3004446&acct=nopgeninfo).

U.S. Environmental Protection Agency. "A Citizen's Guide to Bioremediation." April 1996. Retrieved September 25, 2008 (http://www.bugsatwork.com/XYCLONYX/EPA_GUIDES/BIO.PDF).

U.S. Environmental Protection Agency. "Environmental Marketing Claims." November 7, 2007. Retrieved September 25, 2008 (http://www.epa.gov/oppt/epp/pubs/claims.htm).

U.S. Environmental Protection Agency. "Hazardous Waste." 2008. Retrieved September 25, 2008 (http://www.epa.gov/epaoswer/osw/hazwaste.htm).

U.S. Environmental Protection Agency. "Municipal Solid Waste Generation, Recycling, and Disposal in the United States: Facts and Figures for 2006." November 2007. Retrieved September 20, 2008 (http://www.epa.gov/epawaste/nonhaz/municipal/pubs/msw06.pdf).

U.S. Environmental Protection Agency. "Wastes." 2008. Retrieved September 20, 2008 (http://www.epa.gov/epawaste/index.htm).

U.S. Environmental Protection Agency and U.S. Department of Energy. "About Energy Star." Retrieved September 23, 2008 (http://www.energystar.gov/index.cfm?c=about.ab_index).

U.S. Geological Survey. "Bioremediation: Nature's Way to a Cleaner Environment." April 1, 1997. Retrieved September 25, 2008 (http://water.usgs.gov/wid/html/bioremed.html#HDR1).

Western Lake Superior Sanitary District. "Household Hazardous Wastes?" 2006. Retrieved September 20, 2008 (http://www.wlssd.duluth.mn.us/uploads/WLSSD_HHW_Guide_2006.pdf).

Zimmer, Catherine (health care specialist for Pollution Prevention, Minnesota Technical Assistance Program, University of Minnesota), in discussion with the author, September 2008.

INDEX

ABOUT THE AUTHOR

Judy Monroe Peterson has earned two master's degrees, including a master's in public health education, and is the author of more than fifty educational books for young people. She is a former health care, technical, and academic librarian and college faculty member; a biologist and research scientist; and a curriculum editor with more than twenty-five years of experience. She has taught courses at 3M, the University of Minnesota, and Lake Superior College. Currently, she is a writer and editor of K–12 and post–high school curriculum materials on a variety of subjects, including biology, life science, the environment, health, and life skills.

PHOTO CREDITS

Cover, p. 1 © www.istockphoto.com/Marcus Clackson; p. 8 © Michael Maloney/San Francisco Chronicle/Corbis; p. 10 © Andres Cristaldo/epa/Corbis; p. 10 (inset) © www.istockphoto.com/Ryan Jones; p. 13 © Mariela Lombard/Zuma Press; p. 14 © www.istockphoto.com/Loretta Hostettler; p. 18 David McNew/Getty Images; p. 20 © www.istockphoto.com/Jody Elliott; pp. 24, 32 © Roger Ressmeyer/Corbis; pp. 28–29 Reuters/Newscom.com; p. 30 © Steve LaBadessa/Zuma Press; p. 39 krtphotos/Newscom.com; p. 41 © Redding Record Searchlight/Zuma Press; p. 42 © Charles O'Rear/Corbis; p. 45 © Jim Sugar/Corbis.

Designer: Nicole Russo; Editor: Kathy Kuhtz Campbell;
Photo Researcher: Amy Feinberg